WEB DEVELOPMENT WITH JQUERY®

Web Development with jQuery®

Richard York

wrox™

A Wiley Brand

Web Development with jQuery®

Published by
John Wiley & Sons, Inc.
10475 Crosspoint Boulevard
Indianapolis, IN 46256
www.wiley.com

Copyright © 2015 by John Wiley & Sons, Inc., Indianapolis, Indiana

Published simultaneously in Canada

ISBN: 978-1-118-86607-8
ISBN: 978-1-118-86599-6 (ebk)
ISBN: 978-1-118-86600-9 (ebk)

Manufactured in the United States of America

10 9 8 7 6 5 4 3 2 1

For general information on our other products and services please contact our Customer Care Department within the United States at (877) 762-2974, outside the United States at (317) 572-3993 or fax (317) 572-4002.

Wiley publishes in a variety of print and electronic formats and by print-on-demand. Some material included with standard print versions of this book may not be included in e-books or in print-on-demand. If this book refers to media such as a CD or DVD that is not included in the version you purchased, you may download this material at http://book support.wiley.com. For more information about Wiley products, visit www.wiley.com.

Library of Congress Control Number: 2014948560

ABOUT THE AUTHOR

RICHARD YORK has written four previous Wrox books, including *Beginning JavaScript and CSS Development with jQuery* (2009).

ABOUT THE CONTRIBUTOR AND TECHNICAL EDITOR

PETER HENDRICKSON has been developing software as a hobby since 1989 and professionally since 2001. He is currently a Manager of Software Engineering at salesforce.com, where he has developed both user interface and middle-tier components for the Salesforce Marketing Cloud. In addition to his work technical editing many chapters of the book, Peter contributed by writing several chapters.

ABOUT THE TECHNICAL EDITOR

NIK DEVEREAUX joined ViaSat in 2003 and is currently a program director for ViaSat's Central Engineering department. He manages the Software Engineering Office and University Partnerships & Recruiting programs. In this role, Nik's primary goal is to grow the size, skill set, and strategic alignment of the entire software engineering community across all business areas and office locations. He received his bachelor's and master's degrees from UC San Diego.

CREDITS

PROJECT EDITOR
John Sleeva

TECHNICAL EDITOR
Peter Hendrickson
Nik Devereaux

PRODUCTION MANAGER
Kathleen Wisor

COPY EDITOR
San Dee Phillips

**MANAGER OF CONTENT DEVELOPMENT &
ASSEMBLY**
Mary Beth Wakefield

MARKETING DIRECTOR
David Mayhew

MARKETING MANAGER
Carrie Sherrill

**PROFESSIONAL TECHNOLOGY &
STRATEGY DIRECTOR**
Barry Pruett

BUSINESS MANAGER
Amy Knies

ASSOCIATE PUBLISHER
Jim Minatel

PROJECT COORDINATOR, COVER
Patrick Redmond

PROOFREADER
Amy Schneider

INDEXER
Johnna VanHoose Dinse

COVER DESIGNER
Wiley

COVER IMAGE
©iStock.com/George Pchemyan

CONTENTS

INTRODUCTION

JQUERY HAS BECOME ESSENTIAL in the world of web development. jQuery's mission as a JavaScript library is simple: It strives to make the lives of web developers easier by making many tasks much easier. jQuery began as a library to patch cross-browser inconsistencies, to make developing in JavaScript easier, while it still provides a lot of cross-browser normalization. As browsers have advanced and filled in holes in compatibility, jQuery has become leaner, more efficient, and better at fulfilling the task of providing an API that makes developing JavaScript easier.

jQuery has the proven capability to reduce many lines of ordinary JavaScript to just a few lines, and, in many cases, just a single line of jQuery-enabled JavaScript. The trade-off is including the additional size and complexity of the jQuery library (and possibly additional related downloads) in the materials your users need to obtain to use your website or application. This is less of a trade-off today as more and more people have access to high-speed Internet. High-speed internet, although still pathetic in the United States when compared to some other nations, has inched up in overall speed. So, the additional download isn't all that much when you consider the big picture.

jQuery strives to remove barriers in JavaScript development by removing redundancy wherever possible. jQuery 1.9 and earlier focus more on normalizing cross-browser JavaScript development in key areas where browsers would otherwise differ, such as Microsoft's Event API and the W3C Event API, and other, more remedial tasks such as getting the mouse cursor's position when an event has taken place. With the normalization efforts taking place in the browsers, jQuery 2.0 can shed a great deal of legacy baggage that focused on bridging things such as event compatibility between Internet Explorer and everyone else. Now, the latest version of Internet Explorer has the standard event API in strict standards rendering mode, so when you include the right Document Type Declaration, there is no need to bridge event support.

jQuery 1.9 should be used if you need to work with older versions of Internet Explorer, such as IE8. Both jQuery 1.9 and jQuery 2.0 work with all the modern browsers, including the latest versions of Safari, Firefox, Google Chrome, and Internet Explorer.

Getting started with jQuery is easy—all you need to do is include a single script in your HTML or XHTML documents to include the base jQuery JavaScript library. Throughout this book, jQuery's API (Application Programming Interface) components are demonstrated in detail and show you how everything within this framework comes together to enable you to rapidly develop web applications.

This book also covers the jQuery UI library, which makes redundant user interface (UI) tasks on the client side easier and more accessible to everyday web developers who might not have much JavaScript programming expertise. The jQuery UI library includes widgets such as dialogs, tabs, accordions, and a datepicker; for a complete demonstration, view the examples available at http://www.jqueryui.com.

A large, thriving community of jQuery plugins is available for free, and a few of the most popular are covered. In addition, you learn how to create your own jQuery plugins, from simple to complex.

WHO THIS BOOK IS FOR

This book is for anyone interested in doing more with less JavaScript. You should have an understanding of JavaScript, as this book doesn't go into detail about JavaScript itself. You need to understand the Document Object Model (DOM) and JavaScript programming syntax. In addition, you need to know your way around CSS and HTML5 or XHTML5, as knowledge of those technologies is also assumed. This book covers primarily programming in JavaScript with jQuery.

A complete beginner might grasp what is taking place in the examples in this book but might not understand certain terminology and programming concepts that would be presented in a beginner's JavaScript guide. So, if you are a beginner and insist with pressing forward, you should do so with a beginning JavaScript book on hand as well. Specifically, consider the following Wrox books for more help with the basics:

➤ *Beginning HTML, XHTML, CSS, and JavaScript* (2009), by Jon Duckett

➤ *Beginning CSS: Cascading Style Sheets for Web Design, 3rd Edition* (2011), by Ian Pouncey and Richard York

➤ *Beginning JavaScript, 4th Edition* (2009), by Paul Wilton and Jeremy McPeak

For further knowledge of JavaScript beyond what is covered in this book, check out *Professional JavaScript for Web Developers, 3rd Edition* (2012), by Nicholas C. Zakas.

WHAT THIS BOOK COVERS

This book covers the jQuery JavaScript framework and the jQuery UI JavaScript framework, in addition to some popular third-party plugins and how to write and use your own third-party plugins. It covers each method exposed by jQuery's API, which contains methods to make common, redundant tasks go more quickly in less code. Some examples are methods that help you to select elements from a markup document through the DOM and methods that help you to traverse through those selections and filter them using jQuery's fine-grained controls. This makes working with the DOM easier and more effortless. It also covers jQuery's event model, which both wraps around the normal W3C event API and provides an API that when used correctly can heavily optimize and reduce complexity in your applications.

Later in the book, you see how to leverage the jQuery UI library to make user interface (UI) widgets. jQuery gives you the ability to break up content among multiple tabs in the same page. You have the ability to customize the look and feel of the tabs, and even to create a polished look and feel by providing different effects when you mouse over tabs and click them. The jQuery UI library also makes it easy to create accordion sidebars. These sidebars have two or more panels, and when you mouse over an item, one pane transitions to another via a smooth, seamless animation wherein the preceding pane collapses and the proceeding pane expands.

The jQuery UI library also gives you the ability to make any element draggable with the mouse cursor; by clicking, holding and moving the mouse, you can move elements around a page to any position you like. It also makes it easy to create drag-and-drop user interfaces. You can use jQuery UI to make droppable zones, where you take elements from other parts of a page and drop them on another, similarly to how you might interact with your operating system's file manager when you want to move a folder from one place to another. You can also make lists that are sortable via drag-and-drop, rearranging elements based on where you drop them. You can have a user interface where you drag the mouse cursor to make a selection, as you would in your operating system's file manager when you want to select more than one file or folder. jQuery UI exposes the ability to resize elements on a page using the mouse. All the things that you can imagine doing on your computer's desktop, or within an application, you can do in a web browser with jQuery UI.

jQuery UI also provides a widget for entering a date into a field using a nice, accessible JavaScript-driven calendar that pops up when you click on an input field.

You can make custom pop-up dialogs that are like virtual pop-up windows, except they don't open a separate browser window—they display using markup, CSS, and JavaScript.

Another widget that jQuery UI provides is a graphical slider bar, similar to your media player's volume control.

As jQuery has done for JavaScript programming in general, jQuery UI strives to do for redundant graphical user interface (GUI) tasks. jQuery UI gives you the ability to make professional user-interface widgets with much less development effort.

If you're interested in reading news about jQuery, how it's evolving, and topics related to web development, you may be interested in reading the official jQuery blog at `blog.jquery.com` or jQuery's creator John Resig's blog at `www.ejohn.org`.

If you need help, you can participate in programming discussions at `p2p.wrox.com`, which you can join for free, to ask programming questions in moderated forums. There are also programming forums provided by the jQuery community, which you can learn more about at `http://docs.jquery.com/Discussion`.

HOW THIS BOOK IS STRUCTURED

This book is divided into four parts: The first covers the basic API exposed by the jQuery library; the second covers the jQuery UI library; and the third covers a few popular jQuery plugins, as well as how to make a more advanced jQuery plugin. Finally, the appendices contain useful reference material.

Part 1: The jQuery API

> **Chapter 1: Introduction to jQuery**—This chapter discusses where jQuery came from and why it is needed. It includes some good programming practices and the specific programming conventions used in this book. The chapter ends with a walkthrough of downloading your first jQuery-enabled JavaScript.

➤ **Chapter 2: Selecting and Filtering**—This chapter introduces jQuery's selector engine, which uses selectors like you have used with CSS to make selections from the DOM. It discusses the various methods that jQuery exposes for working with a selection to give you fine-grained control over what elements you're working with from the DOM. It talks about methods that enable you to select ancestor elements, parent elements, sibling elements, and descendant elements; how to remove elements from a selection, how to add elements to a selection, and how to reduce a selection to a specific subset of elements.

➤ **Chapter 3: Events**—This chapter discusses jQuery's event wrapper methods, how to attach event handlers that don't have built-in wrapper methods, how to remove event handlers, how to attach persistent event handlers, how to create custom events, and how to namespace your events for easier reference.

➤ **Chapter 4: Manipulating Content and Attributes**—You learn how to use the methods that jQuery exposes for working with content, text, and HTML, and element attributes. jQuery provides methods for doing just about everything you'll want to do to an element.

➤ **Chapter 5: Iteration of Arrays and Objects**—This is about how you can enumerate over a selection of elements or an array using jQuery. As with everything else, jQuery provides an easier way that requires fewer lines of code to loop over the contents of an array or a selection of elements from the DOM.

➤ **Chapter 6: CSS**—You learn about the methods that jQuery exposes for working with CSS properties and declarations. jQuery provides intuitive and versatile methods that enable you to manipulate CSS in a variety of ways.

➤ **Chapter 7: AJAX**—An elaboration on the methods that jQuery exposes for making AJAX requests from a server, which enable you to request server content without working directly with the `XMLHttpRequest` object and supports handling server responses in a variety of formats.

➤ **Chapter 8: Animation and Easing Effects**—This covers the methods jQuery provides for animating elements, including showing and hiding via a simple animation, fading in and fading out, sliding up and sliding down, using completely custom animation, and a variety of easing effects that you can use to control the flow of time in an animation.

➤ **Chapter 9: Plugins**—How to make your own jQuery plugins.

➤ **Chapter 10: Scrollbars**—An explanation of making containers scrollable, including getting and setting the scroll position.

➤ **Chapter 11: HTML5 Drag and Drop**—The official W3C drag-and drop API for dragging and dropping elements within a browser window. This API is considerably different from the Draggable and Droppable jQuery UI plugins because it enables drag and drop between completely different browser windows or applications. Also introduced is the W3C drag-and-drop file upload specification.

Part II: jQuery UI

➤ **Chapter 12: Draggable and Droppable**—You learn how to implement the Draggable and the Droppable jQuery UI plugins to create drag-and-drop API, an alternative to the HTML5 drag-and-drop API introduced in Chapter 11.

➤ **Chapter 13: Sortable**—How you can make lists sortable using drag-and-drop.

➤ **Chapter 14: Selectable**—Learn about the portion of the jQuery UI library that enables you to make a selection by drawing a box with your mouse, just like you might do in your OS's file management application.

➤ **Chapter 15: Accordion**—See how to make a polished-looking sidebar that has panes that transition like an accordion. When you mouse over an element, one pane collapses via an animation, and another one expands, also via an animation.

➤ **Chapter 16: Datepicker**—You make a standard form input field into a Datepicker using jQuery's Datepicker widget.

➤ **Chapter 17: Dialog**—You create virtual pop-up windows, using the jQuery UI library, that look and act like real pop-up windows but are entirely contained in the same web page that launches them and are built using pure markup, CSS, and JavaScript.

➤ **Chapter 18: Tabs**—The jQuery UI tab component, which enables you to take a document and split it into several tabs and navigate between those tabs without needing to load another page.

Part III: Popular Third-Party jQuery Plugins

➤ **Chapter 19: Tablesorter**—An introduction to a third-party jQuery plugin used for sorting HTML tables by one or more columns.

➤ **Chapter 20: Creating an Interactive Slideshow**—You set up a slideshow plugin, a more complicated example of creating a jQuery plugin, which you can then expand on.

➤ **Chapter 21: Working with HTML5 Audio and Video**—Covers the MediaElement plugin, which bridges audio and video support across desktop and mobile platforms for various popular media formats, such as H.264 and MP3 audio.

➤ **Chapter 22: Creating a Simple WYSIWYG Editor**—Discusses the contenteditable attribute and the various components needed to make a text editor inside the browser.

Part IV: Appendices

➤ **Appendix A**—This appendix contains the answers to chapter exercises.

➤ **Appendix B–U**—These appendices contain reference materials for jQuery and jQuery UI.

WHAT YOU NEED TO USE THIS BOOK

To make use of the examples in this book, you need the following:

- ➤ Several Internet browsers to test your web pages
- ➤ Text-editing software or your favorite IDE

Designing content for websites requires reaching more than one type of audience. Some of your audience may use different operating systems or different browsers other than those you installed on your computer. This book focuses on the most popular browsers available at the time of this writing:

- ➤ Microsoft Internet Explorer 10 or newer for Windows
- ➤ Safari 7 or newer for Mac OS X
- ➤ Firefox 30 or newer for Mac OS X, Windows, or Linux
- ➤ Google Chrome 36 or newer for Mac OS X, Windows, or Linux

It is likely that some or most of the examples will work in older versions of these browsers, but that has not been tested.

CONVENTIONS

To help you get the most from the text and keep track of what's happening, you can find a number of conventions throughout the book.

> **WARNING** *Boxes such as this one hold important, not-to-be forgotten information that is directly relevant to the surrounding text.*

> **NOTE** *Notes, tips, hints, tricks, and asides to the current discussion are offset and placed in italics like this.*

As for styles in the text:

- ➤ We *highlight* with italics new terms and important words when we introduce them.
- ➤ We show keyboard strokes like this: Ctrl+A.

➤ We show URLs and code within the text like so: `persistence.properties`.

➤ We present code in the following way:

```
We use a monofont type with no highlighting for most code examples.
```

SOURCE CODE

As you work through the examples, you may choose either to type in all the code manually or to use the source code files that accompany the book. All the source code used in this book is available for download at `www.wrox.com/go/webdevwithjquery`. Click the Download Code link on the book's detail page to obtain all the source code for the book.

> **NOTE** *Because many books have similar titles, you may find it easiest to search by ISBN; this book's ISBN is 978-1-118-86607-8.*

After you download the code, just decompress it with your favorite compression tool. Alternatively, you can go to the main Wrox code download page at `www.wrox.com/dynamic/books/download.aspx` to see the code available for this book and all other Wrox books.

ERRATA

We make every effort to ensure that there are no errors in the text or in the code. However, no one is perfect, and mistakes do occur. If you find an error in one of our books, such as a spelling mistake or faulty piece of code, we would be grateful for your feedback. By sending in errata you may save another reader hours of frustration, and at the same time, you can help us provide even higher-quality information.

To find the errata page for this book, go to `www.wrox.com` and locate the title using the Search box or one of the title lists. Then, on the Book Search Results page, click the Errata link. On this page, you can view all errata that have been submitted for this book and posted by Wrox editors.

> **NOTE** *A complete book list including links to errata is also available at* `www.wrox.com/misc-pages/booklist.shtml`.

If you don't spot "your" error on the Errata page, click the Errata Form link and complete the form to send us the error you have found. We'll check the information and, if appropriate, post a message to the book's Errata page and fix the problem in subsequent editions of the book.

P2P.WROX.COM

For author and peer discussion, join the P2P forums at p2p.wrox.com. The forums are a web-based system for you to post messages relating to Wrox books and related technologies and interact with other readers and technology users. The forums offer a subscription feature to e-mail you topics of interest of your choosing when new posts are made to the forums. Wrox authors, editors, other industry experts, and your fellow readers are present on these forums.

At http://p2p.wrox.com, you can find several different forums to help you not only as you read this book, but also as you develop your own applications. To join the forums, just follow these steps:

1. Go to p2p.wrox.com and click the Register link.

2. Read the terms of use and click Agree.

3. Complete the required information to join as well as any optional information you want to provide and click Submit.

4. You will receive an e-mail with information describing how to verify your account and complete the joining process.

> **NOTE** *You can read messages in the forums without joining P2P, but to post your own messages, you must join.*

After you join, you can post new messages and respond to messages other users post. You can read messages at any time on the web. If you want to have new messages from a particular forum e-mailed to you, click the Subscribe to This Forum icon by the forum name in the forum listing.

For more information about how to use the Wrox P2P, be sure to read the P2P FAQs for answers to questions about how the forum software works as well as many common questions specific to P2P and Wrox books. To read the FAQs, click the FAQ link on any P2P page.

Web Development with jQuery®

PART 1
The jQuery API

1

Introduction to jQuery

JavaScript frameworks have arisen as necessary and useful companions for client-side web development. Just a few years ago, JavaScript frameworks were needed to pave over the many inconsistencies present with cross-platform web development. Before Microsoft got its act together and gave us IE with vastly improved standards support, there was more often than not the IE way and the standard way. Frameworks like jQuery helped immensely to fill in the holes between standard and nonstandard. Today jQuery is a phenomenally popular, leading JavaScript framework and application development platform. It is leaner; it is faster loading; and it comes loaded with features that make the life of a JavaScript application developer much easier. No longer is JavaScript an afterthought, grafted onto stateless HTML. It is used more and more to be the foundation and the primary driving force of not only web development but also application development, from desktop to tablets and smartphones.

Thanks to renewed vigor in the browser and platform wars of the big tech giants, JavaScript has also become much leaner and faster. Today, the leading browser makers are delivering JavaScript capabilities that take the good ole reliable, interpreted language of JavaScript and instantly transform it into cached machine byte code that can be executed blazingly fast. Because of the collective advances and one-upmanship of Apple, Google, Mozilla, and Microsoft, today we have JavaScript that has never performed better.

When this book was first written in 2009, jQuery was emerging as the de facto standard JavaScript framework and application platform. Today jQuery sits atop the heap as a global leader facilitating cutting-edge web and application development from mom-and-pop shops to Fortune 500 companies. It is baked into iOS and Android apps and mobile websites both with and without the popular jQuery Mobile framework add-on, and it runs the websites of some of the world's biggest companies, such as Amazon, Apple, *The New York Times*, Google, BBC, Twitter, and IBM.

For years JavaScript frameworks have paved over the craters and inconsistencies of cross-browser web development to create a seamless, enjoyable client-side programming experience. Today, with Internet Explorer 11 and its underlying Trident engine, Microsoft finally has a world-class standards-compliant web browser that's caught up with competing offerings from Apple's Safari and world-leading, underlying, open-source WebKit, Google's Chrome browser and newly forked from WebKit Blink engine, and Mozilla's Firefox powered by the Gecko engine. Web developers have never had better platforms on which to build modern, fully standards-compliant applications.

One of jQuery's biggest innovations was its fantastic DOM querying tool using familiar CSS selector syntax. This component, now called Sizzle, is now a separate open-source component included within the larger open-source jQuery framework. It contains jQuery's added on CSS pseudo-class selectors and the full DOM querying CSS selector engine that works in browsers as old as IE6 as well as new browsers. It uses the native JavaScript document, `querySelectorAll()` function call, which makes DOM queries using CSS selectors fast, when it is available. Sizzle is one of the biggest driving forces that makes jQuery web development super easy and has thus attracted a large number of developers to the jQuery world.

Another feature that makes jQuery web development very easy and attractive is its support for chained method calls. Where the API supports it, you can call one method after another by chaining method calls on the backs of one another. This is what a chained method call looks like using jQuery:

```
$('<div/>')
    .addClass('selected')
    .attr({
        id : 'body',
        title : 'Welcome to jQuery'
    })
    .text("Hello, World!");
```

In the preceding example, a `<div>` element is created with jQuery. jQuery is contained within the dollar sign variable, `$`, which is a JavaScript variable just one character long. This variable contains the entire jQuery framework and is the starting point for everything that you can do with jQuery. The statement `$('<div/>')` creates the `<div>` element, and then you see multiple method calls following that statement. `.addClass('selected')` adds the class attribute to the `<div>` element. Then there is a call to `.attr()`, which adds two additional attributes to the `<div>` element, an `id` attribute and a `title` attribute, and then the call to `.text()` fills the `<div>` element with plain text content. With this little snippet of code, you have four separate method calls all strung together to form a single expression spanning multiple lines. This brief sample of what jQuery can do results in the creation of a `<div>` element that can be inserted into the DOM that looks like this:

```
<div class="selected" id="body" title="Welcome to jQuery">Hello, World</
div>
```

jQuery packs a powerful punch; it helps you develop better JavaScript applications by facilitating powerful DOM interaction and manipulation with less code than you would use with a pure JavaScript approach. This is what is meant by jQuery's motto, "Write less, do more." Compare the snippet of jQuery that I presented with the following, which creates the same `<div>` element with pure JavaScript:

```
var div = document.createElement('div');

div.className = 'selected';
div.id = 'body';
```

```
div.title = 'Welcome to jQuery';

var text = document.createTextNode ("Hello, World!");

div.appendChild(div);
```

As you can see, jQuery is much less verbose. It wraps around traditional, native JavaScript APIs to help you as a developer get more done with JavaScript using less code, allowing application development to go more quickly.

In this chapter I present the following information:

➤ What jQuery can do for you

➤ Who develops jQuery?

➤ Where and how to get jQuery

➤ How to install and use jQuery for the first time

➤ XHTML and CSS programming conventions

➤ JavaScript programming conventions

WHAT JQUERY CAN DO FOR YOU

As presented in the last section, jQuery makes many tasks easier. Its simplistic, chainable, and comprehensive API has the capability to completely change the way you write JavaScript. With the goals of doing more with less code, jQuery really shines in the following areas:

➤ jQuery makes iterating and traversing the DOM much easier via its various built-in methods.

➤ jQuery makes selecting items from the DOM easier via its sophisticated, built-in, and ubiquitous capability to use selectors, just like you would use in CSS.

➤ jQuery makes it easy to add your own custom methods via its simple-to-understand plug-in architecture.

➤ jQuery helps reduce redundancy in navigation and UI functionality, like tabs, CSS, and markup-based pop-up dialogs, animations, and transitions, and lots of other things.

Is jQuery the only JavaScript framework? No, certainly not. You can pick from several JavaScript frameworks: Yahoo UI, Prototype, SproutCore, Dojo, and so on. I like jQuery because I enjoy its simplicity and lack of verbosity. However, among the other frameworks, you'll find that there is a lot of similarity, and each provides its own advantages in terms of unifying Event APIs, providing sophisticated selector and traversal implementations, and providing simple interfaces for redundant JavaScript-driven UI tasks. Across the entire web, including websites that don't use any JavaScript frameworks, jQuery can be found on as many as half of all websites. So, jQuery definitely has the benefit of a ubiquitous, de facto standard. Based on its popularity, you're extremely likely to run into other developers who have experience with and know how to use jQuery.

Another aspect of jQuery programming I enjoy is that jQuery doesn't seek to impose its own opinions about programming onto you, its user. Some frameworks, ExtJS in particular, seek to completely circumvent traditional JavaScript, HTML, and CSS web development with complicated Model–View–Controller (MVC) implementations that seek to auto-generate the HTML and CSS portions for you, which is perfectly fine, if that's how you like to program. jQuery does not impose any kind of programming paradigm on you, the user. Combined with tools that are designed to work well with it, such as Mustache.js and Backbone.js, a more reasonable programming paradigm can be achieved alongside the popular MVC-based programming pattern, in which you still have control over the HTML and CSS that you create and use.

In past years, what initially drew developers to jQuery-based web development was its incredibly simple way of erasing the lines between browsers. It presented a unified API for event handling, whereas before JavaScript frameworks came along, you had a clumsy fragmented approach in which Microsoft had one way for IE and the other browsers had the standard way. jQuery made cross-browser web development easy and seamless. Today, developers continue to flock to jQuery, no longer because of fragmentation because those issues have been slowly resolved over the last four years, but simply because it is leaner and easier to understand and use than native JavaScript programming. Finally, Microsoft has implemented the standard event-handling model in Internet Explorer that everyone else has been using for more than a decade. The latest version of jQuery, version 2.0, sheds the legacy baggage that facilitated that cross-browser web development, allowing jQuery to become leaner and faster.

That's not to say that there are no more cross-browser issues. There are still areas of JavaScript development in which there are multiple approaches. Thankfully, these areas are becoming fewer and fewer. Cross-browser issues exist more today in cutting-edge CSS where browsers make brand-new, experimental features available using vendor-prefixed CSS properties. One of the most frustrating examples is that of gradients in CSS, where to implement the feature correctly in modern and legacy browsers, you have up to seven different ways of writing the same gradient:

➤ WebKit's extremely syntactically verbose first stab at CSS gradients: `-webkit-gradient`

➤ WebKit's implementation of the revised standard: `-webkit-linear-gradient` and `-webkit-radial-gradient`

➤ The current W3C CSS3 standard: `linear-gradient` and `radial-gradient`

➤ Microsoft's vendor-prefixed standards-compliant implementation of the W3C standard: `-ms-linear-gradient` and `-ms-radial-gradient`

➤ Microsoft's proprietary implementation of gradients found in the old `filter` and `-ms-filter` properties

➤ Mozilla's implementation: `-moz-linear-gradient` and `-moz-radial-gradient`

➤ Opera's implementation previous to their adoption of Google's WebKit fork (now Blink) engine: `-o-linear-gradient` and `-o-radial-gradient`

As you can see, the situation with using cutting-edge CSS that is still working its way through the standardization process is not pleasant for web developers. Unfortunately, rather than adopting a comprehensive approach, most web developers stop with the `-webkit-` variants, and they don't bother implementing the variants supported by other browsers. This, in part, is what persuaded Opera to discontinue development of its own Presto engine in favor of Google's Blink fork of WebKit. This used to be the kind of thing developers needed a framework like jQuery to solve. This particular situation is solved, by the way, by using server-side dynamically generated CSS template solutions, or even a client-side jQuery plugin.

The beauty of jQuery is that it can solve problems like vendor-specific CSS gradients as well as the remaining cross-browser issues that exist in JavaScript through its comprehensive and easy-to-use plugin ecosystem. Several great third-party jQuery plugins are presented later in this book.

WHO DEVELOPS JQUERY?

I won't spend a lot of time talking about the history of JavaScript frameworks, why they exist, and so on. I prefer to get straight to the point. That said, a brief mention of the people involved with developing jQuery is in order.

jQuery's original creator is John Resig, whose website is located at www.ejohn.org. John resides in Brooklyn, New York, and is presently the Dean of Computer Science at Khan Academy. John still helps with defining the direction and goals of the jQuery project, but jQuery has largely been transitioned to a large team of people. You can learn more about these people and what roles they played in jQuery's development at https://jquery.org/team/.

OBTAINING JQUERY

jQuery is a free, Open Source JavaScript Framework. The current stable, production release version, as of this writing, is 1.10.2 and 2.0.3. The difference in these two versions of jQuery largely revolve around legacy browser support; the 2.0 release of jQuery dispenses with the huge amount of legacy baggage it needed to facilitate support with older versions of Internet Explorer.

I use version 1.10.2 throughout the course of this book, for maximum browser compatibility. Getting jQuery is extremely easy—all you have to do is go to www.jquery.com and click the Download jQuery link. You'll see two options for downloading either the 1.x version or the 2.x version:

- ➤ A compressed production version
- ➤ An uncompressed development version

The uncompressed development version is recommended for use while you are developing. This version can facilitate doing back traces with web developer tools in any of the major browsers. You can walk through the JavaScript chain of execution and see what code is executing in nice, human-readable code. The compressed production version is recommended for use on production websites where size is a huge consideration; the file is compressed to remove all the extra whitespace so that it downloads quickly.

INSTALLING JQUERY

Throughout this book, I will refer to the jQuery script as though it is installed at the following path: www.example.com/jQuery/jQuery.js.

Therefore, if I were using the domain example.com, jQuery would have this path from the document root, /jQuery/jQuery.js. You do not have to install jQuery at this exact path. You can move jQuery wherever you like, but don't forget to update the path.

HELLO, WORLD IN JQUERY

In the following example you learn how to install jQuery and execute a remedial "Hello, World" jQuery-based JavaScript application. To start, follow these steps:

1. Download the jQuery script from www.jquery.com. Alternatively, I have also provided the jQuery script in this book's source code download materials available for free from www.wrox.com/go/webdevwithjquery.

2. Enter the following XHTML document, and save the document as **Example 1-1.html**. Adjust your path to jQuery appropriately; the path that I use reflects the path needed for the example to work when opened in a browser via the source code materials download made available for this book.

```
<!DOCTYPE HTML>
<html xmlns="http://www.w3.org/1999/xhtml">
    <head>
        <meta http-equiv="content-type"
            content="application/xhtml+xml; charset=utf-8" />
        <meta http-equiv="content-language" content="en-us" />
        <title>Hello, World</title>
        <script type='text/javascript' src='../jQuery.js'></
script>
        <script type='text/javascript' src='Example 1-1.js'>
            </script>
        <link type='text/css' href='Example 1-1.css'
            rel='stylesheet' />
    </head>
    <body>

    </body>
</html>
```

3. Enter the following JavaScript document, and save the document as **Example 1-1.js**:

```
$(document).ready(
    function()
    {
        $('body').append(
            $('<div/>')
                .addClass('selected')
```

```
                    .attr({
                        id : 'body',
                        title : 'Welcome to jQuery'
                    })
                    .text(
                        "Hello, World!"
                    )
            );
        }
    );
);
```

4. Enter the following CSS document, and save the document as **Example 1-1.css**:

    ```css
    body {
            margin: 0;
            padding: 20px;
            font: 14px Helvetica, Arial, sans-serif;
    }
    div.selected {
            background: blue;
            color: white;
            padding: 5px;
            display: inline-block;
    }
    ```

The preceding code results in the screen shot that you see in Figure 1-1 if the installation were unsuccessful. If installation were not successful, the page appears blank.

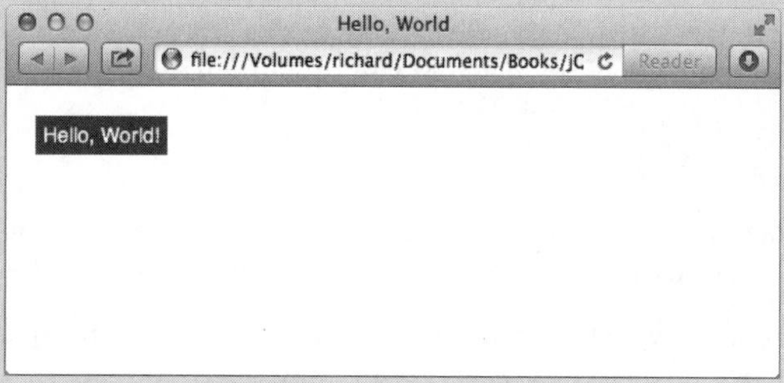

FIGURE 1-1

In the preceding example, you installed and tested your installation of the jQuery framework. The JavaScript that you included is executed when the document's onready event is fired, which is executed as soon as the DOM is fully loaded: all markup, JavaScript, and CSS, but not images. The callback function attached to the onready event then creates a <div> element with the *selected* class name and contains the text *Hello, World!*

You have now used jQuery for the first time.

PROGRAMMING CONVENTIONS

In web development, it's common for professional software engineers, web designers, and web developers—and anyone with a job title whose day-to-day activities encompass the maintenance of source code—to adopt standards and conventions with regard to how the source code is written. Standardization bodies like the W3C, which define the languages that you use to create websites, already decide on some standards for you. Some standards are not written but are rather de facto standards. De facto standards are standards that have become accepted throughout the industry, despite not appearing in any official document developed by a standards organization.

Throughout this book, I talk about standards, de facto and official, and how to develop and design web-based documents and even web-based applications that take those standards into account. For example, I talk extensively about how to separate behavior (JavaScript) from presentation (CSS) and structure (XHTML). JavaScript written in this way is commonly referred to as *nonintrusive* JavaScript—it's nonintrusive because it supplements the content of a web document, and, were it turned off, the document would still be functional. CSS is used to handle all the presentational aspects of the document. And the structure of the document lives in semantically written XHTML. XHTML that is *semantically written* is organized meaningfully with the right markup elements and contains little, if any, presentational components directly in the markup.

In addition to standards, I discuss how to develop web-based documents, taking into account different browser inconsistencies, discrepancies, and idiosyncrasies. There is some interactive functionality that nearly every browser handles differently; in those situations, other web professionals have already pioneered de facto standards that are used to bring all browsers into accord. The idea of a JavaScript foundational framework has become more popular and increasingly a dependency for HTML5 applications, like the ones you'll learn to develop using the jQuery framework.

Before I begin the discussion of how to use jQuery, the coming sections provide a generalized overview of programming conventions and good practice that you should follow.

Markup and CSS Conventions

It's important that your web documents be well organized, cleanly written, and appropriately named and stored. This requires discipline and even an obsessive attention to the tiniest of details.

The following is a list of rules to abide by when creating XHTML and CSS documents:

➤ When selecting id and class names, make sure that they are descriptive and are contained in a namespace. You never know when you might need to combine one project with another—namespaces help you to prevent conflicts.

➤ When defining CSS, avoid using generic type selectors. Make your CSS more specific. This can also help with preventing conflicts.

➤ Organize your files in a coherent manner. Group files from the same project in the same folder; separate multiple projects with multiple folders. Avoid creating huge file dumps that make it difficult to locate and associate files.

➤ Avoid inaccessible markup. Stay away from frames, where possible. Organize your markup using semantically appropriate elements. Place paragraphs in <p> elements. Place lists in <ul> or <ol> elements. Use <h1> through <h6> for headings, and so on.

➤ If you can, also consider the loading efficiency of your documents. For development, use small, modularized files organized by the component; combine and compress those modularized files for a live production site.

Id and Class Naming Conventions

Most web developers don't think too much about the topics of namespacing and naming conventions. Naming conventions are just as important in your markup id and class names as namespacing is important in programming languages.

First, what is namespacing, and why do you need to do it? *Namespacing* is the concept of making your programs, source code, and so on tailored to a particular naming convention, in an effort to make your programs more portable and more capable of living in diverse, foreign programming environments. In other words, if you want to directly insert a web application into your document, you want to be sure that the class and id names, style sheets and script, and all the bits that make your web application what it is do not conflict with any applications that are already present in the document. Your applications should be fully self-contained and self-sufficient and not collide or conflict with any elements already present in a document.

What are some common id names that people use in style sheets? Think first about what the typical components of a web application are. There's a body. There may be one or more columns. There may be a header and a footer, and there are lots of components that can potentially be identified as generic, redundant pieces that all web applications may have. Then, it stands to reason that plenty of websites are probably using id and class names like *body, header, footer, column, left, right,* and so on. If you name an element with the id or class name *body,* you have a good chance of conflicting with an overwhelming majority of websites in existence today. To avoid this type of conflict, it's considered good practice to prefix id and class names within a web application to avoid conflicts and namespace collisions. If you write an application called *tagger,* you might namespace that application by prefixing all your id and class names with the word *tagger.* For example, you might have *taggerBody, taggerHeader, taggerFooter,* and so on. It may be possible, however, that someone has already written an application called *tagger.* To be safe, you might do a web search on the name you've chosen for your application to make sure that no one's already using that name. Typically, simply prefixing your id and class names with your application's name is enough.

In addition, it also helps to prefix id and class names with type selectors in style sheets. *Type* selectors help you narrow down what to look for when modifying or maintaining a document. For example, the id selector #thisId is ambiguous. You don't know what kind of element thisId is, and thus would likely have to scan the entire document to find it. But div#thisId is more specific. By including the div in the selector, you instantly know you're looking for a <div> element. Including the type in the selector also helps you in another way: When dealing with class names, you can have the same class name applied to different types of elements. Although I may not condone that as good practice, at least in the style sheet, you can control which element gets which style. `span.someClass` and `div.someClass` are selectors that differentiate style based on the type of element, whereas `.someClass` is more ambiguous and applies to any element.

Id and class names should also be descriptive of their purpose in a semantically meaningful way. Keep in mind that an id name can potentially be used in a URL as an HTML anchor. Which is better: `www.example.com/index.html#left` or `www.example.com/index.html#exampleRelatedDocuments`? The latter id anchor is namespaced `example` for *example.com*, and `RelatedDocuments` is the name of the element; thus, the latter URL includes more information about what purpose the element serves and greatly increases the maintainability of the document in a very intuitive way. In addition, the latter has more benefit in terms of search engine optimization (SEO). The former is too ambiguous and won't provide much in the way of SEO. Think of each of your id and class names as though it is part of the URL of your document. Give each id and class name that you create semantic names that convey meaning and purpose.

Generic Type Selectors

Generic type selectors are style-sheet rules that look something like this:

```
a {
    color: #29629E;
}
```

In the preceding style-sheet rule, you see what's probably a pretty common scenario, changing the color of every link in a document via a generic type selector that refers to all `<a>` elements. Generic type selectors should be avoided for the same reason that it is good to namespace id and class names within a document, avoiding conflicts when multiple scripts or style sheets are combined in the same document. Instead, it's best practice to apply id or class names to these elements, or at the very least place them in a container that has an id or class name, and only use descendant selectors when referencing those elements via a style sheet.

```
div#exampleBanner a {
    color: #29629E;
}
```

The preceding example avoids the pitfalls introduced by using a blanket, generic selector style-sheet rule by limiting the scope of the style-sheet rule's application. Now, only `<a>` elements that are descendants of a `<div>` with the id name *exampleBanner* receive the declaration `color: #29629E;`.

Storing and Organizing Files

How files are organized and stored is important to the maintainability of a document. You should maintain your documents in an easy-to-understand, easy-to-learn directory hierarchy. Different people have different approaches to storing and organizing files, obviously. What matters is that there is an organization scheme, rather than none at all. Some choose to store documents by type and then separate them by application, whereas others prefer to separate by application first and then sort by type.

Avoid Making Documents Inaccessible

Accessibility is also an important factor to consider in the design of a web document. You should do your best to make your JavaScript nonintrusive, but also avoid taking away a document's accessibility by either script or markup.

➤ Avoid using frames.

➤ Limit the number of images to those that actually contribute to the content of a document. With the CSS3, Data URIs and SVG standards, much more of what used to be required image content for the design of a site no longer has to be included in images and can be programmed with either CSS3 or SVG (for example, gradients or inner or drop shadows). When you have to use images, try to contain as much of the design as possible in CSS background images. Make available double-resolution images for retina or high-resolution devices. And keep images that directly contribute to the content in `<img />` elements. Be sure to include `alt` attributes that describe the image for each `<img />` element.

➤ Place content in semantically appropriate markup containers—use `<p>` for paragraphs, `<h1>` through `<h6>` for headings. Use the new HTML5/XHTML5 elements designed to make semantic content more semantic: `<heading>`, `<article>`, `<aside>`, `<summary>`, to name just a few.

➤ Make the design high contrast when possible. Imagine what the document would look like through the eyes of someone with poor vision. Can you easily read the content?

➤ Avoid wandering too far away from established user-interface conventions. Can you distinguish hyperlinks from normal content?

➤ Consider making the content keyboard-accessible. Can you navigate without a pointing device?

➤ Make the content more unobtrusive. Can you use the website without Flash and JavaScript functionality? JavaScript and Flash should enhance web content in a complementary way, not be a requirement.

➤ Avoid placing a large number of links at the beginning of every document. If you were listening to the content being read to you, rather than seeing it visually, would the experience be enjoyable?

Accessibility should be practiced to the point of becoming an automatic reflex. It should be cemented in your development practices in a fundamental way in the same way that namespacing and file organization are. Although other best practices can become second nature easily, it's also easy to get into the habit of ignoring accessibility, so a conscious effort must be made to periodically review accessibility and ingrain accessibility in the development process.

Efficiency in Markup and CSS

Markup and CSS in a complex website can easily become large and bloated and drag down overall loading and execution times more and more. This can become particularly troublesome as the overall popularity of a site increases. As the complexity of a website increases, it becomes necessary to look into ways of streamlining the content. It's best to limit the number of external files being loaded, but all CSS and JavaScript should be included in at least one external file. Were JavaScript and CSS included directly in a document, the initial loading time would improve, but you'd also lose the advantage of separately caching JavaScript and CSS on the client side.

For the best of the best in efficiency, combine the following concepts:

➤ Server-side gzip compression. You should test your website with this feature enabled and disabled because it has some trade-offs involved. See if gzip compression is right for you. In my experience gzip may make files load more quickly, but it can also delay when you see content because it prevents incremental rendering from occurring. It is usually more important that your users see content as quickly as possible.

➤ Aggressive client-side caching; this makes subsequent page loads much faster.

➤ Automatic compression of markup content by removing excess whitespace and comments from the markup source.

➤ Automatic compression and consolidation of multiple CSS and JavaScript files by removing all excess whitespace and comments from each file. Appropriately combining files further decreases load times by reducing HTTP latency.

When the preceding items are combined, you make the loading times of a web document the best possible; however, there are some caveats to consider that may at first seem contradictory:

➤ Maintainable markup should be written in a neat and organized manner. It should be well spaced and indented and contain line breaks where appropriate.

➤ Good programming practice means modularized development, so break up your CSS and JavaScript by component and application. Make small, easy-to-digest chunks. This will speed up your ability to maintain and extend projects.

➤ Client-side caching can lead to headaches when updates are made to CSS or script files. Browsers will continue to use the old version of the CSS and script files after an update is made, when caching is working correctly.

The good news is that all the preceding caveats can be overcome. The bad news is that it's not particularly easy to overcome them.

The best way to implement efficiency in markup, JavaScript, and CSS documents is to make the efficiency automatic. That is to say, write server-side applications that handle efficiency tasks for you. A well-designed, professional content management system can work out those bits for you. It can allow you to make your JavaScript, markup, and CSS documents modularized and separate them based on the task each is designed to perform but automatically combine and compress those documents for you.

Unfortunately, not everyone can use a professional content management system to serve their content. For those individuals, there are some compromises to be made:

➤ JavaScript and CSS can be hand-compressed using a web-based utility like Dean Edwards's packer, `http://dean.edwards.name/packer`. Development can continue to be modularized, and the compression and consolidation portion of development simply becomes a manual task.

➤ You can limit the amount of whitespace you use in a document. Indent content with two spaces instead of four.

Overcoming the headaches with document caching, however, is a much easier task. You can force a browser to update a document by changing its path. For example, say you have the following script included in your markup:

```
<script src='/script/my.js' type='text/javascript'></script>
```

You change the path from /script/my.js to /script/my.js?lastModified=09/16/07. The latter references the same, my.js, but is technically a different path to the browser, and the browser, consequently, will force refreshing of its cached copy of the document. The *?lastModified=09/16/07* portion of the path is the *query string* portion of the path. The query string begins with a question mark and then contains one or more query string variables. Query string variables are used by a server-side programming language or client-side JavaScript to pass information from one document to another. In this example, there is no information being passed per se. You're including the time of the last modification, although I could have just as easily included the revision, or even a random string of characters. The inclusion of a query string in this example has only one purpose: to force the browser into refreshing the cached version of the document.

The same can be done with CSS:

```
<link type='text/css' rel='stylesheet' href='/styles/
my.css?lastModified=09/16/07' />
```

In the preceding snippet of markup that includes an external CSS document, the query string is used to force a refresh of the browser's cached copy of the style sheet my.css.

The next section talks about some conventions specific to JavaScript.

JavaScript Conventions

In JavaScript, several things should be considered bad practice and avoided:

➤ Include all script in external documents—JavaScript code should be included only in external script files. Script should not be embedded in markup documents or be included inline, directly on markup elements.

➤ Write clean, consistent code—JavaScript code should be neatly formatted and organized in a consistent, predicable way.

➤ Namespace JavaScript code—JavaScript variables, functions, objects, and the like should be namespaced to minimize potential namespace conflicts and collisions with other JavaScript applications.

➤ Avoid browser detection—Browser detection should be avoided where possible. Instead, detect specific browser features.

The next sections present cursory, generalized overviews of each of the preceding concepts.

Include All Script in External Documents

Part of making JavaScript nonobtrusive means making JavaScript complementary and supplemental, rather than required and mandatory. This concept is explored in detail throughout this book; however, it should be noted why this is the best approach.

Consider the following code example:

```
<!DOCTYPE HTML>
<html xmlns="http://www.w3.org/1999/xhtml">
    <head>
        <meta http-equiv="content-type"
            content="application/xhtml+xml; charset=utf-8" />
        <meta http-equiv="content-language" content="en-us" />
        <title>Hello, World</title>
    <link type='text/css' href='Example 1-2.css' rel='stylesheet' />
    </head>
    <body>
        <p>
            <img src="pumpkin.jpg" alt="Pumpkin" />
            <a href="javascript:void(0);"
                onclick="window.open(
                    'pumpkin.jpg',
                    'picture',
                    'scrollbars=no,width=300,height=280,resizable=yes');">
                Open Picture
            </a>
        </p>
    </body>
</html>
```

Combine the preceding markup with the following style sheet:

```
img {
    display: block;
    margin: 10px auto;
    width: 100px;
    border: 1px solid rgb(128, 128, 128);
}
body {
    font: 14px sans-serif;
}
p {
    width: 150px;
    text-align: center;
}
```

The preceding code gives you something like what you see in Figure 1-2.

In Figure 1-2, you see what is probably a common scenario: You have a thumbnail, and you can click to see a bigger version of the thumbnail. This is the kind of thing that JavaScript works well for—giving you the bigger version in a separate pop-up window that doesn't have any controls.

Now examine why what I did in Figure 1-2 was the wrong way to go about adding this functionality.

FIGURE 1-2

Here are the problems with this approach:

➤ If JavaScript is disabled, viewing the larger picture doesn't work.

  ➤ JavaScript can be disabled out of personal preference.

  ➤ JavaScript can be disabled because of company policy.

➤ Placing the JavaScript directly in the markup document adds unnecessary bloat and complexity to the markup document.

The overwhelming point in all this is that inline JavaScript is a bad way to approach adding complementary, interactive functionality to a web document.

Here is a better approach to the application presented in Figure 1-2. First, take the inline JavaScript out of the markup and replace it with a reference to an externally loaded JavaScript. The following example names the externally loaded JavaScript `Example 1-3.js`:

```
<!DOCTYPE HTML>
<html xmlns="http://www.w3.org/1999/xhtml">
    <head>
        <meta http-equiv="content-type"
            content="application/xhtml+xml; charset=utf-8" />
        <meta http-equiv="content-language" content="en-us" />
        <title>Pumpkin Head</title>
        <script type='text/javascript' src='../jQuery.js'></script>
        <script type='text/javascript' src='Example 1-3.js'></script>
        <link type='text/css' href='Example 1-3.css' rel='stylesheet' />
    </head>
    <body>
        <p>
```

```
<img src="pumpkin.jpg" alt="Pumpkin" />
<a href="pumpkin.jpg" id="examplePumpkin" target="_blank">
    Open Picture
</a>
        </p>
    </body>
</html>
```

Then in the externally loaded JavaScript you do something like the following:

```
$(document).ready(
    function()
    {
        $('a#examplePumpkin').click(
            function(event)
            {
                event.preventDefault();

                window.open(
                    'pumpkin.jpg',
                    'Pumpkin',
                    'scrollbars=no,width=300,height=280,resizable=yes'
                );
            }
        );

    }
);
```

With the preceding bits of code, you get the results that you see in Figure 1-3.

FIGURE 1-3

This is an example of nonobtrusive JavaScript. Nonobtrusive JavaScript provides extended, interactive functionality within a web document, but does not do so in a way that obstructs using the document in a plain-vanilla manner. That is to say, with JavaScript disabled, you can still use the website and get what you need from it.

In the preceding example, the JavaScript is moved to an external document called *Example 1-3.js*. Within *Example 1-3.js* jQuery is used to call upon an <a> element with the id name *examplePumpkin*, and this in turn opens the pop-up window. If JavaScript is disabled, the picture is still opened in another window, but if JavaScript is disabled, you just can't control the size of the window or whether it has controls.

So far, the user clicks an <a> element and gets a pop-up window. You want the window to pop up instead of initiating the default action that occurs when a user clicks a link, which instead of doing nothing, is now for the browser to navigate to the document defined in the href attribute of the <a> element, also in a new window. This default action is prevented with the call to event.preventDefault().

In this simple example, you've seen how a simple example can become something a little more complex, but not much more complex. With a little further thought and attention to detail, a simple enhancement can continue to function if the user has disabled script in his browser.

Write Clean, Consistent Code

It's important to follow some predetermined criteria for producing clean, consistent, well-organized code. In the professional world, most programmers have a particular way they like to see their code formatted. Earlier in this section, I talked about how indenting and spacing markup and CSS documents can help you more easily catch errors in those documents and make those documents more maintainable. Well, the same can be applied to JavaScript. Here I talk about each of the programming conventions that I follow for writing JavaScript source code.

Indenting and Line Length

It's a good idea to indent your code so that it's easier to read and maintain. Take the following, for example:

```
window.onload=function(){var nodes=document.getElementsByTagName('a');
for(var i = 0,length=nodes.length;i<length;i++){nodes[i].onclick=
function(event){window.open(this.href,"picture",
"scrollbars=no,width=300,height=280,resizable=yes");
event? event.preventDefault():(window.event.returnValue=false);};};}};
```

In the preceding block of code, you see the contents of *Example 1-3.js* presented above in this section, formatted without any indenting or spacing. Now, imagine that the preceding code is 10,000 lines of code spread out over many files, all formatted the same way. It's not a bad idea to reduce spacing for a live, production script; in fact, many professionals use compression routines specifically for this. But those same professionals don't maintain their scripts in the compressed format and often have a rigid programming standard to which every script they produce must conform.

A common, fairly universal programming standard is setting the size of an indentation to four spaces, although some use just two spaces or other values. This is in addition to setting a blanket rule that tabs cannot be used in place of individual spaces, even though, technically, a tab character results in less bytes added to a file when compared to four individual space characters. The "no tab" rule exists because of the wide variance in the interpretation of what a tab character is in text applications. Some text applications say that a tab character is equal to eight individual spaces. Some text applications say that a tab character is equal to four individual spaces, whereas others still let you explicitly define how big a tab character is. These variances have led to the tab character being unreliable for spacing purposes in code. Most professional integrated developer environments (IDEs) let you define the [Tab] key on a keyboard as individual spaces, in addition to letting you define how many spaces to insert.

Some examples of IDEs are Coda, Adobe Dreamweaver, Eclipse, Zend Studio, and Microsoft Visual Studio: These are all development environments for either directly writing or generating source code. In addition, most IDEs try to guess what you mean when writing a source document by intelligently adjusting the number of spaces. For example, when you press [Return] to begin a new line in your source code document, the IDE can indent the new line with at least as much space as the preceding line. Most IDEs behave this way by default. Dreamweaver automatically inserts two spaces when you press the [Tab] key. Coda, Eclipse, and Zend Studio can all be configured to insert spaces instead of tab characters when you press the [Tab] key.

Throughout this book, I use four spaces for a [Tab] key, although limited space may sometimes require that I use two characters. Generally, the professional standard for client-side source code is two characters because four characters makes file sizes much larger. I've stuck with four because concerns about file size and bandwidth usage can be addressed by compressing your source code when it's used on a production website.

Control Structures

Control structures include programming statements that begin with the keywords if, else, switch, case, for, while, try, catch, and so on. Control structure programming statements are the building blocks of any programming language. Now see how control structure statements should be formatted with regard to popular programming standards and guidelines.

Although, ultimately, different people have different preferences for how to write source code, there are two prevailing methods for formatting control structures in use by the majority of the professional programming community.

The following convention, which is formally called *K&R Style*, is included in Sun's Coding Standards Guidelines for Java:

```
if (condition) {
    something = 1;
} else if (another) {
    something = 2;
} else {
    something = 3;
}
```

In the preceding code example, you see that the curly braces and the parentheses are used as markers for indention.

Compare the preceding to the next convention, which is known as *Allman Style*, which is the default in Microsoft Visual Studio:

```
if (condition)
{
    something = 1;
}
else if (another)
{
    something = 2;
}
else
{
    something = 3;
}
```

In Allman Style, all the curly braces line up in the source code, which makes it easier to detect when one is missing, in addition to preventing typos like missing curly braces from occurring in the first place because you have a visual aid for their placement. It also lends itself nicely to having more space between lines of code, making things easier to read.

When function calls, like window.open in the example, are long, sometimes the function call is broken up over multiple lines to make it easier to read. To the browser,

```
window.open(
    this.href,
    "picture",
    "scrollbars=no,width=300,height=280,resizable=yes"
);
```

and

```
window.open(this.href, "picture", "scrollbars=no,width=300,height=280,resizable=yes");
```

are exactly the same. The former example just makes it easier for humans to parse the arguments present in the function call.

Sometimes these two conventions are mixed to form a third convention, which is known as the *One True Brace* convention. This convention is defined in the Coding Standards Guidelines for PHP's PEAR repository.

```
window.onload = function()
{
    var nodes = document.getElementsByTagName('a');

    for (var counter = 0, length = nodes.length; counter < length; counter++) {
        nodes[counter].onclick = function(event) {
            window.open(
                this.href,
                "picture",
                "scrollbars=no,width=300,height=280,resizable=yes"
            );
```

```
                         event? event.preventDefault() : (window.event.returnValue = false);
            };
        }
    };
```

In the One True Brace convention, the function assigned to `window.onload` follows the Allman Style, while the code within it follows K&R Style.

When I write JavaScript code, I prefer a mixture of Allman Style and K&R Style. I use Allman Style for all function and class definitions as well as control structures, and I use K&R Style for array and object definitions (JSON), and function calls. In practice this looks something like this:

```
$(document).ready(
    function()
    {
        $('a#examplePumpkin').click(
            function(event)
            {
                event.preventDefault();

                window.open(
                    'pumpkin.jpg',
                    'Pumpkin',
                    'scrollbars=no,width=300,height=280,resizable=yes'
                );
            }
        );

    }
);
```

Which programming convention you use is, of course, a matter of personal taste. Often which convention to use can lead to endless battles among programming teams; sometimes people have different tastes. How you indent your code can be a touchy and personal topic. You should use whichever convention makes the most sense for you. Although the methods I've showcased are the most popular, there are a multitude of variations that exist out there in the real world. You can find more information about programming indention styles on Wikipedia at `http://en.wikipedia.org/wiki/Indent_style`.

Optional Curly Braces and Semicolons

In the previous conventions, you'll note that there is always a single space between the keyword that begins the control structure, like `if` and the opening parenthesis. The following is a `switch` control structure using the first convention:

```
switch (variable) {
    case 1:
        condition = 'this';
        break;

    case 2:
        condition = 'that';
```

```
        break;

    default:
        condition = 'those';
}
```

Note in the preceding that no `break` statement appears in the default case. As the default, a break is implied, and it is not necessary to include the `break` statement. I tend to deviate from the norm with how I prefer `switch` control structures to be written.

```
switch (variable)
{
    case 1:
    {
        condition = 'this';
        break;
    };
    case 2:
    {
        condition = 'that';
        break;
    };
    default:
    {
        condition = 'those';
    };
}
```

I like to add curly braces around each `case` in the `switch` statement; I do this because I believe it makes the `switch` statement easier to read and flow better to my eyes; however, ultimately, these are not necessary. Concerning optional curly braces, I always include them, even if they're technically optional. The same goes for semicolons. Terminating each line with a semicolon is technically optional in JavaScript, although there are some circumstances in which you won't be able to omit it. I include all optional semicolons and curly braces, as I think that this not only makes the code cleaner, more organized, and consistent, but also gives you a technical benefit. If you want to compress your code to remove all additional white space, comments, and so on, these optional bits suddenly are no longer optional, but needed to keep the program functional after it's been compressed. In the following example, you can see what I mean by optional components:

```
if (condition)
    something = 1
else if (another)
    something = 2
else
    something = 3
```

In JavaScript, the preceding code is perfectly valid. The semicolon is implied where there is a line break. And as long as there is only a single statement being executed, technically you don't have to include curly braces. However, the above fails when it is compressed:

```
if (condition) something = 1 else if (another) something = 2 else something = 3
```

The preceding fails with a syntax error when you try to execute it. It fails because the script interpreter has no idea where you intend one statement to end and the next to begin. The language could probably be extended to guess in some circumstances, but it's better to just be as explicit as possible. Some combination and compression tools such as *require.js* do their best to fill missing bits and are actually very good at it.

Something else that you might think is odd is the inclusion of a semicolon after some function definitions. You'll see this in JavaScript because a function can be a type of data, just like a number is a type of data or a string is a type of data. In JavaScript, it's possible to pass a function around as you would a number or a string. You can assign a function to a variable and execute the function later. You've already seen an example of this, and here it is again in the following code:

```javascript
window.onload = function()
{
    var nodes = document.getElementsByTagName('a');

    for (var counter = 0, length = nodes.length; counter < length; counter++) {
        nodes[counter].onclick = function(event) {
            window.open(
                this.href,
                "picture",
                "scrollbars=no,width=300,height=280,resizable=yes"
            );
            event? event.preventDefault() : (window.event.returnValue = false);
        };
    }
};
```

In the preceding code, you can see that a function is assigned to the `onload` event of the `window` object. The function definition is terminated with a semicolon. Again, that semicolon is technically optional in this example, but I include it because I want the code to work if it gets compressed, and I think that it makes the code more consistent, organized, and easier to follow.

Naming Variables, Functions, Objects

Variable naming is also accounted for in the coding standards I follow throughout this book. I always use the `camelCase` convention when naming variables, functions, objects, or anything that I can potentially invent a name for. This is contrasted with underscore naming conventions, for example, `underscores_separate_words`.

Namespace JavaScript Code

It's important to think about the big picture when writing an application. Whether you're writing an application for your own use or writing an application that will be deployed in varying environments that you have no control over, you're likely to run into one problem at some point in your career: naming conflicts. I touched on this topic when I talked about namespacing class and id names in your CSS and markup. The same principles are also applicable to JavaScript. Your script applications need to run without invading the global namespace too much. I say "too much" because you need to invade it somewhat, but you need to do so in a controlled and intelligent way. As you may have done for your markup and CSS, namespacing your JavaScript may be as simple as sticking to object-oriented code, wrapping all your programs in just one or a handful of objects and then naming those objects in the global namespace in a noninvasive way. A common approach is to namespace those objects with a prefix of some kind that doesn't infringe on some other existing project. One example is how the jQuery JavaScript framework is namespaced. jQuery does a lot, but for all the code that's included in jQuery, there are precious few intrusions made on the global namespace, the "jQuery" object, and the dollar sign method the jQuery object is aliased to. All the functionality that jQuery provides is provided through those objects, and one of those two, the dollar sign variable can be turned off. (As it turns out this is a common thing for frameworks to do, to bind to a variable named $, so the ability of turning it off allows jQuery to be installed alongside other JavaScript frameworks.)

Without a well-thought-out approach to the namespacing problem, it's possible that your application may cause conflicts with others. It's best to just assume that everything you place in the global namespace will cause a conflict, and thus set out to make as minimal as possible an intrusion into the global namespace.

Avoid Browser Detection

Browser detection can be a real annoyance. You're surfing the web using your favorite browser, and you hit a website that locks you out—not because your web browser is technically incapable, but because it didn't match what the website's creators presupposed would be capable. So, I propose the following:

➤ Make no assumptions about the capabilities of a visitor's browser.

➤ Test for feature compatibility, rather than a browser name or browser version.

➤ Account for the official standards and the de facto standards. (Official standards should take precedence—de facto standards will either become or be replaced by the former.)

➤ The world is always changing—what's most popular today may not remain the most popular in the months and years to come.

➤ It may be time to turn to a framework for some compatibility bridging.

Anyone remember a company called Netscape? At one time, Netscape was the dominant, de facto standard. Now Netscape holds virtually nothing of the world market share, and Chrome, Firefox, Safari, and Internet Explorer are dominant. Another great example: At its most popular, IE held more than 90 percent of the market. Now IE holds 50 percent or less, and other browsers all hold the remaining 50 percent. On mobile, Safari and Chrome are the overwhelming dominant market leaders because they power the browsers on iOS and Android platforms. The browser market can and does fluctuate and change. In the real world, there are a lot of people who use less popular browsers. Some browsers hold 2 percent or less. Two percent may sound small at first glance, but keep in mind that can be 2 percent of a very large number, and thus itself be a very large number. According to www.internetworldstats.com, in 2013, as I write this, there are just more than 2.4 billion Internet users worldwide, which is 34.3 percent of the world's population. Therefore, the so-called less popular browsers aren't really doing too shabby in the grand scheme of things, and although 2 percent sounds small, it's actually a pretty large base of users. Throughout this book I present numerous examples to you of how to avoid using browser detection and use feature detection instead.

SUMMARY

jQuery takes what would otherwise be a more complex or verbose task in traditional JavaScript, and it makes it much easier, sometimes reducing many lines to one or a few. Throughout this book, you will learn about what jQuery has to offer and how to use its simple, easy-to-understand API to write spectacular, professional-appearing web applications.

In this chapter, I talked a little about what jQuery is, where it comes from, and who develops and maintains it, and I showed you how to install it and begin using it. In the next chapter, you get right down to business, learning about jQuery's powerful implementation of the Selectors API and its world-class Event API.

If you are interested in learning more about jQuery's origins, visit www.jquery.com and www.ejohn.org.

This chapter also covered some things that a good programmer will want to get into the habit of doing, such as adopting a formal programming convention and avoiding conflicts with others' code through using a namespace of some sort (whether that be via a feature provided by the language, or through prefixing the names that you use that make an impact on the global namespace). I've shown a few of the practices that I have adopted for myself; although I should emphasize that it doesn't matter what programming convention you adopt, but rather that you adopt one. The premise of a programming convention is that you have a set of rules that you can follow to format your code so that it is neat, organized, and easy to follow. My conventions might not be what you want, but there are many others to choose from.

You should avoid detecting the user's browser, especially when it may lead to one group or another being locked out from functionality.

Your code should take advantage of client-side caching and the increase in performance it provides.

In my opinion, it is better to write code in neatly organized modules and combine those into a larger script later using server-side programming.

Finally, it is also important that you adopt standards for the presentation and maintenance of client-side markup and CSS. Choose either XHTML5 or HTML5, both of which are accepted standards. I prefer XHTML, although it may be too strict for your taste.

Selecting and Filtering

This chapter talks about jQuery's sophisticated implementation of the Selectors API, which provides the ability to select elements in the DOM using CSS selectors. jQuery's Selectors API allows you to select one or more elements from the DOM using a selector; then either you can use that result set, or you can pass those elements on to be filtered down to a more specific result set.

If you've never heard of a selector before, then I recommend that you have a look at my book *Beginning CSS: Cascading Style Sheets for Web Design, 3rd Edition*, which has extensive coverage of selectors.

In CSS, you can apply style to one or more elements by writing a style sheet. You choose which elements to style based on the syntax that appears in the first part of a CSS rule, before the first curly brace, which is known as the selector. Here is a sample CSS selector:

```
div#exampleFormWrapper form#exampleSummaryDialog {
    display: block;
    position: absolute;
    z-index: 1;
    top: 22px;
    left: 301px;
    right: 0;
    bottom: 24px;
    width: auto;
    margin: 0;
    border: none;
    border-bottom: 1px solid rgb(180, 180, 180);
}
```

Using markup and CSS, you can assign id and class names to elements, and you can control the presentational aspects of elements specifically using selectors. In jQuery, the concept of selectors as applied to CSS is also applied to the concept of the *Document Object Model* (DOM). In the DOM, you have available to you every element that exists in the markup of your document, and you can traverse the DOM and select the elements you want to work with using selectors, just like you use in your CSS style sheets.

After you select elements from the DOM, you can apply behavior to them. You can listen to events and make something happen when a user clicks an element, for example. You can make something happen when the user's mouse cursor comes over or leaves an element. Basically, you can make your web documents look and behave more like desktop applications. You are no longer limited to static content as you are with markup and CSS alone—you can apply behavior as well.

This chapter describes how to use jQuery's Selectors API to retrieve elements from a document, in addition to providing some practical examples of usage. It also describes how you can chain calls in jQuery. One use for this is filtering a selection, which you would do to reduce a larger selection of elements down to a smaller selection. Finally, it discusses how jQuery's Event API works in relation to the W3C's Event API and Microsoft's event model as it was implemented up to IE8. IE9 and newer all have support for the standard W3C event model, in addition to Microsoft's older, proprietary event model.

THE ORIGIN OF THE SELECTORS API

The concept of a Selectors API was first dreamed up by Dean Edwards, a JavaScript guru who first created a Selectors API in JavaScript in a free, open-source package he called *cssQuery*. Not long after Dean pioneered the idea and produced a working, proof-of-concept implementation of that idea, it was taken up and expanded upon by John Resig (and other JavaScript framework authors, mutually exclusive to John's efforts) and implemented in his jQuery framework. This led to some back-and-forth collaboration and competition between Dean, John, and other JavaScript framework authors, which resulted in much-needed performance boosts in these ad-hoc implementations, which at their conception were quite slow in some scenarios.

Not long after Dean came up with the concept of a Selectors API, W3C members and editors Anne van Kesteren and Lachlan Hunt drafted it into a specification for the W3C. The official W3C Selectors API involves two methods, one for selecting a single element called `document.querySelector()` and one for selecting multiple elements called `document.querySelectorAll()`.

> **NOTE** *The names for the official API were under considerable debate for quite some time because no browser makers could agree on the names used. The names were finally put to a vote, with these names being the ones decided on. The controversy surrounding the names was not without merit, as this API is quite possibly the most important change to JavaScript that will have a lasting impact for years to come. It's important in that, in one fell swoop, it replaces methods like* `document.getElementById`, `document.all`, *and* `document.getElementsByTagName`, *which are no longer needed—because these methods let you use selector syntax, you can select by id, by tag name, by class name, or by context, via whatever selectors the browser already supports for CSS.*

`document.querySelector` and `document.querySelectorAll` are both implemented natively in Chrome, Safari, Firefox, and IE (back to IE8).

The great thing about jQuery and other JavaScript frameworks is that they had their own versions of the Selectors API already implemented prior to its native inclusion in browsers, which allows them to use the native implementation, if it is available. Using the native implementation makes selecting elements screamingly fast. Otherwise, if the user has an older browser, the framework can fall back on its own, slower, JavaScript-based implementation. This means that when using a JavaScript framework like jQuery, the Selectors API is ubiquitously available across all platforms it supports. jQuery 1.9 supports IE back to version 6 and should be used if you need compatibility with the older versions of IE, in addition to all other popular browsers, of course. jQuery 2.0 drops support for the older versions of Internet Explorer and supports only IE9 onward. jQuery 1.9 keeps support for those legacy browsers and the way legacy browsers do things. jQuery 2.0 is a clean break with the past and supports only the newer versions of browsers with excellent support for standards.

USING THE SELECTORS API

Using the Selectors API in jQuery is easy. As explained in Chapter 1, "Introduction to jQuery," everything that you want to do with jQuery originates from a single, simply named object called $ (a single dollar sign). You can also use "jQuery" in place of the dollar sign, but from here on throughout this book, I will use only the dollar sign, and I will refer to it either as "the dollar sign object" or "the dollar sign method," depending on context, because it is really both a method and an object at the same time.

The dollar sign is both a method and an object because it can be used like a function call, but it also has member properties and methods that you can call. The dollar sign is named after a single dollar sign for one reason only, and that is to reduce the amount of code that you have to write.

Here's a simple example of how you would use this method with a selector to add a click behavior to a collection of links. Basically, the object of the following code is to force the links to open in a new window, instead of using the `target` attribute, which can sometimes be left out when content is managed, and because of this it's easy to abstract away its use by putting in a little JavaScript that follows a few rules that most companies tend to want when it comes to the question of when to open a link in a new window.

Say that you have a markup document that looks like this. (You can try this example for yourself; it's available as *Example 2-1* in the book's download materials.)

```
<!DOCTYPE HTML>
<html xmlns="http://www.w3.org/1999/xhtml">
    <head>
        <meta http-equiv="content-type"
            content="application/xhtml+xml; charset=utf-8" />
        <meta http-equiv="content-language" content="en-us" />
        <title>Links</title>
        <script type='text/javascript' src='../jQuery.js'></script>
        <script type='text/javascript' src='Example 2-1.js'></script>
        <link type='text/css' href='Example 2-1.css' rel='stylesheet' />
    </head>
    <body>
        <ul id="exampleFavoriteLinks">
```

```
            <li><a href="http://www.wrox.com/">Wrox</a></li>
            <li><a href="http://www.daringfireball.com/">Daring Fireball</a></li>
            <li><a href="http://www.apple.com/">Apple</a></li>
            <li><a href="http://www.jquery.com/">jQuery</a></li>
            <li><a href="Example 2-2.html">Example 2-2</a></li>
            <li><a href="Example 2-3.html">Example 2-3</a></li>
        </ul>
    </body>
</html>
```

In the preceding markup document, you have a simple unordered list that contains six links. You take that markup and put it with the following CSS:

```
body {
    font: 16px Helvetica, Arial, sans-serif;
}
ul {
    list-style: none;
    margin: 10px;
    padding: 10px;
    border: 1px solid green;
}
a {
    text-decoration: none;
    color: green;
}
a:hover {
    text-decoration: underline;
}
```

The preceding CSS document does little more than make that list look a little prettier—it neither adds to or takes away from the example.

Finally, you add the following JavaScript document to the markup:

```
$(document).ready(
    function()
    {
        $('a').click(
            function(event)
            {
                var node = $(this);

                var target = node.attr('target');
                var href = node.attr('href');

                if (target === undefined && href !== undefined)
                {
                    switch (true)
                    {
                        case href.indexOf('http://') !== -1:
                        case href.indexOf('https://') !== -1:
                        case href.indexOf('.pdf') !== -1:
                        {
                            node.attr('target', '_blank')
```

```
                                        .addClass('exampleLinkAutoTarget');

                            break;
                        }
                    }
                }
            }
        )
    }
);
```

The preceding code, all put together, should look something like what you see in Figure 2-1.

FIGURE 2-1

When you click a link to an external website in the example, you see those links open in a new window or tab, depending on how you have your browser's preferences set up to handle new windows.

In the preceding example, you use JavaScript to force the links in the `<ul>` element with the id name `exampleFavoriteLinks` to open in a new window or tab. To do this, in the JavaScript, you wrote a bit of jQuery that is executed at the document ready event.

```
$(document).ready(
    function()
    {
```

As I touched on briefly in Chapter 1, jQuery provides its own event called ready, which is fired as soon as the DOM has finished loading, which is different from the onload or load event in that with the load event, you have to wait for all the images to load too before that event will fire. Most of the time, you don't need to wait so long; you just want to start working with the document and adding behavior as soon as the DOM has finished loading. That's what the first line of code does.

Now that the DOM is loaded, you want to add behaviors to the document using script. The first item is an example of jQuery's Selectors API in action: it is a function call to the dollar sign method that uses a selector that picks up all <a> elements.

```
$('a')
```

When those <a> elements are selected, you more than likely want to do something with them. In this example, you add a click event to each of the <a> elements that you selected. The click event is added via a click method that is unique to jQuery:

```
$('a').click(
function(event)
{
```

What you see here is an example of how jQuery lets you chain methods together. First, you selected a bunch of <a> elements; now, you're applying a click event directly to each of those <a> elements via a new method called click() that's chained to the end of your selection.

Within the click() method, you are passing a single anonymous (that is, nameless) function (these are also called closures or lambda functions) that contains the instructions that you want to be executed when each <a> element is clicked by a user.

```
function(event)
{
    var node = $(this);

    var target = node.attr('target');
    var href = node.attr('href');

    if (target === undefined && href !== undefined)
    {
        switch (true)
        {
            case href.indexOf('http://') !== -1:
            case href.indexOf('https://') !== -1:
            case href.indexOf('.pdf') !== -1:
            {
                node.attr('target', '_blank')
                    .addClass('exampleLinkAutoTarget');

                break;
            }
        }
    }
}
```

The anonymous function contains one argument, event, which represents the event object. The event object is just like what you would use with the standard W3C Event API, and Internet

Explorer 8 and earlier using jQuery 1.9; this event object is automatically patched by jQuery so that older versions of IE support the same standard event model that all the other browsers do. IE9 and later have all this functionality built in and no longer need the patches.

The next line takes this and wraps it in a call to jQuery. By default, events are set up so that this references the element the event is attached to. When an event occurs, jQuery leaves this default behavior in place, so by default, you're working with traditional JavaScript within the event callback function. To work with jQuery again, you have to explicitly say that you want to work with jQuery, and one way to do that is to simply wrap this in a call to jQuery.

```
var node = $(this);
```

If you had not wrapped this in a call to jQuery, the subsequent call to attr(), a jQuery function, would have failed.

The next line verifies whether the <a> element has a target attribute or an href attribute. If no target attribute is set, the call to attr('target') will return undefined, and likewise for the href attribute.

```
if (target === undefined && href !== undefined)
```

Next, after it is determined that there is no target attribute and there is an href attribute, the value of the href attribute is examined to see whether a new window should be opened when the link is clicked. This is done with a switch statement. Switching on true will cause the program to execute the first case statement where the expression placed beside the case statement evaluates true, and that is the case if the value of href contains the following:

➤ http://, a non-secure web link to a third-party website

➤ https://, a secure web link to a third-party website

Or if the link contains the .pdf document extension.

With these rules and some additional logic put in place throughout your website, it becomes possible to fish out links to third-party websites and to PDF documents and to make those particular links open in a new window. This works if all the links on your website are written as relative or absolute links without the host name portion of the URL—for example http://www.example.com/, which is the hostname portion of the URL. If some links might contain your own hostname, then you would need to rewrite the logic presented here to filter out those links so that links within your website won't trigger false positives and open in a new window. You learn how to do that in the next section.

This is a simple but practical explanation of one possible way to use the Selectors API, to select all the links on a given page. But what if you want to filter out some of the selected elements based on other criteria, or what if you want to narrow a selection based on elements further down the tree? This is discussed in the next section.

FILTERING A SELECTION

jQuery is innovative in the way that it returns itself, by default, for every method call to it where it makes sense. After you make a selection, that selection is returned as the context of an object that can call upon any other jQuery method and that jQuery method can take the previous selection and do something more with it. You can do this with virtually any language, which is to say, create an object and have the methods of that object return the object itself.

In this section you take a look at the various methods that jQuery provides for modifying a selection in the context of another selection.

Working Within the Context of a Selection

This section introduces a few of jQuery's methods: find(), each(), is(), and val(). This discussion begins with a method used to search for other elements in the context of an existing selection called find(). As I present to you an example of one way you might use the find() method, you also see in the same example each(), is(), and val(). I provide you with a detailed introduction to each(), is(), and val() later in this section in the context of the explanation for *Example 2-2* because I could not begin a discussion about find() without also introducing these other methods. However, to start this leg of your journey into jQuery, you have a look at the find() method, how you might use it, and more important, some techniques you'll want to employ and some behavior you'll want to avoid when you make use of it.

jQuery's find() method enables you to perform a selection within a selection. Another way of saying this is that it lets you search within the context of a selection. A selection, as you have already seen, can contain one element or many elements. Most of the methods that jQuery provides are done with the consistent assumption that a selection can contain just one or many elements. find() is no different; it can be used with a selection containing one or more elements, and it operates to search within the context of every element present in a selection. So, if you have a selection containing just one <form> element, and you use find() on that selection, you'll be looking within just that one <form> element. If you have a selection containing multiple <form> elements, and you use find(), find() will be carried out in the context of each of the <form> elements present in the original selection. So, the first takeaway from using find() is that it can be carried out with selections large and small, and using it can become large and unwieldy quickly.

You use find() if you know that an element (or a collection of elements) contains another element (or collection of elements) somewhere down the DOM tree starting with the pivot of that initial selection. The key thing to remember when turning to find() in your toolbox is that you don't know how far down the tree this additional element or collection of elements might be. For example, if you know that your second selection will be children or siblings of your initial selection, you're better off using the jQuery methods children() or siblings() because they're faster for that situation.

find() is a bit of a blunt instrument; it works well and can even be fairly efficient to very efficient depending on the scenario in which it is used, but it is one of the most general-purpose methods of filtering a selection that jQuery provides. Because the DOM can be either large and very complex, or very small and simple, when selecting elements using the jQuery Selectors API in general, without yet even contemplating the best uses of the find() method, it is best to take a step back and remember a few basic things to keep your scripts fast, optimized, and ready to deal with any scenario. First, remember to construct your documents with appropriate and strategically placed unique id names. Id names are meant to be unique; class names are not meant to be unique. Because id names are meant to be unique, if you create a document with unique id names, the browser can use an efficient index to look up any element by the id name in the DOM. Therefore, when you do a selection using jQuery, the fastest possible selection that you can make is one that involves the use of an id name.

Of course, the concept of having unique id names is not something the browser can enforce; you must enforce this when you create your documents. If you don't consciously consider this, the browser will happily allow you to create multiple elements with the same id name. If you do create multiple elements with the same id name, you miss out on the benefits of optimizations that involve narrowing the scope of possible elements in a selection by using the id name as an initial selector. If you use unique id names, then similarly to a database, the browser can build a fast index to access those elements in the DOM. Because it can find those elements quickly, applications built on top of optimizations using id names can also be much quicker.

Think of the DOM like a database table. Even if you aren't familiar with relational databases (like MySQL, SQL Lite, Postgres SQL, or Microsoft SQL Server), the analogy is helpful to understand a little something about how computers organize information for efficient lookup. Like this book, if you want to locate information about a particular topic quickly, your best bet is going to be the book's index section. It has information broken down by topics and phrases, sorted alphabetically, and provides a listing of pages those topics or phrases appear on. Relational databases work much the same way; they contain a warehouse of information, but they need indexes of their own to find information quickly. A relational database has a collection of physical locations on the hard disk, and indexes, just like with physical books, help provide a way of looking up that information quickly. The document object model is no different. It is a collection of HTML elements, and those elements each have attributes that can be used to organize that data. The DOM is also organized like a tree; it has a root element, <html>, and from there it branches, adding children and children of children until the entire DOM is mapped. So, when you provide extra metadata like id and class names, you are providing a way to identify those elements in the DOM, using both JavaScript and CSS. Of course, you don't have to always use id or class names. Sometimes you can use just the name of the element itself to identify the element, and sometimes you need only a handful of class or id names to meaningfully organize your document in a way that makes it easy to style with CSS or program with JavaScript. You can also identify elements using HTML attributes, which is more common in my experience, with elements such as <input> elements, where you might want to apply style based on whether an element is a text input or a password input. And now with HTML5, we have a dozen or so possible types of inputs.

When it comes to the DOM, however, it is best to design your dynamic, interactive applications in the most efficient way possible, and more often than not, that starts with a selection involving an id name. The second most efficient way to select an element will be using class names. Class names differ from id names in that class names can be applied to many elements. Elements with the same class name should share some common characteristics. You should be essentially saying that elements with the same class name are the same, but they appear multiple times in your document. One example might be a class name that applies to an element that serves as a container for labels for input elements. You might have many such labels in your document, and each label will have the same characteristics in terms of its look and feel. You might have a few variations on the look and feel to accommodate edge cases in the visual layout. For those edge cases you might invent a few new class names that can modify the base look and feel for those situations.

Whatever the situation you are creating an application to accommodate, your id and class names should be designed to aid in both efficient styling with CSS and efficient lookup using the DOM in JavaScript. You want your application to find these elements as quickly as possible, using the least amount of additional metadata that is necessary. This will feel like a statement that is at odds with itself, and in some ways it is. You don't want to be too liberal in creating and assigning id and class names because that will make your document more bulky. When it comes to bandwidth, you want to create a document that is the smallest it can be, while also being as programmatically efficient and optimized as it can be. jQuery is just a tool that enables you to access the DOM, and it allows you lots of ways to interact with the DOM. However, it is up to you as the program's architect to make that application efficient, organized, and well designed so that it loads and executes as quickly as possible. In terms of web applications, it is always important to show the user some content as fast as possible. A few seconds can mean the difference between users delighting in and using your website and web applications, or users pressing the back button and taking their attention elsewhere.

The first of many filtering and traversal methods that you examine in this chapter is a method called find(). Its purpose is to look within an existing selection to find other elements in that selection. Those elements can be children of the element, or elements, that you selected or far-off descendants deep down the DOM tree from that initial selection. The initial selection can be one or many elements, and find() will look inside each of them to locate the additional element or elements that you are looking for. As mentioned in the opening for this section, a great thing about jQuery is that it never assumes (whenever practical and possible) that you want to work with only a single element. If you select several elements, it will work with several elements at once. If you select a single element, it will work with only that one element, but it will treat that one element as an array containing one element.

If you examine the object that a jQuery selection returns, you'll *always* see an array, and that is *always* the case for jQuery methods that are meant to return something related to a selection. When you aren't working with a selection, but are instead using a method that is meant to return a string or some other data, for example, the HTML source or text source of an element, or the value of an attribute—in those situations, jQuery takes the first element of the selection, if the selection contains multiple elements, and it gives you what you are asking for in the context of that first element. So, you must be proactive and take into account what a selection might return and assume that most of the time, your selection could possibly return multiple elements.

As already stated, it is best to start with a selection that is as narrow as possible so that the browser can quickly locate that element in the DOM. *Example 2-2* presents you with a simplified and to-the-point overview of one way you might use find() to locate elements within the context of an existing selection. As with most of the examples present in this book, you can try out the example by manually typing it into a text editor, or you can obtain the example's source code with the book's free downloadable materials available from www.wrox.com/go/webdevwithjquery. This example begins with *Example 2-2.html*:

```
<!DOCTYPE HTML>
<html xmlns="http://www.w3.org/1999/xhtml">
    <head>
        <meta http-equiv="content-type"
            content="application/xhtml+xml; charset=utf-8" />
        <meta http-equiv="content-language" content="en-us" />
        <title>Contact Form</title>
        <script type='text/javascript' src='../jQuery.js'></script>
        <script type='text/javascript' src='Example 2-2.js'></script>
        <link type='text/css' href='Example 2-2.css' rel='stylesheet' />
    </head>
    <body>
        <form id='contactNewsletterForm' method='get'
            action='Example 2-2 Submitted.html'>
            <div>
                <label for='contactFirstName'>First Name:</label>
                <input type='text'
```

```
                                id='contactFirstName'
                                name='contactFirstName'
                                size='25'
                                maxlength='50'
                                required='required' />
                </div>
                <div>
                    <label for='contactLastName'>Last Name:</label>
                    <input type='text'
                                id='contactLastName'
                                name='contactLastName'
                                size='25'
                                maxlength='50'
                                required='required' />
                </div>
                <div>
                    <input type='checkbox'
                                id='contactNewsletter'
                                name='contactNewsletter'
                                value='1' />
                    <label for='contactNewsletter'>
                        Subscribe to newsletter?
                    </label>
                </div>
                <div>
                    <input type='submit'
                                id='contactNewsletterFormSubmit'
                                name='contactNewsletterFormSubmit'
                                value='Go' />
                </div>
            </form>
        </body>
    </html>
```

The preceding markup contains a simple newsletter sign-up form. It is combined with the following CSS, *Example 2-2.css*:

```
body {
    font: 16px Helvetica, Arial, sans-serif;
}
form#contactNewsletterForm {
    margin: 10px;
    padding: 10px;
    border: 1px solid black;
    background: yellow;
}
form#contactNewsletterForm div {
    padding: 5px;
}
```

The following JavaScript, *Example 2-2.js*, is used to validate that required input has been provided in the text input fields, and it disables the submit button upon pressing it, which prevents the user from pressing the submit button multiple times in the event that the action of submitting the form takes longer than desired.

```javascript
var contactNewsletterForm = {

    ready : function()
    {
        $('input#contactNewsletterFormSubmit').click(
            function(event)
            {
                var input = $(this);

                input.attr('disabled', true);

                if (!contactNewsletterForm.validate())
                {
                    alert("Please provide both your first and last name");

                    input.removeAttr('disabled');

                    event.preventDefault();
                }
                else
                {
                    $('form#contactNewsletterForm').submit();
                }
            }
        );
    },

    validate : function()
    {
        var hasRequiredValues = true;

        $('form#contactNewsletterForm').find('input, select, textarea').each(
            function()
            {
                var node = $(this);

                if (node.is('[required]'))
                {
                    var value = node.val();

                    if (!value)
                    {
                        hasRequiredValues = false;
                        return false;
                    }
                }
            }
        );

        return hasRequiredValues;
    }
};

$(document).ready(
    function()
    {
```

```
            contactNewsletterForm.ready();
        }
    );
```

This form is then submitted to the following HTML page, called *Example 2-2 Submitted.html*, which just confirms that the form was submitted. In the real world, this HTML form would more than likely go to a server-side program that would also validate input and actually perform the action of signing up the user for the newsletter. For this simplified example, you omit that part of the process and focus only on the client-side components.

```
<!DOCTYPE HTML>
<html xmlns="http://www.w3.org/1999/xhtml">
    <head>
        <meta http-equiv="content-type"
            content="application/xhtml+xml; charset=utf-8" />
        <meta http-equiv="content-language" content="en-us" />
        <title>Contact Form</title>
        <script type='text/javascript' src='../jQuery.js'></script>
        <script type='text/javascript' src='Example 2-2.js'></script>
        <link type='text/css' href='Example 2-2.css' rel='stylesheet' />
    </head>
    <body>
        <p>
            Thank you for submitting the form.
        </p>
    </body>
</html>
```

The source code in the preceding examples results in the output that you see in Figure 2-2.

FIGURE 2-2

In *Example 2-2*, you see one way you might use the find() method, to validate input for a simple newsletter sign-up form. The text inputs in the HTML form use the HTML5 required attribute to indicate that they are required fields; some browsers with support for HTML5 fields and attributes will already prevent the user from submitting the form without required input. The JavaScript that you implement with this example provides a little more functionality; however, it also prevents the form from being submitted multiple times. In *Example 2-2.js*, you create a simple JavaScript object literal; this is one way of creating a simple JavaScript custom object. An object called contactNewsletterForm is created, which contains the logic necessary for your newsletter sign-up form. It contains two methods, one called ready() and one called validate(). The ready() method is executed when the document's DOMContentLoaded event has fired, which as you already know is mapped to the jQuery event with the much simpler name of ready. So, as soon as the DOM has loaded, this event will be called, and you can do things with the DOM. contactNewsletterForm.ready() attaches a single event to the submit button. It does this by first selecting the <input> with an id selector, input#contactNewsletterFormSubmit, and then it calls the method click() to attach an onclick event to that <input> element. This allows you to intercept and control what happens when the user clicks the submit button.

```
ready : function()
{
    $('input#contactNewsletterFormSubmit').click(
        function(event)
        {
            var input = $(this);

            input.attr('disabled', true);

            if (!contactNewsletterForm.validate())
            {
                alert("Please provide both your first and last name");

                input.removeAttr('disabled');

                event.preventDefault();
            }
            else
            {
                $('form#contactNewsletterForm').submit();
            }
        }
    );
},
```

Within the function that is attached to the click event of the submit button, the first thing you do is create a variable called input with a call to jQuery with the special this keyword as its first and only argument. As mentioned earlier in this chapter, when an event is called, this refers to the element the event occurred on, but this is not jQuery-enabled. To make it jQuery-capable, all you have to do is to call jQuery with this as the argument. This is how you enable any element in the JavaScript DOM to be jQuery-enabled, not just the special this keyword in the context of events.

```
var input = $(this);
```

Next, you disable the submit button so that the user cannot become impatient and click it repeatedly, sending multiple requests to join your newsletter to your server.

```
input.attr('disabled', true);
```

Another way of setting the `disabled` attribute is to call the `attr()` method like this:

```
input.attr('disabled', 'disabled');
```

And you might prefer this method because it is also technically the way that XHTML says that boolean HTML attributes should be done. But jQuery supports doing this either way, by passing a boolean `true` or `false` or by passing the value *disabled*. Likewise, to disable the `disabled` attribute, you can either pass false in a call, such as `attr('disabled', false)`, or you can remove the attribute all together by calling `removeAttr('disabled')`.

In the next line you make a call to `contactNewsletterForm.validate()` to see if the form validates. This method returns a boolean value that indicates either yes, all the required fields have been provided, or no, there is missing data.

```
if (!contactNewsletterForm.validate())
{
```

If all the required data has not been provided, then users sees an `alert()` message, asking them to provide both their first and last names.

```
alert("Please provide both your first and last name");
```

Then the submit button is re-enabled so that users can attempt to submit the form again.

```
input.removeAttr('disabled');
```

I do this by removing the `disabled` attribute, but as mentioned before you can also call `attr('disabled', false)` and this provides the same functionality. Finally, the `preventDefault()` method is called on the `event` object to prevent the default action of the submit button, which is to submit the form.

```
event.preventDefault();
```

If, however, all the data has been provided, then the form is submitted by calling `submit()` on the `<form>` element. You might wonder why this is necessary. Because `event.preventDefault()` is supposed to prevent the default action, wouldn't not calling it allow the default action? In this case, it would not because the default action is also prevented by disabling the submit button by enabling the `disabled` attribute, and because the button has been disabled, you now have to explicitly submit the form.

```
}
else
{
    $('form#contactNewsletterForm').submit();
}
```

Next, you examine what happens inside the `validate()` method. First, you set up a variable that keeps track of whether the required fields have been provided. You start off by assuming that the user did provide every required field by assigning `true` to the variable `hasRequiredValues`. Then you make a selection, and you select the `<form>` element with the id name `contactNewsletterForm`. As presented earlier in this section, it's good to establish a context for your selections, as this can speed up selections tremendously. In this case, this newsletter sign-up form could be part of a much larger document. You don't want to make the mistake of assuming that your code will or will not be part of a much larger document; it's better to always plan for the most flexible approach possible. Your client or employer might change its mind and decide that it wants to move a form, or include a form, to or within places that you hadn't anticipated when you first built your form. In these situations, it's best to have flexible programming that can adapt to changes quickly and seamlessly. Part of providing the best foundation for flexible (and reusable) programming like this is to establish good naming conventions, as discussed back in Chapter 1. Don't choose names that are too simple and could easily conflict with other features. You may be annoyed by the verbosity of the names, but you will be pleased with the ease with which you can move and integrate features within your website or web-based application.

```
validate : function()
{
    var hasRequiredValues = true;

    $('form#contactNewsletterForm').find('input, select, textarea').each(
        function()
        {
            var node = $(this);

            if (node.is('[required]'))
            {
                var value = node.val();

                if (!value)
                {
                    hasRequiredValues = false;
                    return false;
                }
            }
        }
    );

    return hasRequiredValues;
}
};
```

So, begin by selecting the form because it has an established id name; it is a pivot point for quickly making other selections. You look inside your `<form>` element for other elements. In this case you search for `<input>`, `<select>`, or `<textarea>` elements; these are all the possible elements that can be contained inside a form where the user can provide or select data (setting aside, of course, the potential for custom input elements). You might notice that your newsletter form has no `<textarea>` or `<select>` elements, and you might be asking yourself, why do I need to look for elements that don't exist? In this case, you're being proactive and simply planning ahead for potential future changes to the form. In addition, your form needs may grow and you might need to rework or adapt this programming logic so that it handles validation for any form you might create by creating a new, reusable form valida-tion component. One way you can plan ahead is to think about how your validation script might be applied, and that includes planning for fields that might not be there yet.

Iterating a Selection with each() and Testing for a Condition with is()

Now that you have selected the various input fields in the context of the <form> element, you use the each() method to iterate over all the elements matching the selection that you made with find(). each() is similar to writing a for loop, or a while loop; it's used to iterate over an array or object. In the context of this example, each() is used to iterate over a selection. In this example, you first select a <form> element, and then you select four <input> elements using the find() method. Now you need to examine each <input> element individually and see whether the user provided data to the input elements that you have designated as required elements. each() is what you use to examine each element, individually. It executes a callback function for each element in the selection. In the context of this example, that means that the function provided to each() is executed four times, one for each of the four <input> elements matched in the call to find().

```
$('form#contactNewsletterForm').find('input, select, textarea').each(
```

Like events, elements are passed to each() in the form of the JavaScript keyword: this. In addition to the keyword this, there is also an alternative way that you can access an element within the function that you provide to each(), and that is by specifying two arguments for the function. The first argument tells you where you are in the collection; it's a counter offset from zero. The second argument is the value or object that you're working with, and it provides the same data that is provided in this. The following code snippet modifies *Example 2-2* so that it specifies these two optional arguments:

```
$('form#contactNewsletterForm').find('input, select, textarea').each(
    function(counter, element)
    {
```

Also like events, the elements passed to each() in the form of this are not jQuery-enabled by default. So, the first thing you do inside the anonymous function that is executed for each element matched via the each() method is to create a variable with a reference to the element that is jQuery-enabled. In this case you create a variable called *node*, which is an easy generic name to use. You could have just as easily called the variable *input*, or something else more specific.

```
var node = $(this);
```

Now that you have a jQuery-enabled reference to the element, you look for the presence of the HTML5 required attribute to see if the field is required, and you do that with a call to the jQuery method is(). In the context of any jQuery selection, is() tells you whether any of the elements in the selection match a selector that you provide to is(). In the context of this selection, you have a single element in that selection, thanks to each(), and that selection is assigned to the variable node. The selection will be one of the four matched <input> elements, going from top to bottom. So the first element each() that comes across is the <input> with the id name contactFirstName, the second element will be the <input> with the id name contactLastName, the third will be the check box, and the last element that each() will operate on is the submit button. The call to is() contains an attribute selector: [required]. Using is(), you are asking, does the element match this selector? Another way of asking this question is does the element match the selector: input[required="required"] (if the element is an <input> element, of course). And is() will return a boolean value telling you whether the element matches the selector you've provided.

```
if (node.is('[required]'))
{
```

In the context of this example, you just want to know whether the element is required, and that is done by using is() to ask whether the element has the required attribute. Because the required attribute is a boolean attribute and its only possible value is required, or to not exist at all, then the simplest way of asking if the element is required is by using the attribute selector [required].

is() can be used to ask any question of an element or collection of elements that can be expressed as a selector. When it comes to multiple elements being present in a selection, the question that you ask using is() is true if it matches any of the elements in the selection. If the selector matches only a single element, but not the other elements, the result is still true. The result is only false if it matches none of the elements present in the selection.

If the element has the required attribute, the expression node.is('[required']) will return true, and the program will then examine the value of the input. The value of the input is retrieved with a call to val(), another jQuery method that does some behind-the-scenes work to make it a lot easier to fetch the value of a field, automatically adjusting its logic based on the type of input field that you are working with. It returns the value of the value attribute in the case of an <input> element (no matter the type); it retrieves the selected <option>'s value attribute in the case of a <select> element; and it retrieves the text content of a <textarea> element.

```
if (node.is('[required]'))
{
    var value = node.val();

    if (!value)
    {
        hasRequiredValues = false;
        return false;
    }
}
```

Next, you do a simple boolean expression on the value to determine whether there is one. If the expression evaluates to false, there is no value, and the variable you set up to keep track of whether all the provided values were provided, hasRequiredValues, is assigned the value false, and then you return false to break out of subsequent each() iterations.

Within the function that you provide to each(), returning true is the same as writing the keyword continue; iteration proceeds to the next element or item, so if you were on the first element, iteration immediately proceeds to the second element. And returning false from the function is the same as writing the break keyword in a for, while, or switch loop, and iteration stops completely. In the context of this example, if you're on the first <input> element when this happens, then the function is never executed for the second, third, or fourth elements.

Finally, after you have examined each <input> element, the function validate() returns the value of the *hasRequiredValues* variable, letting your click event know definitively whether all the required values have been provided.

```
return hasRequiredValues;
```

In this section, you got to know jQuery a little better with some in-depth explanations of and an example using the methods find(), each(), is(), and val(). The next section continues along the lines of examples of how to traverse the DOM using jQuery with an introduction to the jQuery methods that allow you to move about the DOM.

Working with an Element's Relatives

jQuery provides you with a comprehensive DOM traversal package. You can easily move from an element to its siblings, its parent or ancestors and as its children and its descendants. In this section, you see an example that introduces how to do all this, as well as how to limit a selection to an element based on its numeric offset position in the selection and how to limit a selection's scope by providing a selector that filters your selection based on what you don't want in the selection. The discussion presented in this section encompasses the following methods of jQuery's API:

➤ parent() and parents() are used to select an element's parent or ancestors.

➤ children() is used to select an element's immediate children.

➤ siblings() is used to select all of an element's surrounding sibling elements.

➤ prev() is used to select an element's immediate preceding sibling.

➤ next() is used to select an element's immediate following sibling.

➤ prevAll() is used to select all siblings coming before an element.

➤ nextAll() is used to select all siblings coming after an element.

➤ not() is used to remove elements from a selection using a selector.

➤ eq() is used to zero in on a single element in a selection by providing its offset position within the selection offset from zero.

You can also go up the DOM tree and select parent or ancestor elements. When programming, the need to go up the DOM tree typically arises because you are in a situation in which you have multiples of something in an application. For example, say you have multiple calendars in an application. This could happen because you provide navigation to move from month to month, and instead of deleting each month and building a new one, you keep each month in the application and move between them as needed. If you click on a day within a month, you might also need to know which month that click occurred in which, so you travel up the DOM from the selected day to discover which month the click occurred on. This isn't the only scenario you might want to select a parent or ancestor. You might also run into this situation when you receive an event on an ambiguous or generic element, and you want to get to an element that provides more meta information, class, id name, or other data.

The need to select children() is usually similar to the need to use the find() method introduced earlier in this chapter. The decision of which to use is based on whether you know if an element is a child, or if it is further down the DOM tree. Using children() if an element is a child provides you with some performance benefits. If the browser knows that you want to look only in the pool of immediate children, then that makes finding that element fast. However, using find(), you're potentially asking the browser to examine every descendant element.

jQuery provides no less than five methods for discovering and working with an element's siblings. Whether you need to move to the next sibling element, previous sibling element, find all preceding or all succeeding sibling elements, or all siblings all together, there's a method that matches the situation.

All jQuery's traversal methods share the characteristic of providing a selector to a traversal method to limit traversal to elements that match the provided selector.

Each of the methods introduced here are presented in the following example. If you have downloaded the book's supplemental materials, you'll find this example in the *Chapter 2* folder named *Example 2-3*.

```
<!DOCTYPE HTML>
<html xmlns="http://www.w3.org/1999/xhtml">
    <head>
        <meta http-equiv="content-type"
            content="application/xhtml+xml; charset=utf-8" />
        <meta http-equiv="content-language" content="en-us" />
        <title>November 2013</title>
        <script type='text/javascript' src='../jQuery.js'></script>
        <script type='text/javascript' src='Example 2-3.js'></script>
        <link type='text/css' href='Example 2-3.css' rel='stylesheet' />
    </head>
    <body>
        <table class="calendarMonth" data-year="2013" data-month="11">
            <thead>
                <tr class="calendarHeading">
                    <th colspan="7">
                        <span class="calendarMonth">November</span>
                        <span class="calendarDay"></span>
                        <span class="calendarYear">2013</span>
                    </th>
                </tr>
                <tr class="calendarWeekdays">
                    <th>Sunday</th>
                    <th>Monday</th>
                    <th>Tuesday</th>
                    <th>Wednesday</th>
                    <th>Thursday</th>
                    <th>Friday</th>
                    <th>Saturday</th>
                </tr>
            </thead>
            <tbody>
                <tr>
                    <td class="calendarLastMonth">27</td>
                    <td class="calendarLastMonth">28</td>
                    <td class="calendarLastMonth">29</td>
                    <td class="calendarLastMonth">30</td>
                    <td class="calendarLastMonth calendarLastMonthLastDay">31</
td>
                    <td class="calendarFirstDay">1</td>
                    <td>2</td>
                </tr>
                <tr>
```

```
                            <td>3</td>
                            <td>4</td>
                            <td>5</td>
                            <td>6</td>
                            <td>7</td>
                            <td>8</td>
                            <td>9</td>
                        </tr>
                        <tr>
                            <td>10</td>
                            <td>11</td>
                            <td>12</td>
                            <td>13</td>
                            <td>14</td>
                            <td>15</td>
                            <td>16</td>
                        </tr>
                        <tr>
                            <td>17</td>
                            <td>18</td>
                            <td>19</td>
                            <td class="calendarToday">20</td>
                            <td>21</td>
                            <td>22</td>
                            <td>23</td>
                        </tr>
                        <tr>
                            <td>24</td>
                            <td>25</td>
                            <td>26</td>
                            <td>27</td>
                            <td>28</td>
                            <td>29</td>
                            <td class="calendarLastDay">30</td>
                        </tr>
                        <tr>
                            <td colspan="7" class="calendarEmptyWeek"></td>
                        </tr>
                    </tbody>
                </table>
            </body>
        </html>
```

The preceding HTML joins up with the following style sheet:

```
html,
body {
    width: 100%;
    height: 100%;
}
body {
    font: 14px Helvetica, Arial, sans-serif;
    margin: 0;
    padding: 0;
    color: rgb(128, 128, 128);
```

```css
        }
        table.calendarMonth {
            table-layout: fixed;
            width: 100%;
            height: 100%;
            border-collapse: collapse;
            empty-cells: show;
        }
        table.calendarMonth tbody {
            user-select: none;
            -webkit-user-select: none;
            -moz-user-select: none;
            -ms-user-select: none;
        }
        table.calendarMonth th {
            font-weight: 200;
            border: 1px solid rgb(224, 224, 224);
            padding: 10px;
        }
        tr.calendarHeading th {
            font: 24px Helvetica, Arial, sans-serif;
        }
        table.calendarMonth td {
            border: 1px solid rgb(224, 224, 224);
            vertical-align: top;
            padding: 10px;
        }
        td.calendarLastMonth,
        td.calendarNextMonth {
            color: rgb(204, 204, 204);
            background: rgb(244, 244, 244);
        }
        td.calendarDaySelected {
            background: yellow;
        }
        tr.calendarWeekSelected {
            background: lightyellow;
        }
        td.calendarToday {
            background: gold;
        }
```

Finally, you apply the following JavaScript, which provides you with an introduction to some of jQuery's various methods that allow you to traverse the DOM, as well as change and manipulate selections.

```javascript
        $(document).ready(
            function()
            {
                var today = $('td.calendarToday');

                var setUpThisWeek = function()
                {
                    $('table.calendarMonth td').removeClass(
                        'calendarYesterday ' +
                        'calendarTomorrow ' +
```

```
        'calendarEarlierThisWeek ' +
        'calendarLaterThisWeek ' +
        'calendarThisWeek'
);

var yesterday = today.prev('td');

// If today occurs at the beginning of the week, look in the
// preceding row for yesterday.
if (!yesterday.length)
{
    var lastWeek = today.parent('tr').prev('tr');

    if (lastWeek.length)
    {
        yesterday = lastWeek.children('td').eq(6);
    }
}

// If today occurs in the first cell of the first row of the
// calendar, yesterday won't be present in this month.
if (yesterday.length)
{
    yesterday.addClass('calendarYesterday');
}

var tomorrow = today.next('td');

// If today occurs at the end of the week, look in the
// proceeding row for tommorrow.
if (!tomorrow.length)
{
    var nextWeek = today.parent('tr').next('tr');

    if (nextWeek.length)
    {
        tomorrow = nextWeek.children('td').eq(0);
    }
}

// If today occurs in the last cell of the last row of
// the calendar, tomorrow won't be present in this month.
if (tomorrow.length)
{
    tomorrow.addClass('calendarTommorow');
}

var laterThisWeek = today.nextAll('td');

if (laterThisWeek.length)
{
    laterThisWeek.addClass('calendarLaterThisWeek');
}

var earlierThisWeek = today.prevAll('td');
```

```
            if (earlierThisWeek.length)
            {
                earlierThisWeek.addClass('calendarEarlierThisWeek');
            }

            today.siblings('td')
                .addClass('calendarThisWeek');
        };

        var selectedDay = null;

        $('table.calendarMonth td')
            .not('td.calendarLastMonth, td.calendarNextMonth')
            .click(
                function()
                {
                    if (selectedDay && selectedDay.length)
                    {
                        selectedDay
                            .removeClass('calendarDaySelected')
                            .parent('tr')
                                .removeClass('calendarWeekSelected');
                    }

                    var day = $(this);

                    selectedDay = day;

                    selectedDay
                        .addClass('calendarDaySelected')

                        .parent('tr')
                            .addClass('calendarWeekSelected');
                    day.parents('table.calendarMonth')
                        .find('span.calendarDay')
                        .text(day.text() + ', ');
                }
            )
            .dblclick(
                function()
                {
                    today.removeClass('calendarToday');
                    today = $(this);
                    today.addClass('calendarToday');

                    setUpThisWeek();
                }
            );

        setUpThisWeek();
    }
);
```

When you load the calendar that you created in *Example 2-3* into a browser, you get the results that you see in Figure 2-3.

FIGURE 2-3

Example 2-3 packs several concepts together to provide a more realistic example of how you might use jQuery's traversal methods. Like all previous examples, you start with the DOMContentReady event.

```
$(document).ready(
    function()
    {
```

The first thing you do when the document is ready is set up a variable to contain a reference to today, which contains the <td> element with the class name calendarToday.

```
var today = $('td.calendarToday');
```

This example uses all class names because the calendar concept is one in which you might expect to have multiple months loaded into the same document at once.

Next, you create a reusable function that sets up some metadata, mostly as an intellectual exercise. The metadata that you create provides a demonstration of jQuery's various methods for working with siblings as well as children, and the eq() method, which allows you to narrow a selection to a single element based on its position offset from zero. Because the method is created inside the function that executes when the document is ready, this method is available from within all the other functions that you create inside the ready() function. The same is true of the variable you created just previous to this called today.

```
var setUpThisWeek = function()
{
```

The first thing you do in the function setUpThisWeek is to remove all the class names that are applied later in this same function. You do this by selecting the <td> elements inside of the <table> with class name calendarMonth, and then calling jQuery's removeClass() method. removeClass() can take a single class name or several. If you provide more than one, you simply separate each individual class name with a single space, just as you would if you were specifying class names using the HTML class attribute. This, in turn, removes any of the specified class names if they are present.

```
$('table.calendarMonth td').removeClass(
    'calendarYesterday ' +
    'calendarTomorrow ' +
    'calendarEarlierThisWeek ' +
    'calendarLaterThisWeek ' +
    'calendarThisWeek'
);
```

Next, you create a variable that will contain a reference to yesterday, and that variable is called yesterday. To capture which day is considered yesterday, you start with the day considered today, which you captured previously. Then you move backward a single table cell to the previous day using jQuery's prev() method, which selects the element immediately preceding the element (or elements) referenced by the current selection. In this case, you are working only with a single element, but as with everything else jQuery can do, it will happily allow you to work with multiple elements at the same time. If the selection had contained multiple elements, prev() would work on them all, and it would provide you with a new selection that would provide all preceding adjacent elements. You also provide a selector to prev(), which would limit the adjacent preceding element to a <td> element. In the context of this example, you could easily have left off that selector and you would have the same result. I have included it for two reasons: the first to provide an example of what it means to provide a selector to these methods, the second to make the code a little more intuitive and easier to follow. Because 'td' is specified as the selector, that gives you as a programmer a cue about what the code is doing and what it's operating on.

```
var yesterday = today.prev('td');
```

If you're writing a real calendar application, you need to take into account every possible situation regarding where today might occur. It could happen at the beginning of a row or the end of a row. If today occurs at the beginning of a row, then there will be no adjacent <td> element preceding the <td> element representing today. In this case the previous assignment to yesterday will be an empty array, and it will have no length. This is how you check for the existence of a selection in jQuery.

If a selection results in nothing, jQuery will return an empty array, and you can then check the length property to see if anything were selected.

```
if (!yesterday.length)
{
```

If there were no adjacent preceding element, you need to move to the previous row. To do that, you start with the <td> representing today, and then you move up the DOM from there to that element's parent element using jQuery's parent() method, which will be a <tr> element. When you arrive at the <tr> element, you move backward in the DOM to the preceding <tr> element. You then look at that <tr> element's children elements using jQuery's children() method, which will, of course, all be <td> elements. You then limit the selection of <td> elements to the very last one using the eq() method. Because we're counting from zero, and there are 7 days in a week, that will make the last <td> element the sixth in the selection. Like last time, you provide selectors to the parent(), children(), and prev() methods just to provide more context and information in your programming.

```
var lastWeek = today.parent('tr').prev('tr');

if (lastWeek.length)
{
    yesterday = lastWeek.children('td').eq(6);
}
}
```

It is still possible that there is no <td> element representing yesterday because today could be the first of the month and thus could occur as the first child of the first <tr> element. So, another check for length ensures that a <td> element has been selected to represent yesterday. When it is determined that a <td> element for yesterday exists, it is assigned the class name calendarYesterday.

```
if (yesterday.length)
{
    yesterday.addClass('calendarYesterday');
}
```

Now that you have figured out which, if any, <td> element will represent yesterday, the next step is figuring out which <td> element will represent tomorrow. This time you move forward a <td> element by using jQuery's next() method on the selection representing today, and this will reference the adjacent following <td> element. Any selection is assigned to a variable called tomorrow.

```
var tomorrow = today.next('td');
```

As with yesterday, you are not certain that there is a <td> element that is adjacent and following the <td> element representing today, so again you check the length property to see if a selection were made.

```
if (!tomorrow.length)
{
```

If there is no <td> element, you again move up the DOM to the parent <tr> element from the <td> element representing today, and you proceed to the next <tr> element using next(). Then you look at that <tr> element's children via children() (if there is a next row in the first place), and you limit the selection to the first `<td>` element of that row by calling `eq(0)`. Zero, this time, represents the first child `<td>` element.

```
var nextWeek = today.parent('tr').next('tr');

if (nextWeek.length)
{
    tomorrow = nextWeek.children('td').eq(0);
}
}
```

When you have determined which element, if any, represents tomorrow, you check to see if you have a selection, and if you do, you add the class name `calendarTomorrow` to that `<td>` element.

```
if (tomorrow.length)
{
    tomorrow.addClass('calendarTommorow');
}
```

The next exercise is to identify all days after today, which will represent *later this week*. That is done by calling `nextAll()` on the selection representing today, which brings back a selection of `<td>` elements, all of which are siblings to the `<td>` element representing today, but all occur after today.

```
var laterThisWeek = today.nextAll('td');

if (laterThisWeek.length)
{
```

If there is a selection of `<td>` elements, those `<td>` elements all receive the class name `calendarLaterThisWeek`.

```
    laterThisWeek.addClass('calendarLaterThisWeek');
}
```

Then, you do the same thing to identify `<td>` elements that will qualify for the phrase *earlier this week*. To identify those elements, you call `prevAll()` on today to select all `<td>` elements preceding the `<td>` element representing today.

```
var earlierThisWeek = today.prevAll('td');

if (earlierThisWeek.length)
{
```

If there are `<td>` elements assigned to the variable `earlierThisWeek`, those `<td>` elements each receive the class name `calendarEarlierThisWeek`.

```
    earlierThisWeek.addClass('calendarEarlierThisWeek');
}
```

Finally, you identify all sibling elements of the `<td>` element representing today using jQuery's `siblings()` method, and those elements are all given the class name `calendarThisWeek`.

```
today.siblings('td')
```

```
                        .addClass('calendarThisWeek');
        };
```

The exercise of sibling discovery that you underwent with the method setUpThisWeek() can be explored using a tool like Web Inspector in Safari or Chrome, Firebug in Firefox, and Developer Tools in IE. Pictured in Figure 2-4 is Web Inspector in Safari, which shows the class names that you assigned for each <td> element representing a day or collection of days in the week surrounding the <td> element that represents today.

FIGURE 2-4

The next hunk of code defines some interactivity with the calendar:

➤ Selecting a day in the calendar

➤ Selecting the week that day occurs within

➤ Setting the selected day in date format in the calendar heading

➤ Changing the day that represents today

The first thing you do is to create a new variable that will keep track of the selected day. This variable is created outside the function that fires when you click each day, so that it can persist and remain present between click events. And that variable is called selectedDay.

```
        var selectedDay = null;
```

You then make a selection that starts out with all the <td> elements that are present in the <table> representing the month.

```
        $('table.calendarMonth td')
```

That selection is then narrowed to exclude the <td> elements that represent the remaining days of last month, or the beginning days of next month, even though this particular example has none of the days of the following month included because it ends evenly, filling all seven of the child spots within the last <tr> element. These <td> elements are excluded from the selection by using jQuery's not() method. The not() method takes an existing selection and subtracts from it using a selector.

The not() method can also take the results of another jQuery selection, such as

```
.not($('td.calendarLastMonth, td.calendarNextMonth'))
```

It can also use direct DOM element objects, such as those returned from JavaScript methods such as document.getElementById(). Finally, you can also use a callback function, which would return one of the preceding, a jQuery selection, or a direct DOM element object reference. This same thing is true of many jQuery API methods; where it makes sense and is possible, you can often use a jQuery selection, which is an array of elements returned from jQuery, a direct DOM object reference, or a callback function.

```
.not('td.calendarLastMonth, td.calendarNextMonth')
```

Having now excluded the elements you don't want selectable in the current month, the remaining <td> elements each receive an onclick event via click() and jQuery's event API, which I cover in more detail in Chapter 3, "Events."

```
.click(
    function()
    {
```

When a click occurs, the first thing that you do is to use the selectedDay variable that you created to keep track of the selected day. You first see if you have stored a selection in this variable by checking the length property. If you have stored a selection, that selection is used to remove the class name calendarDaySelected from the last <td> element that was given this class name, and you remove the class name calendarWeekSelected from the last <tr> element to have received that class name. This ensures that only one <td> element has that class name with any given click, and is the only selected day, and that element's parent <tr> element is the only <tr> element to be the selected week. Sans this logic, you would potentially be selecting many <td> and many <tr> elements as the selected day and week, respectively.

```
if (selectedDay && selectedDay.length)
{
    selectedDay
        .removeClass('calendarDaySelected')
        .parent('tr')
            .removeClass('calendarWeekSelected');
}
```

Following the selected day logic, you assign a variable called day with $(this), which is the element currently experiencing the click event made jQuery-able.

```
var day = $(this);
```

The day is then assigned to selectedDay, where it will persist and remain until the next click event occurs.

```
selectedDay = day;
```

The selected day then receives the class name calendarDaySelected, and then its parent <tr> element also receives the class name calendarWeekSelected.

```
selectedDay
    .addClass('calendarDaySelected')
    .parent('tr')
        .addClass('calendarWeekSelected');
```

Then you travel up the DOM from the selected day all the way to the <td> element's ancestor <table> element. You go from there to find the <span> with class name calendarDay, which is then assigned text content. That in turn places the selected day in the calendar header in date format, for example, *November 23, 2013*. The call to day.text() returns the text content of the selected day; in this case this is the number representing the day of the month, and that is appended to a string containing a comma and a space. The parents() method is used to go from an element to that element's parent or ancestor, allowing you to go all the way up the DOM tree to the root <html> element. The selector that you provide to parents() tells the parents() method what element or elements you want to include as you travel up the DOM tree. If you were to also include the jQuery proprietary :first pseudo-class in that selector, such as, table.calendarMonth:first, this would also trigger the parents() method to halt the search when it comes to the first element that matches the provided selector, and it would therefore also provide you with better performance than the selector that I used, which causes jQuery to examine the entire DOM ancestry so that it is sure it has matched every possible element.

```
day.parents('table.calendarMonth')
    .find('span.calendarDay')
    .text(day.text() + ', ');
            }
        )
```

The next event that you create is a double-click event using jQuery's dblclick() method. Creating this event enables you to change the day that is considered to be *today*.

```
.dblclick(
    function()
    {
```

To change the element considered to be today, you first remove the class name calendarToday from the present <td> element with that moniker. You assign the double-clicked <td> element to today. You add the class name calendarToday to the new element.

```
today.removeClass('calendarToday');
today = $(this);
today.addClass('calendarToday');
```

Then you call setUpThisWeek() again to recalculate which days are considered yesterday, tomorrow, earlier this week, later this week, and this week.

```
                    setUpThisWeek();
            }
        );
```

Finally, the last thing that you do within the anonymous function assigned to the `ready()` event is to call `setUpThisWeek()`, which sets up the week relative to the element considered today when the document is initially loaded.

```
        setUpThisWeek();
```

The last concepts presented in this chapter are just some notes about two additional methods that jQuery provides. In my own experience, I haven't had a cause to use these methods often, but they may be useful to you. Those two methods are `slice()` and `add()`.

SLICING A SELECTION

The `slice()` method is similar to the `eq()` method; it selects a subset of a selection based on the offset position of elements in a selection. It does this using one or two arguments. If you provide just one argument, you provide the starting point for the slice. Take the following example of the places of Middle Earth:

```
<!DOCTYPE HTML>
<html xmlns="http://www.w3.org/1999/xhtml">
    <head>
        <meta http-equiv="content-type"
            content="application/xhtml+xml; charset=utf-8" />
        <meta http-equiv="content-language" content="en-us" />
        <title>Places in Middle-Earth</title>
    </head>
    <body>
        <ul>
            <li>The Shire</li>
            <li>Fangorn Forest</li>
            <li>Rohan</li>
            <li>Gondor</li>
            <li>Mordor</li>
        </ul>
    </body>
</html>
```

Using `$('li').slice(1)`, the argument 1 indicates where the slice begins, so `slice(1)` would include all elements from `<li>Fangorn Forest</li>` to `<li>Mordor</li>`. Therefore, using a single argument, counting from zero, your selection includes that element onward.

When supplying two arguments, the first argument is the offset position of the first element you'd like to include in the resulting selection counting from zero, and the second argument is the offset position of the last element you'd like to include in the resulting selection, also offset from zero. This creates a new selection where the elements in that selection include a range of elements starting with that first element and ending with the last element. So, `slice(0, 2)` would start with element number zero and end with element number 1. The selection goes from 0–2, but it does not include element #2 itself. So, this selection will include `<li>The Shire</li>` and `<li>Fangorn Forest</li>`.

ADDING TO A SELECTION

Finally, I introduce you to the add() method. The add() method is the inverse to the not() method, and it is used to add to an existing selection. The following HTML, again, represents places in Middle Earth:

```
<!DOCTYPE HTML>
<html xmlns="http://www.w3.org/1999/xhtml">
    <head>
        <meta http-equiv="content-type"
            content="application/xhtml+xml; charset=utf-8" />
        <meta http-equiv="content-language" content="en-us" />
        <title>Places in Middle-Earth</title>
    </head>
    <body>
        <ul id='middleEarthPlaces'>
            <li>The Shire</li>
            <li>Fangorn Forest</li>
            <li>Rohan</li>
            <li>Gondor</li>
            <li>Mordor</li>
        </ul>
        <ul id='middleEarthMorePlaces'>
            <li>Osgiliath</li>
            <li>Minas Tirith</li>
            <li>Mirkwood Forest</li>
        </ul>
    </body>
</html>
```

A simple demonstration of the add() method is to make an initial selection, such as `$('ul#middleEarthPlaces li')`, which selects all the `<li>` elements in the first `<ul>` element. Then you can add to that selection with a class like this:

```
$('ul#middleEarthPlaces li').add('ul#middleEarthMorePlaces li');
```

The resulting selection now includes all the `<li>` elements present in the document because you first selected the `<li>` elements in the first `<ul>` element, and then you added to that selection the `<li>` elements of the second `<ul>` element.

Like the not() method, you can add elements to a selection using the result of a jQuery selection, just like this:

```
$('ul#middleEarthPlaces li').add($('ul#middleEarthMorePlaces li'));
```

You can also use direct DOM object references, like this:

```
$('ul#middleEarthPlaces li').add(
    document.getElementById('middleEarthMorePlaces').childNodes
);
```

And you can use callback functions that return either jQuery selections or direct DOM object references:

```
$('ul#middleEarthPlaces li').add(
    function()
    {
        return document.getElementById('middleEarthMorePlaces').childNodes;
    }
);
```

The add() method allows you to add elements to a selection using any of these methods. In Chapter 4, "Manipulating Content and Attributes," you'll learn how you can even use a string containing HTML to add to a selection.

> **NOTE** *Appendix C, "Selecting, Traversing, and Filtering," provides a reference for all jQuery's selection and filtering methods.*

SUMMARY

In this chapter, you've seen some examples that give you a comprehensive overview of jQuery's selection and filtering abilities. You learned how jQuery provides ridiculously fine-grained control over selecting elements from the DOM, so fine-grained that you'll often find that there are multiple ways to achieve the same results.

jQuery's selection and filtering methods go much further than what you get with JavaScript alone, which more often than not would take several lines of code to come to the same level of control over a selection.

jQuery harnesses the power, ease, familiarity, and convenience of selectors to help you get anywhere in the DOM you want to go. The selector syntax, you'll find, is the same as what you're used to using with CSS; jQuery even supports a few extensions of its own. See Appendix B, "jQuery Selectors," for a full listing of selector syntax supported by jQuery.

jQuery's filtering methods let you select descendants using the find() method, ancestors using the parents() method, and siblings using the siblings(), prev(), prevAll(), next(), and nextAll() methods. You can add elements using the add() method or exclude elements using the not() method. And you can also get even more specific using the slice() and eq() methods. See Appendix C for a full list of methods related to selection and filtering.

EXERCISES

1. What other client-side technology does jQuery have a lot in common with in terms of its fine-grained control over the selection of elements from the markup source?

2. If you wanted to select an element from the DOM using jQuery based on an ancestral relationship, which method would you use?

3. If you want to swap an element's position in the DOM with its preceding sibling, what jQuery method would help with that application?

4. If you have selected an element and want to select one of that element's descendants from the DOM, what methods does jQuery provide that would give you the results you seek?

5. If you made a selection but later wanted to remove one or more elements from that selection, what jQuery method would you use?

6. If you wanted to select only a single element from a broader selection, what jQuery method would you use?

7. List all the methods that jQuery provides for working with sibling elements.

8. How would you add elements to a selection using jQuery?

Events

jQuery offers a powerful and comprehensive event API. jQuery's event API provides wrapper methods that accommodate most events in JavaScript. jQuery's event API also provides the capability to attach events it doesn't explicitly support via its event methods. The jQuery event API even has the capability to apply events to elements that might not even exist in the document yet. Events can be neatly organized and namespaced within jQuery, another feature it offers above and beyond the baseline provided by JavaScript. Your events can be neatly organized into named categories, which make it a lot easier to manage events. Having named events also makes it possible to easily remove them.

In this chapter, you learn everything you need to know to work with jQuery's event API. You learn how to use jQuery's event wrapper methods such as click() or hover(). You also learn how to use methods such as on() and off(). You can use the on() and off() methods to attach an event handler function to any event, whether it is a native JavaScript event or a custom event that you've created. The on() and off() methods can also attach events to elements that might not even exist in the document yet. In addition, on() and off() can name and organize events, which is useful if you need to manage or remove events as easily as creating them. You also learn how to create completely custom events for your applications by virtue of the trigger() method as well as the on() and off() methods. Custom events can make your own applications highly extensible and flexible.

THE VARIOUS EVENT WRAPPER METHODS

jQuery's event API started with the goal of providing a bridge between the different browsers' disparate methods for dealing with event attachment. There was a time in the not-so-distant past that there was the Microsoft way of dealing with events, and then there was the standardized way of dealing with events. Because of Microsoft's work on Internet Explorer, this is no longer an issue, and you have to worry about this only if you need to support those older versions of Internet Explorer that don't support the standard way of attaching events. Thankfully, jQuery already deals with the browser differences for you. The jQuery 1.x branch provides legacy support for versions of Internet Explorer that don't support the standardized way.

The jQuery 2.x branch does away with things such as legacy support for older versions of Internet Explorer, so the 2.x branch will not provide universal event support.

With the differences in browser support safely behind us for the most part, the jQuery event API has taken up the task of making it easier to work with events in JavaScript in general, and it succeeds well at doing so. The first collection of methods you take a look at in this chapter are a collection of methods that provide API wrappers around the most-used events in JavaScript. These methods make it possible to do two things:

➤   To easily attach a callback function to an event

➤   To easily trigger an event

You can find a comprehensive list of event methods in Appendix D, "Events."

The following example demonstrates the jQuery event wrapper method, click(). Remember, this and all examples are available for free with the book's source code download materials from www.wrox.com/go/webdevwithjquery. This example is available in the accompanying materials as *Example 3-1.html*.

```html
<!DOCTYPE HTML>
<html lang='en'>
    <head>
        <meta http-equiv='X-UA-Compatible' content='IE=Edge' />
        <meta charset='utf-8' />
        <title>Finder</title>
        <script src='../jQuery.js'></script>
        <script src='../jQueryUI.js'></script>
        <script src='Example 3-1.js'></script>
        <link href='Example 3-1.css' rel='stylesheet' />
    </head>
    <body>
        <div id='finderFiles'>
            <div class='finderDirectory' data-path='/Applications'>
                <div class='finderIcon'></div>
                <div class='finderDirectoryName'>
                    <span>Applications</span>
                </div>
            </div>
            <div class='finderDirectory' data-path='/Library'>
                <div class='finderIcon'></div>
                <div class='finderDirectoryName'>
                    <span>Library</span>
                </div>
            </div>
            <div class='finderDirectory' data-path='/Network'>
                <div class='finderIcon'></div>
                <div class='finderDirectoryName'>
                    <span>Network</span>
                </div>
            </div>
            <div class='finderDirectory' data-path='/Sites'>
                <div class='finderIcon'></div>
                <div class='finderDirectoryName'>
                    <span>Sites</span>
```

```
                        </div>
                    </div>
                    <div class='finderDirectory' data-path='/System'>
                        <div class='finderIcon'></div>
                        <div class='finderDirectoryName'>
                            <span>System</span>
                        </div>
                    </div>
                    <div class='finderDirectory' data-path='/Users'>
                        <div class='finderIcon'></div>
                        <div class='finderDirectoryName'>
                            <span>Users</span>
                        </div>
                    </div>
                </div>
            </div>
        </body>
    </html>
```

The preceding HTML is styled with the following style sheet, *Example 3-1.css*.

```
html,
body {
    width: 100%;
    height: 100%;
}
body {
    font: 12px "Lucida Grande", Arial, sans-serif;
    background: rgb(189, 189, 189) url('images/Bottom.png') repeat-x bottom;
    color: rgb(50, 50, 50);
    margin: 0;
    padding: 0;
}
div#finderFiles {
    border-bottom: 1px solid rgb(64, 64, 64);
    background: #fff;
    position: absolute;
    top: 0;
    right: 0;
    bottom: 23px;
    left: 0;
    overflow: auto;
    user-select: none;
    -webkit-user-select: none;
    -moz-user-select: none;
    -ms-user-select: none;
}
div.finderDirectory {
    float: left;
    width: 150px;
    height: 100px;
    overflow: hidden;
}
div.finderIcon {
    background: url('images/Folder 48x48.png') no-repeat center;
```

```
        background-size: 48px 48px;
        height: 56px;
        width: 54px;
        margin: 10px auto 3px auto;
    }
    div.finderIconSelected {
        background-color: rgb(204, 204, 204);
        border-radius: 5px;
    }
    div.finderDirectoryName {
        text-align: center;
    }
    span.finderDirectoryNameSelected {
        background: rgb(56, 117, 215);
        border-radius: 8px;
        color: white;
        padding: 1px 7px;
    }
```

Finally, the JavaScript in *Example 3-1.js* adds some selection functionality to the folders that you created.

```
$(document).ready(
    function()
    {
        $('div.finderDirectory, div.finderFile').click(
            function(event)
            {
                $('div.finderIconSelected')
                    .removeClass('finderIconSelected');

                $('span.finderDirectoryNameSelected')
                    .removeClass('finderDirectoryNameSelected');

                $(this).find('div.finderIcon')
                    .addClass('finderIconSelected');

                $(this).find('div.finderDirectoryName span')
                    .addClass('finderDirectoryNameSelected');
            }
        );

        $('div.finderDirectory, div.finderFile')
            .filter(':first')
            .click();
    }
);
```

The collection of files that make up *Example 3-1* results in what you see in Figure 3-1, when the file is loaded into Safari.

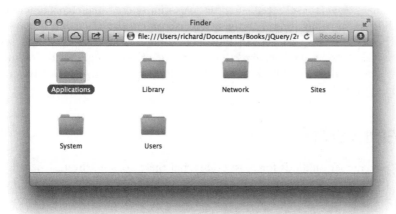

FIGURE 3-1

Example 3-1 demonstrates a simple use of the click() method both to attach a callback method and to trigger the event. Most of jQuery's event wrapper methods work exactly like this, with just a few exceptions, which are events such as hover(), which accept multiple callback methods: one for the mouseover event and one for the mouseout event.

The document ready() event method is also an example of a wrapper event method, which jQuery creates for the DOMContentLoaded event.

In the example, you attach the callback function. You start by selecting all the <div> elements in the document with the class names finderDirectory and finderFile.

```
$('div.finderDirectory, div.finderFile').click(
    function(event)
    {
        $('div.finderIconSelected')
            .removeClass('finderIconSelected');

        $('span.finderDirectoryNameSelected')
            .removeClass('finderDirectoryNameSelected');

        $(this).find('div.finderIcon')
            .addClass('finderIconSelected');

        $(this).find('div.finderDirectoryName span')
            .addClass('finderDirectoryNameSelected');
    }
);
```

When a click event fires and the callback function is executed, there is a bit of logic that handles visually selecting a file or a folder. You start by removing a selection, which is to say you select the

<div> element with class name `finderIconSelected`, and then you remove the `finderIconSelected` class name from it. You then do the same thing with the <span> element with class name `finderDirectoryNameSelected`. Then the function selects and adds those same class names, `finderIconSelected` and `finderDirectoryNameSelected`, to elements that exist inside the element that the event fires on. That element, the element the event fires on, is made available within the callback function within the object stored in the `this` keyword.

ATTACHING OTHER EVENTS

jQuery's event API provides wrapper methods for most events, but there are some events that there are no methods for. Which events, you might ask? Events like those found in the HTML5 drag-and-drop API, for example. There are no jQuery-provided `dragstart()` or `drop()` methods like there are jQuery-provided `click()` or `mouseover()` methods.

For those events, you need to use the `on()` and `off()` methods, which attach event handlers to any named event. The following example takes the script in *Example 3-1.js* and rewrites it to use the `on()`, `off()`, and `trigger()` methods instead of the respective built-in methods for each of the events.

```
$(document).on(
    'DOMContentLoaded',
    function()
    {
        $('div.finderDirectory, div.finderFile').on(
            'click',
            function(event)
            {
                $('div.finderIconSelected')
                    .removeClass('finderIconSelected');

                $('span.finderDirectoryNameSelected')
                    .removeClass('finderDirectoryNameSelected');

                $(this).find('div.finderIcon')
                    .addClass('finderIconSelected');

                $(this).find('div.finderDirectoryName span')
                    .addClass('finderDirectoryNameSelected');
            }
        );

        $('div.finderDirectory, div.finderFile')
            .filter(':first')
            .trigger('click');
    }
);
```

This example is identical in functionality to *Example 3-1*; you can find it in the source materials as *Example 3-2*.

Instead of `$(document).ready()`, `$(document).on('DOMContentLoaded')` provides identical functionality. You can think of jQuery's `on()` method as being close to the standard `addEventListener()`

method that you'd use in JavaScript if you weren't working with a JavaScript framework. It simply has more features built into it to make working with events a lot easier.

Instead of $('div.finderDirectory, div.finderFile').click(), you use $('div.finderDirectory, div.finderFile').on('click'). Finally, to trigger an event to be fired, instead of just calling the event method, like click(), you call the trigger() method with the event name as its argument, such as, trigger('click').

ATTACHING PERSISTENT EVENT HANDLERS

A convenient and cool feature of jQuery's on() and off() methods is the concept of attaching events to nodes in the DOM that might not even exist when you create the event handler. Internally, this feature works by attaching an event to a node that is higher up the DOM tree and thus does exist at the time the event handler is processed and attached.

For example, you might attach a click event to the document object. Then, by providing a selector to the second argument of the on() method, you create a persistent event handler that applies to only the nodes described by the selector. Those nodes described by the selector can exist or not exist at the time the event handler is created; the only catch is the nodes must exist inside the object the event handler is attached to.

Then using event propagation, the event takes place and bubbles up the DOM tree to the element the event handler is attached to. jQuery continuously looks at the event.target property to see if the node that received the event is described by the selector that you provide. If it is, then it applies the event handler.

The following example, which can be found in the source materials as *Example 3-3*, takes the previous two examples and implements the concept of persistent events. (jQuery's documentation has also referred to this concept as *live* events.) You begin with modifying the HTML so that some files can be added after the event handler is created.

```html
<!DOCTYPE HTML>
<html lang='en'>
    <head>
        <meta http-equiv='X-UA-Compatible' content='IE=Edge' />
        <meta charset='utf-8' />
        <title>Finder</title>
        <script src='../jQuery.js'></script>
        <script src='../jQueryUI.js'></script>
        <script src='Example 3-3.js'></script>
        <link href='Example 3-3.css' rel='stylesheet' />
    </head>
    <body>
        <div id='finderFiles'>
            <div class='finderDirectory finderNode' data-path='/Applications'>
                <div class='finderIcon'></div>
                <div class='finderDirectoryName'>
                    <span>Applications</span>
                </div>
            </div>
            <div class='finderDirectory finderNode' data-path='/Library'>
```

```
                    <div class='finderIcon'></div>
                    <div class='finderDirectoryName'>
                        <span>Library</span>
                    </div>
                </div>
                <div class='finderDirectory finderNode' data-path='/Network'>
                    <div class='finderIcon'></div>
                    <div class='finderDirectoryName'>
                        <span>Network</span>
                    </div>
                </div>
                <div class='finderDirectory finderNode' data-path='/Sites'>
                    <div class='finderIcon'></div>
                    <div class='finderDirectoryName'>
                        <span>Sites</span>
                    </div>
                </div>
                <div class='finderDirectory finderNode' data-path='/System'>
                    <div class='finderIcon'></div>
                    <div class='finderDirectoryName'>
                        <span>System</span>
                    </div>
                </div>
                <div class='finderDirectory finderNode' data-path='/Users'>
                    <div class='finderIcon'></div>
                    <div class='finderDirectoryName'>
                        <span>Users</span>
                    </div>
                </div>
            </div>
            <div id='finderAdditionalFiles'>
                <div class='finderFile finderNode' data-path='/index.html'>
                    <div class='finderIcon'></div>
                    <div class='finderFileName'>
                        <span>index.html</span>
                    </div>
                </div>
                <div class='finderFile finderNode' data-path='/Departments.html'>
                    <div class='finderIcon'></div>
                    <div class='finderFileName'>
                        <span>Departments.html</span>
                    </div>
                </div>
                <div class='finderFile finderNode' data-path='/Documents.html'>
                    <div class='finderIcon'></div>
                    <div class='finderFileName'>
                        <span>Documents.html</span>
                    </div>
                </div>
            </div>
        </body>
    </html>
```

The style sheet that you used for the previous two examples is modified a bit as well to add class names for file nodes and directory nodes.

```css
html,
body {
    width: 100%;
    height: 100%;
}
body {
    font: 12px "Lucida Grande", Arial, sans-serif;
    background: rgb(189, 189, 189) url('images/Bottom.png') repeat-x bottom;
    color: rgb(50, 50, 50);
    margin: 0;
    padding: 0;
}
div#finderFiles {
    border-bottom: 1px solid rgb(64, 64, 64);
    background: #fff;
    position: absolute;
    top: 0;
    right: 0;
    bottom: 23px;
    left: 0;
    overflow: auto;
    user-select: none;
    -webkit-user-select: none;
    -moz-user-select: none;
    -ms-user-select: none;
}
div#finderAdditionalFiles {
    display: none;
}
div.finderDirectory,
div.finderFile {
    float: left;
    width: 150px;
    height: 100px;
    overflow: hidden;
}
div.finderIcon {
    background: url('images/Folder 48x48.png') no-repeat center;
    background-size: 48px 48px;
    height: 56px;
    width: 54px;
    margin: 10px auto 3px auto;
}
div.finderFile div.finderIcon {
    background-image: url('images/Safari Document.png');
}
div.finderIconSelected {
    background-color: rgb(204, 204, 204);
```

```
        border-radius: 5px;
}
div.finderDirectoryName,
div.finderFileName {
        text-align: center;
}
span.finderDirectoryNameSelected,
span.finderFileNameSelected {
        background: rgb(56, 117, 215);
        border-radius: 8px;
        color: white;
        padding: 1px 7px;
}
```

And finally, the JavaScript is modified to use a persistent event, as well as to add some new files when you double-click anywhere on the document to test the concept of a persistent event handler.

```
$(document).on(
    'DOMContentLoaded',
    function()
    {
        $('div#finderFiles').on(
            'click',
            'div.finderDirectory, div.finderFile',
            function(event)
            {
                $('div.finderIconSelected')
                    .removeClass('finderIconSelected');

                $('span.finderDirectoryNameSelected')
                    .removeClass('finderDirectoryNameSelected');

                $('span.finderFileNameSelected')
                    .removeClass('finderFileNameSelected');

                $(this).find('div.finderIcon')
                    .addClass('finderIconSelected');

                $(this).find('div.finderDirectoryName span')
                    .addClass('finderDirectoryNameSelected');

                $(this).find('div.finderFileName span')
                    .addClass('finderFileNameSelected');
            }
        );

        $('div#finderFiles div.finderNode:first')
            .trigger('click');

        var addedAdditionalFiles = false;

        $('body').dblclick(
            function()
            {
                if (addedAdditionalFiles)
```

```
                    {
                        return;
                    }

                    $('div#finderAdditionalFiles > div.finderFile').each(
                        function()
                        {
                            $('div#finderFiles').append(
                                $(this).clone()
                            );
                        }
                    );

                    addedAdditionalFiles = true;
                }
            );
        }
    );
```

When the code is loaded into a browser and a dblclick event is dispatched, you can see results similar to Figure 3-2.

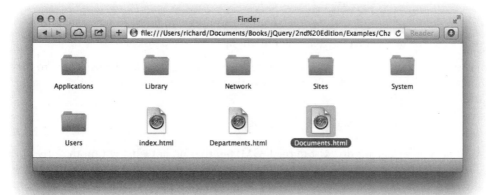

FIGURE 3-2

This example rewrites *Example 3-2* to include a persistent event handler and some additional HTML to test that persistent event handler. The click event handler is attached to the <div> element with the id name finderFiles. This is done because that <div> element will always exist. The second argument, the selector 'div.finderDirectory, div.finderFile', sets up the persistent event handler. The event is attached to the <div> with the id name finderFiles, but the selector argument keeps the event handler from being executed unless the event originates on an element matching the selector.

```
        $('div#finderFiles').on(
            'click',
            'div.finderDirectory, div.finderFile',
            function(event)
            {
                $('div.finderIconSelected')
```

```
                              .removeClass('finderIconSelected');

                $('span.finderDirectoryNameSelected')
                    .removeClass('finderDirectoryNameSelected');

                $('span.finderFileNameSelected')
                    .removeClass('finderFileNameSelected');

                $(this).find('div.finderIcon')
                    .addClass('finderIconSelected');

                $(this).find('div.finderDirectoryName span')
                    .addClass('finderDirectoryNameSelected');

                $(this).find('div.finderFileName span')
                    .addClass('finderFileNameSelected');
        }
    );
```

The event handler is given some new code to deal with the semantics of having files in addition to directories.

```
        $('div#finderFiles div.finderNode:first')
            .trigger('click');
```

The event is triggered on the first <div> element with the class name finderNode.

Next, you set up a variable to keep track of whether the additional files have been added to the entire collection of files and folders, which tests whether an element has to exist for a persistent event handler to get applied.

```
        var addedAdditionalFiles = false;
```

Technically, these new elements do exist in the DOM, but they do not exist within the <div> element that acts as a container for directory and file nodes, and thus, the requisite events associated with file and directory nodes are not yet applied.

```
        $('body').dblclick(
            function()
            {
                if (addedAdditionalFiles)
                {
                    return;
                }

                $('div#finderAdditionalFiles > div.finderFile').each(
                    function()
                    {
                        $('div#finderFiles').append(
                            $(this).clone()
                        );
                    }
                );
```

```
                  addedAdditionalFiles = true;
           }
      );
```

First, you check the variable addedAdditionalFiles; if that variable is true, then execution of the dblclick handler returns. If addedAdditionalFiles is false, then you look inside the <div> with the id name finderAdditionalFiles for some extra <div> elements with class names finderFile, and each of those are added to the other <div> element with the id name finderFiles.

When you click one of the new <div> elements, you notice that selection happens without any additional effort. This is what it means to use a persistent event handler; the event continues to work when new elements are added that match the selector argument. Still using the file manager metaphor, this makes it possible to attach just one event handler for many files or folders, instead of an event handler for each file and folder. If you have a lot of files and folders in the DOM, this also has the advantage of substantially increasing performance. So, persistent event handlers benefit you in two key ways.

1. The element does not have to exist when the event handler is created. The element can be created later; it just has to match the selector that you provide to the on() method.

2. Client-side browser performance can be substantially boosted because you can reduce the number of event handlers that you need for a given event to just one from potentially many.

REMOVING EVENT HANDLERS

The on() method has a companion method called off(), which removes event handlers from a document. jQuery also provides a useful way of discerning which events should be removed by virtue of its capability to namespace event handlers.

Within a more complicated client-side application, you can quickly lose track of which scripts create which event handlers. This is easily remedied by the introduction of named events by jQuery.

The syntax used to name an event is simple: In the argument where you name the event, you add a dot and then the name that you want to use. The syntax works similarly to class names. And like class names, using multiple dots will allow you to refer to multiple names. And referring to any one name refers to any event using that name (even if that event has multiple names attached to it).

The following example, which can be found in the source materials as *Example 3-4*, demonstrates how to work with named events, as well as how to dynamically apply and remove an event handler. You begin with the same HTML that you worked with in preceding examples; you add two new buttons to dynamically apply and remove events.

```
<!DOCTYPE HTML>
<html lang='en'>
   <head>
      <meta http-equiv='X-UA-Compatible' content='IE=Edge' />
      <meta charset='utf-8' />
      <title>Finder</title>
```

```
        <script src='../jQuery.js'></script>
        <script src='../jQueryUI.js'></script>
        <script src='Example 3-4.js'></script>
        <link href='Example 3-4.css' rel='stylesheet' />
    </head>
    <body>
        <div id='finderFiles'>
            <div class='finderDirectory finderNode' data-path='/Applications'>
                <div class='finderIcon'></div>
                <div class='finderDirectoryName'>
                    <span>Applications</span>
                </div>
            </div>
            <div class='finderDirectory finderNode' data-path='/Library'>
                <div class='finderIcon'></div>
                <div class='finderDirectoryName'>
                    <span>Library</span>
                </div>
            </div>
            <div class='finderDirectory finderNode' data-path='/Network'>
                <div class='finderIcon'></div>
                <div class='finderDirectoryName'>
                    <span>Network</span>
                </div>
            </div>
            <div class='finderDirectory finderNode' data-path='/Sites'>
                <div class='finderIcon'></div>
                <div class='finderDirectoryName'>
                    <span>Sites</span>
                </div>
            </div>
            <div class='finderDirectory finderNode' data-path='/System'>
                <div class='finderIcon'></div>
                <div class='finderDirectoryName'>
                    <span>System</span>
                </div>
            </div>
            <div class='finderDirectory finderNode' data-path='/Users'>
                <div class='finderIcon'></div>
                <div class='finderDirectoryName'>
                    <span>Users</span>
                </div>
            </div>
            <div class='finderFile finderNode' data-path='/index.html'>
                <div class='finderIcon'></div>
                <div class='finderFileName'>
                    <span>index.html</span>
                </div>
            </div>
            <div class='finderFile finderNode' data-path='/Departments.html'>
                <div class='finderIcon'></div>
                <div class='finderFileName'>
                    <span>Departments.html</span>
```

```
                    </div>
                </div>
                <div class='finderFile finderNode' data-path='/Documents.html'>
                    <div class='finderIcon'></div>
                    <div class='finderFileName'>
                        <span>Documents.html</span>
                    </div>
                </div>
            </div>
            <div id='finderActions'>
                <button id='finderApplyEventHandler'>
                    Apply Event Handler
                </button>
                <button id='finderRemoveEventHandler'>
                    Remove Event Handler
                </button>
            </div>
        </body>
    </html>
```

The following CSS is applied to the HTML document; it adds some new CSS:

```
html,
body {
    width: 100%;
    height: 100%;
}
body {
    font: 12px "Lucida Grande", Arial, sans-serif;
    background: rgb(189, 189, 189) url('images/Bottom.png') repeat-x bottom;
    color: rgb(50, 50, 50);
    margin: 0;
    padding: 0;
}
div#finderFiles {
    border-bottom: 1px solid rgb(64, 64, 64);
    background: #fff;
    position: absolute;
    z-index: 1;
    top: 0;
    right: 0;
    bottom: 23px;
    left: 0;
    overflow: auto;
    user-select: none;
    -webkit-user-select: none;
    -moz-user-select: none;
    -ms-user-select: none;
}
div#finderAdditionalFiles {
    display: none;
}
div.finderDirectory,
```

```css
div.finderFile {
    float: left;
    width: 150px;
    height: 100px;
    overflow: hidden;
}
div.finderIcon {
    background: url('images/Folder 48x48.png') no-repeat center;
    background-size: 48px 48px;
    height: 56px;
    width: 54px;
    margin: 10px auto 3px auto;
}
div.finderFile div.finderIcon {
    background-image: url('images/Safari Document.png');
}
div.finderIconSelected {
    background-color: rgb(204, 204, 204);
    border-radius: 5px;
}
div.finderDirectoryName,
div.finderFileName {
    text-align: center;
}
span.finderDirectoryNameSelected,
span.finderFileNameSelected {
    background: rgb(56, 117, 215);
    border-radius: 8px;
    color: white;
    padding: 1px 7px;
}
div#finderActions {
    position: absolute;
    bottom: 1px;
    right: 10px;
    z-index: 2;
}
```

The following JavaScript demonstrates how to apply and remove event handlers at will:

```javascript
$(document).on(
    'DOMContentLoaded',
    function()
    {
        var eventHandlerActive = false;

        function applyEventHandler()
        {
            if (eventHandlerActive)
            {
                return;
            }

            $('div#finderFiles').on(
```

```
            'click.finder',
            'div.finderDirectory, div.finderFile',
            function(event)
            {
                $('div.finderIconSelected')
                    .removeClass('finderIconSelected');

                $('span.finderDirectoryNameSelected')
                    .removeClass('finderDirectoryNameSelected');

                $('span.finderFileNameSelected')
                    .removeClass('finderFileNameSelected');

                $(this).find('div.finderIcon')
                    .addClass('finderIconSelected');

                $(this).find('div.finderDirectoryName span')
                    .addClass('finderDirectoryNameSelected');

                $(this).find('div.finderFileName span')
                    .addClass('finderFileNameSelected');
            }
        );

        eventHandlerActive = true;
    }

    function removeEventHandler()
    {
        $('div#finderFiles').off('click.finder');

        eventHandlerActive = false;
    }

    $('div#finderFiles div.finderNode:first')
        .trigger('click');

    applyEventHandler();

    $('button#finderApplyEventHandler').click(
        function()
        {
            applyEventHandler();
        }
    );

    $('button#finderRemoveEventHandler').click(
        function()
        {
            removeEventHandler();
        }
    );
    }
);
```

The preceding example adds two new buttons to the window, which you can see as shown in Figure 3-3.

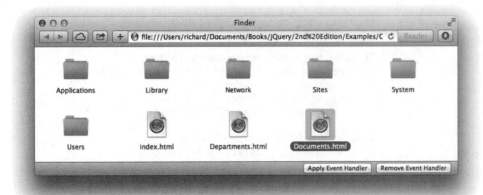

FIGURE 3-3

In *Example 3-4*, the click event handler is applied using the *applyEventHandler* method, which uses jQuery's on() method with a named event handler click.finder. The event is specified as usual, and then a dot is inserted, and any name you like is added after the dot (any name following the same naming conventions as class or id names). You can also use multiple names if you like; in this example, you could have also used click.finder.selection.

The example also adds a button and a method to remove the click event handler. The off() method is called with the same event and event name as was used in the call to the on() method. $('div.finderFiles').off('click.finder') completely removes the event handler.

CREATING CUSTOM EVENTS

Custom events are created using the same methods that you use to attach standard events: on(), off(), and trigger(). The only difference is that custom events require custom names. Custom names should simply require whatever you intend the event to provide.

Following are some examples of custom events from the context of a file manager application:

➤ An upload event can be created and used to execute a callback handler after a file upload has been completed.

➤ A folderUpdate event can be created and used to execute a callback handler when the files and folders displayed in the file manager are changed.

➤ A fileRename event can be created and used to execute a callback handler when a file is renamed.

Custom events exist to fulfill the need of providing more flexibility and extensibility in your applications. This, in turn, makes it possible to drop your application into the page where the user can attach custom event handlers to accommodate their imagined uses for your application. Custom events are demonstrated in the following example, which can be found as *Example 3-5* in the source materials:

```html
<!DOCTYPE HTML>
<html lang='en'>
    <head>
        <meta http-equiv='X-UA-Compatible' content='IE=Edge' />
        <meta charset='utf-8' />
        <title>Finder</title>
        <script src='../jQuery.js'></script>
        <script src='../jQueryUI.js'></script>
        <script src='Example 3-5.js'></script>
        <link href='Example 3-5.css' rel='stylesheet' />
    </head>
    <body>
        <div id='finderFiles'>
            <div class='finderDirectory finderNode' data-path='/Applications'>
                <div class='finderIcon'></div>
                <div class='finderDirectoryName'>
                    <span>Applications</span>
                </div>
            </div>
            <div class='finderDirectory finderNode' data-path='/Library'>
                <div class='finderIcon'></div>
                <div class='finderDirectoryName'>
                    <span>Library</span>
                </div>
            </div>
            <div class='finderDirectory finderNode' data-path='/Network'>
                <div class='finderIcon'></div>
                <div class='finderDirectoryName'>
                    <span>Network</span>
                </div>
            </div>
            <div class='finderDirectory finderNode' data-path='/Sites'>
                <div class='finderIcon'></div>
                <div class='finderDirectoryName'>
                    <span>Sites</span>
                </div>
            </div>
            <div class='finderDirectory finderNode' data-path='/System'>
                <div class='finderIcon'></div>
                <div class='finderDirectoryName'>
                    <span>System</span>
                </div>
            </div>
            <div class='finderDirectory finderNode' data-path='/Users'>
                <div class='finderIcon'></div>
```

```
                    <div class='finderDirectoryName'>
                        <span>Users</span>
                    </div>
                </div>
            </div>
            <div id='finderAdditionalFiles'>
                <div class='finderFile finderNode' data-path='/index.html'>
                    <div class='finderIcon'></div>
                    <div class='finderFileName'>
                        <span>index.html</span>
                    </div>
                </div>
                <div class='finderFile finderNode' data-path='/Departments.html'>
                    <div class='finderIcon'></div>
                    <div class='finderFileName'>
                        <span>Departments.html</span>
                    </div>
                </div>
                <div class='finderFile finderNode' data-path='/Documents.html'>
                    <div class='finderIcon'></div>
                    <div class='finderFileName'>
                        <span>Documents.html</span>
                    </div>
                </div>
            </div>
        </body>
    </html>
```

The preceding HTML is joined by the following style sheet:

```
html,
body {
    width: 100%;
    height: 100%;
}
body {
    font: 12px "Lucida Grande", Arial, sans-serif;
    background: rgb(189, 189, 189) url('images/Bottom.png') repeat-x bottom;
    color: rgb(50, 50, 50);
    margin: 0;
    padding: 0;
}
div#finderFiles {
    border-bottom: 1px solid rgb(64, 64, 64);
    background: #fff;
    position: absolute;
    top: 0;
    right: 0;
    bottom: 23px;
    left: 0;
    overflow: auto;
    user-select: none;
    -webkit-user-select: none;
    -moz-user-select: none;
```

```css
    -ms-user-select: none;
}
div#finderAdditionalFiles {
    display: none;
}
div.finderDirectory,
div.finderFile {
    float: left;
    width: 150px;
    height: 100px;
    overflow: hidden;
}
div.finderIcon {
    background: url('images/Folder 48x48.png') no-repeat center;
    background-size: 48px 48px;
    height: 56px;
    width: 54px;
    margin: 10px auto 3px auto;
}
div.finderFile div.finderIcon {
    background-image: url('images/Safari Document.png');
}
div.finderIconSelected {
    background-color: rgb(204, 204, 204);
    border-radius: 5px;
}
div.finderDirectoryName,
div.finderFileName {
    text-align: center;
}
span.finderDirectoryNameSelected,
span.finderFileNameSelected {
    background: rgb(56, 117, 215);
    border-radius: 8px;
    color: white;
    padding: 1px 7px;
}
```

And finally, this example is topped off with the following JavaScript, which implements a custom event handler and a trigger for that event handler.

```javascript
$(document).on(
    'DOMContentLoaded',
    function()
    {
        $('div#finderFiles')
            .on(
                'click.finder',
                'div.finderDirectory, div.finderFile',
                function(event)
                {
                    $('div.finderIconSelected')
                        .removeClass('finderIconSelected');
```

```
                    $('span.finderDirectoryNameSelected')
                        .removeClass('finderDirectoryNameSelected');

                    $('span.finderFileNameSelected')
                        .removeClass('finderFileNameSelected');

                    $(this).find('div.finderIcon')
                        .addClass('finderIconSelected');

                    $(this).find('div.finderDirectoryName span')
                        .addClass('finderDirectoryNameSelected');

                    $(this).find('div.finderFileName span')
                        .addClass('finderFileNameSelected');
                }
            )
            .on(
                'appendFile.finder',
                'div.finderDirectory, div.finderFile',
                function(event, file)
                {
                    console.log(file.path);
                    console.log($(this));
                }
            );

    $('div#finderFiles div.finderNode:first')
        .trigger('click.finder');

    var addedAdditionalFiles = false;

    $('body').dblclick(
        function()
        {
            if (addedAdditionalFiles)
            {
                return;
            }

            $('div#finderAdditionalFiles > div.finderFile').each(
                function()
                {
                    var file = $(this).clone();

                    $('div#finderFiles').append(file);

                    file.trigger(
                        'appendFile.finder', {
                            path : file.data('path')
                        }
                    );
                }
            );
```

```
                addedAdditionalFiles = true;
            }
        );
    }
);
```

The preceding example's results are shown in Figure 3-4.

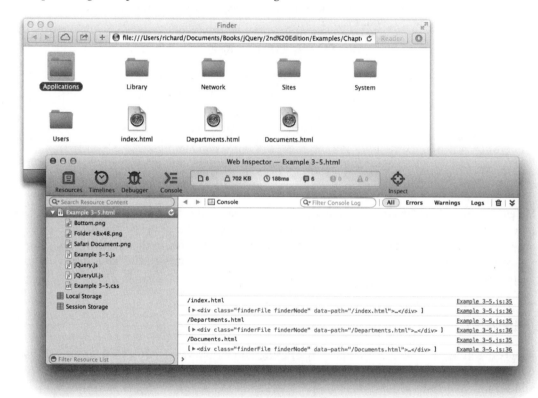

FIGURE 3-4

In *Example 3-5*, you begin by adding a custom event handler. That custom event handler is reproduced here.

```
.on(
    'appendFile.finder',
    'div.finderDirectory, div.finderFile',
    function(event, file)
    {
        console.log(file.path);
        console.log($(this));
    }
);
```

The new custom event handler creates the appendFile.finder event on <div> elements with class names finderDirectory or finderFile. The custom event is namespaced to finder so that the appendFile event name can be applied to other things, if necessary.

And then when a dblclick event is dispatched on the file management window, and the additional files are appended to the document, for each of those files or folders, the appendFile event is fired with a call to trigger().

```
$('div#finderAdditionalFiles > div.finderFile').each(
    function()
    {
        var file = $(this).clone();

        $('div#finderFiles').append(file);

        file.trigger(
            'appendFile.finder', {
                path : file.data('path')
            }
        );
    }
);
```

When the appendFile.finder event is fired off, you can pass data into the event by passing an object literal to the second argument. This data is then passed back to the event handler in its second argument. The contents of the second argument and this are printed to the JavaScript console so that you can observe that custom events work similarly to native ones and allow custom data to be passed back to the handler.

SUMMARY

jQuery events are a flexible and simple way of using JavaScript events. jQuery's APIs provide both wrapper methods for common JavaScript events, as well as more detailed APIs in the on(), off(), and trigger() methods.

If you want to use a browser event that jQuery does not provide a wrapper for, you must use on(), off(), or trigger() to use one of those events, for example, the HTML5 drag-and-drop API (which is discussed in Chapter 11, "HTML5 Drag and Drop").

If you provide a selector to the on() method, you can create persistent or live event handlers. It becomes possible to apply event handlers for elements that don't exist yet. It also becomes possible to greatly reduce the number of event handlers applied within an application because with live or persistent events, events can be applied to just a single element further up the DOM tree.

Event handlers can be namespaced by adding a dot and name to the name of the event. Events can be given multiple names, if you like, and this works similarly to how class names work in CSS selectors.

Event handlers can be absolutely controlled, added, and removed at will. The off() method provides the mechanism to remove an event. Removing an event requires calling the off() method with the name of the event or the event namespace, or both.

Calling an event wrapper method with no arguments, for example calling click() as well as calling trigger(), can trigger an event handler.

Custom events can be created and used with the standard jQuery event API. The on(), off(), and trigger() methods can all create custom events. You also saw some examples in this chapter of some custom events you might apply to a file manager application.

EXERCISES

1. Name all the methods you can use to attach a mouseover event using jQuery.

    Extra Credit: How would you attach both a mouseover and mouseout event using the same method? Hint: This answer can be found in Appendix D.

2. What method would you use to attach any browser event not already provided as a wrapper method?

3. What event property is used as the basis for determining what element has received an event using jQuery's persistent or live events? Explain what happens.

4. How do you use a persistent or live event to create an event handler?

5. How do you name an instance of an event handler? How do you apply multiple names to an instance of an event handler?

6. What method is used to remove an event handler?

7. Can an event handler be removed by virtue of its named instance only?

8. Name two ways to fire a click event handler using script.

9. How do you create a custom event handler? How do you send data to a custom event handler?

Manipulating Content and Attributes

jQuery is thorough; it provides everything you can imagine for working with content in the DOM. In Chapter 2, "Selecting and Filtering," you saw how jQuery made it easy to fetch elements from the DOM via its fine-grained support for selecting and filtering selections. Then in Chapter 3, "Events," you saw how jQuery wraps and extends the W3C event model to make it less verbose while also providing vastly more functionality. This chapter continues the discussion of jQuery's API components with an in-depth look at the methods that jQuery makes available for manipulating content and attributes. No longer do you have to worry about whether a browser supports the `innerText` or `textContent` properties, or the `outerHTML` property, or what the standard DOM method of removing an element from a document is. (You should know how to do those things anyway.) jQuery paves right over these verbose and sometimes fragmented methods with a rock-solid API that just works.

This chapter covers how you can shuffle DOM content around, doing things like replacing one element with another, inserting new text or HTML, appending or prepending content, cloning content, and getting rid of content.

It also covers how you manipulate attributes using jQuery, another area that jQuery makes smooth and easy by providing all the methods you'd need to use in the library. Or maybe you've had an occasion to want to save custom data with an element; jQuery provides this, too.

SETTING, RETRIEVING, AND REMOVING ATTRIBUTES

Working with attributes is easy with jQuery. Like everything you do with jQuery, first you make a selection, and then after you've made a selection, you can do something with that selection, like setting or accessing attributes. Setting attributes on a selection sets those attributes on every element that you've selected. You can set the value of one or more attributes on one or more elements, simultaneously. Retrieving an attribute's value is also easy; after you've made a selection, accessing an attribute's value provides you with the attribute value of the first element in the selection. Finally, removing attributes is just as straightforward: When you remove an attribute, it removes that attribute from each element in the selection. If you attempt to retrieve an attribute after removing it, it returns undefined.

The following document, which appears in the source code download from www.wrox.com/go/ webdevwithjquery as *Example 4-1*, demonstrates these concepts:

```html
<!DOCTYPE HTML>
<html lang='en'>
    <head>
        <meta http-equiv='X-UA-Compatible' content='IE=Edge' />
        <meta charset='utf-8' />
        <title>The Marx Brothers</title>
        <script src='../jQuery.js'></script>
        <script src='../jQueryUI.js'></script>
        <script src='Example 4-1.js'></script>
        <link href='Example 4-1.css' rel='stylesheet' />
    </head>
    <body id='documentAttributes'>
        <form action='javascript:void(0);' method='get'>
            <ul>
                <li>
                    <input type='radio'
                            name='documentAttributeMarx'
                            id='documentAttributeGrouchoMarx'
                            value='Groucho' />
                    <label for='documentAttributeGrouchoMarx'>
                        Groucho
                    </label>
                </li>
                <li>
                    <input type='radio'
                            name='documentAttributeMarx'
                            id='documentAttributeChicoMarx'
                            value='Chico' />
                    <label for='documentAttributeChicoMarx'>
                        Chico
                    </label>
                </li>
                <li>
                    <input type='radio'
                            name='documentAttributeMarx'
                            id='documentAttributeHarpoMarx'
                            value='Harpo' />
                    <label for='documentAttributeHarpoMarx'>
                        Harpo
                    </label>
                </li>
                <li>
                    <input type='radio'
                            name='documentAttributeMarx'
```

```
                    id='documentAttributeZeppoMarx'
                    value='Zeppo' />
                <label for='documentAttributeZeppoMarx'>
                    Zeppo
                </label>
            </li>
        </ul>
        <p>
            <button id='documentSetAttribute'>
                Set Attribute
            </button>
            <button id='documentRetrieveAttribute'>
                Retrieve Attribute
            </button>
            <button id='documentRemoveAttribute'>
                Remove Attribute
            </button>
        </p>
    </form>
</body>
</html>
```

The following style sheet is linked to the preceding document:

```
body {
    font: 12px "Lucida Grande", Arial, sans-serif;
    color: rgb(50, 50, 50);
    margin: 0;
    padding: 15px;
}
body#documentAttributes ul {
    list-style: none;
    margin: 0;
    padding: 0;
}
body#documentAttributes ul li.disabled label {
    opacity: 0.5;
}
```

And the following JavaScript is also linked to the preceding document:

```
$(document).ready(
    function()
    {
        var getCheckbox = function()
        {
            var input = $('input[name="documentAttributeMarx"]:checked');

            if (input && input.length)
            {
                return input;
            }
```

```
        $('input[name="documentAttributeMarx"]:first')
            .attr('checked', true);

        return getCheckbox();
};

$('button#documentSetAttribute').click(
    function(event)
    {
        event.preventDefault();

        var input = getCheckbox();

        input
            .attr('disabled', true)
            .parent('li')
            .addClass('disabled');
    }
);

$('button#documentRetrieveAttribute').click(
    function(event)
    {
        event.preventDefault();

        var input = getCheckbox();

        alert('Disabled: ' + input.attr('disabled'));
    }
);

$('button#documentRemoveAttribute').click(
    function(event)
    {
        event.preventDefault();

        var input = getCheckbox();

        input
            .removeAttr('disabled')
            .parent('li')
            .removeClass('disabled');
    }
);
    }
);
```

The preceding example demonstrates how you use jQuery's attr() and removeAttr() methods to set the disabled attribute on the selected radio <input> element. The preceding example produces something similar to what you see in Figure 4-1, upon clicking the Set Attribute button.

FIGURE 4-1

In the JavaScript source code, the first thing you do is set up a reusable method to retrieve the correct check box element. This method is aptly named getCheckbox().

```
var getCheckbox = function()
{
    var input = $('input[name="documentAttributeMarx"]:checked');

    if (input && input.length)
    {
        return input;
    }

    return $('input[name="documentAttributeMarx"]:first')
        .attr('checked', true);
};
```

First, you use a selector to find the right set of check boxes, which is done with an attribute selector, input[name="documentAttributeMarx"], and then is further narrowed down using jQuery's :checked pseudo-class. The attribute selector selects all four radio <input> elements, and then the selection is immediately narrowed to include only those with the checked="checked" attribute, indicating a user selection. The function makes sure that an element was found with the line input && input.length; if there is an <input> element, it is returned. If there is no <input> element, the check box collection is selected again and this time is narrowed to the first item present in the selection using jQuery's :first pseudo-class. The first item is explicitly checked with attr('checked', true). You can also use attr('checked', 'checked'), if you like; both methods result in the check box being checked. The method then returns the first <input> element, ensuring that the method works whether an <input> element is checked.

The next block of code handles what happens when you click the button labeled Set Attribute:

```
$('button#documentSetAttribute').click(
    function(event)
    {
        event.preventDefault();

        var input = getCheckbox();

        input
            .attr('disabled', true)
            .parent('li')
            .addClass('disabled');
    }
);
```

The Set Attribute button disables the selected radio box with the `disabled="disabled"` attribute and then adds the `disabled` class name to its parent `<li>` element. Adding the disabled class name to the parent `<li>` element allows the opacity of the `<label>` to be manipulated to further provide the impression of the item being disabled.

The second button, labeled Retrieve Attribute, retrieves the current value of the `disabled` attribute. Because this is a boolean attribute, its possible values are either "`disabled`" or `undefined`. Figure 4-2 shows retrieval with the `disabled` attribute applied.

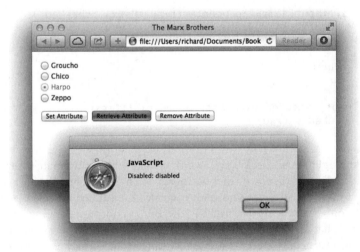

FIGURE 4-2

Retrieving the attribute is as simple as calling `attr('disabled')` on the selection.

```
$('button#documentRetrieveAttribute').click(
    function(event)
    {
        event.preventDefault();
```

```
                var input = getCheckbox();

                alert('Disabled: ' + input.attr('disabled'));
            }
        );
```

The third block of code removes the disabled attribute with the removeAttr() method.

```
        $('button#documentRemoveAttribute').click(
            function(event)
            {
                event.preventDefault();

                var input = getCheckbox();

                input
                    .removeAttr('disabled')
                    .parent('li')
                    .removeClass('disabled');
            }
        );
```

The removeAttr('disabled') method completely removes the disabled attribute from the DOM. When working with boolean HTML attributes, jQuery also allows setting a boolean value using the attr() method, so attr('disabled', false) is functionally the same as removeAttr('disabled'). After removing the disabled attribute, you have the result in Figure 4-3.

FIGURE 4-3

When you attempt to retrieve the value of the disabled attribute after using either removeAttr('disabled') or attr('disabled', false), you get a result of undefined, as shown in Figure 4-4.

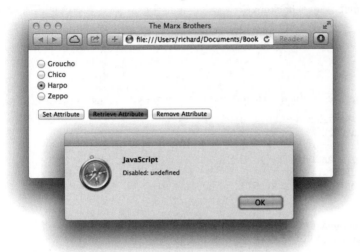

FIGURE 4-4

SETTING MULTIPLE ATTRIBUTES

Setting multiple attributes is done by providing a JavaScript Object Literal to the attr() method, which is demonstrated in the following example:

```
var input = $('<input/>').attr({
    type : 'radio',
    name : 'documentAttributeMarx',
    id : 'documentAttributeGrouchoMarx',
    value : 'Groucho'
});
```

The preceding example creates a new <input> element using jQuery identical to this one in HTML:

```
<input type='radio'
       name='documentAttributeMarx'
       id='documentAttributeGrouchoMarx'
       value='Groucho' />
```

Passing a string such as '<input/>' tells jQuery to create a new element by parsing the snippet of HTML you've passed to it. In this example, you create a single new element, which can then be manipulated using jQuery's various API methods: You call the attr() method and pass an object containing the type, name, id, and value attributes and their corresponding values.

The resulting element assigned to the variable named *input* can then be further operated on with other API methods or inserted into the document using the various methods you learn about later in this chapter, such as html(), prepend(), append(), and so on.

MANIPULATING CLASS NAMES

In earlier chapters, you've seen examples of the addClass(), hasClass(), removeClass(), and toggleClass() methods that jQuery uses to manipulate class names.

It is considered best practice in client-side web development to avoid placing style declarations directly in your JavaScript code and instead maintain a separation of behavior and presentation by placing styles in CSS and manipulating the class names of elements for situations in which you require a dynamic change of style. This is considered best practice for a reason: It keeps things neatly organized and obvious; you don't need to search for style changes in JavaScript or HTML, only in the style sheets. Because all your presentation is neatly contained in CSS, your behaviors in JavaScript, and your structure in HTML, your documents become easier to manage because it's more predictable where to look to make a modification. If your styles are scattered inline in HTML, in the JavaScript, and in style sheets, then it becomes an order of magnitude more difficult to change the presentation of a document because now you have to track down which document contains the change. No big deal for a small web page, but when you scale up to a large website or application, those conventions come into play.

The following example demonstrates the four methods jQuery provides to manipulate and check for the existence of one or more class names. This example appears in the source code download materials from www.wrox.com/go/webdevwithjquery as *Example 4-2*.

```html
<!DOCTYPE HTML>
<html lang='en'>
    <head>
        <meta http-equiv='X-UA-Compatible' content='IE=Edge' />
        <meta charset='utf-8' />
        <title>John Lennon Albums</title>
        <script src='../jQuery.js'></script>
        <script src='../jQueryUI.js'></script>
        <script src='Example 4-2.js'></script>
        <link href='Example 4-2.css' rel='stylesheet' />
    </head>
    <body>
        <form action='javascript:void(0);' method='get'>
            <h4>John Lennon Albums</h4>
            <table>
                <thead>
                    <tr>
                        <th>Title</th>
                        <th>Year</th>
                    </tr>
                </thead>
                <tbody>
                    <tr>
                        <td>John Lennon/Plastic Ono Band</td>
                        <td>1970</td>
                    </tr>
                    <tr>
                        <td>Imagine</td>
                        <td>1971</td>
```

```
                </tr>
                <tr>
                    <td>Some Time in New York City</td>
                    <td>1972</td>
                </tr>
                <tr>
                    <td>Mind Games</td>
                    <td>1973</td>
                </tr>
                <tr>
                    <td>Walls and Bridges</td>
                    <td>1974</td>
                </tr>
                <tr>
                    <td>Rock 'n Roll</td>
                    <td>1975</td>
                </tr>
                <tr>
                    <td>Double Fantasy</td>
                    <td>1980</td>
                </tr>
            </tbody>
        </table>
        <p>
            <button id='documentAddClass'>
                Add Class
            </button>
            <button id='documentHasClass'>
                Has Class
            </button>
            <button id='documentRemoveClass'>
                Remove Class
            </button>
            <button id='documentToggleClass'>
                Toggle Class
            </button>
        </p>
    </form>
</body>
</html>
```

The preceding HTML is styled with the following style sheet:

```
body {
    font: 12px "Lucida Grande", Arial, sans-serif;
    color: rgb(50, 50, 50);
    margin: 0;
    padding: 15px;
}
table.johnLennonAlbums {
    table-layout: fixed;
    width: 500px;
    border: 1px solid black;
    border-collapse: collapse;
}
table.johnLennonAlbums th,
```

```
table.johnLennonAlbums td {
    padding: 3px;
    border: 1px solid black;
}
table.johnLennonAlbums th {
    text-align: left;
    background: lightgreen;
}
table.johnLennonAlbums tbody tr:hover {
    background: lightblue;
}
```

The various jQuery methods for working with class names are demonstrated in the following script:

```
$(document).ready(
    function()
    {
        $('button#documentAddClass').click(
            function(event)
            {
                event.preventDefault();

                $('table').addClass('johnLennonAlbums');
            }
        );

        $('button#documentHasClass').click(
            function(event)
            {
                event.preventDefault();

                if ($('table').hasClass('johnLennonAlbums'))
                {
                    alert('The <table> has the class johnLennonAlbums');
                }
                else
                {
                    alert('The <table> does not have the class
johnLennonAlbums');
                }
            }
        );

        $('button#documentRemoveClass').click(
            function(event)
            {
                event.preventDefault();

                $('table').removeClass('johnLennonAlbums');
            }
        );

        $('button#documentToggleClass').click(
            function(event)
            {
                event.preventDefault();
```

```
                    $('table').toggleClass('johnLennonAlbums');
            }
        );
    }
);
```

Figure 4-5 shows the preceding example in Safari on a Mac.

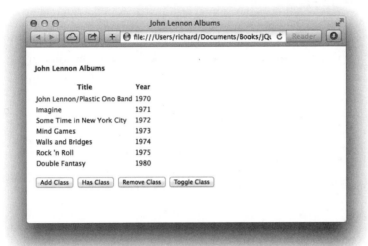

FIGURE 4-5

Clicking the Add Class button provides a styled table, as shown in Figure 4-6.

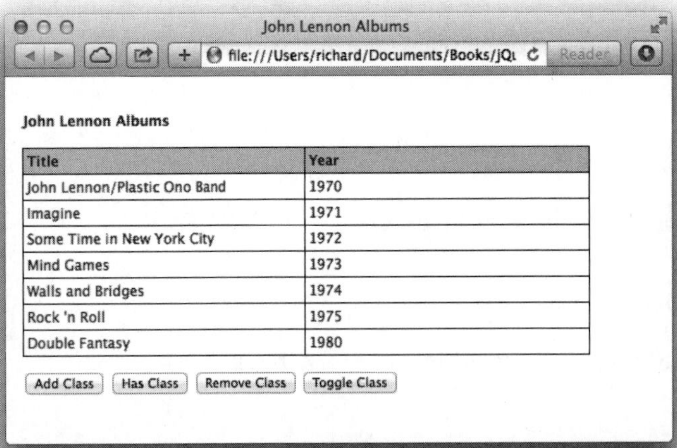

FIGURE 4-6

In the JavaScript created for *Example 4-2*, you attach four events to each of the four <button> elements present in the HTML document. The first event adds the class name johnLennonAlbums to the <table> element. jQuery adds only this class name once; if it is already present, nothing happens. The addClass() method can take one or more class names. If you want to add multiple class names, a space character should separate each class name.

```
$('button#documentAddClass').click(
    function(event)
    {
        event.preventDefault();

        $('table').addClass('johnLennonAlbums');
    }
);
```

The hasClass() method, demonstrated by the event attached to the second <button> element, checks for the existence of one or more class names. If the class is present, the method returns true. If the class is missing, the method returns false. In *Example 4-2*, an alert() message is displayed for each boolean condition. The hasClass() method is the only class method jQuery provides that does not accept multiple class names.

```
$('button#documentHasClass').click(
    function(event)
    {
        event.preventDefault();

        if ($('table').hasClass('johnLennonAlbums'))
        {
            alert('The <table> has the class johnLennonAlbums');
        }
        else
        {
            alert('The <table> does not have the class
johnLennonAlbums');
        }
    }
);
```

Figure 4-7 shows the alert message displayed when the class is present.

The removeClass() method is demonstrated by pressing the third <button> element; it removes a class if it has been added. If the class does not exist, nothing happens. Like the addClass() method, the removeClass() method can accept multiple class names, and also like the addClass() method, you separate multiple class names with a space character. When the class is removed, you see the same table shown in Figure 4-5.

```
$('button#documentRemoveClass').click(
    function(event)
    {
        event.preventDefault();

        $('table').removeClass('johnLennonAlbums');
    }
);
```

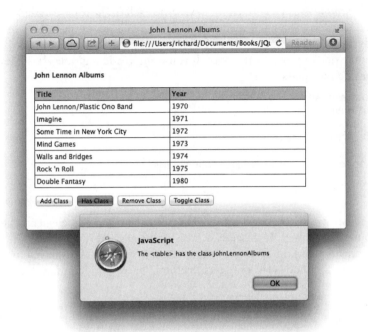

FIGURE 4-7

The `toggleClass()` method is demonstrated by pressing the fourth and final `<button>` element. If the class is present, it is removed. If the class is missing, then it is added. Like the `addClass()` and `removeClass()` methods, the `toggleClass()` method can accept one or more class names; a space character separates multiple class names.

```
$('button#documentToggleClass').click(
    function(event)
    {
        event.preventDefault();

        $('table').toggleClass('johnLennonAlbums');
    }
);
```

MANIPULATING HTML AND TEXT CONTENT

jQuery provides a method for just about everything. Its unique, innovative approach to JavaScript reinvents how you program JavaScript. This reinvention is required because jQuery methods define some ground rules that can be expected to be universal among all its methods. For example, one ground rule that becomes more obvious as you learn more about how jQuery works is how wherever it is possible, its methods work on one or more elements. You never have to distinguish between whether you want to work with just one or a lot of elements, because jQuery always assumes the possibility of an array.

Because jQuery always assumes the possibility of an array, it eliminates redundant code that has historically always been required to iterate over an array or list of several elements. You can chain methods onto one another, and you can perform complex operations on just one or many elements at the same time. One thing you may ask yourself while working with jQuery is, how do I access standard or de facto standard DOM methods and properties? In many cases, you don't need to directly access DOM properties or methods because jQuery provides equivalent and, in most cases, less verbose methods that are designed to work seamlessly with jQuery's chainable model of programming. And not only are jQuery's methods less verbose, they also attempt to fix as many cross-browser stability and reliability issues as possible.

One such property that jQuery replaces is the de facto standard innerHTML property. The innerHTML property and many of Microsoft's extensions to the DOM are on their way to standardization in the HTML5 specification. The innerHTML property is one of the few Microsoft extensions to the DOM that has been ubiquitously adopted among browser makers.

Rather than relying exclusively on the implementation of Microsoft's de facto standard innerHTML property and similar properties, jQuery provides a variety of methods that assist you in manipulating HTML and text content. This section discusses the following methods offered in jQuery's API:

➤ The html() method sets or gets the HTML content of one or more elements.

➤ The text() method gets or sets the text content for one or more elements.

➤ The append() and prepend() methods let you append or prepend content. You will learn about how these methods are actually better than the native de facto standard alternative, innerHTML.

➤ The after() and before() methods let you place content beside other elements (as opposed to appending or prepending the content inside those elements).

➤ insertAfter() and insertBefore() methods let you modify a document by taking one selection of elements and inserting those elements beside another selection of elements.

➤ The wrap(), wrapAll(), and wrapInner() methods give you the ability to wrap one or more elements with other elements.

➤ The unwrap() method removes a parent element, leaving its descendant elements in place of the parent.

The following sections describe and demonstrate how the preceding methods work, to give you expertise in understanding how content manipulation in jQuery works.

Getting, Setting, and Removing Content

The simplest methods that jQuery provides for content manipulation are the html() and text() methods. If you make a selection and call one of these methods without any arguments, jQuery simply returns the text or HTML content of the first matched element in a jQuery selection. The following example, *Example 4-3*, demonstrates how this works:

```
<!DOCTYPE HTML>
<html lang='en'>
    <head>
        <meta http-equiv='X-UA-Compatible' content='IE=Edge' />
        <meta charset='utf-8' />
        <title>Groucho Marx Quote</title>
        <script src='../jQuery.js'></script>
        <script src='../jQueryUI.js'></script>
        <script src='Example 4-3.js'></script>
        <link href='Example 4-3.css' rel='stylesheet' />
    </head>
    <body>
        <p>
            Before I speak, I have something important to say. <i>- Groucho Marx</i>
        </p>
    </body>
</html>
```

The preceding document is linked to the following style sheet:

```
body {
    font: 12px "Lucida Grande", Arial, sans-serif;
    color: rgb(50, 50, 50);
    margin: 0;
    padding: 15px;
}
```

The following script demonstrates how you can use the html() and text() methods and what to expect in the output that you get back:

```
$(document).ready(
    function()
    {
        console.log('HTML: ' + $('p').html());
        console.log('Text: ' + $('p').text());
    }
);
```

Figure 4-8 shows that the html() method has returned the <i> element in the results, but the text() method has left that out. In this sense, you find that the html() method is similar to the innerHTML property, and the text() method is similar to the innerText or textContent properties.

Setting Text or HTML Content

Setting content works similarly: All you have to do is provide the content that you want to set as the value for the element (or elements) in the first argument to the text() or html() method. Which method you use, of course, depends on whether you want HTML tags to be expanded as HTML. The following example, *Example 4-4*, demonstrates how to set text or HTML content:

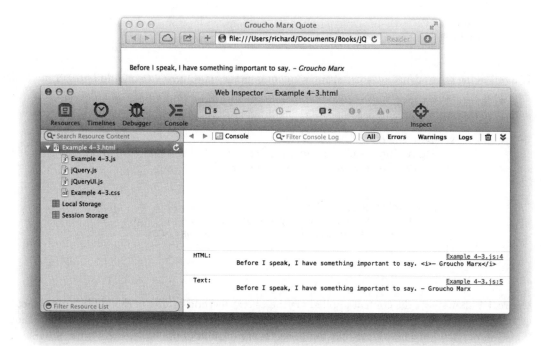

FIGURE 4-8

```html
<!DOCTYPE HTML>
<html lang='en'>
    <head>
        <meta http-equiv='X-UA-Compatible' content='IE=Edge' />
        <meta charset='utf-8' />
        <title>Groucho Marx Quotes</title>
        <script src='../jQuery.js'></script>
        <script src='../jQueryUI.js'></script>
        <script src='Example 4-4.js'></script>
        <link href='Example 4-4.css' rel='stylesheet' />
    </head>
    <body>
        <p>
            Before I speak, I have something important to say. <i>- Groucho Marx</i>
        </p>
        <p id='grouchoQuote1'></p>
        <p id='grouchoQuote2'></p>
    </body>
</html>
```

The following style sheet is applied to the preceding HTML document:

```css
body {
    font: 12px "Lucida Grande", Arial, sans-serif;
    color: rgb(50, 50, 50);
```

```
        margin: 0;
        padding: 15px;
}
```

The following script demonstrates setting element content via jQuery's text() and html() methods:

```
$(document).ready(
    function()
    {
        $('p#grouchoQuote1').text(
            'Getting older is no problem. You just have to ' +
            'live long enough. <i>- Groucho Marx</i>'
        );

        $('p#grouchoQuote2').html(
            'I have had a perfectly wonderful evening, but ' +
            'this wasn&rsquo;t it. <i>- Groucho Marx</i>'
        );
    }
);
```

Figure 4-9 shows how the content applied via the text() method results in the HTML tags being ignored and showing through in the rendered output of the <p> element with id name grouchoQuote1. It also shows how the HTML tags are expanded in the content of the <p> element with id name grouchoQuote2, which is applied using jQuery's html() method.

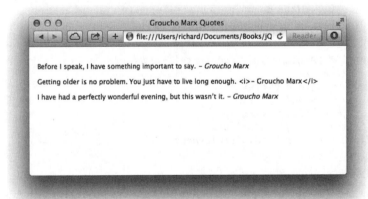

FIGURE 4-9

Setting Text or HTML Content for Multiple Items

Although you probably usually think about text or HTML content being applied only to a single element at a time, jQuery's text() and html() methods will apply that text or HTML content to one or more elements. The following example, *Example 4-5*, demonstrates what happens when you apply HTML content to a selection that includes multiple elements:

```
<!DOCTYPE HTML>
<html lang='en'>
    <head>
        <meta http-equiv='X-UA-Compatible' content='IE=Edge' />
```

```
            <meta charset='utf-8' />
            <title>Groucho Marx Quotes</title>
            <script src='../jQuery.js'></script>
            <script src='../jQueryUI.js'></script>
            <script src='Example 4-5.js'></script>
            <link href='Example 4-5.css' rel='stylesheet' />
        </head>
        <body>
            <p>
                Before I speak, I have something important to say. <i>- Groucho Marx</i>
            </p>
            <p id='grouchoQuote1'></p>
            <p id='grouchoQuote2'></p>
        </body>
    </html>
```

The following CSS is linked to the preceding HTML document:

```
body {
    font: 12px "Lucida Grande", Arial, sans-serif;
    color: rgb(50, 50, 50);
    margin: 0;
    padding: 15px;
}
```

The following script applies HTML content to all the <p> elements in the document:

```
$(document).ready(
    function()
    {
        $('p').html(
            'Quote me as saying I was mis-quoted. ' +
            '<i>- Groucho Marx</i>'
        );
    }
);
```

Figure 4-10 shows a screen shot of the output. You see that the quote applied in the script has been applied to all three <p> elements, replacing whatever content was present previously, if any.

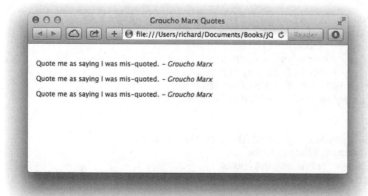

FIGURE 4-10

As you can see in Figure 4-10, jQuery applies the HTML content depending on your selection. If you've selected several elements, the content modification has been applied to several elements, and if you've selected only a single element, your content modifications have been applied to only a single element.

Removing Content

Removing content can also be done with jQuery's `text()` and `html()` elements. All you have to do to remove an element is to call either method with an empty string, that is, `text('')` or `html('')`. That isn't the only way to remove content from a document, however, and you'll see alternative methods for doing this later in this chapter.

Appending and Prepending Content

The word *prepend* is a term more or less invented by the technical programming world. (It does have some use outside that world.) It means to prefix or add some content to the beginning of something else. In fact, you won't find the word *prepend* in many dictionaries, and if you do, you'll find that the definition offers: "(transitive) To premeditate; to weigh up mentally." This doesn't match up with the way it's used in the technical programming community, in which this word is meant to be the opposite of *append*, which, of course, means "to add to the end of something."

This term has come out of the technical programming world by virtue of the flexible nature of computing when compared to the world of print. In the print world, modifying a hard-copy body of work is difficult to do. You have to renumber pages, possibly renumber chapters, and rewrite the table of contents and the index. Without a computer, that's an enormous amount of work. So in the print world, it's easier to add to a printed body of work by *appending*, or tacking on new content to the end. It's not always done that way, but it's one possible explanation for why the world never actually needed a word like *prepend* until the existence of computers made the action a necessity. In the technical world, it's easy to glue something onto the beginning of something else, so we made a new word to describe that action.

The following example, *Example 4-6*, demonstrates jQuery's `append()` and `prepend()` methods:

```html
<!DOCTYPE HTML>
<html lang='en'>
    <head>
        <meta http-equiv='X-UA-Compatible' content='IE=Edge' />
        <meta charset='utf-8' />
        <title>John Lennon Albums</title>
        <script src='../jQuery.js'></script>
        <script src='../jQueryUI.js'></script>
        <script src='Example 4-6.js'></script>
        <link href='Example 4-6.css' rel='stylesheet' />
    </head>
    <body>
        <form action='javascript:void(0);' method='get'>
            <h4>John Lennon Albums</h4>
            <table class='johnLennonAlbums'>
                <thead>
                    <tr>
                        <th>Title</th>
```

```
                            <th>Year</th>
                        </tr>
                    </thead>
                    <tbody>
                        <tr>
                            <td>Imagine</td>
                            <td>1971</td>
                        </tr>
                        <tr>
                            <td>Some Time in New York City</td>
                            <td>1972</td>
                        </tr>
                        <tr>
                            <td>Mind Games</td>
                            <td>1973</td>
                        </tr>
                        <tr>
                            <td>Walls and Bridges</td>
                            <td>1974</td>
                        </tr>
                        <tr>
                            <td>Rock 'n Roll</td>
                            <td>1975</td>
                        </tr>
                    </tbody>
                </table>
                <p>
                    <button id='documentAppend'>
                        Append
                    </button>
                    <button id='documentPrepend'>
                        Prepend
                    </button>
                </p>
            </form>
        </body>
</html>
```

The preceding code is linked to the following style sheet:

```
body {
    font: 12px "Lucida Grande", Arial, sans-serif;
    color: rgb(50, 50, 50);
    margin: 0;
    padding: 15px;
}
table.johnLennonAlbums {
    table-layout: fixed;
    width: 500px;
    border: 1px solid black;
    border-collapse: collapse;
}
table.johnLennonAlbums th,
table.johnLennonAlbums td {
    padding: 3px;
```

```
        border: 1px solid black;
    }
    table.johnLennonAlbums th {
        text-align: left;
        background: lightgreen;
    }
    table.johnLennonAlbums tbody tr:hover {
        background: lightblue;
    }
```

The following script demonstrates the prepend() and append() methods:

```
$(document).ready(
    function()
    {
        $('button#documentAppend').click(
            function(event)
            {
                event.preventDefault();

                if (!$('tr#johnLennonDoubleFantasy').length)
                {
                    $('table tbody').append(
                        "<tr id='johnLennonDoubleFantasy'>\n" +
                            "<td>Double Fantasy</td>\n" +
                            "<td>1980</td>\n" +
                        "</tr>\n"
                    );
                }
            }
        );

        $('button#documentPrepend').click(
            function(event)
            {
                event.preventDefault();

                if (!$('tr#johnLennonPlasticOnoBand').length)
                {
                    $('table tbody').prepend(
                        "<tr id='johnLennonPlasticOnoBand'>\n" +
                            "<td>John Lennon/Plastic Ono Band</td>\n" +
                            "<td>1970</td>\n" +
                        "</tr>\n"
                    );
                }
            }
        );
    }
);
```

In the preceding example, to append HTML content to the <tbody> element, you use jQuery's append() method, which adds the *Double Fantasy* album's entry to the <tbody> element when you click the Append button. In addition, when you tap the Prepend button, the John Lennon/Plastic Ono Band entry is added to the beginning of the <tbody> element. Figure 4-11 shows the example at page load, minus the additional entries.

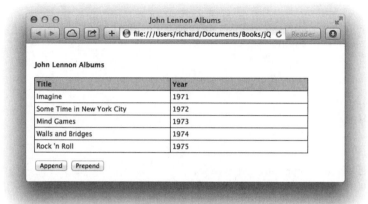

FIGURE 4-11

Inserting Beside Content

With the append() and prepend() methods, you're adding to content *within* an element. With the before() and after() methods, you are inserting content *beside* an element. The before() and after() methods are demonstrated in the following document *(Example 4-7)*:

```
<!DOCTYPE HTML>
<html lang='en'>
    <head>
        <meta http-equiv='X-UA-Compatible' content='IE=Edge' />
        <meta charset='utf-8' />
        <title>Groucho Marx Quote</title>
        <script src='../jQuery.js'></script>
        <script src='../jQueryUI.js'></script>
        <script src='Example 4-7.js'></script>
        <link href='Example 4-7.css' rel='stylesheet' />
    </head>
    <body>
        <p>
            Why, I'd horse-whip you, if I had a horse.
        </p>
    </body>
</html>
```

The following style sheet is applied to the preceding document:

```
body {
    font: 12px "Lucida Grande", Arial, sans-serif;
    color: rgb(50, 50, 50);
    margin: 0;
```

```
        padding: 15px;
    }
    p.quoteAttribution {
        font-style: italic;
    }
```

The following JavaScript demonstrates how content can be inserted before and after the <p> element, via the respective before() and after() methods:

```
$(document).ready(
    function()
    {
        $('p').before(
            '<h4>Quote</h4>'
        );

        $('p').after(
            "<p class='quoteAttribution'>\n" +
            " - Groucho Marx\n" +
            "</p>\n"
        );
    }
);
```

Figure 4-12 shows what happens when you load the preceding document in a browser.

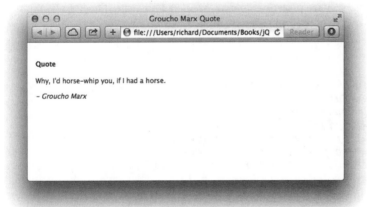

FIGURE 4-12

The content passed to the before() method is inserted before the <p> element, and the content passed to the after() method is inserted after the <p> element.

Inserting Beside Content via a Selection

The before() and after() methods are used to insert content beside elements. The insertBefore() and insertAfter() methods do the same function, but instead of passing content directly to these methods, as you did with the before() and after() methods, you use a selector to reference another element in your document that you want inserted beside another element. In addition, the logic is reversed in how you write the script that does the insert beside action. The following document, which can be found as *Example 4-8* in the source materials, demonstrates how you might use the insertBefore() and insertAfter() methods:

```html
<!DOCTYPE HTML>
<html lang='en'>
    <head>
        <meta http-equiv='X-UA-Compatible' content='IE=Edge' />
        <meta charset='utf-8' />
        <title>John Lennon and Paul McCartney Albums</title>
        <script src='../jQuery.js'></script>
        <script src='../jQueryUI.js'></script>
        <script src='Example 4-8.js'></script>
        <link href='Example 4-8.css' rel='stylesheet' />
    </head>
    <body>
        <!-- Template Items -->
        <table id='seventiesAlbumsTemplate'>
            <thead>
                <tr>
                    <th>Title</th>
                    <th>Year</th>
                </tr>
            </thead>
            <tfoot>
                <tr>
                    <th>Title</th>
                    <th>Year</th>
                </tr>
            </tfoot>
        </table>
        <!-- Main Content -->
        <h4>John Lennon &lsquo;70s Albums</h4>
        <table class='seventiesAlbums'>
            <tbody>
                <tr>
                    <td>John Lennon/Plastic Ono Band</td>
                    <td>1970</td>
                </tr>
                <tr>
                    <td>Imagine</td>
                    <td>1971</td>
                </tr>
                <tr>
                    <td>Some Time in New York City</td>
                    <td>1972</td>
                </tr>
                <tr>
                    <td>Mind Games</td>
                    <td>1973</td>
                </tr>
                <tr>
                    <td>Walls and Bridges</td>
```

```
                    <td>1974</td>
                </tr>
                <tr>
                    <td>Rock &#039;n Roll</td>
                    <td>1975</td>
                </tr>
            </tbody>
        </table>
        <h4>Paul McCartney &lsquo;70s Albums</h4>
        <table class='seventiesAlbums'>
            <tbody>
                <tr>
                    <td>McCartney</td>
                    <td>1970</td>
                </tr>
                <tr>
                    <td>RAM</td>
                    <td>1971</td>
                </tr>
                <tr>
                    <td>Wild Life</td>
                    <td>1971</td>
                </tr>
                <tr>
                    <td>Red Rose Speedway</td>
                    <td>1973</td>
                </tr>
                <tr>
                    <td>Band on the Run</td>
                    <td>1973</td>
                </tr>
                <tr>
                    <td>Venus and Mars</td>
                    <td>1975</td>
                </tr>
                <tr>
                    <td>At the Speed of Sound</td>
                    <td>1976</td>
                </tr>
                <tr>
                    <td>Thrillington (As Percy Thrillington)</td>
                    <td>1977</td>
                </tr>
                <tr>
                    <td>Londontown</td>
                    <td>1978</td>
                </tr>
                <tr>
                    <td>Wings Greatest</td>
                    <td>1978</td>
                </tr>
                <tr>
```

```
                        <td>Back To The Egg</td>
                        <td>1979</td>
                    </tr>
                </tbody>
            </table>
        </body>
    </html>
```

The following style sheet is applied to the preceding markup document:

```css
body {
    font: 12px "Lucida Grande", Arial, sans-serif;
    color: rgb(50, 50, 50);
    margin: 0;
    padding: 15px;
}
table.seventiesAlbums {
    table-layout: fixed;
    width: 500px;
    border: 1px solid black;
    border-collapse: collapse;
}
table.seventiesAlbums th,
table.seventiesAlbums td {
    padding: 3px;
    border: 1px solid black;
}
table.seventiesAlbums th {
    text-align: left;
    background: lightgreen;
}
table.seventiesAlbums tbody tr:hover {
    background: lightblue;
}
table#seventiesAlbumsTemplate {
    display: none;
}
```

The following script demonstrates how you use the `insertBefore()` and `insertAfter()` methods with selectors to duplicate content in a document:

```javascript
$(document).ready(
    function()
    {
        $('table#seventiesAlbumsTemplate thead')
            .insertBefore('table.seventiesAlbums tbody');

        $('table#seventiesAlbumsTemplate tfoot')
            .insertAfter('table.seventiesAlbums tbody');
    }
);
```

Figure 4-13 shows the results of the preceding document in Safari.

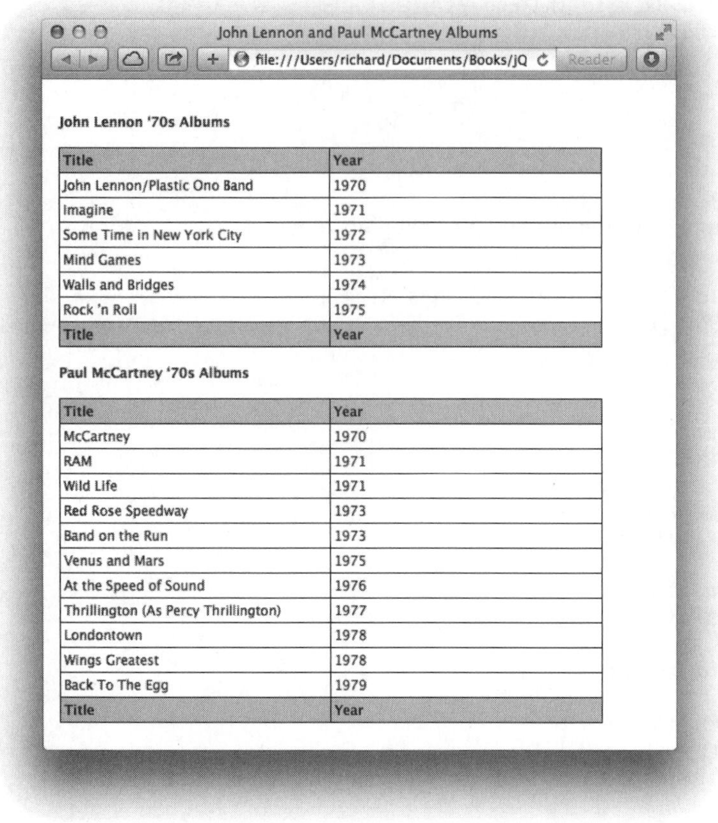

John Lennon '70s Albums

Title	Year
John Lennon/Plastic Ono Band	1970
Imagine	1971
Some Time in New York City	1972
Mind Games	1973
Walls and Bridges	1974
Rock 'n Roll	1975
Title	Year

Paul McCartney '70s Albums

Title	Year
McCartney	1970
RAM	1971
Wild Life	1971
Red Rose Speedway	1973
Band on the Run	1973
Venus and Mars	1975
At the Speed of Sound	1976
Thrillington (As Percy Thrillington)	1977
Londontown	1978
Wings Greatest	1978
Back To The Egg	1979
Title	Year

FIGURE 4-13

In the preceding example, you can see that the `<thead>` and `<tfoot>` elements contained within the hidden (using the `display: none;` CSS declaration) `<table>` element with id name `seventiesAlbumsTemplate` are duplicated to the other two `<table>` elements using jQuery. You start the script with the logic reversed; that is to say, you do the opposite of what you did with the `before()` and `after()` methods, where you first selected the element that you wanted to insert content beside and then provided the content to be inserted beside the selected element(s) within the `before()` or `after()` methods. This time, you begin with a selection of existing content within the document that you want to insert beside another element. In the script, you have the following:

```
$('table#seventiesAlbumsTemplate thead')
    .insertBefore('table.seventiesAlbums tbody');
```

The preceding line begins with selecting the `<thead>` element contained in the `<table>` with id name `seventiesAlbumsTemplate`. You want to duplicate that `<thead>` element to the other two tables and use that content as a template. To do that, you call the `insertBefore()` method and then pass a selector to that method. The selector that you pass is the element before which you want the original selection, `<thead>`, to be inserted. The selector first references `<table>` elements with the class name seventiesAlbums and then selects the descendant <tbody> element. So, in plain English, the script says, "Take the <thead> element in the hidden table and duplicate and insert that <thead> element before the <tbody> elements of the other two tables containing discography information for 1970s era albums of two former Beatles." The other line does the same thing:

```
$('table#seventiesAlbumsTemplate tfoot')
    .insertAfter('table.seventiesAlbums tbody');
```

However this time, you take the <tfoot> element from the hidden table and duplicate and insert that element after the <tbody> element of the other two tables. Essentially, the insertBefore() and insertAfter() methods make it easier to do templating.

Wrapping Content

In jQuery, *wrapping* an element means creating a new element and placing an existing element within a document inside that new element.

jQuery provides a few methods for wrapping content, that is to say, methods that take one or more elements and place those elements within container elements to change the structural hierarchy of a document. The methods that jQuery provides that enable you to wrap content are wrap(), wrapAll(), and wrapInner(). jQuery provides a single method to do the reverse to unwrap an element, and that method is called unwrap(). The following sections demonstrate how to use these methods.

Wrapping a Selection of Elements Individually

jQuery's wrap() method wraps each element matched in a selection individually. That is, if your selection matches five different elements, jQuery's wrap() method makes five separate wrappers. To better illustrate how this works, the following code, *Example 4-9*, demonstrates how the wrap() method wraps three <p> elements within <div> elements:

```
<!DOCTYPE HTML>
<html lang='en'>
    <head>
        <meta http-equiv='X-UA-Compatible' content='IE=Edge' />
        <meta charset='utf-8' />
        <title>Mitch Hedberg Quotes</title>
        <script src='../jQuery.js'></script>
        <script src='../jQueryUI.js'></script>
        <script src='Example 4-9.js'></script>
        <link href='Example 4-9.css' rel='stylesheet' />
    </head>
    <body>
        <h4>Mitch Hedberg Quotes</h4>
        <p>
            Dogs are forever in the push up position.
        </p>
        <p>
            I haven&rsquo;t slept for ten days, because that would be too long.
        </p>
        <p>
            I once saw a forklift lift a crate of forks. And it was way
            too literal for me.
```

```
        </p>
      </body>
</html>
```

The following style sheet is applied to the preceding markup document:

```css
body {
    font: 12px "Lucida Grande", Arial, sans-serif;
    color: rgb(50, 50, 50);
    margin: 0;
    padding: 15px;
}
div {
    padding: 5px;
    border: 1px dashed black;
    background: orange;
    margin: 5px 0;
}
div p {
    margin: 5px;
}
```

The following script demonstrates jQuery's `wrap` method:

```javascript
$(document).ready(
    function()
    {
        $('p').wrap('<div/>');
    }
);
```

In Figure 4-14, you see that each `<p>` element is wrapped in a `<div>` element, which is made obvious by the styles applied in the style sheet. Each `<div>` has a distinct border, margin, and background color applied to make it obvious that a `<div>` exists.

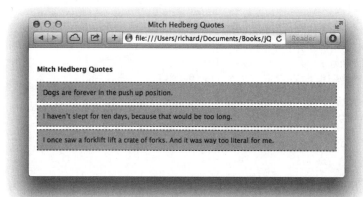

FIGURE 4-14

The preceding example makes it obvious that jQuery's wrap() method is used to wrap each element present in a selection individually.

Wrapping a Collection of Elements

Whereas the wrap() method wraps each item present in a selection individually, jQuery's wrapAll() method wraps all items present in a selection within a single wrapper. The following document presents the same markup and style sheet as you saw in the last section for the demonstration of the wrap() method. The only item that is changed is that the wrapAll() method is used instead of the wrap() method.

In the following script, *Example 4-10*, which uses the same markup and style sheet as *Example 4-9*, you see that the wrap() method has been swapped for the wrapAll() method:

```
$(document).ready(
    function()
    {
        $('p').wrapAll('<div/>');
    }
);
```

Figure 4-15 shows that instead of each <p> element being individually wrapped in a <div> element, you find that all three <p> elements are wrapped with a single <div> element, as made obvious again by the styles used in your style sheet.

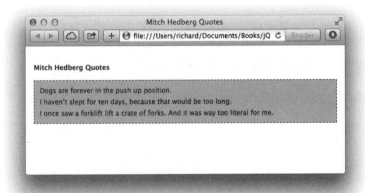

FIGURE 4-15

As you can see in the preceding example, the wrapAll() method takes a selection of elements and collectively wraps the whole selection with a single wrapper element.

Wrapping an Element's Contents

The last wrapper method demonstrates the wrapInner() method, which wraps an element's contents. This method works similarly to the wrap() method in that a wrapper is applied to each item in a selection, but instead of the selected element being placed in a wrapper, its contents are placed in a wrapper. The following document, *Example 4-11*, which is the same document you saw in the last two examples, demonstrates how the wrapInner() method compares and contrasts with the wrap() and wrapAll() methods:

```
<!DOCTYPE HTML>
<html lang='en'>
    <head>
        <meta http-equiv='X-UA-Compatible' content='IE=Edge' />
        <meta charset='utf-8' />
        <title>Mitch Hedberg Quotes</title>
        <script src='../jQuery.js'></script>
        <script src='../jQueryUI.js'></script>
        <script src='Example 4-11.js'></script>
        <link href='Example 4-11.css' rel='stylesheet' />
    </head>
    <body>
        <h4>Mitch Hedberg Quotes</h4>
        <p>
            Dogs are forever in the push up position.
        </p>
        <p>
            I haven&rsquo;t slept for ten days, because that would be too long.
        </p>
        <p>
            I once saw a forklift lift a crate of forks. And it was way
            too literal for me.
        </p>
    </body>
</html>
```

The following style sheet is applied to the preceding markup document:

```
body {
    font: 12px "Lucida Grande", Arial, sans-serif;
    color: rgb(50, 50, 50);
    margin: 0;
    padding: 15px;
}
span {
    background: yellow;
}
p {
    margin: 5px;
}
```

In the following script, you see that the only change from the preceding two examples is that the wrapInner() method is used instead of the wrap() or wrapAll() methods:

```
$(document).ready(
```

```
        function()
        {
            $('p').wrapInner('<span/>');
        }
);
```

In Figure 4-16, you see that the contents of all three <p> elements are each wrapped with <span> tags, making the contents of each <p> element styled with yellow backgrounds, appearing to highlight the content of all three paragraphs.

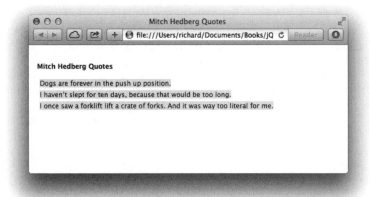

FIGURE 4-16

As demonstrated by what you see in Figure 4-16, the wrapInner() method takes the contents of each individual element present in a selection and places that content in a wrapper.

Unwrapping Elements

Unwrapping elements using the unwrap() method means removing the parent element from one or more elements and placing those element(s) in its place. The following example, *Example 4-12*, demonstrates jQuery's unwrap() method in the context of the preceding wrapping examples that have been presented thus far.

```
<!DOCTYPE HTML>
<html lang='en'>
    <head>
        <meta http-equiv='X-UA-Compatible' content='IE=Edge' />
        <meta charset='utf-8' />
        <title>Mitch Hedberg Quotes</title>
        <script src='../jQuery.js'></script>
        <script src='../jQueryUI.js'></script>
        <script src='Example 4-12.js'></script>
        <link href='Example 4-12.css' rel='stylesheet' />
    </head>
```

```
<body>
    <h4>Mitch Hedberg Quotes</h4>
    <div>
        <p>
            Dogs are forever in the push up position.
        </p>
    </div>
    <div>
        <p>
            I haven&rsquo;t slept for ten days, because that would be too long.
        </p>
    </div>
    <div>
        <p>
            I once saw a forklift lift a crate of forks. And it was way
            too literal for me.
        </p>
    </div>
</body>
</html>
```

The HTML document is joined with the following style sheet:

```
body {
    font: 12px "Lucida Grande", Arial, sans-serif;
    color: rgb(50, 50, 50);
    margin: 0;
    padding: 15px;
}
div {
    padding: 5px;
    border: 1px dashed black;
    background: orange;
    margin: 5px 0;
}
p {
    margin: 5px;
}
```

Then, the following JavaScript unwraps each <p> element from its parent <div> element.

```
$(document).ready(
    function()
    {
        $('p').unwrap();
    }
);
```

The JavaScript removes each <div> element from the document, which results in the HTML structure shown in Figure 4-17.

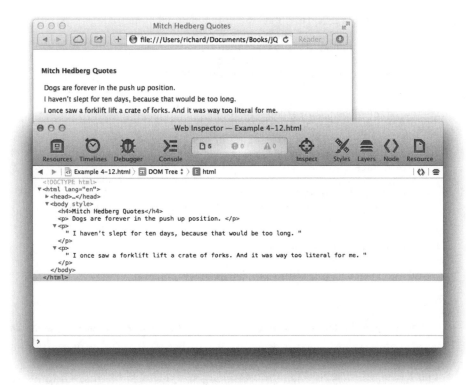

FIGURE 4-17

REPLACING ELEMENTS

This section discusses two methods, jQuery's `replaceWith()` and `replaceAll()`. The jQuery's `replaceWith()` method replaces a selection with whatever HTML content you specify. This works similarly to jQuery's `html()` method, but whereas the `html()` method sets an element's contents, jQuery's `replaceWith()` method replaces the element and its content. This can be thought to be similar to Microsoft's (now de facto standard) `outerHTML` property, for the portion of the `outerHTML` property that can set or replace content.

The `replaceAll()` method is similar to the `insertBefore()` and `insertAfter()` methods that you observed earlier in this chapter; it reverses the logic and is intended to be used with HTML content already in the document, such as HTML you might reuse as a template.

The following document, *Example 4-13*, demonstrates how jQuery's `replaceWith()` and `replaceAll()` methods work:

```
<!DOCTYPE HTML>
<html lang='en'>
    <head>
        <meta http-equiv='X-UA-Compatible' content='IE=Edge' />
        <meta charset='utf-8' />
```

```
        <title>Mitch Hedberg Quotes</title>
        <script src='../jQuery.js'></script>
        <script src='../jQueryUI.js'></script>
        <script src='Example 4-13.js'></script>
        <link href='Example 4-13.css' rel='stylesheet' />
    </head>
    <body>
        <div id='mitchHedbergQuoteTemplate'>
            <p id='mitchHedbergQuote3'>
                I&rsquo;m sick of following my dreams. I&rsquo;m just going
                to ask them where they&rsquo;re goin&rsquo;, and hook up with
                them later.
            </p>
            <p id='mitchHedbergQuote4'>
                My fake plants died because I did not pretend to water them.
            </p>
        </div>
        <h4>Mitch Hedberg Quotes</h4>
        <p>
            <input type='submit' id='mitchHedbergQuoteReveal1' value='View Quote'
/>
        </p>
        <p>
            <input type='submit' id='mitchHedbergQuoteReveal2' value='View Quote'
/>
        </p>
        <p>
            <input type='submit' id='mitchHedbergQuoteReveal3' value='View Quote'
/>
        </p>
        <p>
            <input type='submit' id='mitchHedbergQuoteReveal4' value='View Quote'
/>
        </p>
    </body>
</html>
```

The following style sheet is applied to the preceding HTML:

```
body {
    font: 12px "Lucida Grande", Arial, sans-serif;
    color: rgb(50, 50, 50);
    margin: 0;
    padding: 15px;
}
div#mitchHedbergQuoteTemplate {
    display: none;
}
p {
    margin: 5px;
}
```

The following script demonstrates how jQuery's `replaceWith()` and `replaceAll()` methods are used to replace elements:

```
$(document).ready(
    function()
    {
        $('input#mitchHedbergQuoteReveal1').click(
            function(event)
            {
                event.preventDefault();

                $(this).replaceWith(
                    "<p>\n" +
                    "    I would imagine that if you could understand \n" +
                    "    Morse code, a tap dancer would drive you crazy.\n" +
                    "</p>\n"
                );
            }
        );

        $('input#mitchHedbergQuoteReveal2').click(
            function(event)
            {
                event.preventDefault();

                $(this).replaceWith(
                    "<p>\n" +
                    "    I&rsquo;d like to get four people who do cart wheels
\n" +
                    "    very good, and make a cart.\n" +
                    "</p>\n"
                );
            }
        );

        $('input#mitchHedbergQuoteReveal3').click(
            function(event)
            {
                $('p#mitchHedbergQuote3').replaceAll(this);
            }
        );

        $('input#mitchHedbergQuoteReveal4').click(
            function(event)
            {
                $('p#mitchHedbergQuote4').replaceAll(this);
            }
        );
    }
);
```

Figure 4-18 shows the results of the preceding example. When you click any of the buttons, you see that the button is replaced with a quote.

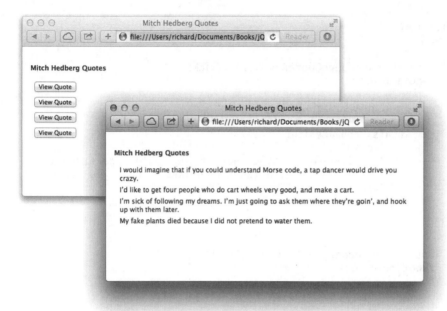

FIGURE 4-18

In the preceding example, you see that a `click` event is attached to each button, and upon clicking any button, the button is replaced with a quote. For the first two buttons, you make a call to `$(this).replaceWith()`, which causes the `<input>` element to be replaced with the HTML content passed to the `replaceWith()` method.

For the second two buttons, the content you want to use for replacement is selected instead of directly provided, as `p#mitchHedbergQuote3`, for example, then the `replaceAll()` method is called, and you provide the item you want to replace as an argument to that method. In the preceding example, you pass the `this` keyword, but you can also use a selector. Essentially, you find that the logic is reversed from the `replaceWith()` method demonstrated earlier in this section.

REMOVING CONTENT

Removing content can be done in a variety of ways. You can, for example, use the `replaceWith()` or `html()` methods in conjunction with an empty string. But jQuery also provides methods that are specifically designated for the removal of content, the `empty()` and the `remove()` methods. The following document, *Example 4-14*, demonstrates how both of these methods are used:

```
<!DOCTYPE HTML>
<html lang='en'>
    <head>
        <meta http-equiv='X-UA-Compatible' content='IE=Edge' />
```

```
        <meta charset='utf-8' />
        <title>John Lennon Albums</title>
        <script src='../jQuery.js'></script>
        <script src='../jQueryUI.js'></script>
        <script src='Example 4-14.js'></script>
        <link href='Example 4-14.css' rel='stylesheet' />
    </head>
<body>
    <form action='javascript:void(0);' method='get'>
        <h4>John Lennon Albums</h4>
        <table class='johnLennonAlbums'>
            <thead>
                <tr>
                    <th>Title</th>
                    <th>Year</th>
                </tr>
            </thead>
            <tbody>
                <tr>
                    <td>John Lennon/Plastic Ono Band</td>
                    <td>1970</td>
                </tr>
                <tr>
                    <td>Imagine</td>
                    <td>1971</td>
                </tr>
                <tr>
                    <td>Some Time in New York City</td>
                    <td>1972</td>
                </tr>
                <tr>
                    <td>Mind Games</td>
                    <td>1973</td>
                </tr>
                <tr>
                    <td>Walls and Bridges</td>
                    <td>1974</td>
                </tr>
                <tr>
                    <td>Rock 'n Roll</td>
                    <td>1975</td>
                </tr>
                <tr>
                    <td>Double Fantasy</td>
                    <td>1980</td>
                </tr>
            </tbody>
        </table>
        <p>
            <button id='documentEmpty'>
                Empty Data
            </button>
            <button id='documentRemove'>
                Remove Content
```

```
                            </button>
                        </p>
                    </form>
                </body>
            </html>
```

The following style sheet is applied to the preceding markup document:

```css
body {
    font: 12px "Lucida Grande", Arial, sans-serif;
    color: rgb(50, 50, 50);
    margin: 0;
    padding: 15px;
}
table.johnLennonAlbums {
    table-layout: fixed;
    width: 500px;
    border: 1px solid black;
    border-collapse: collapse;
}
table.johnLennonAlbums th,
table.johnLennonAlbums td {
    padding: 3px;
    border: 1px solid black;
}
table.johnLennonAlbums th {
    text-align: left;
    background: lightgreen;
}
table.johnLennonAlbums tbody tr:hover {
    background: lightblue;
}
```

The following script demonstrates both the `empty()` and the `remove()` methods:

```javascript
$(document).ready(
    function()
    {
        $('button#documentEmpty').click(
            function(event)
            {
                event.preventDefault();

                $('td').empty();
            }
        );

        $('button#documentRemove').click(
            function(event)
            {
                event.preventDefault();
```

```
                $('h4, table').remove();
            }
        );
    }
);
```

Figure 4-19 shows the result of the preceding example.

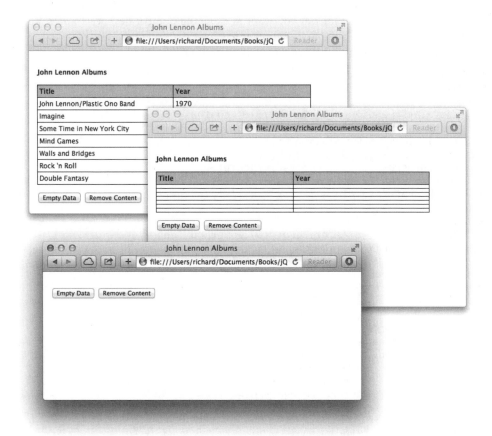

FIGURE 4-19

The preceding example shows what happens when you use jQuery's empty() method. This is essentially the same as passing an empty string to the html() method—all the element's children elements, whether HTML elements or text, are removed.

The preceding example also demonstrates jQuery's remove() method, which deletes the items specified in the selection. It should be noted, however, that those items still exist within jQuery, and you can continue to work with those items by chaining subsequent jQuery methods to the remove() method. You can also pass a selector to the remove() method, which acts as a filter. Any items specified in a selector provided to the remove() method are preserved and are not removed from the document.

CLONING CONTENT

jQuery provides a method called clone() for cloning (copying) content. jQuery's clone() method, unlike the DOM cloneNode() method, automatically assumes that you want to copy the element and all its descendants, so you don't have to worry about specifying whether you want to clone descendant elements. Also unlike the DOM cloneNode() method, you have the option of cloning the element's event handlers (as well as those of descendant elements), which cannot be done with JavaScript's DOM manipulation methods. If you want to clone the element's event handlers, all you have to do is specify boolean true as the first argument to jQuery's clone() method. The following document, *Example 4-15*, demonstrates jQuery's clone() method:

```
<!DOCTYPE HTML>
<html lang='en'>
    <head>
        <meta http-equiv='X-UA-Compatible' content='IE=Edge' />
        <meta charset='utf-8' />
        <title>John Lennon Albums</title>
        <script src='../jQuery.js'></script>
        <script src='../jQueryUI.js'></script>
        <script src='Example 4-15.js'></script>
        <link href='Example 4-15.css' rel='stylesheet' />
    </head>
    <body>
        <form action='javascript:void(0);' method='get'>
            <h4>John Lennon Albums</h4>
            <table class='johnLennonAlbums'>
                <thead>
                    <tr>
                        <th>Title</th>
                        <th>Year</th>
                    </tr>
                </thead>
                <tbody>
                    <tr id='johnLennonAlbumTemplate'>
                        <td contenteditable='true'></td>
                        <td contenteditable='true'></td>
                    </tr>
                    <tr>
                        <td>John Lennon/Plastic Ono Band</td>
                        <td>1970</td>
                    </tr>
                    <tr>
                        <td>Imagine</td>
                        <td>1971</td>
                    </tr>
                    <tr>
                        <td>Some Time in New York City</td>
                        <td>1972</td>
                    </tr>
                    <tr>
                        <td>Mind Games</td>
                        <td>1973</td>
                    </tr>
```

```
            <tr>
                <td>Walls and Bridges</td>
                <td>1974</td>
            </tr>
        </tbody>
    </table>
    <p>
        <button id='documentAddRow'>
            Add a Row
        </button>
    </p>
    </form>
</body>
</html>
```

The following style sheet is linked to the preceding document:

```
body {
    font: 12px "Lucida Grande", Arial, sans-serif;
    color: rgb(50, 50, 50);
    margin: 0;
    padding: 15px;
}
table.johnLennonAlbums {
    table-layout: fixed;
    width: 500px;
    border: 1px solid black;
    border-collapse: collapse;
}
table.johnLennonAlbums th,
table.johnLennonAlbums td {
    padding: 3px;
    border: 1px solid black;
}
table.johnLennonAlbums th {
    text-align: left;
    background: lightgreen;
}
table.johnLennonAlbums tbody tr:hover {
    background: lightblue;
}
tr#johnLennonAlbumTemplate {
    display: none;
}
```

The following script demonstrates jQuery's clone() method:

```
$(document).ready(
    function()
    {
        $('button#documentAddRow').click(
            function(event)
            {
                event.preventDefault();
```

```
                    var tr = $('tr#johnLennonAlbumTemplate').clone(true);

                    tr.removeAttr('id');

                    $('table.johnLennonAlbums tbody').append(tr);

                    tr.children('td:first').focus();
            }
        );
    }
);
```

Figure 4-20 shows the preceding example. When you click the Add a Row button, a new row is added to the table to input a new John Lennon album.

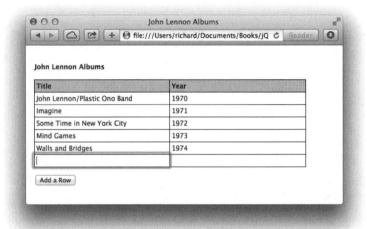

FIGURE 4-20

The following line clones the template <tr> element, with id name *johnLennonAlbumTemplate*.

```
                    var tr = $('tr#johnLennonAlbumTemplate').clone(true);
```

If any event handlers are attached to the <tr>, or the <td> elements it contains, those event handlers are carried over to the new duplicated <tr> element because the first argument provided to the clone() method is set to true.

The id attribute is removed so that the new <tr> element isn't treated like the template <tr> element, which is not displayed in the document.

```
                    tr.removeAttr('id');
```

The new <tr> element is appended to the <tbody> element using the append() method.

```
                    $('table.johnLennonAlbums tbody').append(tr);
```

Finally, the first <td> element is set to focus automatically, so you don't have to click it to enter the new album's data.

```
tr.children('td:first').focus();
```

SUMMARY

In this chapter, you learned about a variety of jQuery's manipulative capabilities. The content discussed in this chapter is documented in detail in Appendix E, "Manipulating Content, Attributes, and Custom Data," and Appendix F, "More Content Manipulation." You began this chapter by learning about jQuery's attribute manipulation method attr(), which enables you to specify attributes in a variety of ways, with the attribute as the first argument, and the value as the second, or via an object literal specifying arguments in key-value pairs, and also by using callback functions. jQuery's removeAttr() method can be used to remove attributes completely.

You also learned how jQuery helps you immensely with manipulating class names. jQuery's addClass() method can add a class name to an element. Its hasClass() method can determine whether a class name is present. Its removeClass() method can remove a class name. And its toggleClass() method can toggle a class name on and off.

You learned about various jQuery methods used to manipulate text and HTML content. You can get or set text or HTML content for elements using jQuery's text() and html() methods. You can append or prepend HTML content to other elements using jQuery's append() or prepend() methods. jQuery's after(), before(), insertAfter(), and insertBefore() methods can all insert content beside other content. And jQuery's wrap(), wrapAll(), and wrapInner() methods can wrap elements with wrapper elements. In addition, the unwrap() method can remove a parent element.

jQuery's replaceWith() and replaceAll() methods can completely replace one or more elements with other content. Its empty() method can completely remove an element's children and descendants. Its remove() methods can remove an element and all its contents from the document. And its clone() method can duplicate content, and optionally, event handlers that exist within that content.

EXERCISES

1. Write sample code that might be used to set both the value and the class attributes of an <input> element.

2. If you want to set the href attribute for an <a> element to www.example.com using jQuery, what might the JavaScript look like?

3. What jQuery method is used to completely remove attributes from elements?

4. What jQuery method would you use to determine whether a class name is present for an element?

5. If an element contains HTM content and you retrieve the content of that element using jQuery's `text()` method, will the HTML tags be present in the returned value?

6. If you set an element's content using jQuery's `text()` method and that content contains HTML tags, will the HTML tags be visible in the rendered output displayed in your browser's viewport?

7. Describe one bug that jQuery's `append()` and `prepend()` methods work around in IE when compared to `innerHTML`.

8. Describe one bug that jQuery's `append()` and `prepend()` methods work around in Firefox when compared to `innerHTML`.

9. If you want to insert existing content within a document before other existing content within a document, what jQuery method might be best suited for this task?

10. What jQuery method might you use if you needed to wrap multiple items in a document in a single element?

11. jQuery's `replaceWith()` method is most similar to what de facto standard JavaScript property?

12. What jQuery method would you use if you want to completely remove an item and all its children from your document?

13. What jQuery function call would you make if you want to duplicate an element and its event handlers and insert the duplicate element elsewhere in the document?

Iteration of Arrays and Objects

This chapter discusses the methods jQuery provides to help you work with looking at the contents of arrays and objects. Historically, working with arrays or objects in JavaScript often required you to come up with your own helper methods and to deal with writing tedious redundant code every time you wanted to enumerate over the contents of an array—for example, creating a counter variable each time you wanted to enumerate over the content of an array.

As you saw in Chapter 4, "Manipulating Content and Attributes," jQuery provides a rich, robust, and helpful API for various tasks associated with manipulating the content in a document. In this chapter, you see that jQuery also does not leave much to be desired in what it offers for dealing with arrays or objects.

ENUMERATING ARRAYS

In this section, you learn how to approach the task of enumerating or iterating over an array of values using jQuery's $.each() method, by calling each() via jQuery and each() directly. The term *enumerate* means to examine items one by one, and the term *iterate* means to do something repeatedly. These terms are often used interchangeably to describe the process of looking at the contents of an array, list, or object. Up to now, when looking at each individual value contained within an array, you might be used to dealing with a loop that looks something like this, which is the way it was been done in JavaScript before frameworks such as jQuery became ubiquitous:

```
var divs = document.getElementsByTagName('div');

for (var counter = 0; counter < divs.length; counter++)
{
    // Do something with each item
    console.log(divs[counter].innerHTML);
}
```

You have an array of items, a static node list, a live node list, or possibly an object. (By the way, in JavaScript, all arrays are objects, but not all objects are arrays.) Then you make a for loop, define a counter, and proceed to iterate over the contents of your array or list. If instead you want to iterate over an object, you'd instead use a for/in construct to look at the properties of the object.

jQuery makes creating a for construct unnecessary by providing a way to iterate over an array or list using a function call instead of a for loop and a callback function that's called for each individual item present in the array or object. Inside that callback function, you can do something with each individual item contained in the array, object, or list.

jQuery provides multiple functions for enumeration, which are covered in this chapter. The function that jQuery provides for basic enumeration is called each(), and it is demonstrated via two possible ways of application, in the following example, *Example 5-1*:

```html
<!DOCTYPE HTML>
<html lang='en'>
    <head>
        <meta http-equiv='X-UA-Compatible' content='IE=Edge' />
        <meta charset='utf-8' />
        <title>The Beatles Discography</title>
        <script src='../jQuery.js'></script>
        <script src='../jQueryUI.js'></script>
        <script src='Example 5-1.js'></script>
        <link href='Example 5-1.css' rel='stylesheet' />
    </head>
    <body>
        <h4>The Beatles</h4>
        <ul id='beatles'>

        </ul>
        <h4>Discography</h4>
        <ul id='beatlesAlbums'>

        </ul>
    </body>
</html>
```

The preceding markup document is linked to the following style sheet:

```css
body {
    font: 12px "Lucida Grande", Arial, sans-serif;
    color: rgb(50, 50, 50);
    margin: 0;
    padding: 0 10px;
}
body ul {
    list-style: none;
    margin: 0 0 10px 0;
    padding: 10px;
    background: yellow;
    width: 250px;
}
```

```css
h4 {
    margin: 10px 0;
}
```

The following script demonstrates jQuery's each() method called both via jQuery and directly.

```javascript
$(document).ready(
    function()
    {
        var beatles = [
            'John Lennon',
            'Paul McCartney',
            'George Harrison',
            'Ringo Starr'
        ];

        var ul = $('ul#beatles');

        // each() called via jQuery
        $(beatles).each(
            function()
            {
                ul.append('<li>' + this + '</li>');
            }
        );

        var albums = [
            'Please Please Me',
            'With the Beatles',
            'A Hard Day\'s Night',
            'Beatles for Sale',
            'Help!',
            'Rubber Soul',
            'Revolver',
            'Sgt. Pepper\'s Lonely Hearts Club Band',
            'Magical Mystery Tour',
            'The Beatles',
            'Yellow Submarine',
            'Abbey Road',
            'Let It Be'
        ];

        ul = $('ul#beatlesAlbums');

        // each() called directly.
        $.each(
            albums,
            function()
            {
                ul.append('<li>' + this + '</li>');
            }
        );
    }
);
```

In the preceding script, you create a couple of arrays, one for `beatles` and one for `albums`. In the first iteration, the variable `beatles` is passed to jQuery's dollar sign method, and then jQuery's `each()` method is chained onto that. You pass a callback function to jQuery's `each()` method, which is executed once for each item in the array; upon each execution, the current item is passed to the callback function; the value is assigned to `this`. You can also define arguments within the callback function to get the current key (a numeric offset in the case of an array or list) or the current value, like so:

```
$(beatles).each(
    function(key, value)
    {
        ul.append('<li>' + value + '</li>');
    }
);
```

For these two arrays, the numeric offset is provided in *key*, the first argument, and the value is provided in the second argument, *value*. The same value is assigned to the special contextual keyword: `this`, which is available only within the callback function itself.

Figure 5-1 shows that both `<ul>` elements are populated with new `<li>` elements via script.

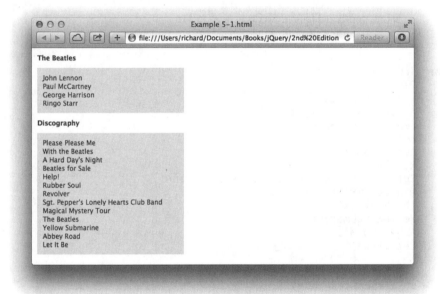

FIGURE 5-1

In the preceding example, you see how jQuery can eliminate the traditional `for` construct that you'd typically use for iterating the contents of an array or list. Instead, you pass an array to jQuery's dollar sign method so that you have the full power of jQuery at your disposal for use with that array. Then you chain a call to jQuery using the `each()` method, which takes a callback function as its only argument. That callback function then is executed once for each item in the array, eliminating the need for a counter because the current item is passed to the function with each iteration in the this keyword. The current index and value can be accessed optionally by providing two arguments to the callback function. Alternatively, you can also call each() directly. Calling each() directly places the array as the first argument and the callback function as the second argument.

Unfortunately, enumerating objects isn't as flexible as enumerating arrays, which is covered in the next section.

Enumerating Objects

Enumerating objects with jQuery is done by calling each() directly; when each() is called via jQuery, jQuery gets confused about what it is supposed to do with the object because jQuery does other things with objects passed to it this way. The following script takes another look at the example presented in Example 5-1, but this time both of the arrays are rewritten as plain objects, so you can observe the differences between enumerating an array and enumerating an object. The same HTML and CSS are used as in *Example 5-1*; you can access this example in the free download materials from www.wrox.com/go/webdevwithjquery. This example is named *Example 5-2*.

```
$(document).ready(
    function()
    {
        var beatles = {
            john : 'John Lennon',
            paul : 'Paul McCartney',
            george : 'George Harrison',
            ringo : 'Ringo Starr'
        };

        var ul = $('ul#beatles');

        // each() called via jQuery
        $(beatles).each(
            function()
            {
                ul.append('<li>' + this + '</li>');
            }
        );

        var albums = {
            1 : 'Please Please Me',
            2 : 'With the Beatles',
            3 : 'A Hard Day\'s Night',
            4 : 'Beatles for Sale',
            5 : 'Help!',
            6 : 'Rubber Soul',
            7 : 'Revolver',
            8 : 'Sgt. Pepper\'s Lonely Hearts Club Band',
            9 : 'Magical Mystery Tour',
            10 : 'The Beatles',
            11 : 'Yellow Submarine',
            12 : 'Abbey Road',
            13 : 'Let It Be'
        };
```

```
ul = $('ul#beatlesAlbums');

if (albums instanceof Array)
{
    console.log("Albums is an array.");
}
else
{
    console.log("Albums is a plain object.");
}

// each() called directly.
$.each(
    albums,
    function()
    {
        ul.append('<li>' + this + '</li>');
    }
);
    }
);
```

In the preceding example you pass an object to jQuery directly and then try to enumerate the object with a call to each(). In Figure 5-2, you can see that the enumeration is not successful. You find that only one item called [object Object]. This means that jQuery passed an object to each(), instead of looking at each of the four properties attached to the object.

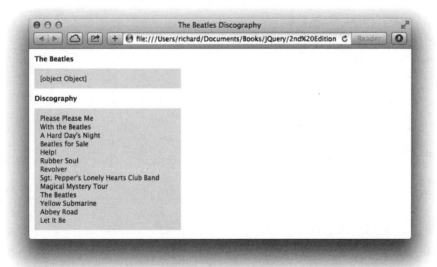

FIGURE 5-2

jQuery can enumerate objects, however, as you can see that the second object is enumerated successfully when the object is passed directly to the each() method as its first argument. If an object is an array, you'll find that the expression (variable instanceof Array) evaluates to true. In this case, the object is not an instanceof Array, so the expression evaluates to false, and the text "Albums is a plain object." is written to the JavaScript console.

> **NOTE** *Emulating the functionality of the* break *and* continue *keywords using jQuery's* each() *method is handled in a very intuitive way. All you have to do is write a* return *statement in your callback function. Returning* false *from your callback function stops iteration, just like using a* break *keyword in a normal loop, and returning* true *continues iteration to the next item immediately, just like using a* continue *keyword.*

Iterating a Selection

jQuery's each() method doesn't have to be applied to an array or object, however; it can also be applied to a selection of elements. The following document, *Example 5-3*, demonstrates how each() can be used to iterate over a selection of elements:

```html
<!DOCTYPE HTML>
<html lang='en'>
    <head>
        <meta http-equiv='X-UA-Compatible' content='IE=Edge' />
        <meta charset='utf-8' />
        <title>Rubber Soul</title>
        <script src='../jQuery.js'></script>
        <script src='../jQueryUI.js'></script>
        <script src='Example 5-3.js'></script>
        <link href='Example 5-3.css' rel='stylesheet' />
    </head>
    <body>
        <h4>Rubber Soul</h4>
        <ul id='rubberSoul'>
            <li>Drive My Car</li>
            <li>Norwegian Wood (This Bird Has Flown)</li>
            <li>You Won't See Me</li>
            <li>Nowhere Man</li>
            <li>Think for Yourself</li>
            <li>The Word</li>
            <li>Michelle</li>
            <li>What Goes On</li>
            <li>Girl</li>
            <li>I'm Looking Through You</li>
            <li>In My Life</li>
            <li>Wait</li>
            <li>If I Needed Someone</li>
            <li>Run for Your Life</li>
        </ul>
    </body>
</html>
```

The following style sheet is applied to the preceding markup document:

```css
body {
    font: 12px "Lucida Grande", Arial, sans-serif;
    color: rgb(50, 50, 50);
    margin: 0;
    padding: 0 10px;
}
ul {
    list-style: none;
    margin: 0 0 10px 0;
    padding: 10px;
    background: yellow;
    width: 250px;
}
ul li {
    padding: 3px;
}
h4 {
    margin: 10px 0;
}
li.rubberSoulEven {
    background: lightyellow;
}
```

In the following script, you see that jQuery's each() method can be chained onto a selection like any other method, and you can iterate over the items of the selection:

```javascript
$(document).ready(
    function()
    {
        $('ul#rubberSoul li').each(
            function(key)
            {
                if (key & 1)
                {
                    $(this).addClass('rubberSoulEven');
                }
            }
        );

    }
);
```

Iterating a selection is essentially the same as iterating an array, only this time when you're working with the callback function, the this keyword contains an individual element from the selection. If you want to use jQuery methods within the callback function, you'll have to wrap the this keyword with a call to the dollar sign method. In the example, each <li> element is selected, iterated using the each() method, and then the even numbered ones are given the class name rubberSoulEven. Figure 5-3 shows the preceding example in a browser.

FIGURE 5-3

FILTERING SELECTIONS AND ARRAYS

Two methods can be associated with filtering an array or a selection in jQuery's API. One method is called filter(), and it is used for filtering items from a selection exclusively. The other method is called grep(), and it is used for filtering items from an array exclusively.

Filtering a Selection

The filter()method removes items from a selection using a selector or a callback function. The following document, *Example 5-4*, demonstrates how filter() can use a selector to reduce items in a selection, and how the end() method can remove a previously used filter:

```
<!DOCTYPE HTML>
<html lang='en'>
    <head>
        <meta http-equiv='X-UA-Compatible' content='IE=Edge' />
        <meta charset='utf-8' />
        <title>Rubber Soul</title>
        <script src='../jQuery.js'></script>
        <script src='../jQueryUI.js'></script>
        <script src='Example 5-4.js'></script>
        <link href='Example 5-4.css' rel='stylesheet' />
    </head>
```

```
<body>
    <h4>Rubber Soul</h4>
    <ul id='rubberSoul'>
        <li class='Paul'>Drive My Car</li>
        <li class='John'>Norwegian Wood (This Bird Has Flown)</li>
        <li class='Paul'>You Won't See Me</li>
        <li class='John'>Nowhere Man</li>
        <li class='George'>Think for Yourself</li>
        <li class='John'>The Word</li>
        <li class='Paul'>Michelle</li>
        <li class='John'>What Goes On</li>
        <li class='John'>Girl</li>
        <li class='Paul'>I'm Looking Through You</li>
        <li class='John'>In My Life</li>
        <li class='John'>Wait</li>
        <li class='George'>If I Needed Someone</li>
        <li class='John'>Run for Your Life</li>
    </ul>
</body>
</html>
```

The preceding markup document includes the following style sheet:

```
body {
    font: 12px "Lucida Grande", Arial, sans-serif;
    color: rgb(50, 50, 50);
    margin: 0;
    padding: 0 10px;
}
ul {
    list-style: none;
    margin: 0 0 10px 0;
    padding: 10px;
    background: yellow;
    width: 250px;
}
ul li {
    padding: 3px;
}
h4 {
    margin: 10px 0;
}
li.rubberSoulJohn {
    background: lightblue;
}
li.rubberSoulPaul {
    background: lightgreen;
}
li.rubberSoulGeorge {
    background: lightyellow;
}
```

The following script demonstrates how the `filter()` method uses a selector to indicate which items should be in the selection:

```
$(document).ready(
    function()
    {
        $('ul#rubberSoul li')
            .filter('li.George')
                .addClass('rubberSoulGeorge')
                .end()
            .filter('li.John')
                .addClass('rubberSoulJohn')
                .end()
            .filter('li.Paul')
                .addClass('rubberSoulPaul')
                .end();
    }
);
```

In the preceding script, the selector `li.George` reduces the selection to include only the `<li>` elements that have a class name of `George`; then the class name `rubberSoulGeorge` is added to each of those `<li>` elements, and the same happens for Paul and John. Just before the time a new `filter()` is attempted, a call to `end()` removes the last filter applied to the selection. Figure 5-4 shows this example in Safari.

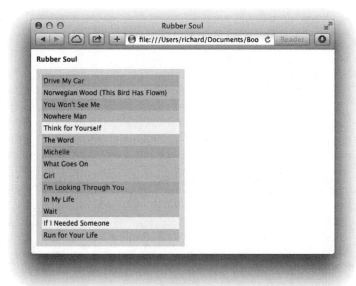

FIGURE 5-4

Filtering a Selection with a Callback Function

Like each(), the filter() method can be used with a callback function. When it is used in this way, filter() is similar to each(), in that it allows a callback function to be specified that is subsequently executed once for every item present in a selection.

With the each() method, you learned that returning a boolean value simulates continue and break statements. With the filter() method, returning a boolean value decides whether an item should be kept or removed from the selection. Returning true keeps the item in the selection, and returning false removes the item from the selection. Using filter() with a callback function is demonstrated in the following document, *Example 5-5*:

```html
<!DOCTYPE HTML>
<html lang='en'>
    <head>
        <meta http-equiv='X-UA-Compatible' content='IE=Edge' />
        <meta charset='utf-8' />
        <title>Rubber Soul</title>
        <script src='../jQuery.js'></script>
        <script src='../jQueryUI.js'></script>
        <script src='Example 5-5.js'></script>
        <link href='Example 5-5.css' rel='stylesheet' />
    </head>
    <body>
        <h4>Rubber Soul</h4>
        <ul id='rubberSoul'>
            <li class='Paul'>Drive My Car</li>
            <li class='John'>Norwegian Wood (This Bird Has Flown)</li>
            <li class='Paul'>You Won't See Me</li>
            <li class='John'>Nowhere Man</li>
            <li class='George'>Think for Yourself</li>
            <li class='John'>The Word</li>
            <li class='Paul'>Michelle</li>
            <li class='John'>What Goes On</li>
            <li class='John'>Girl</li>
            <li class='Paul'>I'm Looking Through You</li>
            <li class='John'>In My Life</li>
            <li class='John'>Wait</li>
            <li class='George'>If I Needed Someone</li>
            <li class='John'>Run for Your Life</li>
        </ul>
    </body>
</html>
```

The preceding markup document links to the following style sheet:

```css
body {
    font: 12px "Lucida Grande", Arial, sans-serif;
    color: rgb(50, 50, 50);
    margin: 0;
    padding: 0 10px;
}
ul {
    list-style: none;
    margin: 0 0 10px 0;
```

```
        padding: 10px;
        background: yellow;
        width: 250px;
    }
    ul li {
        padding: 3px;
    }
    h4 {
        margin: 10px 0;
    }
    li.rubberSoulJohnAndPaul {
        background: lightblue;
    }
```

The following script demonstrates how jQuery's `filter()` method can use a callback function to reduce items present in a selection:

```
$(document).ready(
    function()
    {
        $('ul#rubberSoul li')
            .filter(
                function()
                {
                    return $(this).hasClass('John') || $(this).hasClass('Paul');
                }
            )
            .addClass('rubberSoulJohnAndPaul');
    }
);
```

In the preceding script, the `filter()` method iterates over each item present in the original selection. It looks at each individual <li> element and checks to see if the <li> element has a class name of John or a class name of Paul; if either class name is present, the callback function returns true, indicating that the item should be kept in the selection. Each item kept in the selection then receives a class name of rubberSoulJohnAndPaul. Figure 5-5 shows a screenshot of this example in Safari. Each song written primarily by John or Paul has a lightblue background.

Filtering an Array

As indicated previously, arrays are filtered using a different method called grep(), which can be called only directly, which is to say, you may call it only as $.grep() or jQuery.grep(). Wrapping an array in the dollar sign method and then calling grep() doesn't work for this utility method. The grep() method would typically be used to directly filter some arbitrary array of items in code, rather than a selection from the DOM because the filter() method already exists explicitly for filtering selections. The following example, *Example 5-6*, demonstrates how grep() is used to filter arrays by creating an array of items from a selection; this is done simply to demonstrate how grep() works:

```
<!DOCTYPE HTML>
<html lang='en'>
    <head>
        <meta http-equiv='X-UA-Compatible' content='IE=Edge' />
        <meta charset='utf-8' />
```

```html
    <title>Rubber Soul</title>
    <script src='../jQuery.js'></script>
    <script src='../jQueryUI.js'></script>
    <script src='Example 5-6.js'></script>
    <link href='Example 5-6.css' rel='stylesheet' />
</head>
<body>
    <h4>Rubber Soul</h4>
    <ul id='rubberSoul'>
        <li class='Paul'>Drive My Car</li>
        <li class='John'>Norwegian Wood (This Bird Has Flown)</li>
        <li class='Paul'>You Won't See Me</li>
        <li class='John'>Nowhere Man</li>
        <li class='George'>Think for Yourself</li>
        <li class='John'>The Word</li>
        <li class='Paul'>Michelle</li>
        <li class='John'>What Goes On</li>
        <li class='John'>Girl</li>
        <li class='Paul'>I'm Looking Through You</li>
        <li class='John'>In My Life</li>
        <li class='John'>Wait</li>
        <li class='George'>If I Needed Someone</li>
        <li class='John'>Run for Your Life</li>
    </ul>
    <ul id='rubberSoulFiltered'>

    </ul>
</body>
</html>
```

FIGURE 5-5

The preceding markup document is linked to the following style sheet:

```css
body {
    font: 12px "Lucida Grande", Arial, sans-serif;
    color: rgb(50, 50, 50);
    margin: 0;
    padding: 0 10px;
}
ul {
    list-style: none;
    margin: 0 0 10px 0;
    padding: 10px;
    background: yellow;
    width: 250px;
}
ul li {
    padding: 3px;
}
h4 {
    margin: 10px 0;
}
li.rubberSoulJohnAndPaul {
    background: lightblue;
}
ul#rubberSoulFiltered {
    display: none;
}
```

The following script demonstrates the grep() method:

```javascript
$(document).ready(
    function()
    {
        var songs = [];

        $('ul#rubberSoul li').each(
            function()
            {
                songs.push(
                    $(this).text()
                );
            }
        );

        var filteredSongs = $.grep(
            songs,
            function(value, key)
            {
                return value.indexOf('You') != -1;
            }
        );

        var ul = $('ul#rubberSoulFiltered');
```

```
$('ul#rubberSoul').hide();
ul.show();

$(filteredSongs).each(
    function()
    {
        ul.append('<li>' + this + '</li>');
    }
);
    }
);
```

The preceding script begins by creating a new array and assigning that array to the variable songs. The script then selects all <li> elements within the <ul> element with id name rubberSoul and assigns the text of each <li> element as a new item in the songs array using push(). The end result is that the songs array contains the titles for all the songs on *Rubber Soul*.

Then, a new variable is created called filteredSongs, which contains a filtered array. The grep() method is called directly as $.grep(), with the songs array as the first argument and a callback function as the second argument. In the callback function, you return a boolean value to indicate whether each item should be kept in the array or removed. Returning true indicates that the value should be kept; returning false indicates that the item should be discarded. You can also change the value being kept as well—simply return the replacement value you want to use, and it replaces any previous value.

In the example, the callback function checks to see if each song title contains the word *You*, using JavaScript's indexOf() method. If it does, the song title is kept; if not, the song title is discarded.

The <ul> element with id name rubberSoul is hidden by selecting it and then making a call to jQuery's hide() method.

Finally, the script iterates over the new filteredSongs array using each(), and the four song titles containing the word *you* are appended as new <li> elements to the <ul> element with id name rubberSoulFiltered. Figure 5-6 shows the results of the preceding example in a browser.

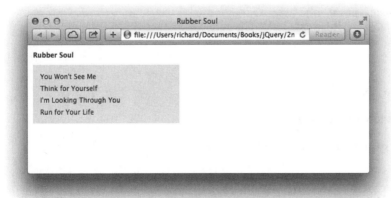

FIGURE 5-6

The grep() method also allows an optional third argument called invert to be specified; if it is set to true, the values of the filtered array are reversed.

> **NOTE** *The arguments provided to the* $.grep() *callback function are reversed;* value *is the first argument and* key *is the second. In addition, the* value *argument is not also provided within* this *when using* $.grep().

MAPPING A SELECTION OR AN ARRAY

As was the case with filtering, there are two different contexts in which you can map one collection of items to another, in a selection or with an arbitrary array of items. This time, however, both contexts use a function that goes by the same name, map(). In the following sections, you learn more about the map() method as applied within either context.

Mapping a Selection

The concept of *mapping* is taking one set of values and modifying one or more of those values to create a new set of values. No items are removed from the set during a mapping, so it's expected that you'll have a set of values of the same length when you finish mapping as when you started—the idea being more or less that you can arbitrarily replace values as needed with new ones that have redundant modifications that must be made to some or all values. The following document, *Example 5-7*, demonstrates how you map a selection with jQuery:

```html
<!DOCTYPE HTML>
<html lang='en'>
    <head>
        <meta http-equiv='X-UA-Compatible' content='IE=Edge' />
        <meta charset='utf-8' />
        <title>Rubber Soul</title>
        <script src='../jQuery.js'></script>
        <script src='../jQueryUI.js'></script>
        <script src='Example 5-7.js'></script>
        <link href='Example 5-7.css' rel='stylesheet' />
    </head>
    <body>
        <h4>Rubber Soul</h4>
        <ul id='rubberSoul'>
            <li class='Paul'>Drive My Car</li>
            <li class='John'>Norwegian Wood (This Bird Has Flown)</li>
            <li class='Paul'>You Won't See Me</li>
            <li class='John'>Nowhere Man</li>
            <li class='George'>Think for Yourself</li>
            <li class='John'>The Word</li>
            <li class='Paul'>Michelle</li>
            <li class='John'>What Goes On</li>
            <li class='John'>Girl</li>
            <li class='Paul'>I'm Looking Through You</li>
            <li class='John'>In My Life</li>
```

```
                <li class='John'>Wait</li>
                <li class='George'>If I Needed Someone</li>
                <li class='John'>Run for Your Life</li>
            </ul>
            <ul id='rubberSoulMapped'>

            </ul>
        </body>
    </html>
```

The preceding markup document is styled with the following style sheet:

```
    body {
        font: 12px "Lucida Grande", Arial, sans-serif;
        color: rgb(50, 50, 50);
        margin: 0;
        padding: 0 10px;
    }
    ul {
        list-style: none;
        margin: 0 0 10px 0;
        padding: 10px;
        background: yellow;
        width: 350px;
    }
    ul li {
        padding: 3px;
    }
    h4 {
        margin: 10px 0;
    }
    ul#rubberSoulMapped {
        display: none;
    }
```

The following script demonstrates how a selection is mapped to a new array:

```
    $(document).ready(
        function()
        {
            var mappedSongs = $('ul#rubberSoul li').map(
                function(key)
                {
                    if ($(this).hasClass('John'))
                    {
                        return $(this).text() + ' <i>John Lennon</i>';
                    }

                    if ($(this).hasClass('Paul'))
                    {
                        return $(this).text() + ' <i>Paul McCartney</i>';
                    }

                    if ($(this).hasClass('George'))
                    {
                        return $(this).text() + ' <i>George Harrison</i>';
                    }
```

```
            }
        );

        $('ul#rubberSoul').hide();

        var ul = $('ul#rubberSoulMapped');
        ul.show();

        $(mappedSongs).each(
            function()
            {
                ul.append('<li>' + this + '</li>');
            }
        );
    }
);
```

The preceding script begins by selecting all <li> elements in the document. Then a call to the map() method is chained onto that selection, and a callback function is provided as the first argument to the map() method.

The callback function provided to the map() method, as with the other methods you've observed in this chapter, passes each item to its callback function in the this keyword. If you need to reference it, the index or key or counter (whatever you choose to call it) is accessible in the first argument that you provide to your callback function. Each item is numbered offset from zero, and that counter is accessible in that first argument. In the preceding example, the first argument is named key.

Inside the callback function, a few expressions look to see what class name each <li> element has. If the <li> element has a class name of John, for example, the callback function returns the name of the song with the HTML <i>John Lennon</i> appended to the end. The callback function attaches the name of the more prominent writer of each song for each song present, building a new array that is assigned to the variable mappedSongs.

The first <ul> list with id name rubberSoul is hidden by selecting it and making a call to jQuery's hide() method and the <ul> with id name rubberSoulMapped is displayed with a call to show().

The each() method is then used to iterate the contents of the mappedSongs variable, appending each mapped value to the second <ul> element with the id name rubberSoulMapped. Figure 5-7 shows the final product.

Mapping an Array

Mapping an array basically employs the same logic that you observed in *Example 5-7* with mapping a selection—you just use an array instead of a selection. So, you can call jQuery's map() method with an array the same way that you called the each() method, by either passing an array to the dollar sign method or by calling the map() method directly, with an array as its first argument and a callback function as its second argument. The following document, *Example 5-8*, shows an example of the map() method as it is applied to an array:

```
<!DOCTYPE HTML>
<html lang='en'>
    <head>
```

```
        <meta http-equiv='X-UA-Compatible' content='IE=Edge' />
        <meta charset='utf-8' />
        <title>Revolver</title>
        <script src='../jQuery.js'></script>
        <script src='../jQueryUI.js'></script>
        <script src='Example 5-8.js'></script>
        <link href='Example 5-8.css' rel='stylesheet' />
    </head>
    <body>
        <h4>Revolver</h4>
        <ul id='revolver'>

        </ul>
    </body>
</html>
```

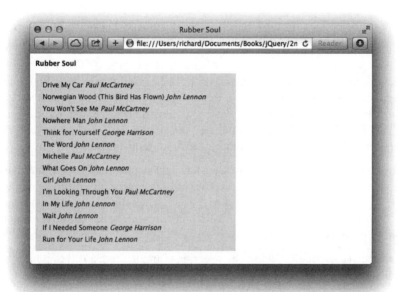

FIGURE 5-7

The following style sheet is applied to the preceding markup:

```
body {
    font: 12px "Lucida Grande", Arial, sans-serif;
    color: rgb(50, 50, 50);
    margin: 0;
    padding: 0 10px;
}
ul {
    list-style: none;
    margin: 0 0 10px 0;
    padding: 10px;
    background: yellow;
}
```

```
        width: 350px;
    }
    ul li {
        padding: 3px;
    }
    h4 {
        margin: 10px 0;
    }
```

The following script demonstrates how jQuery's map() method is used with an array instead of a selection:

```
$(document).ready(
    function()
    {
        var songs = [
                'Taxman',
                'Eleanor Rigby',
                'I\'m Only Sleeping',
                'Love You To',
                'Here, There and Everywhere',
                'Yellow Submarine',
                'She Said, She Said',
                'Good Day Sunshine',
                'And Your Bird Can Sing',
                'For No One',
                'Doctor Robert',
                'I Want to Tell You',
                'Got to Get You into My Life',
                'Tomorrow Never Knows'
            ];

        var mappedSongs = $(songs).map(
            function(key)
            {
                var track = key + 1;

                return (track < 10? '0' + track : track) + ' ' + this;
            }
        );

        $(mappedSongs).each(
            function()
            {
                $('ul#revolver').append('<li>' + this + '</li>');
            }
        );
    }
);
```

In the preceding script, a collection of song titles of the Beatles' album *Revolver* is placed in an array and assigned to the variable songs.

The songs variable is then passed to a call to the dollar sign method, and the map() method is called.

In the callback function passed to the `map()` method, a variable called `track` is created by incrementing the key's value by one; it's used as a counter for the track number. The callback function then checks to see if `track` is less than 10 using a ternary expression. If it is, a leading zero is prepended to the value; otherwise, no leading zero is prepended. This portion becomes the track number.

A single space is inserted between the track number and the song title, and the new array containing song titles with track numbers prefixed is assigned to the variable `mappedSongs`.

Finally, the array assigned to the `mappedSongs` variable is iterated using the `each()` method, and the modified song titles with track name prefixes are appended as `<li>` elements to the `<ul>` element in the document. The result of the preceding example appears in Figure 5-8.

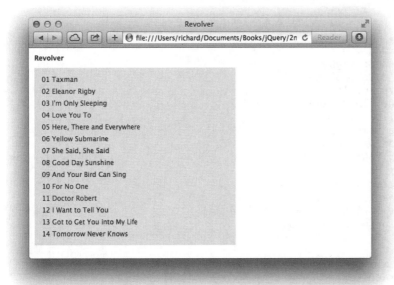

FIGURE 5-8

ARRAY UTILITY METHODS

jQuery also provides a few utility methods that are useful for probing information from an array. The following sections briefly cover each of jQuery's utility methods:

➤ `$.makeArray(data)`—Transforms any data into a true array

➤ `$.inArray(needle, haystack)`—Finds the index associated with the first occurrence of needle within the haystack

➤ `$.merge(first, second)`—Merges two arrays together

Most of jQuery's array utility methods must be called directly, using the dollar sign dot function name, as you see documented in the preceding list. All the methods covered in this chapter are documented in the Quick Reference that appears in Appendix I, "Utilities," as well as Appendix C, "Selecting, Traversing, and Filtering." Appendix I contains utility methods, and Appendix C contains jQuery methods that exist for filtering or traversing a selection.

Making an Array

jQuery's makeArray() method does just what the name implies; it takes any data and transforms it into a true array. The following example, *Example 5-9*, shows how a string, an object, or a number can be made into an array using this method:

```html
<!DOCTYPE HTML>
<html lang='en'>
    <head>
        <meta http-equiv='X-UA-Compatible' content='IE=Edge' />
        <meta charset='utf-8' />
        <title>$.makeArray()</title>
        <script src='../jQuery.js'></script>
        <script src='../jQueryUI.js'></script>
        <script src='Example 5-9.js'></script>
    </head>
    <body>

    </body>
</html>
```

The following JavaScript is included in the preceding markup document.

```javascript
$(document).ready(
    function()
    {
        var name = 'The Beatles';

        var madeArray = $.makeArray(name);

        console.log('Transforming a string.');
        console.log('Type: ' + typeof(madeArray));
        console.log('Is Array? ' + (madeArray instanceof Array? 'yes' : 'no'));
        console.log(madeArray);

        var madeArray = {
            band1 : "The Beatles",
            band2 : "Electric Light Orchestra",
            band3 : "The Moody Blues",
            band4 : "Radiohead"
        };

        madeArray = $.makeArray(madeArray);

        console.log('Transforming an object.');
        console.log('Type: ' + typeof(madeArray));
        console.log('Is Array? ' + (madeArray instanceof Array? 'yes' : 'no'));
        console.log(madeArray);
```

```
        var madeArray = 1;

        madeArray = $.makeArray(madeArray);

        console.log('Transforming a number.');
        console.log('Type: ' + typeof(madeArray));
        console.log('Is Array? ' + (madeArray instanceof Array? 'yes' : 'no'));
        console.log(madeArray);
    }
);
```

The preceding code writes data to the JavaScript console like that shown in Figure 5-9.

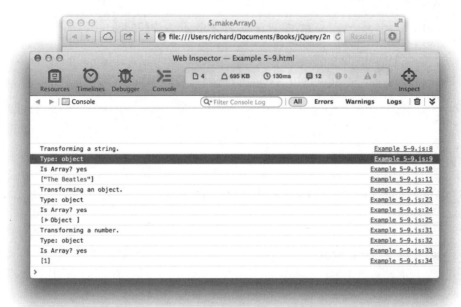

FIGURE 5-9

In the script, the string *The Beatles* is assigned to the variable name. The variable name is passed to makeArray(), and the result is assigned to the variable madeArray. Then, you check the typeof of the object madeArray, which will be object now instead of string. The expression madeArray instanceof Array will also report true, and then the content of madeArray is dumped to the console for visual inspection.

The process is repeated for an object and a number, each time resulting in an array.

Finding a Value Within an Array

jQuery's inArray() method works just like JavaScript's indexOf() method. It returns the position of an item within an array. If it is present, offset from zero, and if the item is not present, the function returns –1 (minus one). The following example, *Example 5-10*, demonstrates how jQuery's inArray() method works:

```html
<!DOCTYPE HTML>
<html lang='en'>
    <head>
        <meta http-equiv='X-UA-Compatible' content='IE=Edge' />
        <meta charset='utf-8' />
        <title>$.inArray()</title>
        <script src='../jQuery.js'></script>
        <script src='../jQueryUI.js'></script>
        <script src='Example 5-10.js'></script>
    </head>
    <body>

    </body>
</html>
```

The following JavaScript demonstrates $.inArray():

```javascript
$(document).ready(
    function()
    {
        var songs = [
                'Taxman',
                'Eleanor Rigby',
                'I\'m Only Sleeping',
                'Love You To',
                'Here, There and Everywhere',
                'Yellow Submarine',
                'She Said, She Said',
                'Good Day Sunshine',
                'And Your Bird Can Sing',
                'For No One',
                'Doctor Robert',
                'I Want to Tell You',
                'Got to Get You into My Life',
                'Tomorrow Never Knows'
        ];

        console.log(
            'Love You To: ' + (
                $.inArray('Love You To', songs)
            )
        );

        console.log(
            'Strawberry Fields Forever: ' + (
                $.inArray('Strawberry Fields Forever', songs)
            )
        );
    }
);
```

The preceding script outputs the messages to the console, as shown in Figure 5-10.

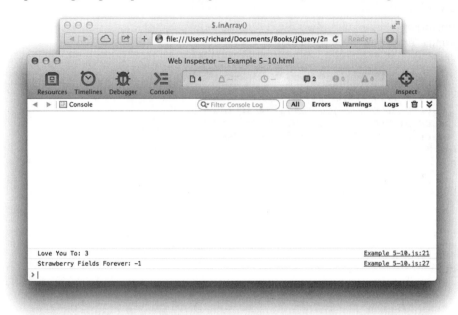

FIGURE 5-10

Merging Two Arrays

jQuery's `$.merge()` method can glue two arrays together to make a single array. The following example, *Example 5-11*, demonstrates how this works:

```html
<!DOCTYPE HTML>
<html lang='en'>
    <head>
        <meta http-equiv='X-UA-Compatible' content='IE=Edge' />
        <meta charset='utf-8' />
        <title>$.merge()</title>
        <script src='../jQuery.js'></script>
        <script src='../jQueryUI.js'></script>
        <script src='Example 5-11.js'></script>
    </head>
    <body>

    </body>
</html>
```

The following script is included in the preceding markup:

```
$(document).ready(
    function()
    {
        var rubberSoul = [
            'Drive My Car',
            'Norwegian Wood (This Bird Has Flown)',
            'You Won\'t See Me',
            'Nowhere Man',
            'Think for Yourself',
            'The Word',
            'Michelle',
            'What Goes On',
            'Girl',
            'I\'m Looking Through You',
            'In My Life',
            'Wait',
            'If I Needed Someone',
            'Run for Your Life'
        ];

        var revolver = [
            'Taxman',
            'Eleanor Rigby',
            'I\'m Only Sleeping',
            'Love You To',
            'Here, There and Everywhere',
            'Yellow Submarine',
            'She Said, She Said',
            'Good Day Sunshine',
            'And Your Bird Can Sing',
            'For No One',
            'Doctor Robert',
            'I Want to Tell You',
            'Got to Get You into My Life',
            'Tomorrow Never Knows'
        ];

        var songs = $.merge(rubberSoul, revolver);

        console.log('Songs :', songs);
    }
);
```

The preceding script results in the console output that you see in Figure 5-11.

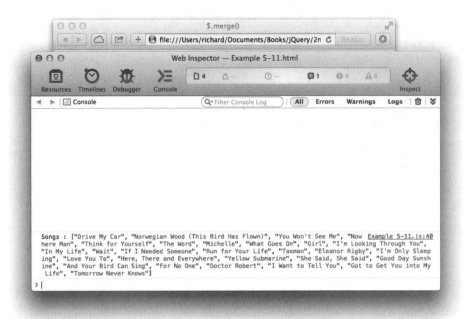

FIGURE 5-11

As you can see, jQuery's merge() method is pretty straightforward, appending the contents of the second array argument to the contents of the first array argument.

SUMMARY

This chapter presented several methods associated with iterating and working with arrays and selections.

You learned how jQuery's each() method is a less-verbose, easier-to-use alternative for iterating over an array, object, or selection when compared to using a for construct and a counter, or a for/in construct for objects. You learned how to emulate break and continue keywords with the each() method by returning a boolean value. You learned that jQuery's each() method can be called directly or chained to a selection or an array that's wrapped in a call to the dollar sign method.

You learned how a selection is filtered using jQuery's filter() method using either a selector or a callback function. An array can be filtered using jQuery's grep() method, which must be called directly.

You learned how one array can be mapped to another array and how one selection can be mapped to an array using jQuery's map() method, which exists to translate one set of values to another set of values.

Finally, you learned about jQuery's various array utility methods. $.makeArray() can turn any data into a true array. $.inArray() can find the position of a value within an array, offset from zero, and works just like JavaScript's indexOf() method, with −1 (minus one) indicating that a value is not present within the array. $.merge() glues two separate arrays together into just one array.

EXERCISES

1. What might the JavaScript code look like if you want to iterate over the following collection of elements using jQuery's each() method?

   ```
   nodes = document.getElementsByTagName('div');
   ```

2. What statement would you write inside a callback function provided to jQuery's each() method if you want to simulate a break statement?

3. When filtering a selection using filter(), what does providing a selector to the filter() method do?

4. When filtering a selection using filter() with a callback function, what does returning true do?

5. What value does a callback function provided to jQuery's grep() method have to return to keep an item in the array?

6. What happens to the value returned by a callback function provided to jQuery's map() method?

7. What does –1 (minus one) mean when returned by jQuery's $.inArray() method?

CSS

When working with CSS from JavaScript, a few minor points of verbosity and inconsistency exist where jQuery can lend a helping hand. jQuery makes it easier to manipulate CSS from JavaScript. jQuery's approach enables you to define styles for multiple CSS properties at once, or one CSS property at a time. But instead of setting CSS properties one element at a time, you can set the style on one or many elements at once.

As mentioned in Chapter 4, "Manipulating Content and Attributes," and in Chapter 1, "Introduction to jQuery," it's generally good practice to avoid mixing style (CSS) with behavior (JavaScript) and structure (HTML). You want to keep CSS, JavaScript, and HTML partitioned as cleanly as possible into their respective documents.

In some cases, however, it is unavoidable to bring presentation into your JavaScript programming; for example, it may have already been done the wrong or more-difficult-to-maintain way long before you ever arrived. In these cases, the style changes dynamically in such a way that it is impractical and unreasonable to keep CSS only in a style sheet and not directly modify style with JavaScript programming. This chapter covers the methods that jQuery exposes that enable you to work with style-sheet properties and values.

WORKING WITH CSS PROPERTIES

Instead of messing around with the `style` property as you may be used to doing with traditional JavaScript, when you want to access style information or modify style information with jQuery, you use jQuery's `css()` method. You can use the `css()` method in three different ways:

➤ To return a property's value from the first element matched in a selection

➤ To set a property's value on one or more elements

➤ To set multiple properties on one or more elements

When you simply want to get a property's value for an element, this is what you do:

```
var backgroundColor = $('div').css('backgroundColor');
```

Note that because you are accessing the property through JavaScript as a string, you have the option of either using camelCase or specifying the property name with a hyphen, as it is done in a style sheet. This is also valid:

```
var backgroundColor = $('div').css('background-color');
```

After you make a selection, you call the css() method chained to the selection with the property that you want the value for. The snippet of code here returns the backgroundColor for the first <div> element of the selection, so if there are five <div> elements present in a document, the preceding code would return the background-color for the first one.

If you want to retrieve multiple properties, you specify an array of properties to retrieve, and an object of property/value pairs are retrieved from the element.

```
var properties = $('div').css([
    'background-color',
    'color',
    'padding',
    'box-shadow'
]);
```

The preceding example returns an object containing the specified properties. Remember, you can always dump the content of a variable to the JavaScript console using the console.log() method, if you want to know what value a variable contains.

If you want to set the value of a single property, that's done like this:

```
$('div').css('background-color', 'lightblue');
```

In the preceding example, the background-color of all <div> elements in the document is set to lightblue.

Setting multiple properties for multiple elements can be done like this:

```
$('div').css({
    backgroundColor : 'lightblue',
    border : '1px solid lightgrey',
    padding : '5px'
});
```

Or this:

```
$('div').css({
    'background-color' : 'lightblue',
    border : '1px solid lightgrey',
    padding : '5px'
});
```

An object literal with key, value pairs is passed to the css() method. In the preceding example, the background-color is set to lightblue, the border is set to 1px solid lightgrey, and the padding is set to 5px for all the <div> elements in the document. You can use hyphenated property names like this as well, but you must place quotes around any property names that contain hyphens.

JQUERY'S PSEUDO-CLASSES

In CSS the pseudo-class marks a condition or state. For example, the :hover pseudo-class is for styling an element when the mouse cursor comes over the element. The styles that you specify for the :hover state are only in effect while the mouse cursor resides above an element. jQuery adds a few pseudo-classes that make more sense in the JavaScript world than in the CSS world.

Some pseudo-classes that jQuery provides are not feasible in CSS. For example, jQuery's :parent pseudo-class moves a selection from one or more elements to the parent element(s) of that/those element(s). This cannot be done in CSS because of the incremental rendering rule. A style sheet must be applied as it is downloaded to a DOM that is being created as it may also be downloading. Because of the incremental rendering rule, which is part of what can make a browser appear to load a page blazingly fast, having to step backward in the DOM poses a technical challenge similar to reversing the flow of a river. If everything is built to flow in one direction, from the bottom up, going from the top to the bottom introduces hurdles, obstacles, and potential glitches. For this reason, the W3C's CSS working group has been resistant to introduce any type of parent or ancestor selector.

In JavaScript, however, there are no such limitations. You're most likely already waiting for the DOM and, by extension, the associated style sheets to be loaded before you do things with the document.

> **NOTE** *All of jQuery's pseudo-class extensions, in addition to the various types of standard selectors supported by jQuery, are documented in Appendix B, "CSS Selectors Supported by jQuery."*

OBTAINING OUTER DIMENSIONS

In traditional JavaScript, when you want to get the width of an element—which includes the CSS width, in addition to border width and padding width—you use the property offsetWidth. Using jQuery, this information is available when you call the method outerWidth(), which provides the offsetWidth of the first element in a selection. This gives you a pixel measurement including width, border, and padding. Likewise, the outerHeight() method does the same with height; it includes CSS height, padding height, and border height.

> **NOTE** *You can also ask for margin length to be included in the return value by setting the first argument to* outerWidth() *or* outerHeight() *to* true.

To demonstrate how you would use the css(), outerWidth(), and outerHeight() methods, the following example, *Example 6-1*, shows you how to make a custom context menu that leverages these methods to set a custom context menu's position within the document. The *context menu* is the menu your browser provides when you click the right button on a three-button mouse, use the two-finger tap gesture on a Mac, or hold down the [Ctrl] key and click also on a Mac. Given the various operating system differences in producing a context menu, the action of producing a context menu will hereafter be referred to as a *contextual click*. This menu pops up at the location of your mouse cursor. You begin with the following XHTML.

```html
<!DOCTYPE HTML>
<html lang='en'>
    <head>
        <meta http-equiv='X-UA-Compatible' content='IE=Edge' />
        <meta charset='utf-8' />
        <title>Context Menu Example</title>
        <script src='../jQuery.js'></script>
        <script src='../jQueryUI.js'></script>
        <script src='Example 6-1.js'></script>
        <link href='Example 6-1.css' rel='stylesheet' />
    </head>
    <body>
        <h4>Context Menu Example</h4>
        <div id='contextMenu'>

        </div>
    </body>
</html>
```

The preceding markup is styled with the following style sheet:

```css
body {
    font: 12px "Lucida Grande", Arial, sans-serif;
    color: rgb(50, 50, 50);
    margin: 0;
    padding: 0 10px;
}
div#contextMenu {
    width: 150px;
    height: 150px;
    background: yellowgreen;
    border: 1px solid gold;
    padding: 10px;
    position: absolute;
    left: 0;
    right: 0;
    display: none;
}
```

The following JavaScript defines the behavior that enables the context menu to function:

```javascript
$(document).ready(
    function()
    {
        var contextMenuOn = false;

        $(document).on(
            'contextmenu',
```

```javascript
function(event)
{
    event.preventDefault();

    var contextMenu = $('div#contextMenu');

    contextMenu.show();

    // The following bit gets the dimensions of the viewport
    // Thanks to quirksmode.org
    var vpx, vpy;

    if (self.innerHeight)
    {
        // all except Explorer
        vpx = self.innerWidth;
        vpy = self.innerHeight;
    }
    else if (document.documentElement &&
             document.documentElement.clientHeight)
    {
        // Explorer 6 Strict Mode
        vpx = document.documentElement.clientWidth;
        vpy = document.documentElement.clientHeight;
    }
    else if (document.body)
    {
        // other Explorers
        vpx = document.body.clientWidth;
        vpy = document.body.clientHeight;
    }

    // Reset offset values to their defaults
    contextMenu.css({
        top : 'auto',
        right : 'auto',
        bottom : 'auto',
        left : 'auto'
    });


    // If the height or width of the context menu is greater than
    // the amount of pixels from the point of click to the right or
    // bottom edge of the viewport adjust the offset accordingly
    if (contextMenu.outerHeight() > (vpy - event.pageY))
    {
        contextMenu.css('bottom', (vpy - event.pageY) + 'px');
    }
    else
    {
        contextMenu.css('top', event.pageY + 'px');
    }
```

```
                    if (contextMenu.outerWidth() > (vpx - event.pageX))
                    {
                        contextMenu.css('right',  (vpx - event.pageX) + 'px');
                    }
                    else
                    {
                        contextMenu.css('left', event.pageX + 'px');
                    }
                }
            );

            $('div#contextMenu').hover(
                function()
                {
                    contextMenuOn = true;
                },
                function()
                {
                    contextMenuOn = false;
                }
            );

            $(document).mousedown(
                function()
                {
                    if (!contextMenuOn)
                    {
                        $('div#contextMenu').hide();
                    }
                }
            );
        }
    );
```

The preceding example produces output similar to Figure 6-1.

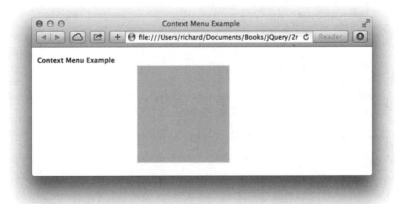

FIGURE 6-1

Before we explain the concepts in this example, consider this. Although replacing the context menu that your browser provides can be used to provide useful functionality that can go much further in making your web-based applications look and feel like desktop applications, you should be cautious about the scenarios that you choose to invoke custom context menu functionality. The context menu is also heavily used by browser users to do simple things like navigate forward or backward from their present location, to reload the current page, or to do other useful tasks associated with using the browser. But if your web application recklessly takes control of the context menu, you risk alienating or annoying your user base because your application prevents the user from accessing and interacting with his browser in the way he normally would. In addition, disabling the browser's context menu will not prevent users from seeing your application's source code because you can still go to the browser's main menu and click the View Source option.

More savvy users can bypass JavaScript by disabling it or even directly access your source code through other means, such as via your browser's cache or by accessing the source code from your website directly from a command line or script. If you're considering disabling the context menu for this purpose, you may want to reconsider publishing your web application for public consumption because this method of preventing access to your website's source code is ineffective and is subject to numerous workarounds. Remember, content you place on the web is, by design, made to be publicly consumed and transportable to browsers of all kinds residing on platforms of all kinds. The key thing to keep in mind is that rendering your markup and executing your JavaScript is entirely optional.

That said, the preceding example takes a `<div>` with perfectly square dimensions that takes the place of your browser's default context menu. When you do a contextual click on the document (anywhere in the browser window), the `<div>` acting as the replacement context menu appears and is positioned based on where the click occurred.

First, you set up the event that fires when the user accesses the context menu. This is done using jQuery's on() method because jQuery does not provide a `contextmenu()` method. It should also be noted that `contextmenu` events can be disabled in Firefox; they are enabled by default.

The following code thus far disables the browser's default context menu when the user tries to access the context menu with the mouse cursor within the document window:

```
$(document).on(
    'contextmenu',
    function(event)
    {
        event.preventDefault();
```

Next, the `<div>` element that acts as the context menu is selected and assigned to the `contextMenu` variable, and that `<div>` element is made visible with jQuery's show() method.

```
var contextMenu = $('div#contextMenu');

contextMenu.show();
```

When you create your own context menu, you want to have the position of your context menu change depending on where in the browser window the context menu is accessed. If the user accesses the context menu close to the left and top sides of the window, you want your context menu to position itself from the left and the top. If the user accesses the context menu from the right and bottom of the window, then you want the context menu to intelligently reposition from the right and bottom and do this without any part of the context menu being obstructed.

To make the context menu so that it dynamically repositions itself depending on where it is accessed, you need to do a little bit of math. The first bits of data that you need to do that math are the dimensions of the viewport. Use the dimensions of the viewport to help determine how the context menu should be positioned relative to the place where the user accesses it. Getting the viewport's dimensions, unfortunately, is one of those fringe areas in which different browsers implement different methods of doing the same thing, and jQuery doesn't provide a neat, unified method of patching over this particular difference. This is less of a nuisance today because recent versions of Internet Explorer have come more in line with the defined standards. The following code intelligently obtains the viewport's dimensions depending on the browser's implementation:

```
// The following bit gets the dimensions of the viewport
// Thanks to quirksmode.org
var vpx, vpy;

if (self.innerHeight)
{
    // all except Explorer
    vpx = self.innerWidth;
    vpy = self.innerHeight;
}
else if (document.documentElement &&
            document.documentElement.clientHeight)
{
    // Explorer 6 Strict Mode
    vpx = document.documentElement.clientWidth;
    vpy = document.documentElement.clientHeight;
}
else if (document.body)
{
    // other Explorers
    vpx = document.body.clientWidth;
    vpy = document.body.clientHeight;
}

// Reset offset values to their defaults
contextMenu.css({
    top : 'auto',
    right : 'auto',
    bottom : 'auto',
    left : 'auto'
});
```

Before you actually position the context menu, you need to reset your context menu's offset positions to the defaults. All four offsets have to be reset because the next portion of code will set at least two of the offset properties to the correct values, and the two that are set can vary depending on where the user accesses the context menu. You don't, for example, want the positions you set the last time the user accessed the context menu to persist to this time because that may create a conflict. To reset each offset position, you use jQuery's css() method to set the top, right, bottom, and left offset properties back to each property's default value, auto.

```
// Reset offset values to their defaults
contextMenu.css({
    top : 'auto',
    right : 'auto',
    bottom : 'auto',
    left : 'auto'
});
```

Now you're ready to mathematically determine the proper position for the context menu. To get the right position, you want to know if the outerHeight() of the <div> element you're using for the menu exceeds the browser's viewport height (specified in the vpy variable) minus the vertical point of the mouse cursor's position (provided in event.pageY), relative to the document. If the outerHeight() is bigger than this calculation, it means that the menu should be positioned from the bottom, rather than from the top; otherwise, the menu would be clipped.

```
// If the height or width of the context menu is greater than
// the amount of pixels from the point of click to the right
// or bottom edge of the viewport adjust the offset accordingly
if (contextMenu.outerHeight() > (vpy - event.pageY))
{
    contextMenu.css('bottom', (vpy - event.pageY) + 'px');
}
else
{
    contextMenu.css('top', event.pageY + 'px');
}
```

The same calculation is done for the horizontal portion. If the outerWidth() of the menu is greater than the width of the viewport (specified in the vpx variable) minus the horizontal coordinate of the mouse cursor's position (provided in event.pageX), relative to the document, the menu should be positioned from the right, rather than the left; otherwise, the menu would be clipped horizontally.

```
if (contextMenu.outerWidth() > (vpx - event.pageX))
{
    contextMenu.css('right', (vpx - event.pageX) + 'px');
}
else
{
    contextMenu.css('left', event.pageX + 'px');
}
```

That's all there is to positioning the context menu correctly based on where the user clicks in the document. The additional code handles revealing and hiding the context menu at the right moments. At the beginning of the document, you declare the following variable:

```
var contextMenuOn = false;
```

The preceding variable is used to track whether the user's mouse cursor is over the context menu when it is active. When the user's mouse cursor leaves the context menu, this variable is set to false; when the user's mouse cursor is present, this variable is set to true. This boolean value is then used to toggle the menu off when the user clicks an area outside the context menu and keeps the menu active when the user clicks the menu itself.

The following code handles the part that sets the contextMenuOn variable to either true or false via passing two event handlers to jQuery's hover() method:

```
$('div#contextMenu').hover(
    function()
    {
        contextMenuOn = true;
    },
    function()
    {
        contextMenuOn = false;
    }
);
```

Then the following code hides the menu when the user clicks anywhere outside the menu because the variable is false in that case and keeps the menu on when the user actually clicks the menu.

```
$(document).mousedown(
    function()
    {
        if (!contextMenuOn)
        {
            $('div#contextMenu').hide();
        }
    }
);
```

jQuery's API as it relates to CSS is documented in Appendix B and Appendix H.

SUMMARY

In this chapter, you learned how to get the value of an element's CSS property using jQuery's css() method. You also learned how to manipulate an element's style using the same css() method, which can be done by passing a property and value to the css() method as two separate strings, or by passing an object literal with one or more property, value pairs.

jQuery provides the offsetHeight and offsetWidth properties by calling the methods outerHeight() or outerWidth(). These methods return an element's pixel width or height, including padding and borders. You can also specifically add margin to the value returned by these methods.

Finally, these methods were reiterated with a real-world-oriented example that shows you how to replace the browser's default context menu with your own. In this situation, you want to use jQuery's css() method to set CSS property values, rather than a style sheet, because the values set are set dynamically.

EXERCISES

1. What script would you use if you want to obtain the value of the color property for a `<div>` element using jQuery?

2. If you want to set the background color of a web page using jQuery, what code would you use?

3. If you need to set padding, a margin, and a border on a set of `<div>` elements using jQuery, what would the code look like?

4. What is the jQuery method that returns an element's pixel width including border and padding dimensions called?

5. If you wanted to obtain a `<div>` element's pixel height including a border, padding, and margins using jQuery, what would the code look like?

7

AJAX

AJAX is the technology that enables you to make arbitrary HTTP requests from JavaScript to obtain new data without the need for reloading a document. *AJAX* stands for Asynchronous JavaScript and XML. The name is misleading, though, because you don't have to use XML, and your requests don't have to be asynchronous. You can have synchronous requests (a request that causes your code to pause execution until the answer is received from the server) that are in the JSON format. XML is just one of many possible formats that you can use to transmit data from a server to client-side JavaScript.

Using AJAX you can make web documents behave much less like documents and much more like completely self-contained desktop applications. With a web-based application, updates are much easier to propagate because everyone upgrades immediately upon their next visit to the website. No longer do companies worry about maintaining legacy software and users—with a web-based application, everyone is pushed to the latest version. It also becomes easier for a user to access these applications. Because a separate installation is not required on every computer where the application's use is wanted, all that is required is a capable browser on top of moderately capable hardware. Browsers strive to blur the line between desktop applications and web-based applications even more because browsers such as Firefox and Google's Chrome browser make it easier to make a web-based application available as a desktop application via placing an icon on the user's desktop, dock, start menu, or quick-launch bar. In Firefox's case, this functionality is experimental, but in the case of Chrome, the feature is already a reality. Then there is Adobe's AIR runtime, which allows you to develop desktop applications using web standards. Because AIR is built on top of WebKit—which is the rendering engine used in Safari, and iOS, among others—AIR can make sophisticated, complex desktop applications using a robust standards-compliant rendering engine. So, if these companies have anything to say about it, web-based applications will become more popular and increasingly take over certain tasks that desktop applications once served.

Another advantage of web-based application development, which some people may perceive as nefarious, is that web-based applications are immune to piracy, at least in the traditional sense. It's impossible to obtain a web-based application's services without payment because a user can simply be locked out if payment is not made, and use of an application can be limited to a single login session at a time. Up until now, this aspect hasn't been much of a problem, though, because web-based applications are often supported with advertisements that make them free.

Then another advantage still is that you can make a web-based application available to many more operating systems and browsers than you might have otherwise with a self-contained desktop application. You can target Safari, Chrome, Firefox, Internet Explorer, and Opera and reach more than 99 percent of your browsing audience easily. Frameworks like jQuery make this even easier because they eliminate many browser inconsistencies and headaches that might otherwise present as roadblocks to cross-browser development.

There are some disadvantages to web-based applications, though, and a fair discussion should include them. Because a web-based application can change so easily, some users will complain, and some might even refuse to adapt. In addition, the speed of a web-based application has not come close to the same speed offered by native programming. Speed is an issue because JavaScript is an interpreted language, even with most browsers rapidly converting JavaScript to machine code and caching it, which is a huge speed increase. JavaScript (along with (X)HTML and CSS) still has network latency as an issue and still has a disadvantage in being an interpreted language that is processed on-the-fly instead of compiled like most of the desktop applications you use every day. On mobile, the speed issue is still enough of a problem to keep most development from web-based languages and browsers; instead most mobile development is done with a native compiled language such as Objective-C, Swift, Java, or .NET. Finally, as a web-based technology, network or server issues can potentially completely shut down user access to your application, although in some development scenarios a network outage can be worked around.

Nonetheless, AJAX has become a powerful and increasingly essential component of web development; this chapter covers jQuery's built-in methods for making AJAX requests. As you would expect, jQuery takes something that is moderately verbose and complex and boils it down into a much simpler, easier-to-grasp API so that you can start writing AJAX-capable web applications much more quickly.

MAKING A SERVER REQUEST

As you're probably already aware, the web works through a protocol called HTTP. When you navigate to a web page, your browser fires off a request to a remote HTTP server that's running Apache, nginx, Microsoft IIS, or some other HTTP server software, using the HTTP communication protocol. AJAX makes it so that you can fire off those HTTP requests programmatically without having to reload the entire web page. After your JavaScript makes a request and receives a response, you can then take that data and manipulate the content that's in front of the user based on the response that you receive. Using the HTTP protocol, there are many ways that you can request data from the server. The most common ways information is transmitted between an HTTP server and client are the GET and POST methods, although there are many more methods that can be implemented as part of a RESTful service. If your server or application is configured to support RESTful calls, you will also have methods such as PUT and DELETE, which I discuss in the section "Sending a REST Request." Before taking a look at REST, you should first be familiar with the most common methods of transmitting an HTTP request using a simple GET or POST request.

What's the Difference Between GET and POST?

At face value, the GET and POST methods seem identical: Both allow you to request a web page and send data along with that request. Most of the time, for AJAX requests, you want to use the GET method because it is slightly faster from a performance standpoint where AJAX is concerned, but there are other differences that you should be aware of that address semantic differences between the two methods, as well as technical and security differences. The following outlines these differences:

➤ The GET method is intended for requests that have no tangible, lasting effect on the state of anything. (The HTTP specification calls this type of request *safe*.) For example, when you make a request and you're simply retrieving data from a database, GET is properly suited for this type of request. If a request results in a change to the database via an insertion, update, or deletion—for example, when managing content or making an order or uploading data— the POST method is best suited. This difference, however, is merely semantic.

➤ Using the POST method causes a browser to automatically prevent resubmitting a form if the user navigates back to a submitted form using the browser's Back button because the POST method is intended to be used for situations in which data manipulation occurs. This is a technical difference put in place to prevent resubmission of form data. But this automatic prevention is ineffective because you still have to design your server-side programs to account for possible resubmissions . . . anything that can go wrong, will! Users can be impatient and click the Submit button multiple times or refresh submitted forms, ignoring a browser's warnings. However, the GET method provides no automatic protection against resubmission. This difference is mostly inconsequential to AJAX programming because there is no way for a user to resubmit a POST request without you specifically designing the ability into your program.

➤ The GET method has a much lower limitation on request length imposed than the POST method. This difference is a technical one that can have an effect on your applications. The limitation of the length a GET request can be varies among browsers, but RFC 2068 states that servers should be cautious about depending on URI lengths greater than 255 bytes. Because GET request data is included as part of the URI (the web page's address), the GET request is actually limited by the length of the URI a browser supports. Internet Explorer can support a URL up to 2,083 characters in length, which is ridiculously long. The POST method, however, theoretically has no limitation on length other than what your server is configured to accept. PHP (a server-side language), for example, is configured to accept a POST request that's 8 MB or less in size, by default. This setting and others, such as how long a script can execute and how much memory it can consume, collectively define how big your POST requests can be in the context of that server-side language. Other server-side languages, no doubt, have similar configuration settings; on the client side, however, a POST request has no hard limitation defined, other than the limits of the client's hardware, network, and server capabilities.

➤ The POST and GET methods can be encoded differently, again a technical difference. I'm not going to go into this difference in great detail because it is outside the scope of this book. This difference applies when you want to upload files via the POST method; I discuss how to perform a file upload via POST in Chapter 11, "HTML5 Drag and Drop." As you will see in Chapter 11, however, when doing a file upload via AJAX APIs provided by the browser, the browser takes care of encoding for you.

The distinction between the POST and GET methods is mostly moot when it comes to making a request originating from an AJAX script. Because the user is not involved with the request, the automatic protection portion becomes unnecessary, which leaves only the semantic differences and the limitations in length. For the most part, you can get away with making GET requests for everything, which has been said to have a slight performance advantage over the POST method. Personally, I tend to honor the semantic differences out of simple habit from years of working with forms in client-side programming.

> **NOTE** *You can find more information about the performance aspect on the Yahoo Developer website at* `http://developer.yahoo.com/performance/rules.html`.

RESTful Requests

REST, or *Representational State Transfer*, makes it possible to distinguish between differing actions based on the specified HTTP transport method. So far you've learned about the GET and POST HTTP transport methods. As stated in the last section, distinguishing between GET and POST is mostly semantic because every HTTP server can handle GET and POST. REST is an architectural decision in how you choose to implement your web services. Instead of GET and POST being merely semantically different, you can choose to enforce technical constraints as well, for example, a server-side application that behaves and handles data differently based on whether you use the GET or POST method. In addition to GET and POST, a REST architecture can implement the PUT and DELETE methods. Finally, in addition to those four methods, some implementations may take things even further by defining additional methods, for example, PATCH.

The differences within which HTTP transport method you specify (GET, POST, PUT, or DELETE) can be enforced on the server side. For example, you can send GET, POST, PUT, or DELETE requests to the same URI location with information specified in the body of the request as JSON, and then the server-side application routes the request and executes different code based on which method is specified. Many developers simply use the URL to do the same thing and don't go beyond GET or POST. It has become increasingly more in fashion, however, to use HTTP to clearly define the purpose of a request, as well as to respond to a request using HTTP error codes. Using a REST approach brings your AJAX applications more into the realm of defined standards by making use of the features defined in the HTTP protocol that have been mostly ignored.

In the section "Sending a REST Request," I present an example of how to send and receive data with jQuery using a REST approach.

Formats Used to Transport Data with an AJAX Request

Although the name implies that you use XML to transport data with an AJAX request, this is entirely optional. In addition to XML, there are two other common ways that data is transmitted from the server to a client-side JavaScript application: JSON (or JavaScript Object Notation) and HTML. You are not limited to these formats, however, because you can conceivably take any data you like from the server and transmit it to the client. These formats are the most popular because JavaScript provides you with tools for working with these types of data. XML can be easily queried using DOM tools and methods, as well as with jQuery's various methods of traversal, filtering, and retrieval. HTML can be sent in incomplete snippets that can be effortlessly inserted into a document using jQuery's html() method.

You can also transmit JavaScript from the server, and the JavaScript will be evaluated in the client-side application, executing it and making whatever variables, functions, objects, and so on available.

The JSON format is a subset of the syntax allowed to create JavaScript object literals, and it is therefore a subset of JavaScript. It is considered to be its own format for data transmission, however. Many popular languages have the ability to both read and send JSON-formatted data.

There are potential security issues associated with JSON that you should consider that result from using eval() to execute JavaScript code from the server. eval() should be used only if you are certain that the data being evaluated cannot be manipulated and cannot contain malicious code. For your web application, you should take precautions before using the eval() method to execute any-thing that has been user-provided because a user can have malicious intentions. Because a portion of your code is available for all to see on the client-side, any user can discover what methods you use to transmit and receive data. If you use JSON to transmit user-supplied data that originates from your input forms, a user can maliciously craft the data submitted in your forms to be executed alongside your JSON-formatted code. One exploit a malicious user can take advantage of in this way would be to execute JavaScript that takes other users' session data and transmits that data back to the malicious user's server. This type of exploit is known as an *XSS (Cross-Site Scripting) vulnerability*, alternatively known as *Cross-Site Scripting Forgery*. Because session data is not tied to a user's computer but, instead, relies on long strings of numbers and letters that are mathematically difficult to reproduce, when a malicious user obtains another user's session id, that malicious user can then impersonate other users and steal their sensitive data or log in to your server and obtain privileged information. So great care and thought must be placed into what code is safe to eval() and what code is not.

Making a GET Request with jQuery

Having talked about some of the inner workings of what an AJAX request is, the next topic for discussion is making your first GET request with AJAX using jQuery.

Of course, AJAX is typically used to create dynamic web applications that have a server-side compo-nent written in something such as PHP, Java, .NET, Ruby, or whatever you like. The server-side portion of this is outside the scope of this book, so, instead of linking an AJAX request to a server-side application, I link these requests to local documents that provide the same response every time. If you'd like to learn more about the server-side components that are involved, Wrox has an excel-lent selection of books covering just about every language.

That said, jQuery makes a few methods available that initiate a GET request from a server; the method that you use depends on the data you're getting. The generic method, which you can use to make any type of GET request, is called, easily enough, get(). Each method is a member of the jQuery object, so you'd call the get() method like this: $.get().

Requesting Data Formatted in XML

The first example I demonstrate shows you how to request data from a server that formats the response as XML. The following source code demonstrates an input form for an address in which the country field causes the state field to be dynamically updated when the country selection is changed and the country's flag is changed as well. Each list of states is dynamically fetched from the server using an AJAX request. However, this happens only for three of the country selections— the United States, Canada, and the United Kingdom—because the information is fed from static XML files rather than a database-driven server. If I were to create an XML file for all 239 country options, I would at least change the flag for that country, even if no administrative subdivision similar to a state exists for that country. The following is the HTML portion of *Example 7-1*:

```html
<!DOCTYPE HTML>
<html lang='en'>
    <head>
        <meta http-equiv='X-UA-Compatible' content='IE=Edge' />
        <meta charset='utf-8' />
        <title>Context Menu Example</title>
        <script src='../jQuery.js'></script>
        <script src='../jQueryUI.js'></script>
        <script src='Example 7-1.js'></script>
        <link href='Example 7-1.css' rel='stylesheet' />
    </head>
    <body>
        <form action='javascript:void(0);' method='post'>
            <fieldset>
                <legend>Address</legend>
<div id='addressCountryWrapper'>
    <label for='addressCountry'>
        <img src='flags/us.png' alt='Country' />
    </label>
    <select id='addressCountry' size='1' name='addressCountry'>
        <option value='0'>Please select a country</option>
        <option value='1'>Afghanistan</option>
        <option value='2'>Albania</option>
        <option value='3'>Algeria</option>
        <option value='4'>American Samoa</option>
         <option value='5'>Andorra</option>
```

The long list of countries has been snipped out. The complete file is available as part of this book's free source code download materials available from www.wrox.com/go/webdevwithjquery.

```html
        <option value='222'>United Kingdom</option>
        <option value='223' selected='selected'>United States</option>
        <option value='224'>United States Minor Outlying Islands</option>
        <option value='225'>Uruguay</option>
        <option value='226'>Uzbekistan</option>
        <option value='227'>Vanuatu</option>
        <option value='228'>Vatican City State (Holy See)</option>
        <option value='229'>Venezuela</option>
        <option value='230'>Vietnam</option>
        <option value='231'>Virgin Islands (British)</option>
        <option value='232'>Virgin Islands (U.S.)</option>
        <option value='233'>Wallis and Futuna Islands</option>
```

```
            <option value='234'>Western Sahara</option>
            <option value='235'>Yemen</option>
            <option value='236'>Yugoslavia</option>
            <option value='237'>Zaire</option>
            <option value='238'>Zambia</option>
            <option value='239'>Zimbabwe</option>
        </select>
    </div>
    <div>
        <label for='addressStreet'>Street Address:</label>
        <textarea name='addressStreet'
                  id='addressStreet'
                  rows='2'
                  cols='50'></textarea>
    </div>
    <div>
        <label for='addressCity'>City:</label>
        <input type='text' name='addressCity' id='addressCity' size='25' />
    </div>
    <div>
        <label for='addressState'>State:</label>
        <select name='addressState' id='addressState'>
        </select>
    </div>
    <div>
        <label for='addressPostalCode'>Postal Code:</label>
        <input type='text'
             name='addressPostalCode'
             id='addressPostalCode'
             size='10' />
    </div>
    <div id='addressButtonWrapper'>
        <input type='submit'
             id='addressButton'
             name='addressButton'
             value='Save' />
    </div>
            </fieldset>
        </form>
    </body>
</html>
```

The preceding HTML is styled with the following CSS:

```
body {
    font: 16px sans-serif;
}
fieldset {
    background: #93cdf9;
    border: 1px solid rgb(200, 200, 200);
}
fieldset div {
    padding: 10px;
    margin: 5px;
}
```

```
fieldset label {
    float: left;
    width: 200px;
    text-align: right;
    padding: 2px 5px 0 0;
}
div#addressCountryWrapper img {
    position: relative;
    top: -4px;
}
div#addressButtonWrapper {
    text-align: right;
}
```

Then, the following JavaScript is included in the preceding HTML document:

```
$(document).ready(
    function()
    {
        $('select#addressCountry').click(
            function()
            {
                $.get(
                    'Example 7-1/' + this.value + '.xml',
                    function(xml)
                    {
                        // Make the XML query-able with jQuery
                        xml = $(xml);

                        // Get the ISO2 value, that's used for the
                        // file name of the flag.
                        var iso2 = xml.find('iso2').text();

                        // Swap out the flag image
                        $('div#addressCountryWrapper img').attr({
                            alt : xml.find('name'),
                            src : 'flags/' + iso2.toLowerCase() + '.png'
                        });

                        // Remove all of the options
                        $('select#addressState').empty();

                        // Set the states...
                        xml.find('state').each(
                            function()
                            {
                                $('select#addressState').append(
                                    $('<option/>')
                                        .attr('value', $(this).attr('id'))
                                        .text($(this).text())
                                );
                            }
                        );
```

```
                             // Change the label
                             $('label[for="addressState"]').text(
                                 xml.find('label').text() + ':'
                             );
                         },
                         'xml'
                     );
                 }
             );

             $('select#addressCountry').click();
         }
     );
```

Then for the AJAX requests to succeed, you need to create some XML files for the response content. When you change the country in the <select> element, an AJAX request is sent via the GET method for the file *Example 7-1/<addressCountry>.xml*, where <addressCountry> is the numeric id of the country selected from the drop-down list. I've prepared XML files for three countries with the ids 38, 222, and 223, those being the respective ids of Canada, the United Kingdom, and the United States. Each XML file looks similar to the following, which is Canada's:

```xml
<?xml version="1.0" encoding="UTF-8" standalone="yes"?>
<country>
    <name>Canada</name>
    <iso2>CA</iso2>
    <iso3>CAN</iso3>
    <label>Province</label>
    <state id='0'> </state>
    <state id="66">Alberta</state>
    <state id="67">British Columbia</state>
    <state id="68">Manitoba</state>
    <state id="69">Newfoundland</state>
    <state id="70">New Brunswick</state>
    <state id="71">Nova Scotia</state>
    <state id="72">Northwest Territories</state>
    <state id="73">Nunavut</state>
    <state id="74">Ontario</state>
    <state id="75">Prince Edward Island</state>
    <state id="76">Quebec</state>
    <state id="77">Saskatchewan</state>
    <state id="78">Yukon Territory</state>
</country>
```

Each XML file is structured identically, providing the country's name, an ISO2 and ISO3 country code, a label, and the list of administrative subdivisions, which I have simply called *states*, even though that's not always technically correct; Canada's are called provinces and the United Kingdom's are called counties.

The preceding example looks like what you see in Figure 7-1, when you select United Kingdom from the country drop-down.

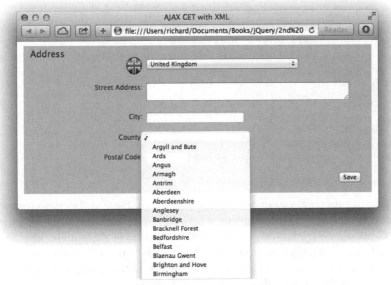

FIGURE 7-1

In the JavaScript file, things get under way with adding a `click` event to the `<select>` element with id name `addressCountry`. Within the handler for the `click` event, you begin your AJAX request using jQuery's `$.get()` method. The first argument specifies the path that you want to request, which is the XML file, dynamically substituting the country id in the filename. The second argument is a callback function that you want to execute when your script has received the server's response, and the third argument is the type of AJAX request that you want to make. For a complete overview of the API of the `$.get()` method, see Appendix G, "AJAX Methods."

The callback method that you specified has one argument specified, `xml`. This variable contains the XML data that the server has sent back. This data is then made into a jQuery object, which makes it much easier to extract data from it:

```
// Make the XML query-able with jQuery
xml = $(xml);
```

The next thing to do is to fetch the ISO2 code from the XML document, which is used to fetch the updated flag for the selected country:

```
// Get the ISO2 value, that's used for the
// file name of the flag.
  var iso2 = xml.find('iso2').text();
```

Just as you would do in a normal HTML document, you can use jQuery's `find()` method to locate the XML element `<iso2>` and retrieve its text content via jQuery's `text()` method. In the context of the three countries I've created XML files for, the `iso2` variable would contain CA for Canada, GB for the United Kingdom, or US for the United States. The next step is to set the `alt` and `src` attributes of the `<img>` element referencing the country flag:

```
// Swap out the flag image
$('div#addressCountryWrapper img').attr({
    alt : xml.find('name'),
    src : 'flags/' + iso2.toLowerCase() + '.png'
});
```

The `<img>` element is located by querying the DOM for a `<div>` element with an id attribute having the value `addressCountryWrapper` and then finding the `<img>` element within. Then the `<img>` element's `src` and `alt` attributes are set using jQuery's `attr()` method, and the path for the flag is defined, taking into account the structure of files in this book's source code download materials. Then the filename is appended, and the ISO2 code is converted to lowercase because each flag image is named using lowercase characters. This may not be a problem for some servers, such as Windows or some Mac servers that are case-insensitive, but UNIX and Linux servers, including some Mac servers (depending on how the Macs have been formatted), are case-sensitive, and having the incorrect case for the filename would cause the image to fail to load.

The next step is to remove all state options. First, query for the `<select>` element with the id name `addressState`, and then call jQuery's `empty()` method to remove all options.

```
// Remove all of the options
$('select#addressState').empty();
```

The next step is to add the administrative subdivisions from the XML file as options. jQuery's `find()` method locates all the `<state>` elements in the XML file. Then you enumerate over each `<state>` element using the `each()` method.

```
// Set the states...
xml.find('state').each(
    function()
    {
```

Now you create each `<option>` element and append each element to the `<select>` element:

```
$('select#addressState').append(
    $('<option/>')
        .attr('value', $(this).attr('id'))
        .text($(this).text())
);
```

Because you're working within the callback function provided to the `each()` method, each `<state>` element is passed to that callback function as `this`, just as it is done with (X)HTML. To access jQuery's methods, you wrap `this` in a call to the jQuery object `$(this)`. You set the value attribute for each `<option>` element, which will be the unique numeric id passed in each `<state>` element as the attribute `id="0"`, where zero is the unique id. To get to that id, all you have to do is call jQuery's `attr()` method with the attribute's name as the first argument. Then all that's left to do is set the option's label, which is done with a simple call to jQuery's `text()` method, which retrieves the text content of the `<state>` element.

The last item is to set the label for the "state." Because Canadians use provinces, Britons use counties, and Americans use states, you need to use the right label, which is provided in the XML file as the `<label>` element. To find the `<label>` element you want to change, you query the DOM for the

`<label>` element with a `for` attribute having the value `addressState`. Then you set that `<label>` element's text content to the text content of the `<label>` element from the XML document.

```
// Change the label
$('label[for="addressState"]').text(
    xml.find('label').text() + ':'
);
```

As you can see with the preceding example, jQuery does not disappoint with its well-thought-out AJAX-handling abilities. With traditional JavaScript and DOM methods, the preceding would have been much more verbose and much more difficult to get working. jQuery's capability to *bind* itself to an XML response makes parsing and working with XML documents just like working with HTML documents: easy.

> **NOTE** *The iTunes-like flags included in the source code download originated from the following website, where you may also obtain higher-quality images:*
>
> `www.bartelme.at/journal/archive/flag_button_devkit/`

Sending Data Along with a Request

Let's say in that last example that you were actually working with a database-driven server; in that case, how you would have constructed the request would be slightly different than in the preceding example. Instead of dynamically creating the filename of the XML file you want to retrieve using the country's id, you would instead need to pass that information separately. jQuery accommodates passing data in the `$.get()` method. In the context of the preceding example, you started out making a call to the `$.get()` method that looked like this, with the extra code snipped out to make the example easier to understand:

```
$.get(
    'Example 7-1/38.xml',
    function(xml)
    {
        // snip
    },
    'xml'
);
```

The first argument is the path of the file you're requesting—this can be any URL value. Typically, you'll want to reference some server-side script that can output data for you. The second argument is the callback function that the server's response XML will be passed to, and the third argument is the type of request being made, which is one of the following strings: `'xml'`, `'html'`, `'script'`, `'json'`, `'jsonp'`, or `'text'`. This argument is set depending on the type of data that you expect coming back from the server.

When you want to send additional data with the request, another argument is added:

```
$.get(
    'Example 7-1/38.xml', {
```

```
                        countryId : 223,
                        iso2 : 'US',
                        iso3 : 'USA',
                        label : 'State'
                },
                function(xml)
                {
                        // snip
                },
                'xml'
        );
```

The new argument comes after the filename and before the function reference, and this is an object literal that contains the data you want to pass along in the GET request to the server. In the preceding example, I've modified the filename to be simply *Example 7-1/38.xml*, and I've created an object literal with four properties, countryId, iso2, iso3, and label. So, behind the scenes, this modification will cause the request to the server to look like this:

```
Example%207-1/38.xml?countryId=223&iso2=US&iso3=USA&label=State
```

jQuery takes the items in the object literal and builds a GET request from them. Because GET requests include data as part of the URL that you are calling, that data gets appended to the end of the URL. The question mark in the URL indicates that what follows is GET request data; then values are passed in name/value pairs, where each name and value is separated by an equals sign. Then if there is more than one value, additional values are appended subsequently by appending an ampersand character to the last name/value pair. Then this data is encoded for transport to the HTTP server. When at the HTTP server, how this data is accessed depends on the server-side language that you're using to read it.

Requesting JSON Formatted Data

This section revisits the example from the last section but this time uses JSON as the format for data transport instead of XML. I could use the same jQuery method, $.get(), to do this and change the last argument from 'xml' to 'json', but jQuery offers another method called $.getJSON() for retrieving JSON-formatted data. This method is just like the $.get() method except that the data format returned by the server is obviously expected to be JSON.

Using JSON as the data transportation format makes the code even leaner and easier to work with than XML, in addition to significantly reducing the size of the response from the server. The following example is the same example that you saw in the last section where when you select Canada, the United States, or the United Kingdom from the drop-down, the flag, administrative subdivisions, and administrative subdivision label all swap out, presenting data relevant to the country you're looking at. The HTML portion remains the same, and just a few modifications are made to the JavaScript portion. This example is available in the source code materials as *Example 7-2*.

```
$(document).ready(
    function()
    {
        $('select#addressCountry').click(
```

```
function()
{
    $.getJSON(
        'Example 7-2/' + this.value + '.json',
        function(json)
        {
            // Swap out the flag image
            $('div#addressCountryWrapper img').attr({
                alt : json.name,
                src : 'flags/' + json.iso2.toLowerCase() + '.png'
            });

            // Remove all of the options
            $('select#addressState').empty();

            // Set the states...
            $.each(
                json.states,
                function(id, state)
                {
                    $('select#addressState').append(
                        $('<option/>')
                            .attr('value', id)
                            .text(state)
                    );
                }
            );

            // Change the label
            $('label[for="addressState"]').text(
                json.label + ':'
            );
        }
    );
}
);

$('select#addressCountry').click();
    }
);
```

In the preceding JavaScript, things function similarly to the example that you saw in the last section where the server response was formatted as XML. However, this time you initiate an AJAX request using the $.getJSON() method instead of the $.get() method. Figure 7-2 shows the results.

These two methods are similar, except that you don't have to specify the last argument, specifying the format of the server response with the $.getJSON() method. Another difference is that you are requesting a file with a .json extension instead of .xml. Also, like in the last example, the file requested depends on which country is selected from the drop-down menu. The JSON object is formatted like so in the file being requested:

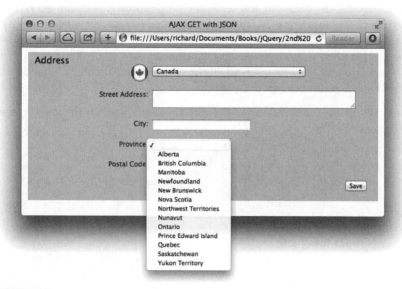

FIGURE 7-2

```
{
    "name" : "Canada",
    "iso2" : "CA",
    "iso3" : "CAN",
    "label" : "Province",
    "states" : {
        "0" : " ",
        "66" : "Alberta",
        "67" : "British Columbia",
        "68" : "Manitoba",
        "69" : "Newfoundland",
        "70" : "New Brunswick",
        "71" : "Nova Scotia",
        "72" : "Northwest Territories",
        "73" : "Nunavut",
        "74" : "Ontario",
        "75" : "Prince Edward Island",
        "76" : "Quebec",
        "77" : "Saskatchewan",
        "78" : "Yukon Territory"
    }
}
```

As you can see, the JSON format uses object literal syntax that you're already familiar with in JavaScript. The whole object is wrapped in curly braces but isn't assigned a name, which makes it easy for frameworks such as jQuery to take the JSON-formatted data and assign it directly to an object. In the JavaScript, the preceding JSON was passed to the event handler for the $.getJSON()

method as the `json` argument. All the data that you see in the JSON-formatted document is available inside that `json` variable. You access the ISO2 information as `json.iso2`, the label as `json.label`, and the states array as `json.states`. Using JSON, you've removed a step that would otherwise be required if you were working with XML data, which is querying the data within the response; with JSON, the data is fed directly to an object and is available immediately. Also note how much leaner the JSON file is compared to the verbose XML document.

Like the `$.get()` method, if you want to pass data to the server, you can provide that data in the same optional data argument.

```
$.getJSON(
    'Example 7-2/38.json', {
        countryId : 223,
        iso2 : 'US',
        iso3 : 'USA',
        label : 'State'
    },
    function(json)
    {

    }
);
```

Making a POST Request

POST requests are identical to GET requests in jQuery, except for the name of the method. Instead of `$.get()`, you use `$.post()`. Because a POST method request is reserved for modifying the state of the data in some way, you're probably more often than not going to want to pass some data along with your POST request, and that data will probably come from a form of some kind. jQuery makes it easy to grab form data and pass that along to the server. The method jQuery provides for this is `serialize()`. The `serialize()` method takes data for the input elements that you specify (which encompasses `<input>`, `<textarea>`, and `<select>` elements) and processes the values in those fields into a query string. If you do not select any elements for serialization, you can instead select a `<form>` element and jQuery automatically serializes all `<input>`, `<textarea>`, and `<select>` elements that it finds within the `<form>` element. The following (*Example 7-3*) is what the updated JavaScript looks like:

```
$(document).ready(
    function()
    {
        $('select#addressCountry').click(
            function()
            {
                $.getJSON(
                    'Example 7-3/' + this.value + '.json',
                    function(json)
                    {
                        // Swap out the flag image
                        $('div#addressCountryWrapper img').attr({
                            alt : json.name,
                            src : 'flags/' + json.iso2.toLowerCase() + '.png'
```

```
                                });

                                // Remove all of the options
                                $('select#addressState').empty();

                                // Set the states...
                                $.each(
                                    json.states,
                                    function(id, state)
                                    {
                                        $('select#addressState').append(
                                            $('<option/>')
                                                .attr('value', id)
                                                .text(state)
                                        );
                                    }
                                );

                                // Change the label
                                $('label[for="addressState"]').text(
                                    json.label + ':'
                                );
                            }
                        );
                    }
                );

                $('select#addressCountry').click();

                $('input#addressButton').click(
                    function(event)
                    {
                        event.preventDefault();

                        $.post(
                            'Example 7-3/POST.json',
                            $('form').serialize(),
                            function(json)
                            {
                                if (parseInt(json) > 0)
                                {
                                    alert('Data posted successfully.');
                                }
                            },
                            'json'
                        );
                    }
                );
            }
        );
    }
);
```

Make the preceding modifications, load up the new document, and click the Save button. You should see something like Figure 7-3.

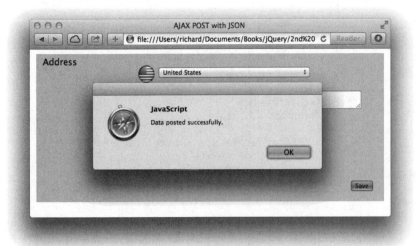

FIGURE 7-3

You've added a new event to the <input> element with the id name addressButton. When you click the <input> element, a POST request is initiated using jQuery's $.post() method. Of course, you have no HTTP server set up to transmit this data to, so, instead, you simply reference a static JSON file that lets you know the POST request succeeded at least as far as requesting the specified document. In the second argument to the $.post() method, you supply the data that you want to transmit to the server, just like you can do with the $.get() and $.getJSON() methods that you saw in the previous two sections. However, in addition to supporting an object literal, you can also provide a serialized string of URL-encoded key, value pairs. This is what the serialize() method provides; it encodes key, value pairs and creates a URL-encoded string from them. It searches within the <form> element for all <input>, <textarea>, and <select> elements automatically when you select a <form> element. You can also tell it specifically which <input>, <textarea>, or <select> elements you want to serialize by explicitly selecting those elements. That selection is then passed to jQuery's serialize() method, which finds the right names and values from the various input elements, formatting that data like so:

```
addressCountry=223
&addressStreet=123+Main+Street
&addressCity=Springfield
&addressState=23
&addressPostalCode=12345
```

This data appears as one unbroken line when it is passed to serialize(); some line breaks have been added here to make the string more readable. This data is now ready to be posted to the server, so all you have to do is pass this formatted data in the data argument of the $.post() method. This also works for jQuery's other AJAX request methods as well, and jQuery is smart enough to know when you're passing an object literal, as I demonstrated previously, and when you're passing a formatted query string, like you are here. Then, on the server side, all you have to do is access the posted data as you would normally work with POST request data.

LOADING HTML SNIPPETS FROM THE SERVER

In the previous sections, you've seen how to request data from the server using the XML and JSON data transport formats. The other popular way of transporting data from the server to the client asynchronously is via HTML snippets. Using this method, you request small chunks of HTML as you need them without the <html>, <head>, and <body> tags.

The following example (*Example 7-4*) demonstrates how to load snippets of HTML with jQuery's load() method:

```html
<!DOCTYPE HTML>
<html lang='en'>
    <head>
        <meta http-equiv='X-UA-Compatible' content='IE=Edge' />
        <meta charset='utf-8' />
        <title>Folder Tree</title>
        <script src='../jQuery.js'></script>
        <script src='../jQueryUI.js'></script>
        <script src='Example 7-4.js'></script>
        <link href='Example 7-4.css' rel='stylesheet' />
    </head>
    <body>
        <div id='folderTree'>
            <ul class='folderTree'>
                <li>
                    <div class='folderTreeDirectory folderTreeRoot'
                        data-id='1'
                        title='/'>
                        <span>Macintosh HD</span>
                    </div>
                    <ul class='folderTreeDirectoryBranchOn' data-id='1'>
                        <li class='folderTreeDirectoryBranch'>
                            <div class='folderTreeDirectory'
                                data-id='5175'
                                title='/Applications'>
                                <div class='folderTreeIcon'></div>
                                <span>Applications</span>
                            </div>
                            <img src='tree/right.png'
                                class='folderTreeHasChildren'
                                data-id='5175'
                                alt='+'
                                title='Click to expand.' />
                            <div class='folderTreeBranchWrapper'>
                            </div>
                        </li>
                        <li class='folderTreeDirectoryBranch folderTreeServer'>
                            <div class='folderTreeDirectory'
                                data-id='5198'
                                title='/Library'>
                                <div class='folderTreeIcon'></div>
                                <span>Library</span>
                            </div>
                            <img src='tree/right.png'
```

```
                                        class='folderTreeHasChildren'
                                        data-id='5198'
                                        alt='+'
                                        title='Click to expand.' />
                                <div class='folderTreeBranchWrapper'></div>
                            </li>
                            <li class='folderTreeDirectoryBranch'>
                                <div class='folderTreeDirectory'
                                    data-id='3667'
                                    title='/System'>
                                    <div class='folderTreeIcon'></div>
                                    <span>System</span>
                                </div>
                                <img src='tree/right.png'
                                    class='folderTreeHasChildren'
                                    data-id='5198'
                                    alt='+'
                                    title='Click to expand.' />
                                <div class='folderTreeBranchWrapper'></div>
                            </li>
                            <li class='folderTreeDirectoryBranch'>
                                <div class='folderTreeDirectory'
                                    data-id='5185'
                                    title='/Users'>
                                    <div class='folderTreeIcon'></div>
                                    <span>Users</span>
                                </div>
                                <img src='tree/right.png'
                                    class='folderTreeHasChildren'
                                    data-id='5185'
                                    alt='+'
                                    title='Click to expand.' />
                                <div class='folderTreeBranchWrapper'></div>
                            </li>
                        </ul>
                    </li>
                </ul>
            </div>
        </body>
</html>
```

This markup is styled with the following style sheet:

```
body {
    font: 13px "Lucida Grande", Arial, sans-serif;
    color: rgb(50, 50, 50);
    background: rgb(214, 221, 229);
    margin: 0;
    padding: 10px;
}
div#folderTree ul {
    list-style: none;
    padding: 0;
    margin: 0;
}
div.folderTreeRoot {
```

```css
        height: 28px;
        background: url('tree/internal.png') no-repeat left 1px;
        padding: 4px 0 0 28px;
    }
    li.folderTreeDirectoryBranch {
        position: relative;
        padding: 0 0 0 20px;
        zoom: 1;
    }
    img.folderTreeHasChildren {
        position: absolute;
        top: 3px;
        left: 0;
    }
    div.folderTreeIcon {
        background: url('tree/folder.png') no-repeat left;
        width: 16px;
        height: 16px;
        margin: 0 5px 0 0;
        float: left;
    }
    div.folderTreeBranchWrapper {
        display: none;
    }
```

Then the following JavaScript demonstrates how folders in a tree structure are loaded asynchronously. Each folder is an HTML snippet that loads separately from the server, which makes the initial download much smaller and the overall application much more efficient.

```javascript
$(document).ready(
    function()
    {
        $('img.folderTreeHasChildren').click(
            function()
            {
                var arrow = 'tree/down.png';

                if (!$(this).next().children('ul').length)
                {
                    $(this).next().load(
                        'Example%207-4/' +
                            $(this)
                                .prev()
                                .data('id') + '.html',
                        function()
                        {
                            $(this)
                                .show()
                                .prev()
                                .attr('src', arrow);
                        }
                    );
                }
                else
                {
```

```
            $(this).next().toggle();

            if ($(this).attr('src').indexOf('down') != -1)
            {
                arrow = 'tree/right.png';
            }

            $(this).attr('src', arrow);
        }
    }
);

}
);
```

All put together, the preceding code looks like Figure 7-4 when it is tested in a browser.

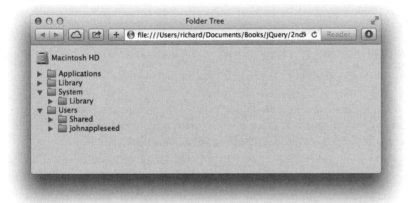

FIGURE 7-4

In the preceding script, a click event is attached to each <img> element in the HTML document. When the user clicks the <img> element, which is a gray arrow, the script first checks to see whether the folder's contents have already been requested, which is done by checking to see if the <img> element's next sibling, the <div> element with class name folderTreeBranchWrapper, has a child <ul> element. Whether that <ul> element exists is determined by the following expression:

```
if (!$(this).next().children('ul').length)
{
```

The next() method traverses the selection from the <img> to the <div> element, and the children() method looks at the children of the <div> method. Then the length property determines how many children <ul> elements exist. If there is a <ul> element, that means the folder's contents have already been requested from the server and loaded into the document. If there is not a <ul> element, then the folder's contents are requests from the server.

Loading directly in the document is done based on a selection. In this script, you select the <div> element with the class name folderTreeBranchWrapper, which is done with the call to $(this)

.next(). this references the <img> element, and next() causes the next sibling element to be selected, which is the <div> element. Then the load() method is chained directly to that selection. By chaining the load() method to the selection, you're telling jQuery where you want the HTML snippet to be inserted in the DOM.

The load() method otherwise works similarly to the other AJAX request methods that jQuery provides: You specify the URL of the document you want to request in the first argument. You can include an optional second argument that includes data that you want to send to the server via a GET request, and the third parameter is a callback function that is executed upon success of the request. Both providing data to send to the server and specifying a callback function are optional—if you like, you can simply call the load() method with only a URL, and that will work just fine as well.

The server responds with a snippet of HTML that is loaded directly into the document. The following is what the HTML snippet being loaded looks like:

```
<ul data-id="31490s">
    <li class="folderTreeDirectoryBranch">
        <div class="folderTreeDirectory" data-id="31491s" title="/Users/Shared">
            <div class="folderTreeIcon"></div>
            <span>Shared</span>
        </div>
        <img src="tree/right.png"
            class="folderTreeHasChildren" data-id="31491s" alt="+"
            title="Click to expand." />
        <div class="folderTreeBranchWrapper"></div>
    </li>
    <li class="folderTreeDirectoryBranch folderTreeServer">
        <div class="folderTreeDirectory" data-id="698482s" title="/Users/
johnappleseed">
            <div class="folderTreeIcon"></div>
            <span>johnappleseed</span>
        </div>
        <img src="tree/right.png"
            class="folderTreeHasChildren" data-id="698482s" alt="+"
            title="Click to expand." />
        <div class="folderTreeBranchWrapper"></div>
    </li>
</ul>
```

The preceding is the HTML snippet that is loaded upon clicking the arrow for the /Users folder. I've prepared HTML snippets for each of the top-level folders. In the source code download for this book, each of these is named using a numeric directory id. For example, /Applications has the id 5175, /Library has the id 5198, and so on. Each of these numeric ids is embedded in the data-id attribute of the <div> element with class name folderTreeDirectory that is present in the structure for each folder. Upon requesting the folder contents, the embedded numeric id is extracted with the following:

```
$(this).prev().data('id')
```

The preceding starts out at the <img> element, where the click originated, which is the $(this) portion of the code. Then you navigate to the preceding sibling with the prev() method and access its id attribute with data('id'). That's used to construct the filename of the HTML snippet to be loaded, which again wouldn't normally be requested as a static HTML file—for this kind of thing, you want a server-side script to do the heavy lifting. Each HTML snippet is located in a subfolder called *Example 7-4.*

After the request is made, the following callback function is executed:

```
function()
{
    $(this)
        .show()
        .prev()
        .attr('src', arrow);
}
```

The callback function is executed within the context of the <div> element with the class name folder-TreeBranchWrapper; this refers to that <div> element. By default, all the <div> elements with the class name folderTreeBranchWrapper are hidden by the inclusion of display: none in the style sheet; calling jQuery's show() method makes the <div> visible. Now all that's left to do is to change the orientation of the arrow from pointing right to pointing down to indicate that the folder is open, which is what the second bit of code in the callback function does. It changes the image referenced in the src attribute of the <div> element's preceding sibling, which is the <img> element housing the arrow.

That leaves what happens if the folder is already loaded:

```
    }
    else
    {
        $(this).next().toggle();

        if ($(this).attr('src').indexOf('down') != -1)
        {
            arrow = 'tree/right.png';
        }

        $(this).attr('src', arrow);
    }
```

If the folder already exists, you want to toggle the display of the folder on and off with each click of the arrow. The call to $(this).next().toggle() does exactly that: If the <div> element is visible, it's made invisible, and vice versa. The second bit of code toggles the orientation of the arrow by toggling between the right.png and down.png images.

DYNAMICALLY LOADING JAVASCRIPT

Another useful and innovative feature of jQuery is its capability to dynamically and asynchronously load JavaScript documents using its AJAX API. As covered in Chapter 1, "Introduction to jQuery," it is a recommended best practice to split JavaScript development into smaller, easier-to-digest modules that have narrowly focused tasks. Another technique that goes hand-in-hand with modular JavaScript development is loading the minimal required JavaScript at the initial page load and dynamically loading additional JavaScript via AJAX as it is needed to save page load time and to make applications more responsive.

In addition to modular JavaScript development, another reason you may want to load JavaScript via AJAX is to have JavaScript that changes dynamically, depending on user actions, or when you need to load more-complex applications that vary depending on user input or context.

Whatever use you find for this functionality, in this section, I walk you through the API that jQuery provides for loading JavaScript via its AJAX interface using the $.getScript() method. The following example demonstrates how to load the entire jQuery UI API asynchronously and then uses that API to produce an animation that transitions between two colors. This is demonstrated in the following document, *Example 7-5*:

```html
<!DOCTYPE HTML>
<html lang='en'>
    <head>
        <meta charset='utf-8' />
        <title>November 2013</title>
        <script type='text/javascript' src='../jQuery.js'></script>
        <script type='text/javascript' src='Example 7-5.js'></script>
        <link type='text/css' href='Example 7-5.css' rel='stylesheet' />
    </head>
    <body>
        <table class="calendarMonth" data-year="2013" data-month="11">
            <thead>
                <tr class="calendarHeading">
                    <th colspan="7">
                        <span class="calendarMonth">November</span>
                        <span class="calendarDay"></span>
                        <span class="calendarYear">2013</span>
                    </th>
                </tr>
                <tr class="calendarWeekdays">
                    <th>Sunday</th>
                    <th>Monday</th>
                    <th>Tuesday</th>
                    <th>Wednesday</th>
                    <th>Thursday</th>
                    <th>Friday</th>
                    <th>Saturday</th>
                </tr>
            </thead>
            <tbody>
                <tr>
                    <td class="calendarLastMonth">27</td>
                    <td class="calendarLastMonth">28</td>
                    <td class="calendarLastMonth">29</td>
                    <td class="calendarLastMonth">30</td>
                    <td class="calendarLastMonth calendarLastMonthLastDay">31</td>
                    <td class="calendarFirstDay">1</td>
                    <td>2</td>
                </tr>
                <tr>
                    <td>3</td>
                    <td>4</td>
                    <td>5</td>
                    <td>6</td>
                    <td>7</td>
                    <td>8</td>
                    <td>9</td>
                </tr>
```

```
            <tr>
                <td>10</td>
                <td>11</td>
                <td>12</td>
                <td>13</td>
                <td>14</td>
                <td>15</td>
                <td>16</td>
            </tr>
            <tr>
                <td>17</td>
                <td>18</td>
                <td>19</td>
                <td class="calendarToday">20</td>
                <td>21</td>
                <td>22</td>
                <td>23</td>
            </tr>
            <tr>
                <td>24</td>
                <td>25</td>
                <td>26</td>
                <td>27</td>
                <td>28</td>
                <td>29</td>
                <td class="calendarLastDay">30</td>
            </tr>
            <tr>
                <td colspan="7" class="calendarEmptyWeek"></td>
            </tr>
        </tbody>
    </table>
    </body>
</html>
```

The preceding HTML is styled with the following style sheet:

```
html,
body {
    width: 100%;
    height: 100%;
}
body {
    font: 14px Helvetica, Arial, sans-serif;
    margin: 0;
    padding: 0;
    color: rgb(128, 128, 128);
}
table.calendarMonth {
    table-layout: fixed;
    width: 100%;
    height: 100%;
    border-collapse: collapse;
    empty-cells: show;
}
table.calendarMonth tbody {
```

```css
    user-select: none;
    -webkit-user-select: none;
    -moz-user-select: none;
    -ms-user-select: none;
}
table.calendarMonth th {
    font-weight: 200;
    border: 1px solid rgb(224, 224, 224);
    padding: 10px;
}
tr.calendarHeading th {
    font: 24px Helvetica, Arial, sans-serif;
}
table.calendarMonth td {
    border: 1px solid rgb(224, 224, 224);
    vertical-align: top;
    padding: 10px;
}
td.calendarLastMonth,
td.calendarNextMonth {
    color: rgb(204, 204, 204);
    background: rgb(244, 244, 244);
}
td.calendarDaySelected {
    background: yellow;
}
tr.calendarWeekSelected {
    background: lightyellow;
}
td.calendarToday {
    background: gold;
}
```

Then the following JavaScript is applied:

```javascript
$(document).ready(
    function()
    {
        $.getScript(
            '../jQueryUI.js',
            function()
            {
                $('table.calendarMonth td:not(td.calendarLastMonth,
                    td.calendarNextMonth)').click(
                    function()
                    {
                        if ($(this).css('background-color') != 'rgb(200, 200,
200)')
                        {
                            $(this).animate({
                                'background-color' : 'rgb(200, 200, 200)'
                            },
                            1000
                            );
                        }
                        else
```

```
                            {
                                $(this).animate({
                                    'background-color' : 'rgb(255, 255, 255)'
                                },
                                1000
                            );
                        }
                    }
                );
            }
        );
    }
);
```

The JavaScript demonstrates how an external script is loaded via jQuery's $.getScript() method. The $.getScript() method takes two arguments: The path to the script that you want to load, and like jQuery's other AJAX request method, it also allows a callback function, which is executed when the script has been loaded and successfully executed.

Figure 7-5 shows a snapshot after the animation that takes place when you click a day in the calendar. The background-color animates from white to rgb(200, 200, 200) (a shade of gray) and when clicked again it animates from rgb(200, 200, 200) back to white, or rgb(255, 255, 255). jQuery animations are covered in more detail in Chapter 8, "Animation and Easing Effects."

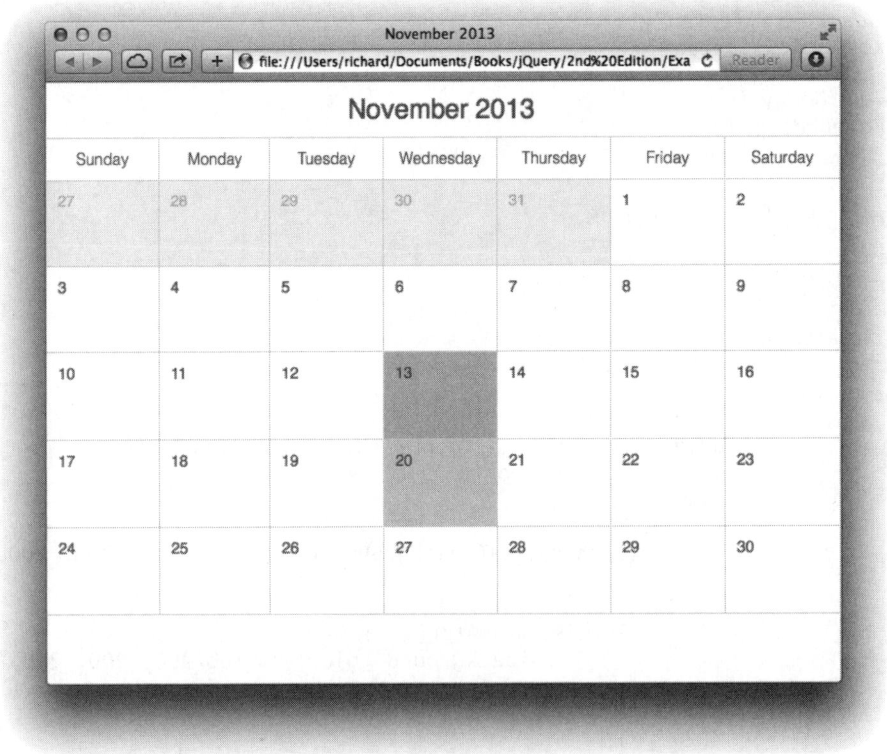

FIGURE 7-5

The script that you load for the example, jQueryUI.js, along with the source code for the example, is available with this book's source code download materials at www.wrox.com/go/webdevwithjquery.

AJAX EVENTS

This section covers what jQuery calls *AJAX events*. AJAX events are milestones that occur during an AJAX request that can give you feedback about the status of your request or allow you to execute code when each milestone occurs. Examples of milestones are when a request starts, when a request stops, when a request has been sent, when a request has failed, when a request is completed, and when a request is completely successful. I don't go into exhaustive detail about each of these events, but Appendix G has a full listing of all the AJAX methods, properties, and AJAX events supported by jQuery.

One example is how to show an activity indicator while some remote content is being fetched. An activity indicator is an animation that shows the user that something is happening, but it gives the user an indication to wait for that something to happen. There are three ways to do this. Two methods enable you to globally set AJAX events for all AJAX requests using jQuery's AJAX methods, and there is one way to set AJAX events per individual request using jQuery's ajax() method. This section describes how to make a loading message using each of these methods.

Adding jQuery AJAX events globally is easy—all you have to do is call jQuery's ajaxSetup() method. First, you need an activity indicator to show that something is taking place. Typically, an animated GIF is good enough to get the job done. In the following snippet, *Example 7-6*, from the folder tree example that I presented previously, I've added an animated GIF to display while activity is taking place:

```html
<!DOCTYPE HTML>
<html lang='en'>
    <head>
        <meta http-equiv='X-UA-Compatible' content='IE=Edge' />
        <meta charset='utf-8' />
        <title>Folder Tree</title>
        <script src='../jQuery.js'></script>
        <script src='../jQueryUI.js'></script>
        <script src='Example 7-6.js'></script>
        <link href='Example 7-6.css' rel='stylesheet' />
    </head>
    <body>
        <div id='folderTree'>
            <ul class='folderTree'>
                <li>
                    <div class='folderTreeDirectory folderTreeRoot'
                        data-id='1'
                        title='/'>
                        <span>Macintosh HD</span>
                    </div>
                    <ul class='folderTreeDirectoryBranchOn' data-id='1'>
                        <li class='folderTreeDirectoryBranch'>
                            <div class='folderTreeDirectory'
                                data-id='5175'
```

```
                    title='/Applications'>
                    <div class='folderTreeIcon'></div>
                    <span>Applications</span>
                </div>
                <img src='tree/right.png'
                    class='folderTreeHasChildren'
                    data-id='5175'
                    alt='+'
                    title='Click to expand.' />
                <div class='folderTreeBranchWrapper'>
                </div>
            </li>
            <li class='folderTreeDirectoryBranch folderTreeServer'>
                <div class='folderTreeDirectory'
                    data-id='5198'
                    title='/Library'>
                    <div class='folderTreeIcon'></div>
                    <span>Library</span>
                </div>
                <img src='tree/right.png'
                    class='folderTreeHasChildren'
                    data-id='5198'
                    alt='+'
                    title='Click to expand.' />
                <div class='folderTreeBranchWrapper'></div>
            </li>
            <li class='folderTreeDirectoryBranch'>
                <div class='folderTreeDirectory'
                    data-id='3667'
                    title='/System'>
                    <div class='folderTreeIcon'></div>
                    <span>System</span>
                </div>
                <img src='tree/right.png'
                    class='folderTreeHasChildren'
                    data-id='5198'
                    alt='+'
                    title='Click to expand.' />
                <div class='folderTreeBranchWrapper'></div>
            </li>
            <li class='folderTreeDirectoryBranch'>
                <div class='folderTreeDirectory'
                    data-id='5185'
                    title='/Users'>
                    <div class='folderTreeIcon'></div>
                    <span>Users</span>
                </div>
                <img src='tree/right.png'
                    class='folderTreeHasChildren'
                    data-id='5185'
                    alt='+'
                    title='Click to expand.' />
                <div class='folderTreeBranchWrapper'></div>
            </li>
```

```
                </ul>
              </li>
            </ul>
        </div>
        <div id='folderActivity'>
            <img src='tree/activity.gif' alt='Activity Indicator' />
        </div>
      </body>
  </html>
```

Then, some CSS is added to the example to put the activity indicator in the lower-right part of
the window.

```
body {
    font: 13px "Lucida Grande", Arial, sans-serif;
    color: rgb(50, 50, 50);
    background: rgb(214, 221, 229);
    margin: 0;
    padding: 10px;
}
div#folderTree ul {
    list-style: none;
    padding: 0;
    margin: 0;
}
div.folderTreeRoot {
    height: 28px;
    background: url('tree/internal.png') no-repeat left 1px;
    padding: 4px 0 0 28px;
}
li.folderTreeDirectoryBranch {
    position: relative;
    padding: 0 0 0 20px;
    zoom: 1;
}
img.folderTreeHasChildren {
    position: absolute;
    top: 3px;
    left: 0;
}
div.folderTreeIcon {
    background: url('tree/folder.png') no-repeat left;
    width: 16px;
    height: 16px;
    margin: 0 5px 0 0;
    float: left;
}
div.folderTreeBranchWrapper {
    display: none;
}
div#folderActivity {
    position: absolute;
    bottom: 5px;
    right: 5px;
```

```
        display: none;
    }
```

Then finally, the JavaScript is modified so that the activity indicator is dynamically revealed when an AJAX request takes place and hidden when the request concludes:

```
$(document).ready(
    function()
    {
        $.ajaxSetup({
            beforeSend : function(event, request, options)
            {
                $('div#folderActivity').show();
            },
            success : function(response, status, request)
            {
                $('div#folderActivity').hide();
            },
            error : function(request, status, error)
            {
                $('div#folderActivity').hide();
            }
        });

        $('img.folderTreeHasChildren').click(
            function()
            {
                var arrow = 'tree/down.png';

                if (!$(this).next().children('ul').length)
                {
                    $(this).next().load(
                        'Example%207-6/' +
                            $(this)
                                .prev()
                                .data('id') + '.html',
                        function()
                        {
                            $(this)
                                .show()
                                .prev()
                                .attr('src', arrow);
                        }
                    );
                }
                else
                {
                    $(this).next().toggle();

                    if ($(this).attr('src').indexOf('down') != -1)
                    {
                        arrow = 'tree/right.png';
```

```
                                }
                            $(this).attr('src', arrow);
                        }
                    }
                );

            }
        );
```

This modification looks like what you see in Figure 7-6, when you make an AJAX request. Because you're requesting a file from your own local computer, the activity indicator will be revealed and hidden almost instantaneously. So this technique is obviously better suited for requesting content from a remote server where there may be some latency.

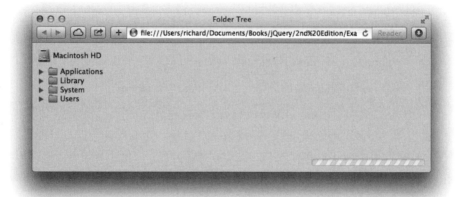

FIGURE 7-6

In the JavaScript, you make a call to `$.ajaxSetup()` to define events called beforeSend, success, and error. Each of these events is defined inside a JavaScript object literal that is passed to the `$.ajax-Setup()` method. By attaching a callback function to the beforeSend property, you are telling jQuery to execute the specified function before every AJAX request. In this case, you cause the activity indicator to be displayed by calling jQuery's show() method. Then, after the request has completed successfully, you hide the activity indicator by attaching a callback function to the success and error events, which, in turn, is executed upon a successful or failed request. (Another way to do this is to attach to the AJAX complete event, which executes when a request is completed, whether it was successful or failed.) These are but a few of the properties that you can specify using this method to define AJAX defaults globally for jQuery. All the options that can be specified here are outlined in detail in Appendix G.

You are not, of course, limited to this use of jQuery's AJAX events. jQuery's AJAX events can also modify the HTTP headers that will be used in the request or to do other low-level things with jQuery's AJAX API.

Using AJAX Event Methods

The preceding example defines events globally using the $.ajaxSetup() method. In the following example, *Example 7-7*, I demonstrate how to do the same using individual jQuery AJAX event methods. Only the script for the preceding example, *Example 7-6*, has been modified:

```
$(document).ready(
    function()
    {
        $(document)
            .ajaxSend(
                function(event, request, options)
                {
                    if (decodeURI(options.url).indexOf('Example 7-7') != -1)
                    {
                        $('div#folderActivity').show();
                    }
                }
            )
            .ajaxSuccess(
                function(response, status, request)
                {
                    if (decodeURI(options.url).indexOf('Example 7-7') != -1)
                    {
                        $('div#folderActivity').hide();
                    }
                }
            )
            .ajaxError(
                function(request, status, error)
                {
                    if (decodeURI(options.url).indexOf('Example 7-7') != -1)
                    {
                        $('div#folderActivity').hide();
                    }
                }
            );

        $('img.folderTreeHasChildren').click(
            function()
            {
                var arrow = 'tree/down.png';

                if (!$(this).next().children('ul').length)
                {
                    $(this).next()
                        .load(
                            'Example%207-7/' +
                                $(this)
                                    .prev()
                                    .data('id') + '.html',
                            function()
                            {
                                $(this)
```

```
                                        .show()
                                        .prev()
                                        .attr('src', arrow);
                                }
                            );
                        }
                        else
                        {
                            $(this).next().toggle();

                            if ($(this).attr('src').indexOf('down') != -1)
                            {
                                arrow = 'tree/right.png';
                            }

                            $(this).attr('src', arrow);
                        }
                    }
                );

            }
        );
```

The preceding modification gives you the same outcome demonstrated by *Example 7-6*, only this time the functions that reveal and hide the activity indicator are attached by using jQuery's AJAX event methods instead of the $.ajaxSetup() method. This example takes things one step further by taking a look at the options.url property, decoding URI encoded characters with a call to decodeURI(), and then limiting the application of the activity indicator based on the URI of the AJAX request. Things are set up similarly to *Example 7-6*; otherwise, you moved the callback function for the beforeSend property to inside the call to the ajaxSend() method, and the callback function for the success property to inside the call to the ajaxSuccess() method, and finally the call for the error property to inside the call to the ajaxError() method. And those methods are, of course, chainable like most of jQuery's other methods, but these methods must be applied to the document object and cannot be attached to just any HTML element object.

Attaching AJAX Events to Individual Requests

The last way that you can attach events is via a call to jQuery's more low-level ajax() method. The ajax() method is used internally, within jQuery, to construct AJAX requests for jQuery's other AJAX request methods, like $.get(), $getJSON(), $.post(), and so on. jQuery's $.ajax() method gives you the ability to set as many low-level AJAX request options as you like. *Example 7-8* demonstrates how to use $.ajax() to mimic the same results as the preceding two examples:

```
$(document).ready(
    function()
    {
        $('img.folderTreeHasChildren').click(
            function()
            {
                var arrow = 'tree/down.png';
```

```
if (!$(this).next().children('ul').length)
{
    var tree = $(this);

    var file = (
        $(this)
            .prev()
            .data('id') + '.html'
    );

    $.ajax({
        beforeSend : function(event, request, options)
        {
            $('div#folderActivity').show();
        },
        success : function(response, status, request)
        {
            $('div#folderActivity').hide();

            tree.attr('src', arrow)
                .next()
                .html(response)
                .show();
        },
        error : function(request, status, error)
        {
            $('div#folderActivity').hide();
        },
        url : 'Example%207-8/' + file,
        dataType : 'html'
    });
}
else
{
    $(this).next().toggle();

    if ($(this).attr('src').indexOf('down') != -1)
    {
        arrow = 'tree/right.png';
    }

    $(this).attr('src', arrow);
}
            }
        );

    }
);
```

The preceding example is functionally identical to the last two examples that you've seen in this section. Just like those other two examples, you are requesting the contents of each folder with each AJAX request, and you're showing an activity indicator that appears while the AJAX request is taking place and is hidden when it completes. Because the $.ajax() method works by calling that method of the jQuery object directly, you have to change your approach from using the load() method. First, because you want to load HTML, you need to remember what element you want to load that HTML into.

```
var tree = $(this);
```

$(this) is assigned to a variable called tree so that you can reference the variable tree from within the callback functions that you assign to the various options of the $.ajax() method. If you remember from *Example 7-4*, this refers to the <img> element containing the arrows that appear beside each folder. The $.ajax() method takes various options defined as an object literal, which are documented in Appendix G. You again define the beforeSend, success, and error options that contain functions that reveal and hide the activity indicator, but this time in the context of the AJAX request that you're making instead of globally.

If your request were successful, the rest of the code carries on like the code from *Example 7-4*. The <img> element is contained in the variable tree. The src of the <img> element is changed to 'tree/down.png'. The response variable in the success method contains the HTML text content of the response containing the subfolders. If this were an XML request, you'd be working with an XML object; if it were JSON, you'd be working with a JSON object. The HTML snippet is loaded into the next sibling <div> element that appears after the <img> element; then that <div> element is made visible with the show() method.

```
success : function(response, status, request)
{
    $('div#folderActivity').hide();

    tree.attr('src', arrow)
        .next()
        .html(response)
        .show();
},
```

jQuery's $.ajax() method allows for a great deal of request customization, which should be used when the other AJAX methods just don't provide the options that you need.

Sending a REST Request

The last example of using the $.ajax() method that I present is how to make and send a REST request. Sending a REST request with jQuery is straightforward; you must configure the type, contentType, dataType, and data properties to set up the REST call. Otherwise, your server must also be properly configured to receive calls to a REST service. This will include setting the Access-Control-Allow-Methods HTTP header on your server, which will allow HTTP request methods other than GET and POST. Properly setting up and configuring a web server to deliver a REST service is outside the scope of this book. You can, however, examine what is required on the client side for such a request utilizing jQuery's $.ajax() method. This is demonstrated in the following document, *Example 7-9*:

```
<!DOCTYPE HTML>
<html lang='en'>
    <head>
        <meta http-equiv='X-UA-Compatible' content='IE=Edge' />
        <meta charset='utf-8' />
```

```
            <title>REST Requests</title>
            <script src='../jQuery.js'></script>
            <script src='../jQueryUI.js'></script>
            <script src='Example 7-9.js'></script>
            <link href='Example 7-9.css' rel='stylesheet' />
        </head>
        <body>
            <form action='javascript:void(0);' method='post'>
                <fieldset>
                    <legend>Address</legend>
    <div id='addressCountryWrapper'>
        <label for='addressCountry'>
            <img src='flags/us.png' alt='Country' />
        </label>
        <select id='addressCountry' size='1' name='addressCountry'>
            <option value='0'>Please select a country</option>
            <option value='1'>Afghanistan</option>
            <option value='2'>Albania</option>
            <option value='3'>Algeria</option>
            <option value='4'>American Samoa</option>
            <option value='5'>Andorra</option>
```

The long list of countries has been snipped out. The complete file is available as part of this book's free source code download materials.

```
            <option value='222'>United Kingdom</option>
            <option value='223' selected='selected'>United States</option>
            <option value='224'>United States Minor Outlying Islands</option>
            <option value='225'>Uruguay</option>
            <option value='226'>Uzbekistan</option>
            <option value='227'>Vanuatu</option>
            <option value='228'>Vatican City State (Holy See)</option>
            <option value='229'>Venezuela</option>
            <option value='230'>Vietnam</option>
            <option value='231'>Virgin Islands (British)</option>
            <option value='232'>Virgin Islands (U.S.)</option>
            <option value='233'>Wallis and Futuna Islands</option>
            <option value='234'>Western Sahara</option>
            <option value='235'>Yemen</option>
            <option value='236'>Yugoslavia</option>
            <option value='237'>Zaire</option>
            <option value='238'>Zambia</option>
            <option value='239'>Zimbabwe</option>
        </select>
    </div>
    <div>
        <label for='addressStreet'>Street Address:</label>
        <textarea name='addressStreet'
                  id='addressStreet'
                  rows='2'
                  cols='50'></textarea>
    </div>
    <div>
        <label for='addressCity'>City:</label>
        <input type='text' name='addressCity' id='addressCity' size='25' />
    </div>
```

```
<div>
    <label for='addressState'>State:</label>
    <select name='addressState' id='addressState'>
    </select>
</div>
<div>
    <label for='addressPostalCode'>Postal Code:</label>
    <input type='text'
           name='addressPostalCode'
           id='addressPostalCode'
           size='10' />
</div>
<div id='addressButtonWrapper'>
    <input type='submit'
           id='addressButton'
           name='addressButton'
           value='Save' />
</div>
            </fieldset>
        </form>
    </body>
</html>
```

The preceding markup is combined with the following style sheet:

```
body {
    font: 12px "Lucida Grande", Arial, sans-serif;
    color: rgb(50, 50, 50);
    margin: 0;
    padding: 0 10px;
}
fieldset {
    background: orange;
    border: 1px solid rgb(200, 200, 200);
}
legend {
    position: relative;
    top: 13px;
    font-size: 16px;
}
fieldset div {
    padding: 5px;
    margin: 3px;
    clear: left;
}
fieldset label {
    float: left;
    width: 200px;
    text-align: right;
    padding: 2px 5px 0 0;
}
div#addressCountryWrapper img {
    position: relative;
    top: -4px;
}
```

```
div#addressButtonWrapper {
    text-align: right;
}
```

Finally, the following JavaScript demonstrates a REST request using the ADD method:

```
$(document).ready(
    function()
    {
        $('select#addressCountry').click(
            function()
            {
                $.getJSON(
                    'Example 7-9/' + this.value + '.json',
                    function(json)
                    {
                        // Swap out the flag image
                        $('div#addressCountryWrapper img').attr({
                            alt : json.name,
                            src : 'flags/' + json.iso2.toLowerCase() + '.png'
                        });

                        // Remove all of the options
                        $('select#addressState').empty();

                        // Set the states...
                        $.each(
                            json.states,
                            function(id, state)
                            {
                                $('select#addressState').append(
                                    $('<option/>')
                                        .attr('value', id)
                                        .text(state)
                                );
                            }
                        );

                        // Change the label
                        $('label[for="addressState"]').text(
                            json.label + ':'
                        );
                    }
                );
            }
        );

        $('select#addressCountry').click();

        $('input#addressButton').click(
            function(event)
            {
                event.preventDefault();

                var data = {
                    country : $('select#addressCountry').val(),
```

```
                    street : $('textarea#addressStreet').val(),
                    city : $('input#addressCity').val(),
                    state : $('select#addressState').val(),
                    postalCode : $('input#addressPostalCode').val()
                };

                $.ajax({
                    url : 'Example%207-9/ADD.json',
                    contentType : "application/json; charset=utf-8",
                    type : 'ADD',
                    dataType : 'json',
                    data : JSON.stringify(data),
                    success : function(json, status, request)
                    {
                        if (parseInt(json) > 0)
                        {
                            alert('Data added successfully.');
                        }
                    },
                    error : function(request, status)
                    {

                    }
                });
            }
        );
    }
);
```

If you use this example with a properly configured server, you will note that the request is sent to the server along with a payload of JSON formatted data that can be decoded into an object on the server side. The screen shot shows submitting data via the ADD method to my own server, which has been configured with the Access-Control-Allow-Methods HTTP header, making it possible to submit REST requests. Figure 7-7 shows the address form.

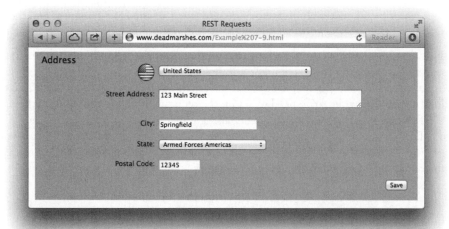

FIGURE 7-7

Figure 7-8 shows Safari's web inspector, which shows the request data sent along to the server.

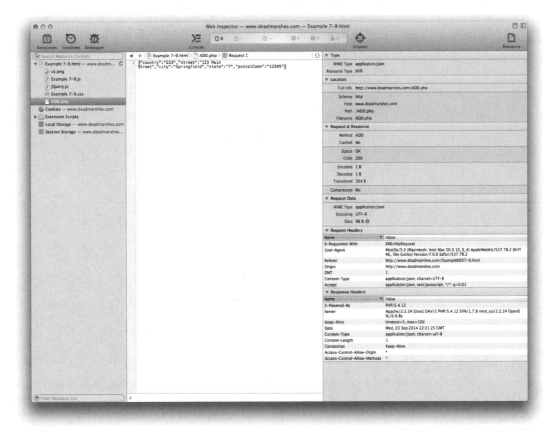

FIGURE 7-8

Figure 7-9 shows a closer look at the web inspector's detailed view of the HTTP request and the server's response.

This example shows you that setting up a REST request on the client side is easy, but you need to have the right server-side configuration to complete an implementation. Implementing a REST service call is as easy as pointing your client-side app to a server configured to handle the additional request methods that REST provides. You need to set up the request to specify the right method, such as GET, POST, DELETE, or ADD, which is done using jQuery's type property with the $.ajax() method. Then if you intend to pass JSON data between the server and client, you also need to set the contentType, dataType, and data properties. The contentType tells the server what to expect in the body of the request. The dataType property tells jQuery what type of data to expect in the server's response, and the data property passes along the data to be placed in the body of the HTTP request to the server. The data assigned to the data property will then be accessible on the server side. In this example, the data is passed with JSON formatting. On the server side, you would then need to decode the JSON formatted data into an object.

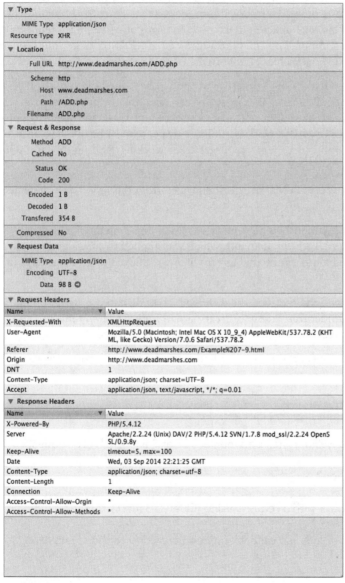

FIGURE 7-9

SUMMARY

This chapter took you on a tour of jQuery's built-in AJAX capabilities. You saw the differences between a GET and a POST HTTP request, learning that a GET request has a limit on its length, in addition to being semantically suited for requests that result in no lasting modification or effect on the server. POST requests, in contrast, should be reserved for requests that shouldn't be arbitrarily repeated and do have some kind of lasting impact on the server. In terms of AJAX, GET requests have a slight performance advantage. In addition, you can take advantage of REST to make your requests even more semantic, adding method verbs such as ADD or DELETE to the existing GET and POST.

jQuery offers the `$.get()` method to make GET requests and the `$.post()` method to make POST requests. When you work with XML, jQuery makes it super-easy to extract information from an XML document by giving you full access to jQuery's various selection methods for querying your XML responses. The JSON format is easier to work with, but extra care must be taken to ensure that you don't make yourself vulnerable to a cross-site forgery. For working with JSON data, jQuery offers the `$.getJSON()` method.

You can use the `load()` method to insert HTML snippets requested from the server into elements that you select with jQuery.

I described how to load script asynchronously with jQuery's `$.getScript()` method. This was demonstrated by loading the jQuery UI API on demand, which was applied to the calendar you made in *Example 7-5*, and provided a nifty animated effect when you clicked the various days in the calendar.

I talked about jQuery's AJAX events and described the different ways you can use AJAX events to add an activity indicator to the folder tree example, creating *Example 7-6*, *Example 7-7*, and *Example 7-8* demonstrating the different ways that AJAX events can be utilized.

Finally, I demonstrated how to use jQuery's `$.ajax()` method to create a request to a server implementing REST services.

EXERCISES

1. For an AJAX request, is there any difference between a GET and a POST HTTP request?

2. What does a REST service provide?

3. How would you provide extra data with a request using jQuery's `$.get()` method?

4. How would you access a JSON object in a callback function provided to the `$.getJSON()` method?

5. Given the following XML, how would you access the contents of the `<response>` element, assuming you used jQuery's `$.get()` method to request the XML document?

   ```
   <?xml version="1.0" encoding="UTF-8" standalone="yes"?>
   <response>Yes!</response>
   ```

6. If you wanted to load an HTML snippet into a selection of elements, what jQuery method would you use?

7. In the following JavaScript, describe the purpose of each property's callback function:

```
$.ajaxSetup({
    beforeSend : function()
    {

    },
    success : function()
    {

    },
    error : function()
    {

    },
    complete : function()
    {

    }
});
```

8. If you wanted to attach AJAX events to apply only in the context of an individual AJAX request, rather than globally, what methods does jQuery provide to attach events in this way?

9. What jQuery method would you use if you wanted to get the value of every input element within a form?

10. How would you go about implementing a client-side request to a REST service providing the DELETE method where you pass a JSON object along to the server within the request? Describe the configuration you would need to accomplish this and then provide example code.

Animation and Easing Effects

jQuery does a lot to make the life of a developer easier, but jQuery does not stop at making it easier to traverse the DOM, or manipulate, or iterate, or all the other cool things you've learned about in the preceding chapters. It also gives you the tools to make your documents look polished, professional, and sophisticated via animation and a plethora of special effects. This chapter presents how to work with the API that jQuery provides for dealing with effects.

As you've seen in examples in previous chapters, jQuery can toggle the display of elements between hidden and displayed states using its show() and hide() methods. What you may not have already learned is that those methods also have the ability to animate between hidden and displayed states via a short animation.

jQuery also gives you the ability to animate an element between hidden and displayed states by animating an element's height, in addition to the ability to fade elements on and off via an animation of an element's opacity, all with a simple and trivial function call.

Finally, jQuery also has the cability to animate objects in your document between arbitrary numeric styles, which gives you the ability to create your own, custom animations.

SHOWING AND HIDING ELEMENTS

jQuery provides three methods for showing and hiding elements: show(), hide(), and toggle(). You've seen examples of show() and hide() in previous chapters. By default, these three methods simply make an object visible or invisible by toggling that element's CSS display property. These methods make it easier to turn elements on or off. What you haven't learned about these properties yet is that you can also supply arguments to these methods that customize an animation of the transition from visible to invisible or vice versa via easings. Easings are algorithms that control how an animation progresses over time. For example, an animation may begin quickly, and as time goes on, the transformation may become slower or faster. An algorithm determines how time is applied to the animation. Easings may be visualized as a single line on a graph that represents how time is altered and applied throughout the duration of an animation. Easings may also alter the animation. For example, an easing that includes bouncing can produce a transition in which the transformation of an object appears to bounce. When animating the width of an object, a bounce easing is apparent as the width becomes smaller, then snaps larger, and then snaps smaller again, giving the appearance of bouncing. The easing in this case applies an algorithm that controls the animation of width over time, with points in time where the animation temporarily goes backward and then forward again until the duration is met to produce the appearance of bouncing.

These easing effects are all prepackaged into presets that you can utilize in your scripts by calling a method in jQuery with an argument or option that references the name of the easing preset. Not all the easing presets are included in the default jQuery download; only 'linear' and 'swing' are included. Additional easings must be downloaded separately from the jQuery UI website at www. jqueryui.com/download/. The examples in this chapter include jQuery UI with all optional easings and UI components included. The jQuery UI file is included in the source code materials download for this book available for free from www.wrox.com/go/webdevwithjquery and is named *jQueryUI.js*.

Potential animations include fading, sliding, swinging, and a whole suite of additional effects. In addition to the animations built in and included with jQuery, you can create your own completely custom animations using jQuery's animate() method, as discussed in the section "Custom Animation."

You can also supply a callback function to any of jQuery's animation methods, which is executed when animation completes. And if that doesn't provide enough flexibility, you can also supply a configuration object that supports a comprehensive list of options that cover additional callback function scenarios, as well as tweaking all aspects of the animation.

The following example demonstrates how to animate show and hide element transitions using jQuery's show(), hide(), and toggle() methods. The toggle() method, as the name implies, encompasses both show() and hide() functionality in a single method, switching back and forth depending on whether the element is visible when animation commences.

```html
<!DOCTYPE HTML>
<html lang='en'>
    <head>
        <meta charset='utf-8' />
        <title>Animation and Effects</title>
        <script src='../jQuery.js'></script>
        <script src='../jQueryUI.js'></script>
        <script src='Example 8-1.js'></script>
        <link href='Example 8-1.css' rel='stylesheet' />
    </head>
    <body>
        <div id='exampleDialogCanvas'>
            <div id='exampleDialog'>
                <h4>Integer Feugiat Fringilla</h4>
                <p>
                    Lorem ipsum dolor sit amet, consectetuer adipiscing elit.
                    Ut vestibulum ornare augue. Fusce non purus vel libero
                    mattis aliquet. Vivamus interdum consequat risus. Integer
                    feugiat fringilla est. Vivamus libero. Vestibulum
                    imperdiet arcu vitae nunc. Nunc est velit, varius sed,
                    faucibus quis.
                </p>
            </div>
        </div>
        <form method='get' action='#'>
            <fieldset>
```

```
<legend>Animation Options</legend>
<div>
    <label for='exampleAnimationEasing'>
        Easing:
    </label>
    <select name='exampleAnimationEasing'
            id='exampleAnimationEasing'>
        <option value='linear'>linear</option>
        <option value='swing'>swing</option>
        <option value='easeInQuad'>easeInQuad</option>
        <option value='easeOutQuad'>easeOutQuad</option>
        <option value='easeInOutQuad'>easeInOutQuad</option>
        <option value='easeInCubic'>easeInCubic</option>
        <option value='easeOutCubic'>easeOutCubic</option>
        <option value='easeInOutCubic'>easeInOutCubic</option>
        <option value='easeInQuart'>easeInQuart</option>
        <option value='easeOutQuart'>easeOutQuart</option>
        <option value='easeInOutQuart'>easeInOutQuart</option>
        <option value='easeInQuint'>easeInQuint</option>
        <option value='easeOutQuint'>easeOutQuint</option>
        <option value='easeInOutQuint'>easeInOutQuint</option>
        <option value='easeInExpo'>easeInExpo</option>
        <option value='easeOutExpo'>easeOutExpo</option>
        <option value='easeInOutExpo'>easeInOutExpo</option>
        <option value='easeInSine'>easeInSine</option>
        <option value='easeOutSine'>easeOutSine</option>
        <option value='easeInOutSine'>easeInOutSine</option>
        <option value='easeInCirc'>easeInCirc</option>
        <option value='easeOutCirc'>easeOutCirc</option>
        <option value='easeInOutCirc'>easeInOutCirc</option>
        <option value='easeInElastic'>easeInElastic</option>
        <option value='easeOutElastic'>easeOutElastic</option>
        <option value='easeInOutElastic'>easeInOutElastic</option>
        <option value='easeInBack'>easeInBack</option>
        <option value='easeOutBack'>easeOutBack</option>
        <option value='easeInOutBack'>easeInOutBack</option>
        <option value='easeInBounce'>easeInBounce</option>
        <option value='easeOutBounce'>easeOutBounce</option>
        <option value='easeInOutBounce'>easeInOutBounce</option>
    </select>
    <label for='exampleAnimationDuration'>
        Duration:
    </label>
    <input type='range'
           value='5000'
           min='100'
           max='10000'
           step='100'
           name='exampleAnimationDuration'
           id='exampleAnimationDuration' />
    <input type='submit'
           name='exampleAnimationShow'
           id='exampleAnimationShow'
           value='Show' />
    <input type='submit'
```

```
                              name='exampleAnimationHide'
                              id='exampleAnimationHide'
                              value='Hide' />
                    <input type='submit'
                              name='exampleAnimationToggle'
                              id='exampleAnimationToggle'
                              value='Toggle' />
              </div>
           </fieldset>
        </form>
     </body>
  </html>
```

The following style sheet is applied to the preceding markup document:

```
body {
    font: 12px 'Lucida Grande', Arial, sans-serif;
    background: #fff;
    color: rgb(50, 50, 50);
}
div#exampleDialogCanvas {
    height: 400px;
    position: relative;
    overflow: hidden;
}
div#exampleDialog {
    box-shadow: 0 7px 100px rgba(0, 0, 0, 0.7);
    border-radius: 4px;
    width: 300px;
    height: 200px;
    position: absolute;
    padding: 10px;
    top: 50%;
    left: 50%;
    z-index: 1;
    margin: -110px 0 0 -160px;
    background: #fff;
}
div#exampleDialog h4 {
    border: 1px solid rgb(50, 50, 50);
    background: lightblue;
    border-radius: 4px;
    padding: 5px;
    margin: 0 0 10px 0;
}
div#exampleDialog p {
    margin: 10px 0;
}
input#exampleAnimationDuration {
    vertical-align: middle;
}
```

The following script demonstrates the animations provided by jQuery's show(), hide(), and toggle() methods:

```
$(document).ready(
    function()
    {
        var animating = false;

        $('input#exampleAnimationShow').click(
            function(event)
            {
                event.preventDefault();

                if (!animating)
                {
                    animating = true;

                    var easing = $('select#exampleAnimationEasing').val();
                    var duration = parseInt($('input#exampleAnimationDuration').val());

                    $('div#exampleDialog').show(
                        duration,
                        easing,
                        function()
                        {
                            animating = false;
                        }
                    );
                }
            }
        );

        $('input#exampleAnimationHide').click(
            function(event)
            {
                event.preventDefault();

                if (!animating)
                {
                    animating = true;

                    var easing = $('select#exampleAnimationEasing').val();
                    var duration = parseInt($('input#exampleAnimationDuration').val());

                    $('div#exampleDialog').hide(
                        duration,
                        easing,
                        function()
                        {
                            animating = false;
                        }
                    );

                }
            }
        );
```

```
$('input#exampleAnimationToggle').click(
    function(event)
    {
        event.preventDefault();

        if (!animating)
        {
            animating = true;

            var easing = $('select#exampleAnimationEasing').val();
            var duration = parseInt($('input#exampleAnimationDuration').val());

            $('div#exampleDialog').toggle(
                duration,
                easing,
                function()
                {
                    animating = false;
                }
            );
        }
    }
);

$('input#exampleAnimationDuration').change(
    function()
    {
        $(this).attr('title', $(this).val());
    }
);
    }
);
```

The preceding example is *Example 8-1* in the source code download materials. Figure 8-1 shows the results of loading up *Example 8-1.html* in a browser.

In *Example 8-1*, you created an application that allows you to test the most-used aspects of the show(), hide(), and toggle() methods. This includes testing every possible type of easing offered in both default jQuery and the various easing extensions offered as part of jQuery UI. All the easings offered by jQuery are specified in the <select> element that you created to make it easy to test each easing.

Along with easing, you also provide a duration to each method that is provided by the <input> range element. The duration argument is specified in milliseconds; 1,000 milliseconds equal 1 second. Aside from providing an integer value representing the number of milliseconds, you can also provide a duration-preset string. jQuery offers three duration-preset strings: 'slow', 'normal', and 'fast'. If no duration is specified, the default duration is the 'normal' preset.

The script that you created begins by setting up a variable to keep track of whether an animation is in progress. The purpose of this variable is to prevent multiple animations from backing up and occurring one after another by repeatedly clicking any of the buttons while an animation is in progress. When an animation is initiated, the animating variable is set to true, which prevents additional animations from occurring while that initial animation is in progress. When an animation completes, the callback function provided to each method is executed and the animating variable is reset to false, which allows a new animation to take place.

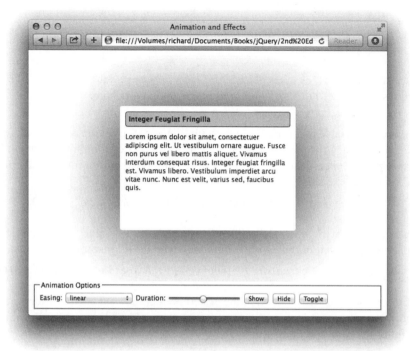

FIGURE 8-1

```
$(document).ready(
    function()
    {
        var animating = false;
```

Next, you set up a click() event on the <input> element with the id name exampleAnimationShow.

```
$('input#exampleAnimationShow').click(
    function(event)
    {
        event.preventDefault();

        if (!animating)
        {
            animating = true;

            var easing = $('select#exampleAnimationEasing').val();
            var duration = parseInt($('input#exampleAnimationDuration').val());

            $('div#exampleDialog').show(
                duration,
                easing,
                function()
                {
                    animating = false;
                }
```

```
            );
        }
    }
);
```

The first thing that happens when a click takes place is the event.preventDefault() method. This prevents the <form> from submitting to the URL specified in the action attribute.

```
animating = true;
```

You then check the animating variable to ensure that an animation is not in progress. If the value of the animating variable is false, then the next statement dependent on that condition is executed. If the value of the animating variable is true, then nothing happens and the callback function supplied to the click() method concludes execution.

```
var easing = $('select#exampleAnimationEasing').val();
```

The value of the <select> element with id name exampleAnimationEasing is assigned to the easing variable, which goes on to be provided in the *easing* argument of the show() method.

```
var duration = parseInt($('input#exampleAnimationDuration').val());
```

Likewise, the value of the <input> element with id name exampleAnimationDuration is converted to an integer data type with parseInt() and assigned to the duration variable. The duration variable then goes on to stand in for the *duration* argument of the show() method.

```
$('div#exampleDialog').show(
    duration,
    easing,
    function()
    {
        animating = false;
    }
);
```

The show() method is applied to the <div> with the id name exampleDialog.

All the arguments provided to the show() method are optional. If the show() method is called with no arguments, no animation takes place and only the CSS display property is set to display the element; for a <div> element the display property would be set to block. If only the *duration* argument is specified, the action of displaying the element is animated via the provided duration with the default easing 'swing'.

The callback function provided to the show() method is executed when the animation has completed. In this case, the callback function resets the value of the animating variable to false so that additional animations can take place.

The remainder of the script repeats the logic of the click() event assigned to the <input> element with the id name exampleAnimationShow on two additional <input> elements. The <input> with id name exampleAnimationHide receives a similar click() event that swaps out the show() method for the hide() method. Likewise, the <input> element with id name exampleAnimationToggle receives a click() event that swaps out the show() method for the toggle() method, which completes this demonstration of the show(), hide(), and toggle() methods.

SLIDING ELEMENTS

jQuery also provides the ability to animate an element by sliding. *Sliding* in jQuery is animating an element's height. *Sliding down* animates an element's height from nothing to its normal height. *Sliding up* animates an element's height from its normal height to nothing. These two actions are accomplished using the slideDown(), slideUp(), and slideToggle() methods.

Sliding is another way to reveal and hide elements—you just use a different animation to accomplish the task. The slideDown(), slideUp(), and slideToggle() methods are demonstrated in the following example, which modifies the document created in *Example 8-1*. This document also appears in the source code download materials as *Example 8-2*. To save space, the following example shows only the differences between *Example 8-1* and *Example 8-2*.

```
<input type='submit'
       name='exampleAnimationShow'
       id='exampleAnimationShow'
       value='Slide Down' />
<input type='submit'
       name='exampleAnimationHide'
       id='exampleAnimationHide'
       value='Slide Up' />
<input type='submit'
       name='exampleAnimationToggle'
       id='exampleAnimationToggle'
       value='Toggle Slide' />
    </div>
</fieldset>
```

In the HTML document, only the value attributes of the submit <input> elements are modified to reflect the updated actions.

The only modification to the style sheet is to the background color of the <h4> element within the dialog. This is done so that you can more easily see a difference between *Example 8-1* and *Example 8-2* when testing the script in a browser.

```
div#exampleDialog h4 {
    border: 1px solid rgb(50, 50, 50);
    background: lightgreen;
    border-radius: 4px;
    padding: 5px;
    margin: 0 0 10px 0;
}
```

The following script replaces the show(), hide(), and toggle() methods from *Example 8-1* with the slideDown(), slideUp(), and slideToggle() methods.

```
$(document).ready(
    function()
    {
        var animating = false;

        $('input#exampleAnimationShow').click(
            function(event)
```

```
    {
        event.preventDefault();

        if (!animating)
        {
            animating = true;

            var easing = $('select#exampleAnimationEasing').val();
            var duration = parseInt($('input#exampleAnimationDuration').val());

            $('div#exampleDialog').slideDown(
                duration,
                easing,
                function()
                {
                    animating = false;
                }
            );
        }
    }
);

$('input#exampleAnimationHide').click(
    function(event)
    {
        event.preventDefault();

        if (!animating)
        {
            animating = true;

            var easing = $('select#exampleAnimationEasing').val();
            var duration = parseInt($('input#exampleAnimationDuration').val());

            $('div#exampleDialog').slideUp(
                duration,
                easing,
                function()
                {
                    animating = false;
                }
            );

        }
    }
);

$('input#exampleAnimationToggle').click(
    function(event)
    {
        event.preventDefault();

        if (!animating)
        {
            animating = true;
```

```
                    var easing = $('select#exampleAnimationEasing').val();
                    var duration = parseInt($('input#exampleAnimationDuration').val());

                    $('div#exampleDialog').slideToggle(
                        duration,
                        easing,
                        function()
                        {
                            animating = false;
                        }
                    );
                }
            }
        );

        $('input#exampleAnimationDuration').change(
            function()
            {
                $(this).attr('title', $(this).val());
            }
        );
    }
);
```

The preceding script results in the document that you see in Figure 8-2.

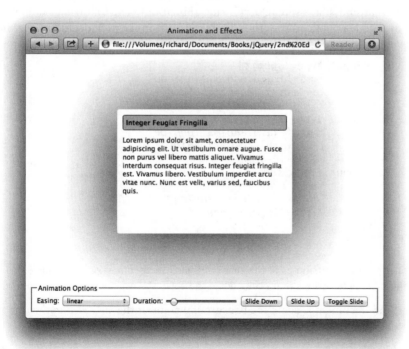

FIGURE 8-2

The preceding example repeats the logic of *Example 8-1*, swapping out show(), hide(), and toggle() for slideDown(), slideUp(), and slideToggle(). The setup is exactly the same, only the animation is different. The arguments provided to these three methods are exactly the same as the arguments provided to show(), hide(), and toggle(). *Example 8-2* allows you to test every possible variation of utilizing the slideDown(), slideUp(), and slideToggle() animations in your own scripts.

Refer to *Example 8-1* for a detailed explanation of the logic taking place in *Example 8-2*. The next section presents a demonstration of the last trio of built-in jQuery methods that provide animations for showing and hiding elements: the fadeIn(), fadeOut(), and fadeToggle() methods.

FADING ELEMENTS

Fading elements is another variation that jQuery offers for revealing and hiding elements via an animation that takes an element from fully opaque to fully transparent or vice versa. After a fade in is started, or a fade out has been completed, the CSS display property is toggled, so an element that has been faded out no longer takes up space in the document, or an element that is fading in is visible in the document.

The API is the same as the methods of the preceding two sections; only the names of those methods and the animation used by those methods are different. jQuery offers three methods for fading elements: fadeIn(), fadeOut(), and fadeToggle().

The following example demonstrates the trio of fading methods provided by jQuery. Again the example is the same concept provided in *Example 8-1* and *Example 8-2*, with only a few tweaks so that you can observe what's possible using jQuery's fade animations. The following example is *Example 8-3* in the source code download materials. Only the portions of each document that have been changed are quoted to conserve space.

```
<input type='submit'
       name='exampleAnimationShow'
       id='exampleAnimationShow'
       value='Fade In' />
<input type='submit'
       name='exampleAnimationHide'
       id='exampleAnimationHide'
       value='Fade Out' />
<input type='submit'
       name='exampleAnimationToggle'
       id='exampleAnimationToggle'
       value='Toggle Fade' />
    </div>
</fieldset>
```

In *Example 8-3.html* only the value attributes of the submit <input> elements have been changed. These are given labels that reflect the fade actions that occur when the submit <input> elements are pressed.

The only change to the CSS document is again the background color of the <h4> element within the dialog; this time the background is set to yellow.

```
div#exampleDialog h4 {
    border: 1px solid rgb(50, 50, 50);
```

```
        background: yellow;
        border-radius: 4px;
        padding: 5px;
        margin: 0 0 10px 0;
    }
```

The following script demonstrates the fadeIn(), fadeOut(), and fadeToggle() methods.

```
$(document).ready(
    function()
    {
        var animating = false;

        $('input#exampleAnimationShow').click(
            function(event)
            {
                event.preventDefault();

                if (!animating)
                {
                    animating = true;

                    var easing = $('select#exampleAnimationEasing').val();
                    var duration = parseInt($('input#exampleAnimationDuration').val());

                    $('div#exampleDialog').fadeIn(
                        duration,
                        easing,
                        function()
                        {
                            animating = false;
                        }
                    );
                }
            }
        );

        $('input#exampleAnimationHide').click(
            function(event)
            {
                event.preventDefault();

                if (!animating)
                {
                    animating = true;

                    var easing = $('select#exampleAnimationEasing').val();
                    var duration = parseInt($('input#exampleAnimationDuration').val());

                    $('div#exampleDialog').fadeOut(
                        duration,
                        easing,
                        function()
```

```
                        {
                            animating = false;
                        }
                    );


                }
            }
        );

        $('input#exampleAnimationToggle').click(
            function(event)
            {
                event.preventDefault();

                if (!animating)
                {
                    animating = true;

                    var easing = $('select#exampleAnimationEasing').val();
                    var duration = parseInt($('input#exampleAnimationDuration').val());

                    $('div#exampleDialog').fadeToggle(
                        duration,
                        easing,
                        function()
                        {
                            animating = false;
                        }
                    );
                }
            }
        );

        $('input#exampleAnimationDuration').change(
            function()
            {
                $(this).attr('title', $(this).val());
            }
        );
    }
);
```

The preceding example results are shown in Figure 8-3.

FIGURE 8-3

CUSTOM ANIMATION

jQuery also provides an API that facilitates custom animation using the `animate()` method. jQuery's `animate()` method transitions any CSS properties with numeric values over the specified *duration*. This makes it possible to arbitrarily animate `width`, `height`, `margin`, `padding`, `border-width`, or any other property with a numeric value. The `animate()` method automatically pulls the starting values from the style properties that are present when animation begins, and those properties are transitioned over the specified *duration* using the specified *easing* algorithm.

The following example, *Example 8-4*, demonstrates how to use the `animate()` method using the same example that you used for the previous three examples. As with *Example 8-3* and *Example 8-2*, only the portions of the HTML document that have been changed from the other examples are provided.

```
<label for='exampleAnimationDuration'>
    Duration:
</label>
<input type='range'
```

```
                            value='5000'
                            min='100'
                            max='10000'
                            step='100'
                            name='exampleAnimationDuration'
                            id='exampleAnimationDuration' />
                  <input type='submit'
                            name='exampleAnimationGrow'
                            id='exampleAnimationGrow'
                            value='Grow' />
                  <input type='submit'
                            name='exampleAnimationShrink'
                            id='exampleAnimationShrink'
                            value='Shrink' />
            </div>
         </fieldset>
```

The following CSS shows only the portion that changes from *Example 8-3*.

```css
div#exampleDialog h4 {
    border: 1px solid rgb(50, 50, 50);
    background: pink;
    border-radius: 4px;
    padding: 5px;
    margin: 0 0 10px 0;
}
```

The following script demonstrates the animate() method.

```javascript
$(document).ready(
    function()
    {
        var animating = false;

        $('input#exampleAnimationGrow').click(
            function(event)
            {
                event.preventDefault();

                if (!animating)
                {
                    animating = true;

                    var easing = $('select#exampleAnimationEasing').val();
                    var duration = parseInt($('input#exampleAnimationDuration').val());

                    $('div#exampleDialog').animate(
                        {
                            width : '400px',
                            height : '350px',
                            marginLeft : '-210px',
                            marginTop : '-185px'
                        },
```

```
                            duration,
                            easing,
                            function()
                            {
                                animating = false;
                            }
                    );
                }
            }
        );

        $('input#exampleAnimationShrink').click(
            function(event)
            {
                event.preventDefault();

                if (!animating)
                {
                    animating = true;

                    var easing = $('select#exampleAnimationEasing').val();
                    var duration = parseInt($('input#exampleAnimationDuration').val());

                    $('div#exampleDialog').animate(
                        {
                            width : '300px',
                            height : '200px',
                            marginLeft : '-160px',
                            marginTop : '-110px'
                        },
                        duration,
                        easing,
                        function()
                        {
                            animating = false;
                        }
                    );

                }
            }
        );

        $('input#exampleAnimationDuration').change(
            function()
            {
                $(this).attr('title', $(this).val());
            }
        );
    }
);
```

The preceding example is shown in Figure 8-4, when you click the *Grow* button.

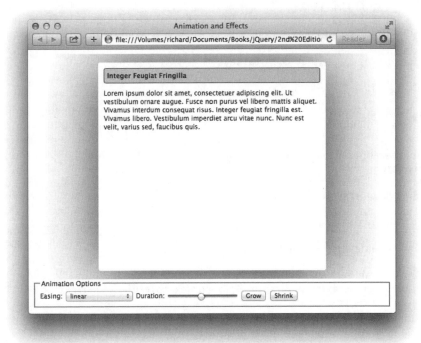

FIGURE 8-4

When you click the *Grow* button, the animate() method animates a transition in the <div> with the id name exampleDialog from the width, height, and margin that are specified in the style sheet.

```
$('div#exampleDialog').animate(
    {
        width : '400px',
        height : '350px',
        marginLeft : '-210px',
        marginTop : '-185px'
    },
    duration,
    easing,
    function()
    {
        animating = false;
    }
);
```

The width is animated from 300px to 400px, the height from 200px to 350px, the margin-left from -160px to -210px, and the margin-top from -110px to -185px. All four of these properties are animated at the same time, at the same rate determined by the *duration* and the *easing* selections. With the exception of the specification of custom CSS properties to animate, the animate() method is otherwise similar to the methods introduced in the earlier sections of this chapter.

Although the `animate()` method is limited to animating numeric CSS properties, jQuery UI provides a jQuery Color plugin as part of jQuery UI for animating transitions between colors as well as numeric values.

The next section covers the options that you can provide to any of jQuery's animation methods to have a more fine-grained control over jQuery animations.

ANIMATION OPTIONS

All jQuery's animation methods—the `animate()` method as well as show(), hide(), toggle(), slideIn(), slideDown(), slideToggle(), fadeIn(), fadeOut(), and fadeToggle()—support providing a simple JavaScript object of key, value pairs in place of the *duration, easing,* and *callback function* arguments, which allows you to fine-tune all aspects of an animation.

The following describes what the method signatures of all these methods look like when using the *options* argument instead of the *duration, easing,* and *callback function* arguments.

➤ `animate(`*properties, options*`)`

➤ `show(`*options*`)`, `hide(`*options*`)`, `toggle(`*options*`)`

➤ `slideDown(`*options*`)`, `slideUp(`*options*`)`, `slideToggle(`*options*`)`

➤ `fadeIn(`*options*`)`, `fadeOut(`*options*`)`, `fadeToggle(`*options*`)`

The options that can be provided in the alternative *options* argument are as follows:

➤ `duration`—The length of the animation. The value will be either an integer representing milliseconds or one of the following strings: `'slow'`, `'normal'`, or `'fast'`.

➤ `easing`—How the transition is animated over time. The value will be a string referencing one of jQuery's built-in easing functions.

➤ `queue`—A boolean value that indicates whether the animation should be placed in jQuery's animation queue. If the value provided to `queue` is `false`, the animation is not queued and it begins immediately. If a string is the value provided, the animation is placed in a queue that is named after the string provided. If a custom queue name is used, the animation will not be started automatically; to start a custom queue, call the `dequeue(`*queueName*`)` method.

➤ `specialEasing`—Applicable only to the `animate()` method. An object that maps CSS properties provided in the *properties* argument to easings. This makes it possible to animate different properties with different easings.

➤ `step function((number)` *now*`, (tween)` *tween*—A callback function that is executed once for each animated property of each animated element, per step of the animation.

➤ `progress function((promise)` *animation*`, (number)` *progress*`, (number)` *remainingMilliseconds*`)` —A callback function that is executed after each step of the animation but is executed only once per animated element regardless of the animated properties.

➤ `complete function()`—A callback function that is executed when the animation has completed.

➤ `start function((promise)` *animation*`)` —A callback function that is executed when the animation starts.

➤ `done function((promise)` *animation*`, (Boolean)` *jumpedToTheEnd*`)` —A callback function that is executed when the animation has completed and its Promise object has been resolved.

➤ `fail function((promise)` *animation*`, (Boolean)` *jumpedToTheEnd*`)` —A callback function that is executed when the animation fails to be completed and its Promise object has been rejected.

➤ `always function((promise)` *animation*`, (Boolean)` *jumpedToTheEnd*`)` —A callback function that is executed when the animation has been completed or stops without completing and its Promise object has either been resolved or rejected.

SUMMARY

In this chapter, you learned how jQuery's animation methods work to hide, display, or transition elements, either by using jQuery's various built-in animations or by making a custom animation.

You learned how jQuery's `hide()`, `show()`, and `toggle()`, as well as all seven additional animation-related methods, can be provided a duration argument, which can be either a string `'slow'`, `'normal'`, or `'fast'`, or an integer representing time specified in milliseconds. When used without any arguments specified, jQuery's `show()`, `hide()`, and `toggle()` methods simply show and hide an element by toggling the CSS `display` property without an animation. Specifying at least the one argument causes these methods to use an animation to transition between the hidden and displayed states.

jQuery offers some alternative animations that essentially provide the same functions as the `show()`, `hide()`, and `toggle()` methods. The `slideDown()`, `slideUp()`, and `slideToggle()` methods animate an element's height to hide and display an element. The `fadeIn()`, `fadeOut()`, and `fadeToggle()` methods animate an element's opacity to hide and display an element.

Finally, you learned how to use the `animate()` method, which transitions between the styles an element already has to styles that you specify in the first argument to the `animate()` method. The styles that can be animated are all of the various CSS properties that allow numeric values.

jQuery effects are documented in detail in Appendix M, "Animation and Easing Effects."

EXERCISES

1. When specifying the duration of an animation, what values are allowed?

2. What does jQuery's `slideDown()` method do?

3. Which methods would you use to display or hide an element using an animation of that element's opacity?

4. What method would you use to create a custom animation?

5. Which easings are provided with jQuery core?

Plugins

Beyond making many scripting tasks much easier, jQuery also makes itself easy to extend with new functionality. This is done with an easy-to-understand Plugin API. Using jQuery's Plugin API, you can make your own chainable jQuery methods and even write entire complex client-side applications completely as jQuery plugins.

There are a lot of things you can do with plugins. Some of the more useful and prominent examples of jQuery plugins are found in the jQuery UI library, which I discuss in more detail in Chapter 12, "Draggable and Droppable." Plugins in the jQuery UI library help you to implement functionality like drag-and-drop or selecting elements, and a variety of other functionality. There is also a thriving third-party development community for jQuery that produces plugins for just about anything you can think of. You'll examine a few third-party jQuery plugins and even write one in Part II, "jQuery UI," of this book. jQuery's thriving plugin community exists largely thanks to how ridiculously easy it is to write plugins for jQuery.

This chapter demonstrates how to use jQuery's Plugin API and covers the basic concepts you need to understand to start writing plugins of your own. Beyond what you learn about jQuery plugin basics in this chapter, you also see more examples that use jQuery's Plugin API later in the book.

WRITING A PLUGIN

jQuery plugins are easy to implement. All you need to do is pass an object literal containing the methods you want to extend jQuery with to the `$.fn.extend()` method.

Writing a Simple jQuery Plugin

Example 9-1 demonstrates how to write a simple jQuery plugin. If you would like to try this example for yourself, you can find it in the Chapter 9 folder with the rest of the book's examples that you can download from www.wrox.com/go/webdevwithjquery.

```
<!DOCTYPE HTML>
<html xmlns="http://www.w3.org/1999/xhtml">
    <head>
```

```
            <meta http-equiv="content-type"
                content="application/xhtml+xml; charset=utf-8" />
            <meta http-equiv="content-language" content="en-us" />
            <title>John Candy Movies</title>
            <script type='text/javascript' src='../jQuery.js'></script>
            <script type='text/javascript' src='Example 9-1.js'></script>
            <link type='text/css' href='Example 9-1.css' rel='stylesheet' />
        </head>
        <body>
            <h2>John Candy Movies</h2>
            <ul class='movieList'>
                <li>The Great Outdoors</li>
                <li>Uncle Buck</li>
                <li>Who&rsquo;s Harry Crumb?</li>
                <li>Canadian Bacon</li>
                <li>Home Alone</li>
                <li>Spaceballs</li>
                <li>Planes, Trains, and Automobiles</li>
            </ul>
            <p>
                <a href='javascript:void(0);' id='movieSelectAll'>Select All</a>
            </p>
        </body>
    </html>
```

The following CSS sets up some basic styling for your jQuery plugin-enabled XHTML 5 document so that you can visually see what happens when you click items in the movie list:

```
body {
    font: 200 16px Helvetica, Arial, sans-serif;
}
h2 {
    font: 200 18px Helvetica, Arial, sans-serif;
    text-decoration: underline;
}
ul.movieList {
    list-style: none;
    margin: 10px;
    padding: 0;
}
ul.movieList li {
    padding: 3px;
}
ul.movieList li.movieSelected {
    background: forestgreen;
    color: white;
}
a {
    text-decoration: none;
    color: green;
}
a:hover {
    text-decoration: underline;
}
```

The following JavaScript provides a simple, to-the-point demonstration of how to use the jQuery Plugin API to write custom plugins for jQuery:

```javascript
$.fn.extend({

    select : function()
    {
        // In a jQuery plugin; 'this' is already a jQuery ready object
        // Performing an operation like addClass() works on one
        // or more items, depending on the selection.
        return this.addClass('movieSelected');
    },

    unselect : function()
    {
        return this.removeClass('movieSelected');
    }
});

var movies = {

    ready : function()
    {
        $('a#movieSelectAll').click(

            function(event)
            {
                event.preventDefault();

                $('ul.movieList li').select();
            }
        );

        $(document).on(
            'click.movieList',
            'ul.movieList li',
            function()
            {
                if ($(this).hasClass('movieSelected'))
                {
                    $(this).unselect();
                }
                else
                {
                    $(this).select();
                }
            }
        );
    }
};

$(document).ready(
    function()
    {
```

```
            movies.ready();
        }
    );
```

The preceding code results in the screen shot that you see in Figure 9-1 when you click individual movie titles.

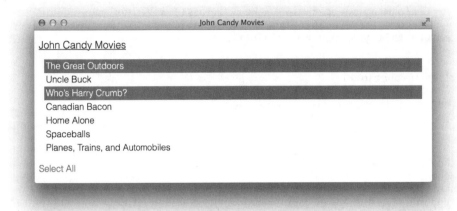

FIGURE 9-1

In the preceding example, you see how jQuery plugins are written using the `$.fn.extend()` method. In essence, a jQuery plugin extends what you can do with an object representing an HTML element. In this case, you're creating two jQuery plugins, one for selecting an element and one for unselecting an element. The selection itself is by virtue of applying a class name to one of the `<li>` elements. If the `<li>` element is selected, it has the class name `movieSelected` applied. If the `<li>` element is not selected, then the class name `movieSelected` is withdrawn. And just so you can visually see that an item is selected, the `movieSelected` class name applies a *forestgreen* background and makes the text *white*. This is a really simple example of what can be done using a jQuery plugin; you take one or more HTML elements and do something directly to those elements. In this example, you're doing selection, but you can do much more complicated things with jQuery plugins. You can have a plugin that adds a calendar to an input element; you can have a plugin that makes an element a drop zone for drag and drop actions. You'll see many more examples of jQuery plugins throughout this book; some are plugins developed by the jQuery Foundation, such as jQuery UI, and others are great third-party plugins that add useful functionality, such as the ability to sort a table, which you'll take a look at in Chapter 20, "Creating an Interactive Slideshow."

The Anatomy of a jQuery Plugin

A jQuery plugin's primary purpose is to do something to an element in the DOM. Within a plugin, the special keyword `this` represents the element or elements that you are working with. In *Example 9-1*, you had two plugins, `select()` and `unselect()`. These jQuery plugins can be called on any HTML element in the DOM through jQuery. The plugin works on one element or many elements.

```
$.fn.extend({

    select : function()
    {
        // In a jQuery plugin; 'this' is already a jQuery ready object
        // Performing an operation like addClass() works on one
        // or more items, depending on the selection.
        return this.addClass('movieSelected');
    },

    unselect : function()
    {
        return this.removeClass('movieSelected');
    }
});
```

As you've been learning throughout the first part of this book, if you have the following jQuery selection

```
$('ul.movieList li')
```

what follows that expression can be any method that jQuery supports. You could call addClass(), for example, and add a class name to every <li> element that selection matches. With jQuery plugins, in addition to all the methods that jQuery supports, such as find(), addClass(), each(), and so on, you can also extend jQuery any way that you see fit with your own custom plugin. In *Example 9-1*, you saw a remedial example, where you're just adding a class name to every element in a selection. The keyword this represents an array, and that array contains every element in the selection. In the example of John Candy movies, this contained an array of seven <li> elements, so when the following plugin executed

```
select : function()
{
    // In a jQuery plugin; 'this' is already a jQuery ready object
    // Performing an operation like addClass() works on one
    // or more items, depending on the selection.
    return this.addClass('movieSelected');
}
```

it did so on this collection of <li> elements:

```
<li>The Great Outdoors</li>
<li>Uncle Buck</li>
<li>Who&rsquo;s Harry Crumb?</li>
<li>Canadian Bacon</li>
<li>Home Alone</li>
<li>Spaceballs</li>
<li>Planes, Trains, and Automobiles</li>
```

And it added the movieSelected class name to those elements, depending on whether you clicked a <li> element directly, or selected them all using the <a> element beneath the list.

Inspecting the Document Object Model

In traditional JavaScript, HTML element objects have always had some built-in properties and methods. These properties and methods make it possible to interact with and manipulate the DOM. jQuery sits in the middle, between traditional JavaScript's built-in DOM and the API it provides for interacting with that DOM. As you've already learned, jQuery simplifies the amount of code you have to write to query and manipulate the DOM. Most of the methods jQuery provides have an analogue in the traditional JavaScript DOM API. Some of the methods you're likely to find in the traditional DOM are methods like appendChild(), which adds a new child element or text node just after the last element or text node. Another is getAttribute(), which returns the value of an attribute. In the context of these two examples, jQuery provides similar methods. Instead of append-Child(), you get a whole spectrum of methods for element placement and DOM manipulation such as after(), insertAfter(), before(), insertBefore(), and all the other methods I introduced to you in Chapter 4, "Manipulating Content and Attributes."

Instead of getAttribute(), setAttribute(), or hasAttributes(), you have attr() and a whole spectrum of CSS attribute selectors. You'll note, however, that the concept of a jQuery plugin builds on the concept of the DOM and the properties and methods that it exposes for working with an element. jQuery plugins extend what you can do with an element and make it possible to define completely custom methods.

In *Example 9-2*, you tweak what you saw in *Example 9-1*, using traditional JavaScript. You examine what properties and methods are attached to the <a> element in the HTML document.

You start with this XHTML 5 document:

```
<!DOCTYPE HTML>
<html xmlns="http://www.w3.org/1999/xhtml">
    <head>
        <meta http-equiv="content-type"
            content="application/xhtml+xml; charset=utf-8" />
        <meta http-equiv="content-language" content="en-us" />
        <title>John Candy Movies</title>
        <script type='text/javascript' src='Example 9-2.js'></script>
        <link type='text/css' href='Example 9-2.css' rel='stylesheet' />
    </head>
    <body>
        <h2>John Candy Movies</h2>
        <ul class='movieList'>
            <li>The Great Outdoors</li>
            <li>Uncle Buck</li>
            <li>Who&rsquo;s Harry Crumb?</li>
            <li>Canadian Bacon</li>
            <li>Home Alone</li>
            <li>Spaceballs</li>
            <li>Planes, Trains, and Automobiles</li>
        </ul>
        <p>
            <a href='javascript:void(0);' id='movieSelectAll'>Select All</a>
        </p>
    </body>
</html>
```

It might seem redundant, but next I include the same CSS that you saw in *Example 9-1* so that you can see all the components of this document, leaving nothing to mystery.

```css
body {
    font: 200 16px Helvetica, Arial, sans-serif;
}
h2 {
    font: 200 18px Helvetica, Arial, sans-serif;
    text-decoration: underline;
}
ul.movieList {
    list-style: none;
    margin: 10px;
    padding: 0;
}
ul.movieList li {
    padding: 3px;
}
ul.movieList li.movieSelected {
    background: forestgreen;
    color: white;
}
a {
    text-decoration: none;
    color: green;
}
a:hover {
    text-decoration: underline;
}
```

Finally, we get to the JavaScript document, *Example 9-2.js*:

```javascript
document.addEventListener(
    'DOMContentLoaded',
    function()
    {
        var a = document.getElementById('movieSelectAll');

        for (var property in a)
        {
            console.log(property);
        }
    }
);
```

In *Example 9-2*, you cast aside jQuery for a moment for the traditional JavaScript Document Object Model. You grab an <a> element from the document and then put it inside a for/in loop to examine what methods and properties are attached to the <a> element.

You can take a look at the structure of jQuery itself by putting something like this (*Example 9-3*) in a JavaScript file:

```javascript
$.fn.extend({

    select : function()
```

```
    {
        // In a jQuery plugin; 'this' is already a jQuery ready object
        // Performing an operation like addClass() works on one
        // or more items, depending on the selection.
        return this.addClass('movieSelected');
    },

    unselect : function()
    {
        return this.removeClass('movieSelected');
    }
});

console.log($.fn);
```

The call to `console.log()` allows you to examine the structure of jQuery itself, both built-in plugins and custom third-party plugins. In Firefox's web console, when you click the console entry that represents `console.log($.fn)`, you see a list expand in the right column that is filled with the names of jQuery plugins, both built-in plugins and custom plugins that have been added via `$.fn.extend()`.

Writing a Context Menu jQuery Plugin

In *Example 9-4*, you write a more complicated jQuery plugin with some of the features that you're used to seeing in jQuery plugins, such as being self-contained, and the ability to apply behavior to an element that has been prepared for use with a jQuery plugin through the application of a particular HTML structure and CSS. In this example, you can see how to transform an unordered list into a custom context menu. To start, download or type in the following XHTML 5 document:

```
<!DOCTYPE HTML>
<html xmlns="http://www.w3.org/1999/xhtml">
    <head>
        <meta http-equiv="content-type"
            content="application/xhtml+xml; charset=utf-8" />
        <meta http-equiv="content-language" content="en-us" />
        <title>Context Menu Plugin</title>
        <script type='text/javascript' src='../jQuery.js'></script>
        <script type='text/javascript' src='Example 9-4.js'></script>
        <link type='text/css' href='Example 9-4.css' rel='stylesheet' />
    </head>
    <body class='contextMenuContainer'>
        <div id='applicationContainer'>
            <p>
                jQuery plugins give you the ability to extend jQuery's functionality,
                quickly and seamlessly.  In this example you see how to make a context
                menu plugin.  It demonstrates some of what you might need to make a
                context menu widget as a self-contained jQuery plugin.
            </p>
            <p class='applicationContextMenuToggles'>
                <span id='applicationContextMenuDisable'>Disable Context Menu</
span> |
```

```
                    <span id='applicationContextMenuEnable'>Enable Context Menu</
span>
            </p>
            <div id='applicationContextMenu'>
                <ul>
                    <li><span>Open</span></li>
                    <li class='contextMenuSeparator'><div></div></li>
                    <li><span>Save</span></li>
                    <li><span>Save As...</span></li>
                    <li class='contextMenuSeparator'><div></div></li>
                    <li class='contextMenuDisabled'><span>Edit</span></li>
                </ul>
            </div>
        </div>
    </body>
</html>
```

The preceding XHTML 5 document sets up the necessary markup structure to begin a context menu plugin. There's a bit of text, a couple of <span> elements that can toggle whether the context menu is enabled, and the structure for the context menu itself. This markup is put together with the following CSS, which styles the context menu to look a lot like a Mac OS X system context menu—which I did because I can.

```
html,
body {
    padding: 0;
    margin: 0;
    width: 100%;
    height: 100%;
}
body {
    font: 12px 'Lucida Grande', Helvetica, Arial, sans-serif;
    background: #fff;
    color: rgb(50, 50, 50);
    line-height: 1.5em;
    -webkit-user-select: none;
    -moz-user-select: none;
    -ms-user-select: none;
    user-select: none;
}
div#applicationContainer {
    width: 400px;
    padding: 20px;
}
div.contextMenu {
    display: none;
    position: absolute;
    z-index: 10;
    top: 0;
    left: 0;
    width: 200px;
    font-size: 14px;
    background: #fff;
    background: rgba(255, 255, 255, 0.95);
```

```
        border: 1px solid rgb(150, 150, 150);
        border: 1px solid rgba(150, 150, 150, 0.95);
        padding: 4px 0;
        box-shadow: 0 5px 25px rgba(100, 100, 100, 0.9);
        border-radius: 5px;
        border-radius: 5px;
        color: #000;
}
div.contextMenu ul {
        list-style: none;
        margin: 0;
        padding: 0;
}
div.contextMenu ul li {
        padding: 2px 0 2px 21px;
        margin: 0;
        height: 15px;
        overflow: hidden;
}
div.contextMenu ul li span {
        position: relative;
        top: -2px;
}
div.contextMenu ul li.contextMenuSeparator {
        padding: 5px 0 8px 0;
        font-size: 0;
        line-height: 0;
        height: auto;
}
li.contextMenuSeparator div {
        font-size: 0;
        line-height: 0;
        padding-top: 1px;
        background: rgb(200, 200, 200);
        margin: 0 1px;
}
body div.contextMenu ul li.contextMenuHover {
    /* Old browsers */
    background: rgb(82, 117, 243);
    /* FF3.6+ */
    background: -moz-linear-gradient(top,  rgb(82, 117, 243) 0%, rgb(3, 57,
242) 100%);
      /* Chrome,Safari4+ */
    background: -webkit-gradient(
        linear, left top, left bottom,
        color-stop(0%, rgb(82, 117, 243)),
        color-stop(100%, rgb(3, 57, 242))
    );
    /* Chrome10+,Safari5.1+ */
    background: -webkit-linear-gradient(top, rgb(82,117,243) 0%, rgb(3, 57,
242) 100%);
    background: -o-linear-gradient(top, rgb(82, 117, 243) 0%, rgb(3, 57, 242)
100%);
      /* IE10+ */
```

```
    background: -ms-linear-gradient(top,  rgb(82, 117, 243) 0%, rgb(3, 57,
242) 100%);
    /* W3C */
    background: linear-gradient(to bottom, rgb(82, 117, 243) 0%, rgb(3, 57,
242) 100%);
    color: white;
}
li.contextMenuDisabled {
    opacity: 0.5;
}
p.applicationContextMenuToggles {
    color: green;
}
p.applicationContextMenuToggles span:hover {
    text-decoration: underline;
    cursor: pointer;
}
```

Finally, the following JavaScript ties everything together and breathes life into this once static, inanimate HTML document.

```
$.fn.extend({

    contextMenu : function()
    {
        var options = arguments[0] !== undefined ? arguments[0] : {};

        var contextMenuIsEnabled = true;

        var contextMenu = this;

        if (typeof options == 'string')
        {
            switch (options)
            {
                case 'disable':
                {
                    contextMenuIsEnabled = false;
                    break;
                }
            }
        }
        else if (typeof options == 'object')
        {
            // You can pass in an object containing options to
            // further customize your context menu.

        }

        function getViewportDimensions()
        {
            var x, y;

            if (self.innerHeight)
```

```
    {
        x = self.innerWidth;
        y = self.innerHeight;
    }
    else if (document.documentElement &&
            document.documentElement.clientHeight)
    {
        x = document.documentElement.clientWidth;
        y = document.documentElement.clientHeight;
    }
    else if (document.body)
    {
        x = document.body.clientWidth;
        y = document.body.clientHeight;
    }

    return {
        x : x,
        y : y
    };
}

if (contextMenuIsEnabled)
{
    // If this is attaching a context menu to multiple elements,
    // iterate over each of them.
    this.find('li')
        .not('li.contextMenuDisabled, li.contextMenuSeparator')
        .bind(
            'mouseover.contextMenu',
            function()
            {
                $(this).addClass('contextMenuHover');
            }
        )
        .bind(
            'mouseout.contextMenu',
            function()
            {
                $(this).removeClass('contextMenuHover');
            }
        );

    if (!this.data('contextMenu'))
    {
        this.data('contextMenu', true)
            .addClass('contextMenu')
            .bind(
                'mouseover.contextMenu',
                function()
                {
                    $(this).data('contextMenu', true);
                }
            )
```

```
        .bind(
            'mouseout.contextMenu',
            function()
            {
                $(this).data('contextMenu', false);
            }
        );

    this.parents('.contextMenuContainer:first')
        .bind(
            'contextmenu.contextMenu',
            function(event)
            {
                event.preventDefault();

                var viewport = getViewportDimensions();

                contextMenu.show();

                contextMenu.css({
                    top : 'auto',
                    right : 'auto',
                    bottom : 'auto',
                    left : 'auto'
                });

                if (contextMenu.outerHeight() >
                    (viewport.y - event.pageY))
                {
                    contextMenu.css(
                        'bottom',
                        (viewport.y - event.pageY) + 'px'
                    );
                }
                else
                {
                    contextMenu.css(
                        'top',
                        event.pageY + 'px'
                    );
                }

                if (contextMenu.outerWidth() >
                    (viewport.x - event.pageX))
                {
                    contextMenu.css(
                        'right',
                        (viewport.x - event.pageX) + 'px'
                    );
                }
                else
                {
                    contextMenu.css(
                        'left',
```

```
                                    event.pageX + 'px'
                            );
                        }
                    }
                );
            }

            if (!$('body').data('contextMenu'))
            {
                $('body').data('contextMenu', true);

                $(document).bind(
                    'mousedown.contextMenu',
                    function()
                    {
                        $('div.contextMenu').each(
                            function()
                            {
                                if (!$(this).data('contextMenu'))
                                {
                                    $(this).hide();
                                }
                            }
                        );
                    }
                );
            }
        }
        else
        {
            this.find('li')
                .not('li.contextMenuDisabled, li.contextMenuSeparator')
                .unbind('mouseover.contextMenu')
                .unbind('mouseout.contextMenu');

            this.data('contextMenu', false)
                .removeClass('contextMenu')
                .unbind('mouseover.contextMenu')
                .unbind('mouseout.contextMenu');

            this.parents('.contextMenuContainer:first')
                .unbind('contextmenu.contextMenu');

            $('body').data('contextMenu', false);

            $(document).unbind('mousedown.contextMenu');
        }

        return this;
    }
});

$(document).ready(
    function()
    {
```

```
$('span#applicationContextMenuDisable').click(
    function(event)
    {
        $('div#applicationContextMenu').contextMenu('disable');
        $('div#applicationContextMenu').hide();
    }
);

$('span#applicationContextMenuEnable').click(
    function()
    {
        $('div#applicationContextMenu').contextMenu();
    }
);

$('div#applicationContextMenu').contextMenu();
    }
);
```

With all three documents in place, you get a fine example of jQuery-enabled interactivity when you load this document into a browser that supports and has enabled the contextmenu event. (By default, all do except legacy Presto engine-based Opera, although it's possible to disable this event in Firefox's advanced preferences.) The contextMenu event, as you might have guessed, replaces the menu that comes up by default wherever you might right-click in this web page with a mouse's right button or a context menu gesture. On Macs, the context menu gesture brings up the context menu when you tap with two fingers on an Apple Wireless Trackpad or MacBook Trackpad (assuming you've enabled the gesture in System Preferences ➪ Trackpad). The result will look something like what you see in Figure 9-2.

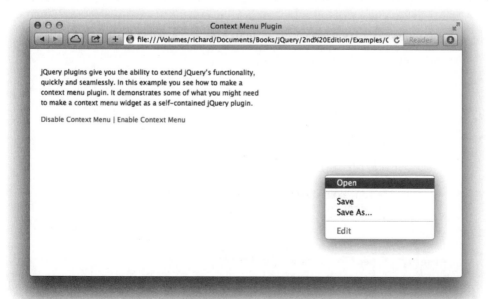

FIGURE 9-2

If you press Disable Context Menu, you should see the default context menu instead. My default context menu is shown in Figure 9-3.

FIGURE 9-3

The remainder of this section picks apart the JavaScript in *Example 9-4* line by line and explains how and why it works.

```
var options = arguments[0] !== undefined ? arguments[0] : {};

var contextMenuIsEnabled = true;

var contextMenu = this;

if (typeof options == 'string')
{
    switch (options)
    {
        case 'disable':
        {
            contextMenuIsEnabled = false;
            break;
        }
    }
}
else if (typeof options == 'object')
{
    // You can pass in an object containing options to
    // further customize your context menu.

}
```

The first chunk of code (preceding this sentence) provides support for passing in some options. To disable the context menu, you pass in the string `'disabled'`, as in `contextMenu('disabled')`. To enable the context menu, you call `contextMenu()` with no arguments.

If you like, you can expand on this example and add some options of your own. The following is the function call that gets everything started:

```
$('div#applicationContextMenu').contextMenu();
```

In the HTML, you set up and structure a `<div>` element that contains a `<ul>` element, and this becomes the context menu:

```
<div id='applicationContextMenu'>
    <ul>
        <li><span>Open</span></li>
        <li class='contextMenuSeparator'><div></div></li>
        <li><span>Save</span></li>
        <li><span>Save As...</span></li>
        <li class='contextMenuSeparator'><div></div></li>
        <li class='contextMenuDisabled'><span>Edit</span></li>
    </ul>
</div>
```

Along with some CSS, this context menu becomes almost indistinguishable from a real Mac OS X system context menu. Also in the HTML document, you define a boundary for this context menu. The context menu will occur only within the confines of this element. In our document, that container became the `<body>` element because it was assigned the `contextMenuContainer` class name. For this plugin to work, the context menu can be placed in any container, so long as it has a parent or ancestor with the `contextMenuContainer` class name. This is all that you need from the standpoint of the HTML structure, a container element with the `contextMenuContainer` class name and the `<div>` element containing a `<ul>` element. Each `<li>` element represents a context menu option.

The next block of code in the JavaScript is a reusable function that gets the dimensions of the viewport. This is made compatible with older versions of Internet Explorer, which use different ways of getting the dimensions of the viewport. The method used by most modern, standards-compliant browsers appears in the first block of code:

```
function getViewportDimensions()
{
    var x, y;

    if (self.innerHeight)
    {
        x = self.innerWidth;
        y = self.innerHeight;
    }
    else if (document.documentElement &&
             document.documentElement.clientHeight)
    {
        x = document.documentElement.clientWidth;
        y = document.documentElement.clientHeight;
    }
    else if (document.body)
```

```
            {
                x = document.body.clientWidth;
                y = document.body.clientHeight;
            }

            return {
                x : x,
                y : y
            };
        }
```

The dimensions of the viewport are needed to reposition the context menu depending on where the user clicks inside the viewport. If the user clicks on the left side of the viewport, the context menu is positioned from the left. If the user clicks near the top of the view port, the context menu is positioned from the top, and if the user clicks near the bottom, the context menu is positioned from the bottom. Using a little math, you attempt to avoid a situation in which the element used for the context menu might appear offscreen. Instead, by analyzing where a user clicks and the proximity to the edges of the viewport, you can reposition based on that data.

```
            if (contextMenuIsEnabled)
            {
```

The preceding block of code detects if contextMenu() is called with no arguments, or in other words, when the context menu is enabled.

First, you set up some mouseover and mouseout events for the <li> elements, but only elements that aren't disabled or separators.

```
            this.find('li')
                .not('li.contextMenuDisabled, li.contextMenuSeparator')
                .bind(
                    'mouseover.contextMenu',
                    function()
                    {
                        $(this).addClass('contextMenuHover');
                    }
                )
                .bind(
                    'mouseout.contextMenu',
                    function()
                    {
                        $(this).removeClass('contextMenuHover');
                    }
            );
```

The call to find('li') finds the <li> elements inside the element acting as the context menu. These receive mouseover and mouseout events that are namespaced for our contextMenu plugin. The entire event is mouseover.contextMenu. The mouseover part is the standard event you are attaching, and the contextMenu part is the name of this application of the mouseover event. As you've learned in all the chapters preceding this one, naming your events is good practice because it isolates the events that you apply into namespaces and makes it much easier to selectively enable and disable events, just as you see here where you bind and unbind events based on the event and the event name. So each <li>

element, except those with `contextMenuDisabled` and `contextMenuSeparator` (filtered out using `not()`) class names receives a `contextMenuHover` class name when the user hovers over those `<li>` elements within the context menu. If you look at the CSS, this causes a CSS gradient to be applied during `mouseover`.

```
if (!this.data('contextMenu'))
{
    this.data('contextMenu', true)
        .addClass('contextMenu')
        .bind(
            'mouseover.contextMenu',
            function()
            {
                $(this).data('contextMenu', true);
            }
        )
        .bind(
            'mouseout.contextMenu',
            function()
            {
                $(this).data('contextMenu', false);
            }
        );
```

As explained earlier in this chapter, `this` refers to the element or elements that are selected. In this case `this` refers directly to this selection:

```
$('div#applicationContextMenu')
```

If you were to do `console.log(this)` in Safari or Chrome, you'd see the HTML source code of `<div id="applicationContextMenu">`. The preceding block of code begins by checking to see if data has been attached to that `<div>` element, under the name `contextMenu`.

```
if (!this.data('contextMenu'))
{
```

If no data is found, data is created.

```
this.data('contextMenu', true)
```

Invisibly, data is attached to the `<div>` element, within jQuery.

Then the `<div>` element is given the class name `contextMenu`.

```
.addClass('contextMenu')
```

That `<div>` element now looks like this:

```
<div id='applicationContainer' class='contextMenu'>
```

And that same `<div>` element receives `mouseover` and `mouseout` events, which themselves set the same data on the `<div>` element, which is used to keep track of whether the context menu is active. If the mouse cursor isn't over the context menu, then the context menu is considered inactive, and if a click occurs while the mouse cursor isn't on top of the context menu, the context menu will be hidden.

Next, the `contextmenu` event is applied, and this happens by traveling up the DOM tree from our `<div>` element to the first element that has the class name `contextMenuContainer`.

```
this.parents('.contextMenuContainer:first')
    .bind(
        'contextmenu.contextMenu',
        function(event)
{
```

The preceding code binds the `contextmenu` event namespaced using our plugin's name, `contextMenu`, to the element with the `contextMenuContainer` class name. The `function` provided, of course, executes when the `contextmenu` event fires. In the first line of that function, the default action, displaying the default system context menu is canceled. The dimensions of the viewport are retrieved from our previously defined function. The `contextMenu` is set to display with a call to `show()`; then the four CSS position properties `top`, `right`, `bottom`, and `left` are all reset to their default value, `auto`. This is important because your code will set two of the four in pairs, but never all four.

```
event.preventDefault();

var viewport = getViewportDimensions();

contextMenu.show();

contextMenu.css({
    top : 'auto',
    right : 'auto',
    bottom : 'auto',
    left : 'auto'
});
```

The remaining of the `contextmenu` event callback function defines the position of the context menu relative to the viewport based on where the user clicked inside that viewport.

```
if (contextMenu.outerHeight() >
    (viewport.y - event.pageY))
{
    contextMenu.css(
        'bottom',
        (viewport.y - event.pageY) + 'px'
    );
}
else
{
    contextMenu.css(
        'top',
        event.pageY + 'px'
    );
}

if (contextMenu.outerWidth() >
    (viewport.x - event.pageX))
```

```
        {
            contextMenu.css(
                'right',
                (viewport.x - event.pageX) + 'px'
            );
        }
        else
        {
            contextMenu.css(
                'left',
                event.pageX + 'px'
            );
        }
}
```

A little bit of math and comparison determines whether it is best to place the context menu from the left or right, and whether from the top or from the bottom is better. The size of the context menu is taken into consideration, along with where the mouse click occurs in relation to the edges of the viewport. The properties event.pageX and event.pageY, obviously provided with all the other event data, are the x,y coordinates of the mouse click in relation to the document. The properties viewport.x and viewport.y contain the width and height of the viewport. Finally, outerHeight() is a jQuery method that gets the height of the context menu including the following CSS properties: height, padding, border-width, and margin. Likewise, outerWidth() provides similar dimensions for width.

Next, an event is attached to the document to track clicks that occur outside the context menu.

```
if (!$('body').data('contextMenu'))
{
    $('body').data('contextMenu', true);

    $(document).bind(
        'mousedown.contextMenu',
        function()
        {
            $('div.contextMenu').each(
                function()
                {
                    if (!$(this).data('contextMenu')
                    {
                        $(this).hide();
                    }
                }
            );
        }
    );
}
```

If the <body> element does not have the data *contextMenu*, or *contextMenu* is set to false, then the event is attached. So that the event cannot be attached multiple times, the *contextMenu* data is set to true on the <body> element to indicate that the event has been attached.

```
$('body').data('contextMenu', true);
```

A mousedown event, again namespaced with the name *contextMenu*, is attached to the document. Whenever a mousedown event occurs, every <div> element with the class name contextMenu is iterated.

```
$(document).bind(
    'mousedown.contextMenu',
    function()
    {
        $('div.contextMenu').each(
            function()
            {
                if (!$(this).data('contextMenu'))
                {
                    $(this).hide();
                }
            }
        );
    }
);
```

If any of those <div> elements doesn't have its contextMenu data set to true, then that <div> element is hidden. Remember earlier in the script that you attached a mouseover and mouseout event to the context menu to track whether the context menu is active, which was done by setting the data contextMenu to a boolean value. This bit of code completes that implementation and makes it possible to close the context menu just by clicking anywhere but on the context menu.

The last block of code is executed when the context menu is disabled, which is done when you click the *Disable Context Menu* option.

```
$('span#applicationContextMenuDisable').click(
    function(event)
    {
        $('div#applicationContextMenu').contextMenu('disable');
        $('div#applicationContextMenu').hide();
    }
);
```

The preceding code causes the last block of code, which disables the context menu, to execute.

```
    }
    else
    {
        this.find('li')
            .not('li.contextMenuDisabled, li.contextMenuSeparator')
            .unbind('mouseover.contextMenu')
            .unbind('mouseout.contextMenu');

        this.data('contextMenu', false)
            .removeClass('contextMenu')
            .unbind('mouseover.contextMenu')
            .unbind('mouseout.contextMenu');

        this.parents('.contextMenuContainer:first')
            .unbind('contextmenu.contextMenu');

        $('body').data('contextMenu', false);
```

```
        $(document).unbind('mousedown.contextMenu');
    }
```

In this block of code, events are removed and data is set to false, reversing all the document changes that you put in place to enable your context menu. Because your events are namespaced using the contextMenu name, only the events that you explicitly attached are removed. If other people attached click or mouseover or other events using other names in other scripts, their events remain untouched and functional.

GOOD PRACTICE FOR JQUERY PLUGIN DEVELOPMENT

There are just a few things you should keep in mind while developing your own jQuery plugins:

➤ It's considered good practice to always expect one or more items to be passed to your plugin (in the jQuery selection preceding the call to your plugin), and to always return the jQuery object, whenever it makes sense and is possible to do so, which makes it possible to chain multiple method calls together.

➤ If you plan on using third-party jQuery plugins, you'll want to consider name-spacing your own plugins in some way so that your naming choices don't conflict with those of third-party plugins. Oftentimes this is done by prefixing a name of some sort to your plugin name, like the name of your company or organization. In the context of your context menu plugin, if that plugin were developed by your company Example, you might end up calling your plugin *exampleContextMenu()*.

➤ Avoid polluting the global namespace. Place all your function calls and variables inside your jQuery plugin. As an added benefit, this can also make your APIs private and callable only by you. Preventing other people from using your private APIs gives you the freedom to change them when you need to because you don't have to worry about supporting the people using those APIs.

➤ If you're interested in developing official third-party jQuery plugins that follow all the recommended best practices published by jQuery's developers, see the document located at http://docs.jquery.com/Plugins/Authoring.

SUMMARY

In this chapter, you learned the basic concepts needed to author your own jQuery plugin. You learned how jQuery plugins are created by passing an object literal to jQuery's $.fn.extend() method.

You learned how jQuery plugins expect to have one or more items passed to them, which are always present in the this keyword.

When you write jQuery plugins, you should return the jQuery object (when it makes sense and is possible to do so) because this preserves jQuery's capability to chain method calls onto one another.

You learned how to write a more complicated, more realistic jQuery plugin example by creating a context menu plugin.

EXERCISES

1. What method do you use to add a plugin to jQuery?

2. How do you list all the plugins in use within jQuery?

3. How would you create a private API for your own use within your jQuery plugin?

4. How are items you've selected with jQuery accessed in your custom plugin?

5. What value should your plugin return?

6. Why is namespacing your event names a good idea?

7. Customize the jQuery contextMenu plugin example to provide one or more options:

    a. Have your contextMenu plugin execute a callback function when the menu is opened and positioned.

    b. Have your contextMenu plugin provide options for the list of items used in the context menu itself.

Scrollbars

jQuery provides functionality to interact with scrollable DOM elements. As discussed in the preceding chapter, plugins can extend jQuery with even more capability. Even a quick web search results in an array of plugins that tout their scrolling merits. Although these plugins can be useful for specific purposes, jQuery handles most common needs.

This chapter focuses on the interactions provided by the jQuery core framework. These interactions include determining the current scrollbar position of a scrollable element as well as setting the scrollbar position. As expected, you could accomplish these tasks using a combination of JavaScript and DOM attributes; however, as usual, jQuery simplifies and standardizes these items.

GETTING THE POSITION OF A SCROLLBAR

Like most of jQuery's functionality, getting the position of a scrollbar is simple:

```
$('div#aScrollableElement').scrollTop();
$('div#aScrollableElement').scrollLeft();
```

As demonstrated by the preceding lines of code, scroll position involves two dimensions: vertical and horizontal. Vertical scroll position is measured in pixels from the top, and horizontal scroll position is measured in pixels from the left.

To showcase the output from these functions, the following example attaches a scroll event handler that displays the scroll position during scrolling. You begin with the XHTML5 base, which is presented in the following markup (*Example 10-1* in the code downloads at www.wrox.com/go/webdevwithjquery):

```
<!DOCTYPE HTML>
<html xmlns='http://www.w3.org/1999/xhtml'>
    <head>
        <meta http-equiv='content-type'
            content='application/xhtml+xml; charset=utf-8' />
        <meta http-equiv='content-language' content='en-us' />
        <title>Scrollbar Position</title>
```

```html
        <script src='../jQuery.js'></script>
        <script src='Example 10-1.js'></script>
        <link href='Example 10-1.css' rel='stylesheet' />
    </head>
    <body>
        <div id='container'>
            <div class='filler'>
                Lorem ipsum dolor sit amet, consectetur adipisicing elit,
                sed do eiusmod tempor incididunt ut labore et dolore magna aliqua.
                Ut enim ad minim veniam, quis nostrud exercitation ullamco laboris
                nisi ut aliquip ex ea commodo consequat. Duis aute irure dolor in
                reprehenderit in voluptate velit esse cillum dolore eu fugiat nulla
                pariatur. Excepteur sint occaecat cupidatat non proident, sunt in
                culpa qui officia deserunt mollit anim id est laborum.
            </div>
        </div>
        <div class='status-bar'>
            <span id='vertical-scroll-label'>
                Current Vertical Scrollbar Position:
            </span>
            <span id='vertical-scroll-value'>0</span>
        </div>
        <div class='status-bar'>
            <span id='horizontal-scroll-label'>
                Current Horizontal Scrollbar Position:
            </span>
            <span id='horizontal-scroll-value'>0</span>
        </div>
    </body>
</html>
```

The following CSS sets up the styling for the scrollbar example:

```css
html,
body {
    width: 100%;
    height: 100%;
}
body {
    font: 12px "Lucida Grande", Arial, sans-serif;
    background: rgb(189, 189, 189);
    color: rgb(50, 50, 50);
    margin: 0;
    padding: 0;
}
div#container {
    border: 1px solid rgb(64, 64, 64);
    background: #fff;
    padding: 5px;
    margin: 0 20px 0 20px;
    width: 200px;
    height: 100px;
    overflow: auto;
}
```

```
}
div.filler {
    margin: 10px;
    padding: 5px;
    width: 400px;
    height: 150px;
    background: rgb(200, 200, 255);
}
div.status-bar {
    margin: 5px 20px 5px 20px;
}
```

The preceding XHTML and CSS are combined with the following JavaScript:

```
$(document).ready(
    function()
    {
        $('div#container')
            .scroll(
                function()
                {
                    $('span#vertical-scroll-value')
                        .text($(this).scrollTop());

                    $('span#horizontal-scroll-value')
                        .text($(this).scrollLeft());
                }
            );
    }
);
```

The preceding source code results in the document that you see in Figure 10-1.

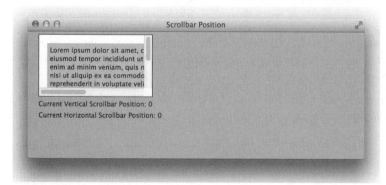

FIGURE 10-1

In the preceding example, you created a scrollable <div> element with content larger than its container. When you scroll that container to view its content, the scrollbar positions are retrieved and displayed on the page.

The markup in this example is straightforward. The scrollable content is contained in the `<div>` element with id name `container`; this container element is needed so that the size of the contents exceeds the size of the container to allow for scrolling.

```
<div id='container'>
```

Within that container, the `<div>` element with the class name `filler` simply contains sample text to help show movement when the container is scrolled.

```
<div class='filler'>
    Lorem ipsum dolor sit amet, consectetur adipisicing elit,
    sed do eiusmod tempor incididunt ut labore et dolore magna aliqua.
    Ut enim ad minim veniam, quis nostrud exercitation ullamco laboris
    nisi ut aliquip ex ea commodo consequat. Duis aute irure dolor in
    reprehenderit in voluptate velit esse cillum dolore eu fugiat nulla
    pariatur. Excepteur sint occaecat cupidatat non proident, sunt in
    culpa qui officia deserunt mollit anim id est laborum.
</div>
```

In addition to the scrollable content, the markup includes two `<div>` elements with the class name `status-bar` for use in displaying the scrollbar position values.

```
<div class='status-bar'>
    <span id='vertical-scroll-label'>
        Current Vertical Scrollbar Position:
    </span>
    <span id='vertical-scroll-value'>0</span>
</div>
<div class='status-bar'>
    <span id='horizontal-scroll-label'>
        Current Horizontal Scrollbar Position:
    </span>
    <span id='horizontal-scroll-value'>0</span>
</div>
```

The style sheet presents this markup in such a fashion that the contents of the container require more space than the container itself so that the browser can provide useful scrollbars for the container. The following reviews each rule in the style sheet and explains why each is needed.

The `<html>` and `<body>` element are each given 100 percent width and height so that these both automatically take up the entire viewport.

```
html,
body {
    width: 100%;
    height: 100%;
}
```

In the next rule, you give the document a Lucida Grande font, which is a Mac font commonly used in Mac applications. If that font isn't available, you can fall back on Arial, which is present in Windows; otherwise, if that font is not present, you fall back on the generic sans-serif font. The background is set to a shade of gray. The font color is set to a dark gray, and finally, the default padding and margin are removed from the `<body>` element, which is necessary to avoid scrollbars that would appear on the viewport due to the application of 100 percent width and height with the preceding stylesheet rule.

```
body {
    font: 12px "Lucida Grande", Arial, sans-serif;
    background: rgb(189, 189, 189);
    color: rgb(50, 50, 50);
    margin: 0;
    padding: 0;
}
```

The next rule positions the <div> element with id name container, which contains the scrollable content. This <div> element is sized to a rather small 200 pixels by 100 pixels, and a small amount of padding and horizontal margin is applied. The background is set to white; there is a dark gray border placed around the container; and finally, the overflow: auto; declaration is added so that scrollbars appear when this element's contents exceed its specified dimensions.

```
div#container {
    border: 1px solid rgb(64, 64, 64);
    background: #fff;
    padding: 5px;
    margin: 0 20px 0 20px;
    width: 200px;
    height: 100px;
    overflow: auto;
}
```

The next rule sets the presentation of the <div> element with the class name filler, setting a small amount of margin and padding as well as a light blue background. More important, the element is sized to 400 pixels by 150 pixels so that it is larger than its container.

```
div.filler {
    margin: 10px;
    padding: 5px;
    width: 400px;
    height: 150px;
    background: rgb(200, 200, 255);
}
```

The next rule simply adds a small amount of margin to the <div> elements with the class name status-bar to add a small amount of space between the elements and to align with the scrollable container.

```
div.status-bar {
    margin: 5px 20px 5px 20px;
}
```

The JavaScript for this example is, as usual, succinct. You start by adding a handler function for the scroll event.

```
$('div#container')
    .scroll(
```

Inside the scroll event, you write some logic for updating the status bars by getting the scrollbar positions. First, you get the scrollTop() value from the scrolled element and use its value to set the innerText of the span#vertical-scroll-value element. Then you similarly get the scrollLeft() value from the scrolled element and use that value to set the innerText of the span#horizontal-scroll-value element.

```
function()
{
    $('span#vertical-scroll-value')
        .text($(this).scrollTop());

    $('span#horizontal-scroll-value')
        .text($(this).scrollLeft());
}
```

With this minimal amount of jQuery, you have retrieved the scrollbar position values of a DOM element while it is being scrolled and updated additional DOM elements to display those values. The remaining examples in this chapter build upon this structure that you created.

SCROLLING TO A PARTICULAR ELEMENT WITHIN A SCROLLING <DIV>

As discussed in the introduction to this chapter, and as is typical with jQuery, the same method used to get the value can also be used to set the value. Therefore, setting the scrollbar positions of a scrollable element is as easy as

```
$('div#aScrollableElement').scrollTop(100);
$('div#aScrollableElement').scrollLeft(100);
```

Again, the values should be specified in pixels when setting the scrollbar positions; as a result, you must calculate the pixel values if you want to scroll directly to an element within a scrollable container. *Example 10-2* shows multiple elements within a scrolling <div> element and the code needed to scroll directly to each:

```
<!DOCTYPE HTML>
<html xmlns='http://www.w3.org/1999/xhtml'>
    <head>
        <meta http-equiv='content-type'
            content='application/xhtml+xml; charset=utf-8' />
        <meta http-equiv='content-language' content='en-us' />
        <title>Scrollbar Position</title>
        <script src='../jQuery.js'></script>
        <script src='Example 10-2.js'></script>
        <link href='Example 10-2.css' rel='stylesheet' />
    </head>
    <body>
        <div id='container'>
            <div class='filler'>
                Lorem ipsum dolor sit amet, consectetur adipisicing elit,
                sed do eiusmod tempor incididunt ut labore et dolore magna aliqua.
```

```
                    Ut enim ad minim veniam, quis nostrud exercitation ullamco laboris
                    nisi ut aliquip ex ea commodo consequat. Duis aute irure dolor in
                    reprehenderit in voluptate velit esse cillum dolore eu fugiat nulla
                    pariatur. Excepteur sint occaecat cupidatat non proident, sunt in
                    culpa qui officia deserunt mollit anim id est laborum.
                </div>
                <div id='block1' class='block'>Block 1</div>
                <div id='block2' class='block'>Block 2</div>
            </div>
            <div class='button-bar'>
                <button class='block-button' data-block='block1'>
                    Go to Block 1
                </button>
                <button class='block-button' data-block='block2'>
                    Go to Block 2
                </button>
            </div>
            <div class='status-bar'>
                <span id='vertical-scroll-label'>
                    Current Vertical Scrollbar Position:
                </span>
                <span id='vertical-scroll-value'>0</span>
            </div>
            <div class='status-bar'>
                <span id='horizontal-scroll-label'>
                    Current Horizontal Scrollbar Position:
                </span>
                <span id='horizontal-scroll-value'>0</span>
            </div>
        </body>
    </html>
```

The preceding HTML is combined with the following CSS:

```
html,
body {
    width: 100%;
    height: 100%;
}
body {
    font: 12px "Lucida Grande", Arial, sans-serif;
    background: rgb(189, 189, 189);
    color: rgb(50, 50, 50);
    margin: 0;
    padding: 0;
}
div#container {
    border: 1px solid rgb(64, 64, 64);
    background: #fff;
    padding: 5px;
    margin: 0 20px 0 20px;
    width: 200px;
    height: 100px;
    overflow: auto;
}
```

```css
div.filler {
    margin: 10px;
    padding: 5px;
    width: 400px;
    height: 150px;
    background: rgb(200, 200, 255);
}
div.status-bar,
div.button-bar {
    margin: 5px 20px 5px 20px;
}
div.block {
    margin: 10px;
    padding: 5px;
    width: 400px;
    height: 70px;
    background-color: rgb(255, 140, 0);
}
```

Finally, you apply the following JavaScript, which extends *Example 10-1* with new code that enables the click event handlers to set scrollbar positions.

```javascript
$(document).ready(
    function()
    {
        $('div#container')
            .scroll(
                function()
                {
                    $('span#vertical-scroll-value')
                        .text($(this).scrollTop());

                    $('span#horizontal-scroll-value')
                        .text($(this).scrollLeft());
                }
            );
        $('button.block-button')
            .click(
                function()
                {
                    $('div#container')
                        .scrollTop($('div#' + $(this).data().block).offset().top
                            - $('div#container').offset().top
                            + $('div#container').scrollTop())
                        .scrollLeft($('div#' + $(this).data().block).offset().left
                            - $('div#container').offset().left
                            + $('div#container').scrollLeft());
                }
            );

    }
);
```

The preceding source code gives you output, as shown in Figure 10-2, in Safari on Mac OS X.

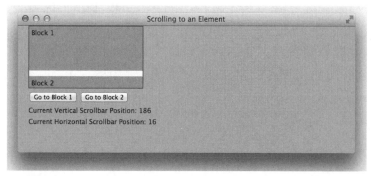

FIGURE 10-2

In the preceding example, you added two elements within the scrollable container, added buttons to reference those new elements, and wired the `click` event of these buttons to set the scrollbar positions of the scrollable container.

The two new `<div>` elements were added within the scrollable container, that is, the `<div>` element with id name `container`.

```
<div id='block1' class='block'>Block 1</div>
<div id='block2' class='block'>Block 2</div>
```

The buttons and their containing `<div>` element were added outside the scrollable container before the status bars. The `data-block` attributes of these buttons were used within the `click` event handlers to reference the appropriate block for the clicked button.

```
<div class='button-bar'>
    <button class='block-button' data-block='block1'>Go to Block 1</button>
    <button class='block-button' data-block='block2'>Go to Block 2</button>
</div>
```

To set up the document for this example, you added a rule to the style sheet for the new elements. In addition to size and spacing, the elements are set to a dark orange color to offset the filler text.

```
div.block {
    margin: 10px;
    padding: 5px;
    width: 400px;
    height: 70px;
    background-color: rgb(255, 140, 0);
}
```

In addition, you reused the status-bar style rules for the new button-bar element to maintain consistency.

```
div.status-bar,
div.button-bar {
    margin: 5px 20px 5px 20px;
}
```

Next, you added a `click` event handler for the new buttons to scroll the scrollable container to the referenced elements within the scrollable container.

```
$('button.block-button')
    .click(
        function()
        {
            $('div#container')
                .scrollTop($('div#' + $(this).data().block).offset().top
                    - $('div#container').offset().top
                    + $('div#container').scrollTop())
                .scrollLeft($('div#' + $(this).data().block).offset().left
                    - $('div#container').offset().left
                    + $('div#container').scrollLeft());

        }
    );
```

Within this event handler, you set the `scrollTop()` value for the `<div>` element with id name container using calculated values. You began with the value of the top edge of the block element specified by the button's `data-block` attribute (relative to the top of the document).

```
$('div#' + $(this).data().block).offset().top
```

From that value, you subtracted the value of the top edge of the scrollable container.

```
$('div#container').offset().top
```

Finally, you added back in the current scroll position of the scrollable container, which has an impact on the first value in this calculation.

```
$('div#container').scrollTop()
```

You followed the same pattern to set the horizontal scrollbar position using `scrollLeft()`.

SCROLLING TO THE TOP

The preceding example demonstrated the functionality of setting the scrollbar positions using calculated values. Scrolling to the top of a scrollable container is a specialized case in which the value to be set is zero. To scroll the container to its top leftmost content, you need only one line of jQuery code:

```
$('div#aScrollableElement').scrollTop(0).scrollLeft(0);
```

jQuery's `scrollTop()` and `scrollLeft()` are fairly tolerant of values outside the logical bounds. This tolerance can be useful when the values are calculated. For instance, fractional values are truncated; most values greater than the maximum possible scrollbar position result in the maximum valid value; and negative or otherwise invalid values result in zero. As a result, the following line also scrolls the container to its top leftmost content:

```
$('div#aScrollableElement').scrollTop('red').scrollLeft('blue');
```

Scrolling a container to its bottom rightmost content can be accomplished by calculating values larger than the maximum possible values or by simply using a value sufficiently large to be reasonably sure of exceeding the maximum but sufficiently small to be valid. Both approaches are demonstrated in the following lines:

```
$('div#aScrollableElement').scrollTop($('div#aScrollableElement')
.prop('scrollHeight')).scrollLeft($('div#aScrollableElement')
.prop('scrollWidth'));
$('div#aScrollableElement').scrollTop(999999999).scrollLeft(999999999);
```

Although the last approach might leave you scratching your head, it is technically more efficient than selecting elements from the DOM and reading their properties.

SUMMARY

In this chapter, you learned how to retrieve and update the scrollbar positions of scrollable content.

Throughout this chapter, you worked on building a page to display the current scroll positions as content was scrolled, discovering in the process the event handler you can specify to execute code during a scrolling operation. You extended the page to set the scroll positions based on elements within the scrollable content.

Finally, you learned how to scroll a container to the limits of its content, including the most common case of scrolling to the top, and you became acquainted with some of the nuances of jQuery's scrollTop() and scrollLeft() methods for values outside the expected ranges.

EXERCISES

1. If you want to retrieve the current scrollbar positions for a scrollable element, which jQuery functions would you use?

2. If you want to scroll the top of a particular element into view within its scrollable container, which three coordinates are needed?

3. Write the function call that you would use to scroll a scrollable element to its top.

4. Describe two general approaches to scroll a scrollable element to its bottom.

5. If an invalid value is specified when setting scrollTop() or scrollLeft(), what value is used by the function?

11

HTML5 Drag and Drop

In this chapter you learn how to use the HTML5 drag-and-drop specification with jQuery. The HTML5 drag-and-drop specification gives you a more powerful drag-and-drop implementation than jQuery UI's implementation in the Draggables and Droppables plugins, which you work with in Chapter 12, "Draggable and Droppable." The HTML5 drag-and-drop specification enables you to drag and drop between multiple browser windows, and even multiple browser windows between completely different browsers. For example, you can initiate a drag in Safari and complete it in Chrome or Firefox. You can also use HTML5 drag and drop to upload documents from your desktop or file manager. You can drag files from your desktop, Finder, Windows Explorer, and such to a browser window, and there you can access the document or documents uploaded through JavaScript and display thumbnails and upload progress meters.

jQuery has nothing built into it that assists with using the HTML5 drag-and-drop specification, but you can use jQuery in an implementation of the HTML5 drag-and-drop API to attach events and manipulate HTML attributes or CSS to enable drag and drop. In the following section you learn more about how the drag-and-drop API came about and see an example implementing it.

IMPLEMENTING DRAG AND DROP

HTML5 drag and drop can be summed up as mostly a collection of JavaScript events. There are some additional CSS/HTML attributes that enable drag and drop depending on the browser. The additional CSS/HTML portion is often criticized for the weird and divergent methods the browser makers have chosen to make it possible to initiate drag and drop. One such critique is an expletive-laden blog post by Peter-Paul Koch on his `quirksmode.org` site: `http://www.quirksmode.org/blog/archives/2009/09/the_html5_drag.html`.

His rant sums up the problems with the HTML5 drag-and-drop API nicely; it basically boils down to it's a bit of a kludge because it was reverse-engineered and based on IE's legacy implementation. And then, in addition, there is the Safari browser team's diversion from the specification with its addition of CSS to instigate drag-and-drop behavior. However, the Safari team has since changed its implementation to match the official HTML 5 specification.

The merits of Koch's rant can be debated, but the frustration he expresses in learning how to use the drag-and-drop API is a common experience. What you learn in this chapter, hopefully, can significantly mitigate the frustration typically experienced when working with the drag-and-drop API for the first time.

The drag-and-drop API works in all modern browsers, and even some of the older ones with the addition of a line or two of legacy-enabling code. The drag-and-drop API originated in IE5. The modern API is a slight modification of the original IE5 API. The API was spec'd out by the Web Hypertext Application Technology Working Group (WHATWG) and later adopted as part of the formal W3C HTML5 specification, when the W3C took over HTML5 from the WHATWG. The IE API was adopted with some tweaks so that existing code already in use could be used without much difficulty.

Following are the drag-and-drop JavaScript events:

➤ dragstart—This event is fired when a drag begins, on the element the drag was initiated on.

➤ dragend—This event is fired when a drag ends, on the element that the drag was initiated on.

➤ dragenter—This event is fired when an element enters the space over the element this event is attached to; it is used to identify an appropriate drop zone for the drag element.

➤ dragleave—This event is fired when an element leaves the space over the element this event is attached to; it is also used to identify an appropriate drop zone for the drag element.

➤ dragover—This event is fired continuously while a draggable element is within the space over the element this event is attached to; this event is also used on the drop side.

➤ drag—This event is fired continuously while the element is dragged, on the element being dragged.

➤ drop—This event is fired when a draggable element is dropped on the element this event is attached to.

You need to implement event listeners for most of these events to implement drag and drop in a document. The following example implements the drag-and-drop API in a browser-based Mac OS Finder inspired file manager. Remember, you can download this book's source code for free from www.wrox.com/go/webdevwithjquery. This example is *Example 11-1.html*.

```
<!DOCTYPE HTML>
<html lang='en'>
    <head>
        <meta http-equiv='X-UA-Compatible' content='IE=Edge' />
        <meta charset='utf-8' />
        <title>Finder</title>
        <script src='../jQuery.js'></script>
        <script src='../jQueryUI.js'></script>
        <script src='Example 11-1.js'></script>
        <link href='Example 11-1.css' rel='stylesheet' />
    </head>
    <body>
        <div id='finderFiles'>
            <div class='finderDirectory' data-path='/Applications'>
                <div class='finderIcon'></div>
```

```
                <div class='finderDirectoryName'>
                    <span>Applications</span>
                </div>
            </div>
            <div class='finderDirectory' data-path='/Library'>
                <div class='finderIcon'></div>
                <div class='finderDirectoryName'>
                    <span>Library</span>
                </div>
            </div>
            <div class='finderDirectory' data-path='/Network'>
                <div class='finderIcon'></div>
                <div class='finderDirectoryName'>
                    <span>Network</span>
                </div>
            </div>
            <div class='finderDirectory' data-path='/Sites'>
                <div class='finderIcon'></div>
                <div class='finderDirectoryName'>
                    <span>Sites</span>
                </div>
            </div>
            <div class='finderDirectory' data-path='/System'>
                <div class='finderIcon'></div>
                <div class='finderDirectoryName'>
                    <span>System</span>
                </div>
            </div>
            <div class='finderDirectory' data-path='/Users'>
                <div class='finderIcon'></div>
                <div class='finderDirectoryName'>
                    <span>Users</span>
                </div>
            </div>
        </div>
    </body>
</html>
```

The preceding HTML is styled with the following style sheet:

```
html,
body {
    width: 100%;
    height: 100%;
}
body {
    font: 12px "Lucida Grande", Arial, sans-serif;
    background: rgb(189, 189, 189) url('images/Bottom.png') repeat-x bottom;
    color: rgb(50, 50, 50);
    margin: 0;
    padding: 0;
}
div#finderFiles {
    border-bottom: 1px solid rgb(64, 64, 64);
    background: #fff;
```

```
        position: absolute;
        top: 0;
        right: 0;
        bottom: 23px;
        left: 0;
        overflow: auto;
        user-select: none;
        -webkit-user-select: none;
        -moz-user-select: none;
        -ms-user-select: none;
    }
div.finderDirectory {
        float: left;
        width: 150px;
        height: 100px;
        overflow: hidden;
    }
div.finderDirectory:-webkit-drag {
        opacity: 0.5;
    }
div.finderIcon {
        background: url('images/Folder 48x48.png') no-repeat center;
        background-size: 48px 48px;
        height: 56px;
        width: 54px;
        margin: 10px auto 3px auto;
    }
div.finderIconSelected,
div.finderDirectoryDrop div.finderIcon  {
        background-color: rgb(204, 204, 204);
        border-radius: 5px;
    }
div.finderDirectoryDrop div.finderIcon {
        background-image: url('images/Open Folder 48x48.png');
    }
div.finderDirectoryName {
        text-align: center;
    }
span.finderDirectoryNameSelected,
div.finderDirectoryDrop div.finderDirectoryName span {
        background: rgb(56, 117, 215);
        border-radius: 8px;
        color: white;
        padding: 1px 7px;
    }
```

Finally, the following JavaScript brings everything to life:

```
$.fn.extend({
    outerHTML : function()
    {
        var temporary = $("<div/>").append($(this).clone());
        var html = temporary.html();

        temporary.remove();
```

```
            return html;
        },

        enableDragAndDrop : function()
        {
            return this.each(
                function()
                {
                    if (typeof this.style.WebkitUserDrag != 'undefined')
                    {
                        this.style.WebkitUserDrag = 'element';
                    }

                    if (typeof this.draggable != 'undefined')
                    {
                        this.draggable = true;
                    }

                    if (typeof this.dragDrop == 'function')
                    {
                        this.dragDrop();
                    }
                }
            );
        }
});

$(document).ready(
    function()
    {
        $(document).on(
            'mousedown.finder',
            'div.finderDirectory, div.finderFile',
            function(event)
            {
                $(this).enableDragAndDrop();

                $('div.finderIconSelected')
                    .removeClass('finderIconSelected');

                $('span.finderDirectoryNameSelected')
                    .removeClass('finderDirectoryNameSelected');

                $(this).find('div.finderIcon')
                    .addClass('finderIconSelected');

                $(this).find('div.finderDirectoryName span')
                    .addClass('finderDirectoryNameSelected');
            }
        );

        $('div.finderDirectory, div.finderFile')
            .on(
                'dragstart.finder',
```

```
            function(event)
            {
                event.stopPropagation();

                var html = $(this).outerHTML();

                var dataTransfer = event.originalEvent.dataTransfer;

                dataTransfer.effectAllowed = 'copyMove';

                try
                {
                    dataTransfer.setData('text/html', html);
                    dataTransfer.setData('text/plain', html);
                }
                catch (error)
                {
                    dataTransfer.setData('Text', html);
                }
            }
        )
        .on(
            'dragend.finder',
            function(event)
            {
                if ($('div.finderDirectoryDrop').length)
                {
                    $(this).removeClass('finderDirectoryDrop');
                    $(this).remove();
                }
            }
        )
        .on(
            'dragenter.finder',
            function(event)
            {
                event.preventDefault();
                event.stopPropagation();
            }
        )
        .on(
            'dragover.finder',
            function(event)
            {
                event.preventDefault();
                event.stopPropagation();

                if ($(this).is('div.finderDirectory'))
                {
                    $(this).addClass('finderDirectoryDrop');
                }
            }
        )
```

```
        .on(
            'dragleave.finder',
            function(event)
            {
                event.preventDefault();
                event.stopPropagation();

                $(this).removeClass('finderDirectoryDrop');
            }
        )
        .on(
            'drop.finder',
            function(event)
            {
                event.preventDefault();
                event.stopPropagation();

                var dataTransfer = event.originalEvent.dataTransfer;

                try
                {
                    var html = dataTransfer.getData('text/html');
                }
                catch (error)
                {
                    var html = dataTransfer.getData('Text');
                }

                html = $(html);
                var drop = $(this);

                var dontAcceptTheDrop = (
                    drop.data('path') == html.data('path') ||
                    drop.is('div.finderFile')
                );

                if (dontAcceptTheDrop)
                {
                    // Prevent file from being dragged onto itself
                    drop.removeClass('finderDirectoryDrop');
                    return;
                }

                if (html.hasClass('finderDirectory finderFile'))
                {
                    // Do something with the dropped file
                    console.log(html);
                }
            }
        );
    }
);
```

Figure 11-1 shows the preceding example results.

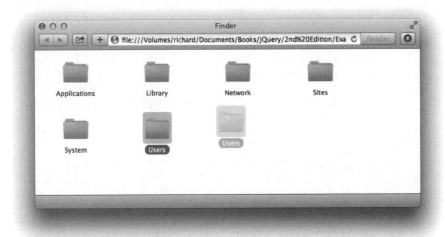

FIGURE 11-1

> **NOTE** *To run this example in Internet Explorer, you should upload the documents to a web server.*

Prerequisite Plugins

This example begins with the creation of two jQuery plugins, $.outerHTML() and $.enableDragAnd-Drop(). The $.outerHTML() plugin is designed to implement IE's native outerHTML property as a jQuery plugin. The purpose of this is to enable easily pasting HTML snippets to the system clipboard using the drag-and-drop API. Using jQuery's existing html() method would get only the content of an element, for example:

```
<div class='finderIcon'></div>
<div class='finderDirectoryName'>
    <span>Sites</span>
</div>
```

Using drag and drop to relocate a complete element, it is instead desirable to have the outer <div> element as well as its content.

```
<div class='finderDirectory' data-path='/Sites'>
    <div class='finderIcon'></div>
    <div class='finderDirectoryName'>
        <span>Sites</span>
    </div>
</div>
```

The $.outerHTML() plugin provided here implements the functionality of the IE property in browsers that haven't implemented the IE property, such as Safari. These snippets can be taken out of the DOM and then reinserted when a successful drag-and-drop operation has taken place.

```
$.fn.extend({
    outerHTML : function()
    {
        var temporary = $("<div/>").append($(this).clone());
        var html = temporary.html();

        temporary.remove();
        return html;
    },
```

The block of code begins with $.fn.extend(), which as you learned in Chapter 9, "Plugins," is used to create jQuery plugins. outerHTML : function() begins the first plugin, which implements outerHTML functionality. The block of markup that you want to retrieve the outerHTML from is cloned using $(this).clone() and is inserted inside a temporary <div> element. The temporary <div> is created using a string "<div/>", which jQuery internally converts to a <div> element object. The cloned object is inserted within the <div> element using the append() method. Then the newly inserted object is retrieved from the newly created <div> element using the html() method and is assigned to the variable named html. The html() method uses the innerHTML property internally, which is implemented universally, in all browsers. Then the temporary <div> element is cleaned up from memory with a call to remove(), which deletes it, and the html source is returned as a string. The HTML snippet that is returned is now portable and can be transported to anywhere that supports rendering HTML, or as plain text, using your operating system's drag-and-drop clipboard. You learn more about the drag-and-drop clipboard later in this section.

The second plugin that you create enables drag and drop using the three different methods that exist for doing so since the drag and drop API was first created by Microsoft with the release of IE5.

```
        enableDragAndDrop : function()
        {
            return this.each(
                function()
                {
                    if (typeof this.style.WebkitUserDrag != 'undefined')
                    {
                        this.style.WebkitUserDrag = 'element';
                    }

                    if (typeof this.draggable != 'undefined')
                    {
                        this.draggable = true;
                    }

                    if (typeof this.dragDrop == 'function')
                    {
                        this.dragDrop();
                    }
                }
            );
        }
```

This plugin does not assume that you are working with just one element. Because it may be desirable to enable drag and drop on many elements at once, it iterates over the potential collection of elements present in this using each(). jQuery *always* passes elements to plugins as an array, never as a single element, to make working with jQuery and writing plugins for jQuery simpler.

Drag-and-drop functionality is first enabled in older WebKit-based browsers, such as Safari and Chrome. (It is worth noting that the order in which these methods are used isn't important, though.) To enable drag and drop in older WebKit-based browsers, the proprietary CSS property -web-kit-user-drag is set to the value *element*. But before you set the value, you first test the CSS property to see if it exists by looking for whether the typeof is *undefined*. If the property exists, the typeof will not be *undefined*, but will instead be *string*.

```
if (typeof this.style.WebkitUserDrag != 'undefined')
{
    this.style.WebkitUserDrag = 'element';
}
```

When you set a proprietary CSS property in JavaScript, the hyphens are omitted, and the first letter is capitalized, so –webkit-user-drag becomes WebkitUserDrag. If it were a property implemented in Firefox, you'd have –moz-user-drag and MozUserDrag, instead.

Next, you check for the existence of the draggable attribute. The draggable attribute is recommended by the W3C HTML 5 drag-and-drop specification as the official way to enable drag and drop. This attribute is supported in the latest versions of Safari, Chrome, Firefox, and Internet Explorer. Like the CSS property, you must check to see if the typeof is not *undefined* to see if the attribute is implemented in the browser.

```
if (typeof this.draggable != 'undefined')
{
    this.draggable = true;
}
```

The draggable attribute is a boolean attribute. Setting it to true enables drag and drop of the element, and setting it to false disables drag and drop. The behavior that you get by setting either the WebkitUserDrag CSS property or draggable attribute is default behavior. Typically, you can move the element around, but nothing happens when you drop it because that behavior has to be defined with JavaScript.

The last method of enabling drag and drop is used for older versions of Internet Explorer. Internet Explorer 9 and later implement the newer HTML 5 drag-and-drop specification and require using the draggable attribute instead of the legacy method used here. To enable drag and drop in IE8 and earlier, first test for the existence of the dragDrop method. Test to see if the typeof the dragDrop method is *function* to find out whether you can use it. (You can also check to see if the typeof is not *undefined* like the CSS property and the HTML attribute, if you like.)

```
if (typeof this.dragDrop == 'function')
{
    this.dragDrop();
}
```

If the dragDrop method exists, simply calling it on the element enables drag and drop on that element in IE8 and earlier.

Event Setup

Now that you have defined these two jQuery plugins, you set up the events that you need to implement the drag-and-drop API.

```
$(document).ready(
    function()
    {
        $(document).on(
            'mousedown.finder',
            'div.finderDirectory, div.finderFile',
            function(event)
            {
                $(this).enableDragAndDrop();

                $('div.finderIconSelected')
                    .removeClass('finderIconSelected');

                $('span.finderDirectoryNameSelected')
                    .removeClass('finderDirectoryNameSelected');

                $(this).find('div.finderIcon')
                    .addClass('finderIconSelected');

                $(this).find('div.finderDirectoryName span')
                    .addClass('finderDirectoryNameSelected');
            }
        );
```

The first event that you create is a mousedown event that enables drag-and-drop functionality on each <div> element with the class names finderDirectory and finderFile. Because it uses the on() method, it is applied automatically when new <div> elements with those class names are added to the DOM. You'll expand on the concept of dynamically applying events to take care of the file or folders added to the folder you're viewing later in this chapter in *Example 11-2*. The mousedown event is applied with an event namespace, *finder*, which you learned about in Chapter 3, "Events." Using jQuery's event namespaces allows you more control over binding and unbinding event handlers. Using the namespace you can unbind only the events in the *finder* namespace, if wanted, without affecting events in other namespaces.

The next thing you do is to begin applying drag-and-drop events to each file and folder <div> element. Along with the CSS property WebkitUserDrag, the HTML attribute draggable, and the dragDrop() method, the application of these events controls what happens when a user drags and drops elements. The drag-and-drop events fire in the following order on the element dragged:

1. dragstart
2. drag
3. dragend

The drag-and-drop events fire in the following order on the drop element:

1. dragenter

2. dragover

3. drop or dragleave

Most of the drag-and-drop events require either event.preventDefault(), or event.stopPropagation(), or both, to block either the default action or to prevent the event from propagating up the DOM tree.

The dragstart event sets the contents of the operating system's drag-and-drop clipboard. It also provides an opportunity to set the effectAllowed property. The effectAllowed property does little more than change the mouse cursor to give the user an indication of what's possible when dragging an element. Because you're working with files and folders, the effectAllowed that makes the most sense is 'copyMove'.

```
$('div.finderDirectory, div.finderFile')
    .on(
        'dragstart.finder',
        function(event)
        {
            event.stopPropagation();

            var html = $(this).outerHTML();

            var dataTransfer = event.originalEvent.dataTransfer;

            dataTransfer.effectAllowed = 'copyMove';

            try
            {
                dataTransfer.setData('text/html', html);
                dataTransfer.setData('text/plain', html);
            }
            catch (error)
            {
                dataTransfer.setData('Text', html);
            }
        }
    )
```

The possible values of the effectAllowed property follow:

➤ none—No operation by drag and drop is permitted.

➤ copy—Only copy by drag and drop is permitted.

➤ move—Only move by drag and drop is permitted.

➤ link—Only link by drag and drop is permitted.

➤ copyMove—Both copy and move are permitted.

➤ copyLink—Both copy and link are permitted.

➤ linkMove—Both link and move are permitted.

➤ all—Copy, link, and move are all permitted.

When two or more operations are supported by the effectAllowed property, the second or third operation is typically invoked by holding down a key on the keyboard.

The system drag-and-drop clipboard is also set in the dragstart event. The clipboard is set by first retrieving the outerHTML() of the element. Then the HTML is copied to the clipboard and identified on the clipboard by the MIME type. In this case, both of the MIME types text/plain and text/html are set. Setting the MIME types allows other applications on your computer to work with the data that you copy to the system clipboard. For example, after copying the HTML to the clipboard in the dragstart event, you can now drag and drop elements outside the browser window to other applications. Any application that supports text/html or text/plain can work with the data copied to the clipboard. You can drag and drop from the browser to a text editor, including editors that only support the text/plain MIME type. You can drag and drop between completely different browsers.

A try / catch exception differentiates between using the setData() method with Internet Explorer's method and the HTML5 standard method. IE supports just two options: 'Text' and 'URL'. All the other browsers use a MIME type. Using an exception automatically switches off to the IE method when using a MIME type fails and throws an error.

The next event that you attach is the dragend event.

```
.on(
    'dragend.finder',
    function(event)
    {
        if ($('div.finderDirectoryDrop').length)
        {
            $(this).removeClass('finderDirectoryDrop');
            $(this).remove();
        }
    }
)
```

The dragend event is fired when the drag has completed, and it is fired on the element that was dragged. There is an issue with the dragend event that is difficult or outright impossible to work with. There is no way of knowing when a drag is completed to an acceptable drop zone when a drag and drop is executed from the browser window to another browser window or an outside application. One potential workaround involves sending an AJAX request to the server from the side receiving the drop and then using web sockets to listen for that drop to occur on the side where the drag originates. But that approach is way over the top for this simple demonstration of the drag-and-drop API.

For drag and drops that originate and terminate in the same browser window, the dragend event looks for the existence of a <div> element with the class name finderDirectoryDrop. If this <div> element is detected, that is an indication that a drag and drop was completed on an acceptable drop zone, which means that the element dragged can be removed from the DOM. Because the element is removed from the DOM, this makes the default action of a drag and drop *move*. If you were to implement a *copy* action, it would then, of course, be desirable to keep the original element. Such an action might be implemented by holding down the Option (Mac) or Ctrl (Windows) key when doing a drag and drop. You'd look for the Option/Alt key by checking whether event.altKey evaluates to true within the `dragstart` event listener. Other options are the Control key, `event.ctrlKey`, the Shift key, `event.shiftKey`, or the Command/Windows key, `event.metaKey`.

The next event attached is the `dragenter` event:

```
.on(
    'dragenter.finder',
    function(event)
    {
        event.preventDefault();
        event.stopPropagation();
    }
)
```

The action taken for the `dragenter` event is simply to prevent the default action and to stop event propagation. The action taken for the `dragover` event is similar:

```
.on(
    'dragover.finder',
    function(event)
    {
        event.preventDefault();
        event.stopPropagation();

        if ($(this).is('div.finderDirectory'))
        {
            $(this).addClass('finderDirectoryDrop');
        }
    }
)
```

The `dragover` event also requires canceling the default action and stopping event propagation. In addition, if the element is a `<div>` element with the classname `finderDirectory`, the classname `finderDirectoryDrop` is added, which changes the icon used for the directory from a closed folder to an open folder.

Likewise, the `dragleave` event also cancels the default action and stops event propagation:

```
.on(
    'dragleave.finder',
    function(event)
    {
        event.preventDefault();
        event.stopPropagation();

        $(this).removeClass('finderDirectoryDrop');
    }
)
```

Then the classname `finderDirectoryDrop` is removed from the `<div>` element, which indicates that the dragging element is no longer over this element.

Finally, the drop event is applied, and it also begins with preventing the default action and stopping event propagation:

```
        .on(
            'drop.finder',
            function(event)
            {
                event.preventDefault();
                event.stopPropagation();

                var dataTransfer = event.originalEvent.dataTransfer;

                try
                {
                    var html = dataTransfer.getData('text/html');
                }
                catch (error)
                {
                    var html = dataTransfer.getData('Text');
                }

                html = $(html);
                var drop = $(this);

                var dontAcceptTheDrop = (
                    drop.data('path') == html.data('path') ||
                    drop.is('div.finderFile')
                );

                if (dontAcceptTheDrop)
                {
                    // Prevent file from being dragged onto itself
                    drop.removeClass('finderDirectoryDrop');
                    return;
                }

                if (html.hasClass('finderDirectory finderFile'))
                {
                    // Do something with the dropped file
                    console.log(html);
                }
            }
        );
```

The drop event listener continues with assigning the dataTransfer object from event.originalEvent. dataTransfer to dataTransfer, which is done to keep the code from getting too wide. The HTML that was copied to the system clipboard under the text/html MIME type during the dragstart event is retrieved from the system clipboard using the getData() method and the same MIME type, text/html. The HTML comes from the clipboard as plain text and is assigned to the html variable. The html variable is converted into a DOM object that jQuery can work with by passing the HTML snippet to the jQuery method, $(html). This makes it possible to do things with the <div> element retrieved from the system clipboard using jQuery methods.

Another try / catch exception is used on the getData() method to differentiate between Internet Explorer's method of retrieving data from the clipboard and the standard way of retrieving data from the clipboard. As you did with setData(), IE requires just 'Text' instead of a MIME type to retrieve data, and using an exception here automatically switches from the MIME type method to the IE method.

> **NOTE** *For security reasons the* `dataTransfer` *object can be accessed only from drag-and-drop event handlers while those drag-and-drop event handlers are firing. This is done to protect users from unauthorized access to their system's clipboard. Access to the* `dataTransfer` *object may also be further limited by the domain name origin (similar to the frame and AJAX cross-domain security limitations).*

Next, the drop element is passed through jQuery, `$(this)`, and assigned to the variable named `drop`.

The variable `dontAcceptTheDrop` checks to see that an element isn't being dropped on itself and that the drop target is a directory, rather than a file. If `dontAcceptTheDrop` is `true`, the `finderDirectory Drop` classname is removed, and execution of the event listener terminates with the call to `return`.

Finally, the `<div>` object created from the HTML snippet is checked to see that it has either the classname `finderDirectory` or `finderFile` as a final validation that the HTML snippet is HTML that you want to work with.

In the next section, you learn how to further extend this example to accept drag-and-drop file uploads, in addition to implementing drag and drop on the folder window. You extend the example to dynamically reapply events to a dragged and dropped file or folder.

IMPLEMENTING DRAG-AND-DROP FILE UPLOADS

File uploads by drag and drop have evolved during the past few years—beginning with only allowing one or more files to be uploaded by drag and drop and then expanding to allowing drag-and-drop downloads. File uploads then expanded again to allow both files and folders to be uploaded by drag and drop. Presently, the latest versions of all the major browsers support file upload by drag and drop. Chrome supports upload of both files and folders, and drag and drop downloads.

In the following example, you build on *Example 11-1*, adding drag-and-drop upload support to it, as well as some other tweaks that improve the drag-and-drop experience. Drag-and-drop uploading is accompanied with thumbnail previews of image files, as well as an upload progress bar. To realistically test the following example, you need to add a server-side script into the mix to receive the uploaded files. The server-side portion of this is not covered by this example, but I have provided a remedial PHP script that you can use to examine uploaded file metadata. This example is available in the book's source code download materials as *Example 11-2*.

```
<!DOCTYPE HTML>
<html lang='en'>
    <head>
        <meta http-equiv='X-UA-Compatible' content='IE=Edge' />
        <meta charset='utf-8' />
        <title>Finder</title>
```

```html
        <script src='../jQuery.js'></script>
        <script src='../jQueryUI.js'></script>
        <script src='Example 11-2.js'></script>
        <link href='Example 11-2.css' rel='stylesheet' />
</head>
<body>
    <div id='finderFiles' data-path='/'>
        <div class='finderDirectory' data-path='/Applications'>
            <div class='finderIcon'></div>
            <div class='finderDirectoryName'>
                <span>Applications</span>
            </div>
        </div>
        <div class='finderDirectory' data-path='/Library'>
            <div class='finderIcon'></div>
            <div class='finderDirectoryName'>
                <span>Library</span>
            </div>
        </div>
        <div class='finderDirectory' data-path='/Network'>
            <div class='finderIcon'></div>
            <div class='finderDirectoryName'>
                <span>Network</span>
            </div>
        </div>
        <div class='finderDirectory' data-path='/Sites'>
            <div class='finderIcon'></div>
            <div class='finderDirectoryName'>
                <span>Sites</span>
            </div>
        </div>
        <div class='finderDirectory' data-path='/System'>
            <div class='finderIcon'></div>
            <div class='finderDirectoryName'>
                <span>System</span>
            </div>
        </div>
        <div class='finderDirectory' data-path='/Users'>
            <div class='finderIcon'></div>
            <div class='finderDirectoryName'>
                <span>Users</span>
            </div>
        </div>
    </div>
    <div id='finderDragAndDropDialogue'>
        <div id='finderDragAndDropDialogueWrapper'>
            <h4>File Upload Queue</h4>
            <div id='finderDragAndDropDialogueProgress'>
                <span>0</span>%
            </div>
            <img id='finderDragAndDropDialogueActivity'
                src='images/Upload Activity.gif'
                alt='Upload Activity' />
            <div id='finderDragAndDropDialogueProgressMeter'>
```

```
                        <div></div>
                    </div>
                    <div id='finderDragAndDropDialogueFiles'>
                        <table>
                            <thead>
                                <tr>
                                    <th class='finderDragAndDropDialogueFileIcon'>
                                    </th>
                                    <th class='finderDragAndDropDialogueFile'>
                                        File
                                     </th>
                                    <th class='finderDragAndDropDialogueFileSize'>
                                        Size
                                    </th>
                                </tr>
                            </thead>
                            <tbody>
                                <tr class='finderDragAndDropDialogueTemplate'>
                                    <td class='finderDragAndDropDialogueFileIcon'>
                                    </td>
                                    <td class='finderDragAndDropDialogueFile'>
                                    </td>
                                    <td class='finderDragAndDropDialogueFileSize'>
                                    </td>
                                </tr>
                            </tbody>
                        </table>
                    </div>
                </div>
            </div>
        </body>
    </html>
```

The preceding file is saved as *Example 11-2.html* and is styled with the following CSS:

```
html,
body {
    width: 100%;
    height: 100%;
}
body {
    font: 12px "Lucida Grande", Arial, sans-serif;
    background:
        rgb(189, 189, 189)
        url('images/Bottom.png')
        repeat-x bottom;
    color: rgb(50, 50, 50);
    margin: 0;
    padding: 0;
}
div#finderFiles {
    border-bottom: 1px solid rgb(64, 64, 64);
    background: #fff;
    position: absolute;
    top: 0;
```

```css
    right: 0;
    bottom: 23px;
    left: 0;
    overflow: auto;
    user-select: none;
    -webkit-user-select: none;
    -moz-user-select: none;
    -ms-user-select: none;
}
div.finderDirectory {
    float: left;
    width: 150px;
    height: 100px;
    overflow: hidden;
}
div.finderDirectory:-webkit-drag {
    opacity: 0.5;
}
div.finderIcon {
    background:
        url('images/Folder 48x48.png')
        no-repeat center;
    background-size: 48px 48px;
    height: 56px;
    width: 54px;
    margin: 10px auto 3px auto;
}
div.finderIconSelected,
div.finderDirectoryDrop > div.finderIcon  {
    background-color: rgb(204, 204, 204);
    border-radius: 5px;
}
div.finderDirectoryDrop > div.finderIcon {
    background-image: url('images/Open Folder 48x48.png');
}
div.finderDirectoryName {
    text-align: center;
}
span.finderDirectoryNameSelected,
div.finderDirectoryDrop > div.finderDirectoryName > span {
    background: rgb(56, 117, 215);
    border-radius: 8px;
    color: white;
    padding: 1px 7px;
}
div#finderDragAndDropDialogue {
    position: fixed;
    width: 500px;
    height: 500px;
    top: 50%;
    left: 50%;
    margin: -250px 0 0 -250px;
    box-shadow: 0 7px 100px rgba(0, 0, 0, 0.6);
    background: #fff;
```

```css
    padding: 1px;
    border-radius: 4px;
    display: none;
}
div#finderDragAndDropDialogue h4 {
    margin: 0;
    padding: 10px;
}
img#finderDragAndDropDialogueActivity {
    position: absolute;
    top: 8px;
    right: 50px;
}
div#finderDragAndDropDialogueProgressMeter {
    position: absolute;
    top: 11px;
    right: 55px;
    width: 210px;
    height: 11px;
    border-radius: 3px;
    border: 1px solid rgb(181, 187, 200);
    display: none;
}
div#finderDragAndDropDialogueProgressMeter div {
    position: absolute;
    top: 0;
    left: 0;
    height: 11px;
    font-size: 0;
    line-height: 0;
    border-top-left-radius: 3px;
    border-bottom-left-radius: 3px;
    background: rgb(225, 228, 233);
    width: 0;
    display: none;
}
div#finderDragAndDropDialogueProgress {
    position: absolute;
    top: 10px;
    right: 10px;
}
div#finderDragAndDropDialogueFiles table {
    table-layout: fixed;
    border-collapse: collapse;
    margin: 0;
    padding: 0;
    width: 100%;
    height: 100%;
}
div#finderDragAndDropDialogueFiles {
    position: absolute;
    overflow: auto;
    top: 35px;
    right: 5px;
```

```css
    bottom: 5px;
    left: 5px;
    border: 1px solid rgb(222, 222, 222);
}
div#finderDragAndDropDialogueFiles table th {
    background: rgb(233, 233, 233);
    border: 1px solid rgb(222, 222, 222);
    text-align: left;
    padding: 5px;
}
div#finderDragAndDropDialogueFiles table td {
    padding: 5px;
    border-left: 1px solid rgb(222, 222, 222);
    border-right: 1px solid rgb(222, 222, 222);
    overflow: hidden;
    text-overflow: ellipsis;
    vertical-align: top;
}
td.finderDragAndDropDialogueFileIcon img {
    max-height: 100px;
}
```

The CSS is saved as *Example 11-2.css*. Finally, the following script and on the following pages completes the HTML drag-and-drop API demo:

```javascript
$.fn.extend({

    outerHTML : function()
    {
        var temporary = $("<div/>").append($(this).clone());
        var html = temporary.html();

        temporary.remove();
        return html;
    },

    enableDragAndDrop : function()
    {
        return this.each(
            function()
            {
                if (typeof this.style.WebkitUserDrag != 'undefined')
                {
                    this.style.WebkitUserDrag = 'element';
                }

                if (typeof this.draggable != 'undefined')
                {
                    this.draggable = true;
                }

                if (typeof this.dragDrop == 'function')
                {
                    this.dragDrop();
```

```
            }
        }
    );
    }
});

dragAndDrop = {

    path : null,

    files : [],

    openProgressDialogue : function(files, path)
    {
        this.path = path;

        $('div#finderDragAndDropDialogue')
            .fadeIn('fast');

        this.files = [];

        $(files).each(
            function(key, file)
            {
                dragAndDrop.addFileToQueue(file);
            }
        );

        if (this.files.length)
        {
            this.upload();
        }
        else
        {
            this.closeProgressDialogue();
        }
    },

    closeProgressDialogue : function()
    {
        // Uncomment this section to automatically close the
        // dialogue after upload

        //$('div#finderDragAndDropDialogue')
        //    .fadeOut('fast');

        //$('div#finderDragAndDropDialogue tbody tr')
        //    .not('tr.finderDragAndDropDialogueTemplate')
        //    .remove();
    },

    addFileToQueue : function(file)
    {
        if (!file.name && file.fileName)
```

```
    {
        file.name = file.fileName;
    }

    if (!file.size && file.fileSize)
    {
        file.size = file.fileSize;
    }

    this.files.push(file);

    var tr = $('tr.finderDragAndDropDialogueTemplate').clone(true);

    tr.removeClass('finderDragAndDropDialogueTemplate');

    // Preview image uploads by showing a thumbnail of the image
    if (file.type.match(/^image\/.*$/) && FileReader)
    {
        var img = document.createElement('img');
        img.file = file;

        tr.find('td.finderDragAndDropDialogueFileIcon')
          .html(img);

        var reader = new FileReader();

        reader.onload = function(event)
        {
            img.src = event.target.result;
        };

        reader.readAsDataURL(file);
    }

    tr.find('td.finderDragAndDropDialogueFile')
      .text(file.name);

    tr.find('td.finderDragAndDropDialogueFileSize')
      .text(this.getFileSize(file.size));

    tr.attr('title', file.name);

    $('div#finderDragAndDropDialogueFiles tbody').append(tr);
},

http : null,

upload : function()
{
    this.http = new XMLHttpRequest();

    if (this.http.upload && this.http.upload.addEventListener)
    {
        this.http.upload.addEventListener(
```

```
                'progress',
                function(event)
                {
                    if (event.lengthComputable)
                    {
                        $('div#finderDragAndDropDialogueProgressMeter')
                            .show();

                        $('div#finderDragAndDropDialogueProgressMeter div')
                            .show();

                        var progress = Math.round(
                            (event.loaded * 100) / event.total
                        );

                        $('div#finderDragAndDropDialogueProgress span')
                            .text(progress);

                        $('div#finderDragAndDropDialogueProgressMeter div')
                            .css('width', progress + '%');
                    }
                },
                false
            );

            this.http.upload.addEventListener(
                'load',
                function(event)
                {
                    $('div#finderDragAndDropDialogueProgress span')
                        .text(100);

                    $('div#finderDragAndDropDialogueProgressMeter div')
                        .css('width', '100%');
                }
            );
        }

        this.http.addEventListener(
            'load',
            function(event)
            {
                // This event is fired when the upload completes and
                // the server-side script /file/upload.json sends back
                // a response.
                dragAndDrop.closeProgressDialogue();

                // If the server-side script sends back a JSON response,
                // this is how you'd access it and do something with it.
                var json = $.parseJSON(dragAndDrop.http.responseText);
            },
            false
        );
```

```javascript
        if (typeof FormData !== 'undefined')
        {
            var form = new FormData();

            // The form object invoked here is a built-in object, provided
            // by the browser; it allows you to specify POST variables
            // in the request for the file upload.
            form.append('path', this.path);

            $(this.files).each(
                function(key, file)
                {
                    form.append('file[]', file);
                    form.append('name[]', file.name);
                    form.append('replaceFile[]', 1);
                }
            );

            // This sends a POST request to the server at the path
            // /file/upload.php. This is the server-side file that will
            // handle the file upload.
            this.http.open('POST', 'file/upload.json');
            this.http.send(form);
        }
        else
        {
            console.log(
                'This browser does not support HTML 5 ' +
                'drag and drop file uploads.'
            );

            this.closeProgressDialogue();
        }
    },

getFileSize : function(bytes)
{
    switch (true)
    {
        case (bytes < Math.pow(2,10)):
        {
            return bytes + ' Bytes';
        }
        case (bytes >= Math.pow(2,10) && bytes < Math.pow(2,20)):
        {
            return Math.round(
                bytes / Math.pow(2,10)
            ) +' KB';
        }
        case (bytes >= Math.pow(2,20) && bytes < Math.pow(2,30)):
        {
            return Math.round(
                (bytes / Math.pow(2,20)) * 10
            ) / 10 + ' MB';
```

```
            }
            case (bytes > Math.pow(2,30)):
            {
                return Math.round(
                    (bytes / Math.pow(2,30)) * 100
                ) / 100 + ' GB';
            }
        }
    },

    applyEvents : function()
    {
        var context = null;

        if (arguments[0])
        {
            context = arguments[0];
        }
        else
        {
            context = $('div.finderDirectory, div.finderFile');
        }

        context
            .on(
                'dragstart.finder',
                function(event)
                {
                    event.stopPropagation();

                    var html = $(this).outerHTML();

                    var dataTransfer = event.originalEvent.dataTransfer;

                    dataTransfer.effectAllowed = 'copyMove';

                    try
                    {
                        dataTransfer.setData('text/html', html);
                        dataTransfer.setData('text/plain', html);
                    }
                    catch (error)
                    {
                        dataTransfer.setData('Text', html);
                    }
                }
            )
            .on(
                'dragend.finder',
                function(event)
                {
                    if ($('div.finderDirectoryDrop').length)
                    {
                        $(this).removeClass('finderDirectoryDrop');
```

```
                $(this).remove();
            }
        }
    )
    .on(
        'dragenter.finder',
        function(event)
        {
            event.preventDefault();
            event.stopPropagation();
        }
    )
    .on(
        'dragover.finder',
        function(event)
        {
            event.preventDefault();
            event.stopPropagation();

            if ($(this).is('div.finderDirectory'))
            {
                $(this).addClass('finderDirectoryDrop');
            }
        }
    )
    .on(
        'dragleave.finder',
        function(event)
        {
            event.preventDefault();
            event.stopPropagation();

            $(this).removeClass('finderDirectoryDrop');
        }
    )
    .on(
        'drop.finder',
        function(event)
        {
            event.preventDefault();
            event.stopPropagation();

            var dataTransfer = event.originalEvent.dataTransfer;
            var drop = $(this);

            if (drop.hasClass('finderDirectory'))
            {
                if (dataTransfer.files && dataTransfer.files.length)
                {
                    // Files dropped from outside the browser
                    dragAndDrop.openProgressDialogue(
                        dataTransfer.files,
                        node.data('path')
                    );
```

```
                    }
                    else
                    {
                        try
                        {
                            var html = dataTransfer.getData('text/html');
                        }
                        catch (error)
                        {
                            var html = dataTransfer.getData('Text');
                        }

                        html = $(html);

                        var dontAcceptTheDrop = (
                            html.data('path') == drop.data('path') ||
                            drop.is('div.finderFile')
                        );

                        if (dontAcceptTheDrop)
                        {
                            // Prevent file from being dragged onto itself
                            drop.removeClass('finderDirectoryDrop');
                            return;
                        }

                        if (html.hasClass('finderDirectory finderFile'))
                        {
                            // Do something with the dropped file
                            console.log(html);
                        }
                    }
                }
            }
        );
    }
};

$(document).ready(
    function()
    {
        $(document).on(
            'mousedown.finder',
            'div.finderDirectory, div.finderFile',
            function(event)
            {
                $(this).enableDragAndDrop();

                $('div.finderIconSelected')
                    .removeClass('finderIconSelected');

                $('span.finderDirectoryNameSelected')
                    .removeClass('finderDirectoryNameSelected');
```

```
            $(this).find('div.finderIcon')
                .addClass('finderIconSelected');

            $(this).find('div.finderDirectoryName span')
                .addClass('finderDirectoryNameSelected');
        }
    );

dragAndDrop.applyEvents();

$('div#finderFiles')
    .on(
        'dragenter.finder',
        function(event)
        {
            event.preventDefault();
            event.stopPropagation();
        }
    )
    .on(
        'dragover.finder',
        function(event)
        {
            event.preventDefault();
            event.stopPropagation();

            $(this).addClass('finderDirectoryDrop');
        }
    )
    .on(
        'dragleave.finder',
        function(event)
        {
            event.preventDefault();
            event.stopPropagation();

            $(this).removeClass('finderDirectoryDrop');
        }
    )
    .on(
        'drop.finder',
        function(event)
        {
            event.preventDefault();
            event.stopPropagation();

            var dataTransfer = event.originalEvent.dataTransfer;
            var drop = $(this);

            if (dataTransfer.files && dataTransfer.files.length)
            {
                dragAndDrop.openProgressDialogue(
                    dataTransfer.files,
                    drop.data('path')
```

```
                );
            }
            else
            {
                try
                {
                    var html = dataTransfer.getData('text/html');
                }
                catch (error)
                {
                    var html = dataTransfer.getData('Text');
                }

                html = $(html);

                if (drop.data('path') == html.data('path'))
                {
                    // Prevent file from being dragged onto itself
                    drop.removeClass('finderDirectoryDrop');
                    return;
                }

                if (!html.hasClass('finderDirectory finderFile'))
                {
                    return;
                }

                var fileExists = false;

                $('div.finderFile, div.finderDirectory').each(
                    function()
                    {
                        if ($(this).data('path') == html.data('path'))
                        {
                            fileExists = true;
                            return false;
                        }
                    }
                );

                if (!fileExists)
                {
                    dragAndDrop.applyEvents(html);
                    drop.append(html);
                }
            }
        }
    );
}
);
```

The preceding JavaScript is saved as *Example 11-2.js*, and loading *Example 11-2.html* in Safari produces the screen shot that you see in Figure 11-2 when you drag some files onto the browser window.

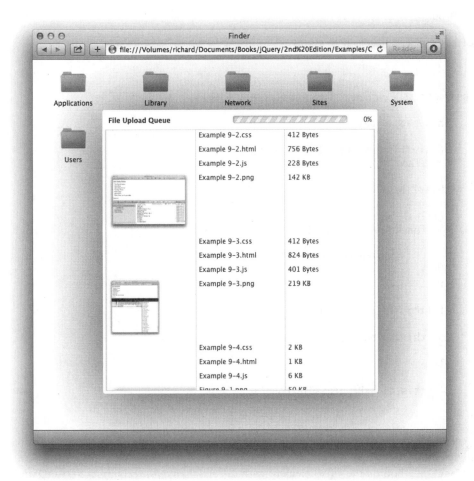

FIGURE 11-2

The example presented in *Example 11-2* is significantly longer than *Example 11-1*, but it offers a more complete implementation of the drag-and-drop API in a web-based file/folder manager paradigm. The following is an examination of the bits and pieces of *Example 11-2* that are new from *Example 11-1*.

Adding the File Information Data Object

The first new piece is the creation of a new JavaScript object called dragAndDrop. This new object holds most of the logic for the implementation of drag-and-drop file uploads. You define two new properties, path and files, which keep track of the current file path that you're uploading to and what files you're uploading to that location. The first method on the new dragAndDrop object that you created is called openProgressDialogue(). (Dialogue is spelled the English way, rather than the American way, which is simply a personal idiosyncrasy.)

```
dragAndDrop = {

    path : null,

    files : [],

    openProgressDialogue : function(files, path)
    {
        this.path = path;

        $('div#finderDragAndDropDialogue')
            .fadeIn('fast');

        this.files = [];

        $(files).each(
            function(key, file)
            {
                dragAndDrop.addFileToQueue(file);
            }
        );

        if (this.files.length)
        {
            this.upload();
        }
        else
        {
            this.closeProgressDialogue();
        }
    },
```

Within the openProgressDialogue() method, you copy the *path* argument, which indicates the path you want to upload the files to, to this.path. And you make the progress dialogue visible by calling the fadeIn('fast') method on the <div> element with the classname *finderDragAndDropDialogue*. The files dragged and dropped for upload are passed in the *files* argument. The *files* variable is an array (it remains an array whether one file is uploaded or many), and it is iterated using jQuery's each() method. The call to dragAndDrop.addFileToQueue() adds the file to the this.files array and also adds the file to the progress dialogue's table so that the user can preview upload progress. If this.files has a length greater than zero, the method this.upload() is called to execute the file upload. If this.files has a length of zero, this.closeProgressDialogue() is called to close the progress dialogue. Logically speaking, the this.closeProgressDialogue() route should be impossible given that the dialogue is not opened unless one or more files are present to upload. This route is represented to cover all bases in implementing a reusable file upload API.

The next method implemented in the dragAndDrop object is the closeProgressDialogue() method.

```
    closeProgressDialogue : function()
    {
        // Uncomment this section to automatically close the
        // dialogue after upload

        //$('div#finderDragAndDropDialogue')
```

```
//      .fadeOut('fast');

//$('div#finderDragAndDropDialogue tbody tr')
//      .not('tr.finderDragAndDropDialogueTemplate')
//      .remove();
},
```

The closeProgressDialogue() method is called automatically when the file upload has completed. It contains some code that you want to uncomment, upon implementing the server-side portion, which closes and resets the progress dialogue.

The following method, addFileToQueue(), sets up the <table> in the progress dialogue with a summary of each file uploaded so that the user can see visual feedback regarding their upload attempt. It creates thumbnails for any images uploaded and adds the files to the this.files array.

```
addFileToQueue : function(file)
{
    if (!file.name && file.fileName)
    {
        file.name = file.fileName;
    }

    if (!file.size && file.fileSize)
    {
        file.size = file.fileSize;
    }
```

The first section normalizes the file object, moving the file.fileName property to file.name and the file.fileSize property to file.size in browsers whose makers preferred the longer property names. Then the file object is added to the this.files array via a call to push().

```
this.files.push(file);
```

The next line of code clones the <tr> element with the classname finderDragAndDropDialogueTemplate with a call to clone(true), which is ultimately added to the <table> with summary data about each file uploaded.

```
var tr = $('tr.finderDragAndDropDialogueTemplate').clone(true);
```

The finderDragAndDropDialogueTemplate classname is removed from the template. The classname hides the template from the user and identifies the <tr> element as a template.

```
tr.removeClass('finderDragAndDropDialogueTemplate');
```

The next line examines the MIME type of the uploaded file by checking to see if the MIME type begins with the string 'image/' using a regular expression, and it checks to see if the FileReader object exists, which is needed to display thumbnails of the uploading image files to the user. At present it is only possible to display thumbnails of image files.

```
// Preview image uploads by showing a thumbnail of the image
if (file.type.match(/^image\/.*$/) && FileReader)
{
```

The thumbnail creation begins by creating a new `<img />` element. The file is assigned to the file property of the `<img />` element.

```
var img = document.createElement('img');
img.file = file;
```

The `<img />` element is added to the `<td>` element with the classname `finderDragAndDropDialogue-FileIcon` with a call to `html()`.

```
tr.find('td.finderDragAndDropDialogueFileIcon')
  .html(img);
```

The `FileReader` object is instantiated, which plays the critical role of reading the file to display the image, which is ultimately scaled down to thumbnail size by the style sheet.

```
var reader = new FileReader();
```

An onload event is created that assigns the `src` attribute of the `<img />` element; each image `src` is created using data URIs. The `FileReader` object provides a base64-encoded data URI representation of the image, which is assigned to the `src` attribute, thus making it possible to preview each image file.

```
reader.onload = function(event)
{
    img.src = event.target.result;
};

reader.readAsDataURL(file);
}
```

Each filename is placed inside the `<td>` with the classname `finderDragAndDropDialogueFile`.

```
tr.find('td.finderDragAndDropDialogueFile')
  .text(file.name);
```

And each file size is converted from bytes to a human-readable number in one of bytes, kilobytes, megabytes, and such depending on the size of the number by virtue of a call to `dragAndDrop.getFileSize()`. The resulting value is placed inside the `<td>` element with the classname `finderDragAndDropDialogueFileSize`.

```
tr.find('td.finderDragAndDropDialogueFileSize')
  .text(this.getFileSize(file.size));
```

The `file.name` is assigned to the `title` attribute of the `<tr>` element.

```
tr.attr('title', file.name);
```

Finally, the completed `<tr>` template is added to the `<tbody>` element.

```
$('div#finderDragAndDropDialogueFiles tbody').append(tr);
},
```

Using a Custom XMLHttpRequest Object

The next property and method provide the data transfer functionality for the uploaded files. This involves setting up a custom XMLHttpRequest object, which is in turn assigned to this.http.

```
http : null,

upload : function()
{
    this.http = new XMLHttpRequest();
```

A series of events is set up to monitor upload progress and to watch out for upload completion. First, you check whether the upload object exists on the XMLHttpRequest (hereafter, I will simply call the XMLHttpRequest object just http), and you check to see whether the addEventListener method exists on the upload object.

```
if (this.http.upload && this.http.upload.addEventListener)
{
```

You next set up an event listener for the progress event on the upload object. This event ultimately tells you the overall progress of the file upload, whether one file is uploaded or many.

```
this.http.upload.addEventListener(
    'progress',
    function(event)
    {
```

The event.lengthComputable property tells you whether there is any progress to report.

```
if (event.lengthComputable)
{
```

The <div> with id name finderDragAndDropDialogueProgressMeter is displayed, as well as the <div> element within that one.

```
$('div#finderDragAndDropDialogueProgressMeter')
    .show();

$('div#finderDragAndDropDialogueProgressMeter div')
    .show();
```

File upload progress is calculated as a rounded percentage from the event.loaded and event.total properties that are provided in the event object.

```
var progress = Math.round(
    (event.loaded * 100) / event.total
);
```

The resulting progress figure is added to the <span> nested with the <div> element with id name finderDragAndDropDialogueProgress.

```
$('div#finderDragAndDropDialogueProgress span')
    .text(progress);
```

Then the <div> nested within the <div> with id name `finderDragAndDropDialogueProgressMeter` is given a percentage width, which also indicates the progress.

```
            $('div#finderDragAndDropDialogueProgressMeter div')
                .css('width', progress + '%');
        }
    },
    false
);
```

Next, a `load` event is attached to the upload object to cover what happens when 100 percent upload progress is reached.

```
        this.http.upload.addEventListener(
            'load',
            function(event)
            {
                $('div#finderDragAndDropDialogueProgress span')
                    .text(100);

                $('div#finderDragAndDropDialogueProgressMeter div')
                    .css('width', '100%');
            }
        );
    }
```

A `load` event is also attached to the `http` object, which is fired when the server side has responded to the upload request.

```
        this.http.addEventListener(
            'load',
            function(event)
            {
                // This event is fired when the upload completes and
                // the server-side script /file/upload.json sends back
                // a response.
```

When the upload request is completed, the progress dialogue is closed with a call to `dragAndDrop.closeProgressDialogue()`.

```
                dragAndDrop.closeProgressDialogue();

                // If the server-side script sends back a JSON response,
                // this is how you'd access it and do something with it.
```

If the server-side sends back a JSON response, it can be read and parsed from the `http.responseText` property, and the application can respond to data in the JSON response appropriately.

```
                var json = $.parseJSON(dragAndDrop.http.responseText);
            },
            false
        );
```

Check for the existence of the FormData object to see if a more recent revision of drag-and-drop upload is supported by your browser. The FormData object is provided by the browser and facilitates the creation of the HTTP request that will ultimately pass the uploaded file data across the Internet. In this example, the FormData object creates a POST request with encoding multipart/form-data. In a traditional file upload, you would have to add multipart/form-data to the <form> element in the enctype attribute. The FormData object takes care of this for you automatically.

```
if (typeof FormData !== 'undefined')
{
    var form = new FormData();

    // The form object invoked here is a built-in object, provided
    // by the browser; it allows you to specify POST variables
    // in the request for the file upload.
```

You can append arguments to the FormData object by using the append() method. The first argument appended is the path argument. This creates a POST variable called path on the server side and signals to the server-side script where you want to upload the files.

```
form.append('path', this.path);
```

Each file is iterated by passing the this.files array to the each() method. The file is passed to the server side in a file[] array. The square brackets are used by PHP to signal the creation of an array. The syntax used to do this might be different in your server-side language of choice. Some additional information is passed on to the server in a name[] variable and the replaceFile[] variable. You can create as many variables as you need.

```
$(this.files).each(
    function(key, file)
    {
        form.append('file[]', file);
        form.append('name[]', file.name);
        form.append('replaceFile[]', 1);
    }
);
```

Finally, the entire POST request including the uploaded file data is sent on to the server-side script for processing. file/upload.json provides a canned JSON response in the absence of a real server-side script.

```
    // This sends a POST request to the server at the path
    // /file/upload.php. This is the server-side file that will
    // handle the file upload.
    this.http.open('POST', 'file/upload.json');
    this.http.send(form);
}
```

If your browser does not support the FormData object, you print a message to the JavaScript console and close the progress dialogue.

```
else
{
```

```
                console.log(
                    'This browser does not support HTML 5 ' +
                    'drag and drop file uploads.'
                );

                this.closeProgressDialogue();
            }
        },
```

Additional Utilities

The remaining methods in the JavaScript act as utilities for simplifying the remaining actions of size calculation, string manipulation, and event application.

The getFileSize() method returns a human-readable representation of file size. The file size in bytes is fed into the method, and a number representing the file size in bytes, kilobytes (KB), megabytes (MB), or gigabytes (GB) is returned. This method uses the Math.pow() method, where Math.pow(2,10) = 1 KB, Math.pow(2,20) = 1 MB, and Math.pow(2,30) = 1 GB.

```
        getFileSize : function(bytes)
        {
            switch (true)
            {
                case (bytes < Math.pow(2,10)):
                {
                    return bytes + ' Bytes';
                }
                case (bytes >= Math.pow(2,10) && bytes < Math.pow(2,20)):
                {
                    return Math.round(
                        bytes / Math.pow(2,10)
                    ) +' KB';
                }
                case (bytes >= Math.pow(2,20) && bytes < Math.pow(2,30)):
                {
                    return Math.round(
                        (bytes / Math.pow(2,20)) * 10
                    ) / 10 + ' MB';
                }
                case (bytes > Math.pow(2,30)):
                {
                    return Math.round(
                        (bytes / Math.pow(2,30)) * 100
                    ) / 100 + ' GB';
                }
            }
        },
```

The applyEvents() method applies all the drag-and-drop events that you first implemented in *Example 11-1*. You start the method by creating a context variable, which decides how the events are applied. If you apply the events to a file or folder object that has been dragged and dropped from outside the browser window, this method applies each drag-and-drop event to the newly moved file or folder object. Otherwise, each event is applied to every file and folder object that is present.

```
applyEvents : function()
{
    var context = null;

    if (arguments[0])
    {
        context = arguments[0];
    }
    else
    {
        context = $('div.finderDirectory, div.finderFile');
    }

    context
```

The dragstart, dragend, dragenter, dragover, and dragleave events remain unchanged from *Example 11-1*. The drop event has been modified to accommodate drag-and-drop file uploads as well as moving around existing files or folders.

```
.on(
    'drop.finder',
    function(event)
    {
        event.preventDefault();
        event.stopPropagation();

        var dataTransfer = event.originalEvent.dataTransfer;
        var drop = $(this);

        if (drop.hasClass('finderDirectory'))
        {
```

If the user has dragged and dropped files for upload to the browser window, the files are present in the dataTransfer.files property, and the files property has a length greater than zero. The files, along with the path of the folder the files were dropped on, passes along to the openProgressDialogue() method for processing and upload.

```
if (dataTransfer.files && dataTransfer.files.length)
{
    // Files dropped from outside the browser
    dragAndDrop.openProgressDialogue(
        dataTransfer.files,
        node.data('path')
    );
}
else
{
    try
    {
        var html = dataTransfer.getData('text/html');
    }
```

```
                    catch (error)
                    {
                        var html = dataTransfer.getData('Text');
                    }

                    html = $(html);
```

Other than file uploads by drag and drop, the `drop` event listener works the same as it did in *Example 11-1.*

Along with the drag-and-drop events that are applied to each file and folder object, a new collection of drag-and-drop events are also applied to the `<div>` element with id name `finderFiles`, which is the folder view taking up nearly all the browser window that holds all the file and folder elements. This `<div>` element receives `dragenter`, `dragover`, and `dragleave` events that are identical to the `dragenter`, `dragover`, and `dragleave` events already placed on `<div>` elements with classnames `finderFile` or `finderDirectory`. This leaves the `drop` event, which is slightly different.

```
        .on(
            'drop.finder',
            function(event)
            {
                event.preventDefault();
                event.stopPropagation();

                var dataTransfer = event.originalEvent.dataTransfer;
                var drop = $(this);
```

As you did with the other drop event, check that the `files` property has a `length` greater than zero, which lets your application know that the user has dropped files onto the browser window.

```
            if (dataTransfer.files && dataTransfer.files.length)
            {
                dragAndDrop.openProgressDialogue(
                    dataTransfer.files,
                    drop.data('path')
                );
            }
            else
            {
                try
                {
                    var html = dataTransfer.getData('text/html');
                }
                catch (error)
                {
                    var html = dataTransfer.getData('Text');
                }

                html = $(html);
```

You also make sure that the folder isn't dropped on itself:

```
            if (drop.data('path') == html.data('path'))
            {
```

```
                    // Prevent file from being dragged onto itself
                    drop.removeClass('finderDirectoryDrop');
                    return;
                }
```

You make sure that the dropped HTML has the `finderDirectory` and `finderFile` class names:

```
                if (!html.hasClass('finderDirectory finderFile'))
                {
                    return;
                }
```

Finally, check that any file or folder dropped onto the directory doesn't already exist in the directory by examining each of the filenames in that directory locally. In this example, the application simply stops when it detects a duplicate file locally. Another approach is upon detecting a duplicate file, you ask users if they wants to replace the duplicate file; then you pass that selection onto the server side, which should also perform validation for existing files or folders. In addition, the same duplicate filename check should be done for drag-and-drop file uploads. I have removed the extra validation in the interest of keeping the script shorter and more to the point.

```
                var fileExists = false;

                $('div.finderFile, div.finderDirectory').each(
                    function()
                    {
                        if ($(this).data('path') == html.data('path'))
                        {
                            fileExists = true;
                            return false;
                        }
                    }
                );
```

If the file or folder does not already exist, you would do something with the dropped HTML here.

```
                if (!fileExists)
                {
                    dragAndDrop.applyEvents(html);
                    drop.append(html);
                }
            }
        }
    );
```

SUMMARY

In this chapter you learned how to use jQuery to leverage the HTML5 drag-and-drop API. You implemented the drag-and-drop API using the CSS property `-webkit-user-drag`, the `draggable` HTML attribute, and the legacy `dragDrop()` method. You also learned how to implement the drag-and-drop API in JavaScript by virtue of attaching listeners to the following events: `dragstart`, `drag`, `dragend`, `dragenter`, `dragover`, `drop`, and `dragleave`.

You also learned how to implement drag-and-drop file uploads using the drag-and-drop API, which includes looking for the `files` property on the `dataTransfer` object. You learned how to preview thumbnails of uploading image files using the `FileReader` object. You learned how to monitor upload progress by attaching `progress` and `load` events to the `upload` property of the `XMLHttpRequest` object. Finally, you learned how to customize an HTTP POST request and submit the file upload to the server side using the `XMLHttpRequest` and `FormData` objects.

EXERCISES

1. Describe how you enable drag-and-drop functionality on an element. Which methods are legacy methods and what browsers do the legacy methods exist for?

2. List the events in the order that they fire that are used to drag an element.

3. List the events in the order that they fire that are used to drop an element.

4. When you implement drag-and-drop file uploads, what property do you look for, and using which event, to detect that a drag-and-drop file upload has taken place? For extra credit, what property would you use if you weren't using jQuery?

5. When implementing a thumbnail preview of image files, what format is used to view preview images?

6. When creating a drag-and-drop file upload, what events can monitor file upload progress? What object do you attach these events to?

7. Which event properties calculate file upload progress percentages?

8. Describe how you would create custom POST variables in the HTTP request that is generated for a drag-and-drop file upload.

9. How do you know that a file upload was successful?

PART II
jQuery UI

12

Draggable and Droppable

Beginning with this chapter, the discussion shifts to the jQuery UI library. The jQuery UI library is a collection of reusable components that enables you create user-interface functionality quickly. The jQuery UI library handles a variety of tasks, such as making elements in a document draggable or making a list of items that you can rearrange by dragging and dropping, and many other UI tasks that you learn about in the remaining chapters of this book.

The jQuery UI library is functionality that exists outside jQuery's core framework you've been using and learning about throughout the preceding chapters of this book. The jQuery UI library is a series of jQuery plugins that handles these different UI tasks. In the spirit of jQuery's API, the library makes certain UI tasks much easier to implement.

You can download jQuery UI library components from `http://ui.jquery.com/download`. The website enables you to customize your download based on which UI components you want to use, and it offers this customization so that you can add the least amount of JavaScript possible, which, in turn, reduces overhead like file size and bandwidth. The source code download for this book is available free from `www.wrox.com/go/webdevwithjquery` and includes the entire jQuery UI package, which comprises all jQuery UI library plugins. For testing and learning purposes, this is fine; however, if you want to use UI library components in a real, production website, you should customize your jQuery UI library download to include only the components that you will use in your application because the entire library is a sizable file weighing in at 229.56 KB packed (all white space, comments, and line breaks removed), or 347.82 KB fully unpacked and uncompressed—a fairly large file download.

This chapter begins coverage of the jQuery UI library with the *Draggable and Droppable* libraries. This contrasts with the coverage presented in Chapter 11, "HTML5 Drag and Drop," which presents how to use HTML5's native drag-and-drop API. The key differences between the HTML5 drag-and-drop API and the jQuery UI's Draggable and Droppable API is that the HTML5 API can be used between multiple, independent browser windows (even different browser windows of completely different browsers), and even between different applications, assuming the applications in question use a browser component such as WebKit (Apple, et al.), Blink (Google, et al.), Gecko (Mozilla), or Trident (Microsoft). HTML5's drag-and-drop API also provides the ability to upload one or more files via drag-and-drop.

The Draggable and Droppable jQuery UI libraries provide similar functionality, but this functionality is limited to working within one browser window. Its functionality does not allow dragged content to leave the boundaries of the browser window. Whichever you choose to use depends upon what your project goals include for functionality.

The Draggable library gives you the ability to make any element on a page draggable. In the most rudimentary sense, that means you can move elements around in a document with your mouse and arrange those elements however you like. The next section introduces the Draggable jQuery UI API.

MAKING ELEMENTS DRAGGABLE

Making an element draggable is easy: First, you need to include the UI library that includes the Draggable plugin; then, after you make a selection with jQuery, you simply chain the method draggable() to the selection, like so:

```
$('div#anElementIdLikeToDrag').draggable();
```

The preceding code makes the <div> element with the id name anElementIdLikeToDrag, a draggable element, which means that you can move the element anywhere in the document with your mouse. The ability to make elements draggable gives you more options in terms of how your applications function, giving you many of the same options that you have developing desktop applications.

The actual code behind the scenes, enabling the drag operation, isn't complex, but it's yet another thing that jQuery allows you to take several lines of code and compress them into little code. In this case, it's a simple function call.

To show you just how easy it is to make an element draggable, the following presents an example in which you create a file manager that looks somewhat like Mac OS X Finder. You begin with the XHTML5 base, which is presented in the following markup (*Example 12-1*):

```
<!DOCTYPE HTML>
<html xmlns='http://www.w3.org/1999/xhtml'>
    <head>
        <meta http-equiv='content-type'
            content='application/xhtml+xml; charset=utf-8' />
        <meta http-equiv='content-language' content='en-us' />
        <title>Finder</title>
        <script src='../jQuery.js'></script>
        <script src='../jQueryUI.js'></script>
        <script src='Example 12-1.js'></script>
        <link href='Example 12-1.css' rel='stylesheet' />
    </head>
    <body>
        <div id='finderFiles'>
            <div class='finderDirectory' data-path='/Applications'>
                <div class='finderIcon'></div>
                <div class='finderDirectoryName'>
                    <span>Applications</span>
                </div>
            </div>
            <div class='finderDirectory' data-path='/Library'>
```

```html
            <div class='finderIcon'></div>
            <div class='finderDirectoryName'>
                <span>Library</span>
            </div>
        </div>
        <div class='finderDirectory' data-path='/Network'>
            <div class='finderIcon'></div>
            <div class='finderDirectoryName'>
                <span>Network</span>
            </div>
        </div>
        <div class='finderDirectory' data-path='/Sites'>
            <div class='finderIcon'></div>
            <div class='finderDirectoryName'>
                <span>Sites</span>
            </div>
        </div>
        <div class='finderDirectory' data-path='/System'>
            <div class='finderIcon'></div>
            <div class='finderDirectoryName'>
                <span>System</span>
            </div>
        </div>
        <div class='finderDirectory' data-path='/Users'>
            <div class='finderIcon'></div>
            <div class='finderDirectoryName'>
                <span>Users</span>
            </div>
        </div>
    </div>
  </body>
</html>
```

The following CSS sets up the styling for the Finder example:

```css
html,
body {
    width: 100%;
    height: 100%;
}
body {
    font: 12px "Lucida Grande", Arial, sans-serif;
    background: rgb(189, 189, 189) url('images/Bottom.png') repeat-x bottom;
    color: rgb(50, 50, 50);
    margin: 0;
    padding: 0;
}
div#finderFiles {
    border-bottom: 1px solid rgb(64, 64, 64);
    background: #fff;
    position: absolute;
    top: 0;
    right: 0;
    bottom: 23px;
    left: 0;
```

```css
        overflow: auto;
    }
    div.finderDirectory {
        float: left;
        width: 150px;
        height: 100px;
        overflow: hidden;
    }
    div.finderIcon {
        background: url('images/Folder 48x48.png') no-repeat center;
        background-size: 48px 48px;
        height: 56px;
        width: 54px;
        margin: 10px auto 3px auto;
    }
    div.finderIconSelected {
        background-color: rgb(196, 196, 196);
        border-radius: 5px;
    }
    div.finderDirectoryName {
        text-align: center;
    }
    span.finderDirectoryNameSelected {
        background: rgb(56, 117, 215);
        border-radius: 8px;
        color: white;
        padding: 1px 7px;
    }
```

The preceding XHTML and CSS are combined with the following JavaScript:

```javascript
$(document).ready(
    function()
    {
        $('div.finderDirectory')
            .mousedown(
                function()
                {
                    $('div.finderIconSelected')
                        .removeClass('finderIconSelected');

                    $('span.finderDirectoryNameSelected')
                        .removeClass('finderDirectoryNameSelected');

                    $(this).find('div.finderIcon')
                        .addClass('finderIconSelected');

                    $(this).find('div.finderDirectoryName span')
                        .addClass('finderDirectoryNameSelected');
                }
            )
            .draggable();
    }
);
```

The preceding source code results in the document that you see in Figure 12-1.

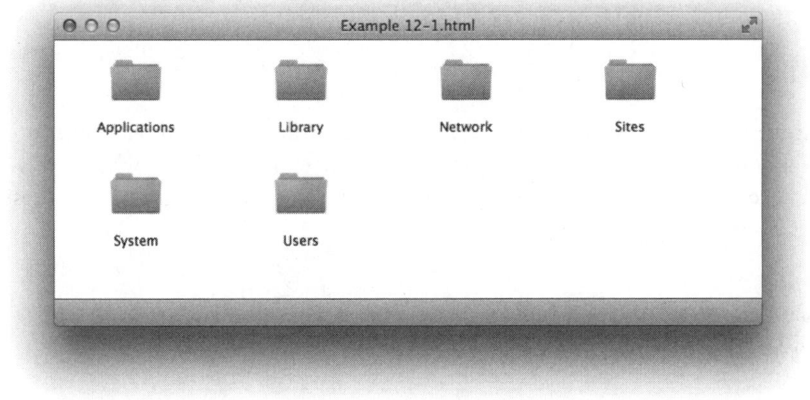

FIGURE 12-1

In the preceding example, you created a layout of folders like that found in Mac OS X Finder. The only difference you'll notice between browsers is that the rounded-corner effect present on selected folders comes through only on newer browsers, whereas older versions of IE and Opera show square corners.

Basically, the gist of this example enables you to select a single folder at a time and drag those folders around to any position in the window.

To make the elements draggable, you included the jQuery UI library, which includes all the jQuery UI plugins, including the Draggable plugin.

```
<script src='../jQueryUI.js'></script>
```

The markup in this example is straightforward. The individual folders are all contained in the <div> element with the id name finderFiles; this container element is needed to assist in controlling the presentation of the folders.

```
<div id='finderFiles'>
```

Each folder resides in a container <div> element with the class name finderDirectory, with the path to the directory contained in the data-path attribute, which could then be used to implement AJAX functionality where the path of the folder is submitted asynchronously to the server and the server responds with the contents of that folder. Each folder has an icon and a name, so markup is put in place for each of these. The reasoning behind this specific structure makes more sense after you examine the style sheet, but you create one <div> element for the icon, which controls the position of the icon and sets the dimensions for the highlighted style. Then the name of the folder is contained in another <div> element, which has the name of the folder nested in a <span> element. The <span> element is used so that when the folder is highlighted, the background is applied to an inline element, and the background hugs the text, even if the text takes up multiple lines (refer to Figure 12-1).

```
<div class='finderDirectory' data-path='/Applications'>
    <div class='finderIcon'></div>
    <div class='finderDirectoryName'>
        <span>Applications</span>
    </div>
</div>
```

The style sheet does all the work of making this raw lump of structural markup into a Finder-imitating document. The following reviews each rule in the style sheet and explains why each is needed. The <html> and <body> element are each given 100 percent width and height so that these both automatically take up the entire viewport.

```
html,
body {
    width: 100%;
    height: 100%;
}
```

In the next rule, you give the Finder a Lucida Grande font, which is a Mac font used for most Apple-created Mac applications. If that font isn't available, you can use Arial, which is present on Windows. If that font is not present, use the generic sans-serif font. The background is set to a shade of gray; then an image is tiled across the bottom of the window so that this document looks a little more like a real Finder window. The font color is set to a dark gray. Finally, the default padding and margin are removed from the <body> element, which is necessary to avoid scrollbars that would appear on the viewport due to the application of 100% width and height with the preceding style sheet rule.

```
body {
    font: 12px "Lucida Grande", Arial, sans-serif;
    background: rgb(189, 189, 189) url('images/Bottom.png') repeat-x bottom;
    color: rgb(50, 50, 50);
    margin: 0;
    padding: 0;
}
```

The next rule positions the <div> element with the id name finderFiles, which contains all the folders. This <div> element is positioned absolutely and is set to take up nearly the entire viewport, except the bottom 23 pixels, and that is done by specifying opposing offset properties, which when present imply width and height. The background is set to white; there is a dark gray border placed across the bottom of the container; and finally, the overflow: auto; declaration is added so that when you have more folders and files than the container can hold, a scrollbar appears so that you can access folders and files off-screen.

```
div#finderFiles {
    border-bottom: 1px solid rgb(64, 64, 64);
    background: #fff;
    position: absolute;
    top: 0;
    right: 0;
    bottom: 23px;
```

```
        left: 0;
        overflow: auto;
    }
```

The remaining style-sheet declarations set up the folders. The next rule puts the folders side by side and gives each fixed dimensions. The `overflow: hidden;` declaration prevents long folder names from extending outside the boundaries of the container.

```
div.finderDirectory {
    float: left;
    width: 150px;
    height: 100px;
    overflow: hidden;
}
```

The next rule handles the display of the folder icon. The `<div>` element sets the dimensions of the icon with the highlighting effect in mind, and the gray background applied to a selected folder is applied to the `<div>` element. The background image is sized using the `background-size` property to limit it to the actual dimensions of the folder's icon. The `background-position` is set to `center` so that it is centered both horizontally and vertically within the solid gray background color when the folder is highlighted. The `<div>` element is adjusted in position using top and bottom margin, and then it is centered inside its container `<div>` element using `margin` with auto as the value of the left and right margins. The result is a folder icon that looks more like a real Finder icon in OS X. Although, if you wanted to mimic Windows Explorer or another file management program, you might choose to deploy some of the same techniques.

```
div.finderIcon {
    background: url('images/Folder 48x48.png') no-repeat center;
    background-size: 48px 48px;
    height: 56px;
    width: 54px;
    margin: 10px auto 3px auto;
}
```

The following rule defines the style for a selected folder. The class name `finderIconSelected` is applied to the `<div>` element with the class name `finderIcon` dynamically using jQuery.

```
div.finderIconSelected {
    background-color: rgb(196, 196, 196);
    border-radius: 5px;
}
```

The next rule centers the name of the folder.

```
div.finderDirectoryName {
    text-align: center;
}
```

And finally, the last rule sets the style for the selected folder's name. A blue background, a little padding, white text, and rounded corners are added to make the folder name look more like the real Finder.

```
span.finderDirectoryNameSelected {
    background: rgb(56, 117, 215);
```

```
    border-radius: 8px;
    color: white;
    padding: 1px 7px;
}
```

And as you've no doubt come to expect, the JavaScript portion of this example is simple. You start with code that's required to make a folder selectable, which is done by adding a mousedown event. A mousedown event is used instead of, say, a click event, because you want a selection to take place even if the user moves the mouse cursor outside the boundaries of the folder while the mouse button is pressed. If users move the cursor while the button is pressed, that causes the element to be dragged. Because of that, you want the folder to be selected to show users that the folder they are dragging is selected.

```
$('div.finderDirectory')
    .mousedown(
```

Inside the mousedown event, you write some logic for selecting the folder. First, you remove the class name finderIconSelected from the div.finderIconSelect element.

Then you repeat the selection; you remove the class name finderDirectoryNameSelected from the span.finderDirectoryNameSelected element.

This series of actions clears any previous selection when a new selection is made.

Now add the class names that you removed to the div.finderIcon and span elements that are selected.

```
function()
{
    $('div.finderIconSelected')
        .removeClass('finderIconSelected');

    $('span.finderDirectoryNameSelected')
        .removeClass('finderDirectoryNameSelected');

    $(this).find('div.finderIcon')
        .addClass('finderIconSelected');

    $(this).find('div.finderDirectoryName span')
        .addClass('finderDirectoryNameSelected');
}
```

Finally, you make each folder draggable by chaining the method draggable() to the call to mousedown().

```
    .draggable();
```

The jQuery UI draggable() method lets you move the folders in the document to any position you like, similar to how Mac OS X's Finder works by default, enabling you to arrange the folders however you like. But the jQuery UI draggable() method enables you to do more than this. In the next section, you learn how to do ghosting and how to add the Droppable API into the mix.

DESIGNATING DROP ZONES FOR DRAGGABLE ELEMENTS

Typically when you implement dragging on elements in your document, you want to designate somewhere for the elements being dragged to be dropped. jQuery UI provides another plugin for handling the drop portion of this; it is called Droppable. The jQuery UI Droppable plugin enables you to create and manipulate a variety of things associated with dropping one element onto another, including what happens while you drag one element over a drop zone and what happens when a drop takes place. jQuery allows you to have precision control over drag-and-drop, which lets you create a basic drag-and-drop implementation or a polished drag-and-drop implementation.

As you've already seen with the Draggable API, jQuery UI provides a concise, easy-to-use API for handling the drop side. To make an element into a droppable element, all you have to do is make a selection and call the `droppable()` method with the appropriate options, just as you did with the `draggable()` method. Options are provided via an object literal consisting of key, value pairs. The following example shows you what a droppable implementation looks like in the context of the Finder clone you've been building throughout this chapter:

```
$('div.finderDirectory')
    .draggable({
        helper: 'clone',
        opacity: 0.5
    })
    .droppable({
        accept: 'div.finderDirectory',
        hoverClass: 'finderDirectoryDrop'
    });
```

In the preceding code, you have a basic example implementation of the Droppable API. Each `<div>` element with the class name `finderDirectory` is made into a drop zone so that any directory can be dragged and dropped onto any other directory. To make the drop portion function properly, you pass some options to the `droppable()` method. The `accept` option lets you specify a selector that will be used to match what elements you want to allow to be dropped onto the drop zone. In this case, you want to allow only `<div>` elements with the class name `finderDirectory` to be dropped. Using this filter, you can add other drag-and-drop functionality within the same document without having conflict between different drag-and-drop implementations.

The `hoverClass` option allows you to change the style of the drop zone as a draggable element is dragged over the droppable element. You simply specify a class name as the value and then set up the appropriate styles in your style sheet.

In the following example (*Example 12-2*), you take the basic concept of the Droppable API that was demonstrated and apply the `droppable()` method to the Finder clone you've been building.

```
<!DOCTYPE HTML>
<html xmlns='http://www.w3.org/1999/xhtml'>
    <head>
        <meta http-equiv='content-type'
            content='application/xhtml+xml; charset=utf-8' />
        <meta http-equiv='content-language' content='en-us' />
        <data-path>Finder</data-path>
        <script src='../jQuery.js'></script>
```

```html
            <script src='../jQueryUI.js'></script>
            <script src='Example 12-2.js'></script>
            <link href='Example 12-2.css' rel='stylesheet' />
        </head>
        <body>
            <div id='finderFiles'>
                <div class='finderDirectory' data-path='/Applications'>
                    <div class='finderIcon'></div>
                    <div class='finderDirectoryName'>
                        <span>Applications</span>
                    </div>
                </div>
                <div class='finderDirectory' data-path='/Library'>
                    <div class='finderIcon'></div>
                    <div class='finderDirectoryName'>
                        <span>Library</span>
                    </div>
                </div>
                <div class='finderDirectory' data-path='/Network'>
                    <div class='finderIcon'></div>
                    <div class='finderDirectoryName'>
                        <span>Network</span>
                    </div>
                </div>
                <div class='finderDirectory' data-path='/Sites'>
                    <div class='finderIcon'></div>
                    <div class='finderDirectoryName'>
                        <span>Sites</span>
                    </div>
                </div>
                <div class='finderDirectory' data-path='/System'>
                    <div class='finderIcon'></div>
                    <div class='finderDirectoryName'>
                        <span>System</span>
                    </div>
                </div>
                <div class='finderDirectory' data-path='/Users'>
                    <div class='finderIcon'></div>
                    <div class='finderDirectoryName'>
                        <span>Users</span>
                    </div>
                </div>
            </div>
        </body>
    </html>
```

The preceding HTML is combined with the following CSS:

```css
html,
body {
    width: 100%;
    height: 100%;
}
body {
    font: 12px "Lucida Grande", Arial, sans-serif;
    background: rgb(189, 189, 189) url('images/Bottom.png') repeat-x bottom;
```

```css
    color: rgb(50, 50, 50);
    margin: 0;
    padding: 0;
}
div#finderFiles {
    border-bottom: 1px solid rgb(64, 64, 64);
    background: #fff;
    position: absolute;
    top: 0;
    right: 0;
    bottom: 23px;
    left: 0;
    overflow: auto;
}
div.finderDirectory {
    float: left;
    width: 150px;
    height: 100px;
    overflow: hidden;
}
div.finderIcon {
    height: 56px;
    width: 54px;
    background: url('images/Folder 48x48.png') no-repeat center;
    background-size: 48px 48px;
    margin: 10px auto 3px auto;
}
div.finderIconSelected,
div.finderDirectoryDrop div.finderIcon {
    background-color: rgb(204, 204, 204);
    border-radius: 5px;
}
div.finderDirectoryDrop div.finderIcon {
    background-image: url('images/Open Folder 48x48.png');
}
div.finderDirectoryName {
    text-align: center;
}
span.finderDirectoryNameSelected,
div.finderDirectoryDrop span.finderDirectoryNameSelected {
    background: rgb(56, 117, 215);
    border-radius: 8px;
    color: white;
    padding: 1px 7px;
}
```

Finally, you apply the following JavaScript, which extends the previous example presented in *Example 12-1* with new code that enables the droppable() API:

```javascript
$(document).ready(
    function()
    {
        $('div.finderDirectory')
            .mousedown(
                function()
                {
```

```
                        $('div.finderIconSelected')
                            .removeClass('finderIconSelected');

                        $('span.finderDirectoryNameSelected')
                            .removeClass('finderDirectoryNameSelected');

                        $(this).find('div.finderIcon')
                            .addClass('finderIconSelected');

                        $(this).find('div.finderDirectoryName span')
                            .addClass('finderDirectoryNameSelected');
                    }
                )
                .draggable({
                    helper : 'clone',
                    opacity : 0.5
                })
                .droppable({
                    accept: 'div.finderDirectory',
                    hoverClass: 'finderDirectoryDrop',
                    drop: function(event, ui)
                    {
                        var path = ui.draggable.data('path');
                        // Do something with the path
                        // For example, make an AJAX call to the server
                        // where the logic for actually moving the file or folder
                        // to the new folder would take place

                        // Remove the element that was dropped.
                        ui.draggable.remove();
                    }
                });
        }
    );
```

The preceding source code gives you output in Safari on Mac OS X, as shown in Figure 12-2.

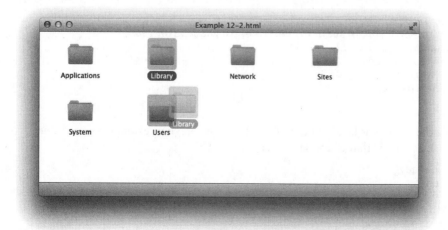

FIGURE 12-2

In the preceding example, you added the jQuery UI `droppable()` method to the Finder clone, which lets you designate areas in which draggable elements can be dropped. The jQuery UI Draggable and Droppable plugins both work in all modern browsers.

To set up the document for the Droppable library, you added a few rules to the style sheet, which define what an element looks like while you drag one element over another. From here on, the action of dragging one element over another element is referred to as the dragover event. jQuery UI simply refers to this event as over, but the native drag-and-drop API from Chapter 11 refers to this event as dragover.

In essence, the style that you use for dragover is simply the same style that you're already using to highlight a folder to indicate its selection, with just one difference: You swap out the default folder icon with an open folder icon. In the JavaScript portion, changing the dragover style in the style sheet is made possible by the addition of the class name, `finderDirectoryDrop`. This class name is added to the `<div>` element with class name `finderDirectory`. jQuery dynamically adds or removes the `finderDirectoryDrop` class name to or from this `<div>` element, allowing you to define a different style upon dragover.

So, you're reusing the "selected folder style" for folders where the dragover event is taking place, with the open folder icon being the only difference. Reusing that style is done simply by adding additional selectors that reference the `<div>` element with the dragover class name `finderDirectoryDrop` to the style sheet.

```
div.finderIconSelected,
div.finderDirectoryDrop div.finderIcon {
    background-color: rgb(204, 204, 204);
    border-radius: 5px;
}
div.finderDirectoryDrop div.finderIcon {
    background-image: url('images/Open Folder 48x48.png');
}
div.finderDirectoryName {
    text-align: center;
}
span.finderDirectoryNameSelected,
div.finderDirectoryDrop span.finderDirectoryNameSelected {
    background: rgb(56, 117, 215);
    border-radius: 8px;
    color: white;
    padding: 1px 7px;
}
```

The preceding reuses the selected folder style for dragover elements. To replace the default folder icon with an open folder icon, you use a more specific selector. The following selector is used to add the default folder icon:

```
div.finderIcon
```

The following selector overrides the preceding selector when a dragover event is taking place, providing an open folder icon instead of the default folder icon:

```
div.finderDirectoryDrop c.finderIcon
```

Next, you pass a few customizations to the `draggable()` method to accomplish two things. The first is that when a user begins to drag a folder icon, you want to use a duplicate of the icon to refer to the item that is being dragged. The second is to make the duplicate semitransparent. This is an effect known as *ghosting*, which creates a UI where when an element is dragged across the screen, a semitransparent duplicate of that element represents what is dragged, which resembles a ghost in appearance.

```
.draggable({
    helper : 'clone',
    opacity : 0.5
})
```

The method of passing a JavaScript object literal containing key, value pairs is a common method used by jQuery plugins to provide customization options. This provides you with fine-grained control over how a plugin works. In the portion of JavaScript that calls `droppable()`, you pass options like `accept`, which lets you filter which elements can be dropped on the droppable element by virtue of a selector.

```
.droppable({
    accept: 'div.finderDirectory',
```

The next option specifies what class name is to be added to the drop element when a `dragover` event takes place. This option causes the class name `finderDirectoryDrop` to be added to the `<div>` element with the class name `finderDirectory` when a `dragover` event takes place.

```
hoverClass: 'finderDirectoryDrop',
```

In the last option passed to the `droppable()` method, you specify a function that is executed when the `drop` event takes place, which occurs when an element has been dragged over a drop zone and the mouse button released. Within this function is where you want to do whatever it is the act of dragging and dropping is intended to provide. In this case, you want to remove the folder being dropped and then make an AJAX call to the server. On the server side, you have code that actually moves the folder to the new location.

```
drop: function(event, ui)
{
    var path = ui.draggable.data('path');
    // Do something with the path
    // For example, make an AJAX call to the server
    // where the logic for actually moving the file or folder
    // to the new folder would take place

    // Remove the element that was dropped.
    ui.draggable.remove();
}
});
```

In the preceding `drop` event, you can access properties associated with the drag-and-drop operation by specifying a second argument in the callback function you provide. The second argument is named ui; then the ui.draggable object gives you access to the element that has been dragged and dropped on this element. If you'd like to examine the ui object in its entirety, you can add console.log(ui); to the code, and the ui object will be output to your browser's debugging console, where you can examine everything it contains.

In the callback function that you assign to the drop option, you access the data-path attribute of the element being dragged, which contains the folder's absolute path. You could then send that path on to the server, along with the path of the folder that the dragged folder has been dropped on and actually move that folder to the new location programmatically. The function ends with the dragged element being deleted with a call to remove(), which would be the final operation that you would do upon implementing a drag-and-drop folder UI.

In the preceding examples, you learned how the jQuery UI draggable() and droppable() methods work in a real-life-oriented demonstration of a drag-and-drop implementation. These methods, combined with what you learned about the native drag-and-drop API in Chapter 11, provide powerful and flexible methods of implementing drag and drop in a browser or application utilizing a browser component.

> **NOTE** *A comprehensive jQuery UI Draggable and Droppable reference is available in Appendix J, including all the options that you can pass to both the* draggable() *and* droppable() *methods and the* ui *object that you can optionally specify in the second argument to draggable and droppable event handlers.*

SUMMARY

In this chapter, you learned how to use the jQuery UI Draggable and Droppable plugins, which you can download à la carte from www.jquery.com. The jQuery website provides à la carte downloading for UI components so that you can include only the plugins that you need to use, which, in turn, helps keep your applications lean and efficient.

Throughout this chapter, you worked on building a file component similar to the one found in Mac OS X's Finder and saw how you can make folders into draggable elements as well as drop zones for draggable elements. You saw how you can control the nuisances of a drag-and-drop implementation via the options that jQuery UI allows you to pass to both the draggable() and droppable() methods, which help you to control what kind of drag operation you want, what the drag element looks like, what the drop element looks like, and the event handlers you can specify to execute code during specific events that take place during a drag-and-drop operation.

The next chapter presents another drag-and-drop UI concept that jQuery provides called *Sortable*.

EXERCISES

1. If you want to have a UI that allows users to drag elements around in a document and position those elements wherever they like, what would you use? (Hint: what function call?)

2. If you want to create draggable elements that work similarly to your operating system's file manager, where the original element remains in place, but when a drag operation starts, you drag around a clone of that element, how would you do that with jQuery UI? Write a sample program that achieves this.

3. If you want to make an element into a drop zone for draggable elements, what function call would you use?

4. Write the function call that you would use to add a class name to a drop zone while an element was being dragged over the top of it.

5. What option would you provide to the droppable() method if you want to limit the drag elements that can be dropped on the drop element? Also, what type of value would you provide to that option?

13

Sortable

Chapter 12, "Draggable and Droppable," introduced how jQuery UI provides plugins that make implementing drag-and-drop UI easy to implement. This chapter presents another jQuery UI plugin, Sortable, which enables you to make items in a list sortable, or "rearrangeable."

In website development you might need to often sort items, and you will probably want to change the order of the items. An example would be the order in which products appear in a navigation or side menu.

Without drag-and-drop, it's still possible to give users the ability to tweak the order of items. You can offer up or down arrows for shifting items in a list, for example, but drag-and-drop sorting is the fastest, most intuitive way to implement this type of user interface.

MAKING A LIST SORTABLE

As you've seen throughout this book, jQuery takes more complex programming tasks and makes them easier. Sometimes, you can do a lot by adding just one line of code or even chaining one additional function call to a selection. When you experience how easy jQuery makes common programming tasks, it becomes nearly impossible to return to JavaScript programming without the convenience offered by frameworks like jQuery. In Chapter 12, you saw how making elements draggable amounts to making a selection and then making a single function call. Making a list of items sortable via drag-and-drop is just as easy—you make a selection of elements, and then you make a single function call. The function that you call in this case is called sortable(). Like the drag-and-drop examples that were presented in Chapter 12, you have the ability to tweak element sortability using fine-grained options that you can pass to the sortable() method with a JavaScript object literal. Each of the options that jQuery UI provides for the Sortable plugin is defined in detail in Appendix K, "Sortable."

All that you need to make this possible is to include the relevant jQuery UI plugin, Sortable, make a selection with jQuery, and then chain a call to the function sortable() onto that selection. The Sortable plugin requires that you select a container element, whose immediate children will be sortable by drag-and-drop. One example of a container is a <ul> element, and the sortable children are the <li> elements contained within that element. The sortable functionality offered by the Sortable plugin works in all modern browsers: IE, Firefox, Safari, and Opera.

The following example puts the concept of sortability into context with a real-world-oriented application, where you sort files through a GUI interface, which you might use in a Content Management System (CMS), to control things such as sorting links in a sidebar or drop-down menu, or the order in which products appear in a catalog. You'll also return to this example throughout this chapter to examine other aspects of file sorting that jQuery UI provides through its Sortable plugin. You begin with the following HTML, which appears as *Example 13-1* in the source materials available at www.wrox.com/go/webdevwithjquery.

```
<!DOCTYPE HTML>
<html xmlns='http://www.w3.org/1999/xhtml'>
    <head>
        <meta http-equiv='content-type'
            content='application/xhtml+xml; charset=utf-8' />
        <meta http-equiv='content-language' content='en-us' />
        <title>Sortable</title>
        <script src='../jQuery.js'></script>
        <script src='../jQueryUI.js'></script>
        <script src='Example 13-1.js'></script>
        <link href='Example 13-1.css' rel='stylesheet' />
    </head>
    <body>
        <ul id='finderCategoryFiles'>
            <li class='finderCategoryFile'>
                <div class='finderCategoryFileIcon'></div>
                <h5 class='finderCategoryFileTitle'>
                    Using CoreImage to Resize and Change Formats on the Fly
                </h5>
                <div class='finderCategoryFilePath'>
                    <a href='/Blog/apple/CoreImage.html'>
                        /Blog/apple/CoreImage.html
                    </a>
                </div>
            </li>
            <li class='finderCategoryFile'>
                <div class='finderCategoryFileIcon'></div>
                <h5 class='finderCategoryFileTitle'>
                    Exploring Polymorphism in PHP
                </h5>
                <div class='finderCategoryFilePath'>
                    <a href='/Blog/php/Polymorphism.html'>
                        /Blog/php/Polymorphism.html
                    </a>
                </div>
            </li>
            <li class='finderCategoryFile'>
                <div class='finderCategoryFileIcon'></div>
                <h5 class='finderCategoryFileTitle'>
                    A PHP Shell Script for Backups
                </h5>
                <div class='finderCategoryFilePath'>
                    <a href='/Blog/php/Backup%20Script.html'>
```

```
                        /Blog/php/Backup Script.html
                    </a>
                </div>
            </li>
            <li class='finderCategoryFile'>
                <div class='finderCategoryFileIcon'></div>
                <h5 class='finderCategoryFileTitle'>
                    HTML 5 DOCTYPE
                </h5>
                <div class='finderCategoryFilePath'>
                    <a href='/Blog/web/html5_doctype.html'>
                        /Blog/web/html5_doctype.html
                    </a>
                </div>
            </li>
            <li class='finderCategoryFile'>
                <div class='finderCategoryFileIcon'></div>
                <h5 class='finderCategoryFileTitle'>
                    First Impressions of IE 8 Beta 2
                </h5>
                <div class='finderCategoryFilePath'>
                    <a href='/Blog/web/ie8_beta2.html'>
                        /Blog/web/ie8_beta2.html
                    </a>
                </div>
            </li>
        </ul>
    </body>
</html>
```

The preceding HTML is joined with the following CSS.

```css
html,
body {
    width: 100%;
    height: 100%;
}
body {
    font: 12px 'Lucida Grande', Arial, sans-serif;
    background: rgb(189, 189, 189)
                url('images/Bottom.png')
                repeat-x
                bottom;
    color: rgb(50, 50, 50);
    margin: 0;
    padding: 0;
}
ul#finderCategoryFiles {
    position: absolute;
    top: 0;
    bottom: 22px;
    left: 0;
    width: 300px;
    border-bottom: 1px solid rgb(64, 64, 64);
    border-right: 1px solid rgb(64, 64, 64);
```

```css
        background: #fff;
        list-style: none;
        margin: 0;
        padding: 0;
}
li.finderCategoryFile {
        clear: both;
        padding: 5px 5px 10px 5px;
        min-height: 48px;
        width: 290px;
}
li.finderCategoryFile h5 {
        font: normal 12px 'Lucida Grande', Arial, sans-serif;
        margin: 0;
}
div.finderCategoryFileIcon {
        float: left;
        width: 48px;
        height: 48px;
        background: url('images/Safari Document.png')
                    no-repeat;
}
h5.finderCategoryFileTitle,
div.finderCategoryFilePath {
        padding-left: 55px;
}
li.finderCategoryFileSelected {
        background: rgb(24, 67, 243)
                    url('images/Selected Item.png')
                    repeat-x
                    bottom;
        color: white;
}
li.finderCategoryFileSelected a {
        color: lightblue;
}
```

Finally, this JavaScript enables sortability.

```javascript
$(document).ready(
    function()
    {
        $('li.finderCategoryFile').mousedown(
            function()
            {
                $('li.finderCategoryFile')
                    .not(this)
                    .removeClass('finderCategoryFileSelected');

                $(this).addClass('finderCategoryFileSelected');
            }
        );
```

```
        $('ul#finderCategoryFiles').sortable();
    }
);
```

The preceding example results in the application you see shown in Figure 13-1.

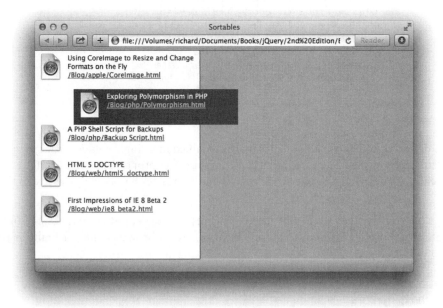

FIGURE 13-1

The preceding example is a demonstration of the jQuery UI Sortable plugin, an application that provides file sorting, which can have a variety of applications, as mentioned just prior to presenting this example.

In this example, you have five files. Each has a file icon, a title, and a clickable link to the file. This is borrowed from Mac OS X for the look and feel of an application that feels more like a native desktop application. If you were to extend this concept, you could also provide alternative templates that mirror the look and feel of other operating systems as well. A server-side language that can detect the user's operating system, combined with different style sheets for each OS, makes that a viable option, which can make your users feel more at home with your web-based application.

In the markup, you set things up so that the content can be styled with CSS. Each file item is represented as a <li> element. Because you work with a list of items, semantically speaking, it makes the most sense to set up your sortable list as a <ul> element, with each list item, <li>, representing each file.

The file icon is placed in a <div> element. You use a <div> so that you can provide the icon via the CSS background property.

The text content is wrapped within an <h5> and a <div> element so that you can control the margin and padding using block elements instead of inline elements like <span>. You can see how this is helpful in the explanation for the style sheet in this example. Then, you also gratuitously give each element class names, which makes it much easier to apply style or behavior to those specific elements, in addition to making it easier to identify the purpose of the element from the standpoint of semantics. Each class name is chosen so that it conveys the exact purpose of the element.

```
<li class='finderCategoryFile'>
    <div class='finderCategoryFileIcon'></div>
    <h5 class='finderCategoryFileTitle'>
        Using CoreImage to Resize and Change Formats on the Fly
    </h5>
    <div class='finderCategoryFilePath'>
        <a href='/Blog/apple/CoreImage.html'>
            /Blog/apple/CoreImage.html
        </a>
    </div>
</li>
```

The application is designed so that sortable elements are contained in a single column that spans the left side. The column is created by using the `top` and `bottom` offset properties in tandem to imply height, which, in turn, lets you have a stretchy column that resizes fluidly with the size of the viewport.

In the style sheet, first, you give the `<html>` and `<body>` elements 100 percent `width` and `height`, and remove any default `margin` or `padding` from the `<body>` element. (Some browsers apply default `margin`; some apply default `padding`.)

```
html,
body {
    width: 100%;
    height: 100%;
}
body {
    font: 12px 'Lucida Grande', Arial, sans-serif;
    background: rgb(189, 189, 189)
                url('images/Bottom.png')
                repeat-x
                bottom;
    color: rgb(50, 50, 50);
    margin: 0;
    padding: 0;
}
```

In the next style-sheet rule, you create the left column by styling the `<ul>` element with the id name `finderCategoryFiles` so that it spans the height of the left side of the document. The declaration `top: 0;` combined with the declaration `bottom: 22px;` causes the `<ul>` element to span the entire height of the viewport, except for the bottom 22 pixels, which has a gradient background applied to that space. The `<ul>` element is given a fixed width of 300 pixels; otherwise, you would have a shrink-to-fit width because the `<ul>` element is absolutely positioned.

```
ul#finderCategoryFiles {
    position: absolute;
    top: 0;
    bottom: 22px;
```

```
            left: 0;
            width: 300px;
            border-bottom: 1px solid rgb(64, 64, 64);
            border-right: 1px solid rgb(64, 64, 64);
            background: #fff;
            list-style: none;
            margin: 0;
            padding: 0;
        }
```

Each <li> element first has the declaration clear: both applied, which is needed to clear the left floating of each file icon (the <div> element with class name finderCategoryFileIcon). Without this declaration, you'd have a jumbled unintelligible mess, as each <li> element tried to float up to the right of the icon of the preceding <li> element, and the <li> element preceding that one float up to the right of the icon of the <li> element before that one, and so on. The clear: both declaration cancels floating so that the icon floats to the left, and only the text content within the <li> element floats up to the right of that icon.

Each <li> element is given a fixed width of 290 pixels. You do this because when you drag a <li> element, the element loses its width and shrinks. It does that because without an explicit width, each <li> element's width is based on the parent, <ul>, element's width. When you drag an <li> element, its parent is no longer the <ul> element but the <body> element. The <li> element is moved with the mouse cursor through CSS. It is positioned absolutely, relative to the viewport, and its position is constantly updated based on where the mouse cursor is going via the jQuery UI Sortable plugin. Otherwise, as an absolutely positioned element, the <li> element would have a shrink-to-fit width, so by giving the <li> element a fixed width, you allow it to maintain its dimensions as it is dragged from one point to another. The min-height property keeps the spacing within the <li> element consistent but also allows each <li> element to expand vertically to accommodate additional text content.

```
    li.finderCategoryFile {
        clear: both;
        padding: 5px 5px 10px 5px;
        min-height: 48px;
        width: 290px;
    }
```

The next item of interest in the style sheet is the icon, which is defined by the following rule:

```
    div.finderCategoryFileIcon {
        float: left;
        width: 48px;
        height: 48px;
        background: url('images/Safari Document.png')
                    no-repeat;
    }
```

In the preceding rule, the <div> element is floated to the left with the declaration float: left;. That declaration causes the text content to float to the right of the icon, as explained previously. The clear: both; declaration of the previous rule cancels this declaration on each <li> element so that only the text content is affected. The icon is set as the background using the background property, and the <div> is given a width and height of 48 pixels, matching the dimensions of the background image.

The last items of interest in the style sheet define the look for selected files. That's done in the following two rules:

```
li.finderCategoryFileSelected {
    background: rgb(24, 67, 243)
                url('images/Selected Item.png')
                repeat-x
                bottom;
    color: white;
}
li.finderCategoryFileSelected a {
    color: lightblue;
}
```

The preceding two rules are for <li> elements with the class name finderCategoryFileSelected. This class name is dynamically added and removed from <li> elements by jQuery. This addition of this class name lets your users see which file is currently selected. Beyond providing a visual cue for selection, this also lets you implement the ability to add a Delete button, which when pressed would remove the selected item or implement some other functionality that is contingent on the selection of an element.

The JavaScript for this example is lean and to the point. The JavaScript basically does two things. It provides the ability to select an <li> element by adding and removing the class name finderCategoryFileSelected as appropriate to indicate selection. And it makes the <li> elements sortable using the jQuery UI Sortable plugin.

When the DOM is ready, the first task is to attach a mousedown event to each <li> element. You can use this event to implement an indication of which element is selected.

```
$('li.finderCategoryFile').mousedown(
    function()
    {
        $('li.finderCategoryFile')
            .not(this)
            .removeClass('finderCategoryFileSelected');

        $(this).addClass('finderCategoryFileSelected');
    }
);
```

The script selects every <li> element with class name finderCategoryFile. The class name is added to the selection, even though as it stands, you could just select every <li> element without a class name and get the same result so that your application can be easily extended. You might bring in more functionality that involves adding <li> elements that are completely unrelated to what you're doing here. Adding the class name to the selector makes the selection more specific and gives you the ability to expand your application's functionality more effortlessly. So every <li> element with class name finderCategoryFile is selected; then the <li> element on which the mousedown event is taking place is filtered out using .not(this), and the class name finderCategoryFileSelected is removed from every <li> element, except the <li> element on which the mousedown event is taking place.

This is actually not the most efficient way to implement selection, especially if you have a long list. Selecting every <li> element is inefficient and can make your script slow if you have a lot of items in the list. So having shown you the wrong way to do a selection, a better approach is to create a variable, and every time a selection is made, store the currently selected element in that variable. The following code is what this approach looks like in the context of *Example 13-1*:

```
$(document).ready(
    function()
    {
        var selectedFile;

        $('li.finderCategoryFile').mousedown(
            function()
            {
                if (selectedFile && selectedFile.length)
                {
                    selectedFile.removeClass('finderCategoryFileSelected');
                }

                selectedFile = $(this);
                selectedFile.addClass('finderCategoryFileSelected');
            }
        );

        $('ul#finderCategoryFiles').sortable();
    }
);
```

The selected item is stored in the variable selectedFile. When the mousedown event fires, the script first checks to see if there is an element stored in the selectedFile variable. If there is, the finder-CategoryFileSelected class name is removed from that element because that element is the previously selected element.

Then the element on which the mousedown event is being fired, referenced by the this keyword, is made into a jQuery object by wrapping this in a call to the dollar sign function, and the class name finderCategoryFileSelected is added to the element on which the mousedown event is being fired. This provides you with a leaner, more efficient selection API.

The last item that happens in the script (and the point of this example) is to make every <li> element sortable with a call to the sortable() method:

```
$('ul#finderCategoryFiles').sortable();
```

The next section introduces some customization into the discussion of the Sortable plugin.

CUSTOMIZING SORTABLE

This section talks about some visual tweaks you can make to sortable lists and how you link one list to another so that you have sorting between multiple, separate lists. The jQuery UI sortable() method, like draggable() and droppable(), enables you to specify an object literal as its first argument, which enables you tweak how sorting works, in addition to providing callback functions that are executed during specific events that occur as sorting is taking place.

> **NOTE** *This section discusses just a few of the options that jQuery UI exposes for its Sortable plugin. You can find a complete list of options in Appendix K.*

The first option presented is `placeholder`, which gives you the ability to style the placeholder that appears within a sortable list as a drag is taking place to indicate where the item will be dropped if the mouse is released. By default (refer to Figure 13-1) you can see that the `placeholder` is simply empty white space, sized relatively to the element being dragged. The `placeholder` option accepts a class name as its value, which, in turn, is applied to the `placeholder` element.

The second option presented describes how you can customize the element being dragged; the process for doing this can also be applied to the jQuery UI `draggable()` method. By default, jQuery UI displays the element the user picked for sorting as the element that the user drags, which, of course, makes sense for most scenarios. You do, however, have the option of using a completely different element for display as the drag element, if you choose. Customizing the element that's displayed during a drag is done with the `helper` option. In jQuery UI, *helper*, as applied to *drag-and-drop*, whether in the Sortable plugin or the Draggable plugin, or other plugins, is the term used for the element that is displayed while a drag is taking place. The `helper` option takes two arguments: The first argument is the event object, and the second argument references the element the user picked for sorting. Aside from completely replacing the element displayed during the `drag` event, you can also use this option to simply tweak the display of the element that the user picked.

In the following example, you extend the file-sorting application that you created in *Example 13-1*, with some options, like the `placeholder` and `helper` options that you learned about in this section. You also add another option that gives you the ability to sort elements between multiple lists.

Using *Example 13-1.html* as the basis, create the following markup document as *Example 13-2.html*:

```
<!DOCTYPE HTML>
<html xmlns='http://www.w3.org/1999/xhtml'>
    <head>
        <meta http-equiv='content-type'
            content='application/xhtml+xml; charset=utf-8' />
        <meta http-equiv='content-language' content='en-us' />
        <title>Sortable</title>
        <script src='../jQuery.js'></script>
        <script src='../jQueryUI.js'></script>
        <script src='Example 13-2.js'></script>
        <link href='Example 13-2.css' rel='stylesheet' />
    </head>
    <body>
        <div id='finderCategoryFileWrapper'>
            <ul id='finderCategoryFiles'>
                <li class='finderCategoryFile'>
                    <div class='finderCategoryFileIcon'></div>
```

```
            <h5 class='finderCategoryFileTitle'>
                Using CoreImage to Resize and Change Formats on the Fly
            </h5>
            <div class='finderCategoryFilePath'>
                <a href='/Blog/apple/CoreImage.html'>
                    /Blog/apple/CoreImage.html
                </a>
            </div>
        </li>
        <li class='finderCategoryFile'>
            <div class='finderCategoryFileIcon'></div>
            <h5 class='finderCategoryFileTitle'>
                Exploring Polymorphism in PHP
            </h5>
            <div class='finderCategoryFilePath'>
                <a href='/Blog/php/Polymorphism.html'>
                    /Blog/php/Polymorphism.html
                </a>
            </div>
        </li>
        <li class='finderCategoryFile'>
            <div class='finderCategoryFileIcon'></div>
            <h5 class='finderCategoryFileTitle'>
                A PHP Shell Script for Backups
            </h5>
            <div class='finderCategoryFilePath'>
                <a href='/Blog/php/Backup%20Script.html'>
                    /Blog/php/Backup Script.html
                </a>
            </div>
        </li>
        <li class='finderCategoryFile'>
            <div class='finderCategoryFileIcon'></div>
            <h5 class='finderCategoryFileTitle'>
                HTML 5 DOCTYPE
            </h5>
            <div class='finderCategoryFilePath'>
                <a href='/Blog/web/html5_doctype.html'>
                    /Blog/web/html5_doctype.html
                </a>
            </div>
        </li>
        <li class='finderCategoryFile'>
            <div class='finderCategoryFileIcon'></div>
            <h5 class='finderCategoryFileTitle'>
                First Impressions of IE 8 Beta 2
            </h5>
            <div class='finderCategoryFilePath'>
                <a href='/Blog/web/ie8_beta2.html'>
                    /Blog/web/ie8_beta2.html
                </a>
            </div>
        </li>
    </ul>
```

```
                        <ul id='finderOtherCategoryFiles'>
                        </ul>
                </div>
        </body>
</html>
```

Using the style sheet in *Example 13-1.css*, make the following modifications and save the results in a new file, as *Example 13-2.css*:

```
html,
body {
    width: 100%;
    height: 100%;
}
body {
    font: normal 12px 'Lucida Grande', Arial, sans-serif;
    background: rgb(189, 189, 189)
                url('images/Bottom.png')
                repeat-x
                bottom;
    color: rgb(50, 50, 50);
    margin: 0;
    padding: 0;
}
div#finderCategoryFileWrapper {
    position: absolute;
    top: 0;
    right: 0;
    bottom: 23px;
    left: 0;
}
ul#finderCategoryFiles,
ul#finderOtherCategoryFiles {
    float: left;
    height: 100%;
    width: 300px;
    border-bottom: 1px solid rgb(64, 64, 64);
    border-right: 1px solid rgb(64, 64, 64);
    background: #fff;
    list-style: none;
    margin: 0;
    padding: 0;
}
li.finderCategoryFile {
    clear: both;
    padding: 5px 5px 10px 5px;
    min-height: 48px;
    width: 290px;
}
li.finderCategoryFile h5 {
    font: normal 12px 'Lucida Grande', Arial, sans-serif;
    margin: 0;
}
div.finderCategoryFileIcon {
    float: left;
```

```css
    width: 48px;
    height: 48px;
    background: url('images/Safari Document.png')
                no-repeat;
}
h5.finderCategoryFileTitle,
div.finderCategoryFilePath {
    padding-left: 55px;
}
li.finderCategoryFileSelected {
    background: rgb(24, 67, 243)
                url('images/Selected Item.png')
                repeat-x
                bottom;
    color: white;
}
li.finderCategoryFileSelected a {
    color: lightblue;
}
.finderCategoryFilePlaceholder {
    background: rgb(230, 230, 230);
    height: 58px;
}
```

Starting with the JavaScript file you created in *Example 13-1.js*, make the following modifications and save the new JavaScript file as *Example 13-2.js*:

```javascript
$(document).ready(
    function()
    {
        var selectedFile;

        $('li.finderCategoryFile').mousedown(
            function()
            {
                if (selectedFile && selectedFile.length)
                {
                    selectedFile.removeClass('finderCategoryFileSelected');
                }

                selectedFile = $(this);
                selectedFile.addClass('finderCategoryFileSelected');
            }
        );

        $('ul#finderCategoryFiles').sortable({
            connectWith : 'ul#finderOtherCategoryFiles',
            placeholder : 'finderCategoryFilePlaceholder',
            opacity : 0.8,
            cursor : 'move'
        });

        $('ul#finderOtherCategoryFiles').sortable({
            connectWith : 'ul#finderCategoryFiles',
            placeholder : 'finderCategoryFilePlaceholder',
```

```
                opacity : 0.8,
                cursor : 'move'
        });
    }
);
```

The preceding gives you something similar to what you see in Figure 13-2.

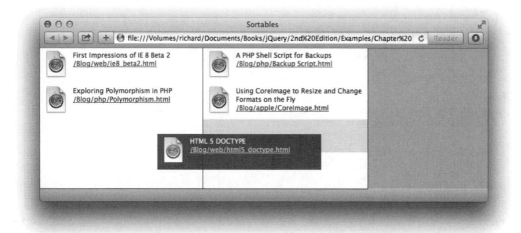

FIGURE 13-2

In *Example 13-2*, you added a few options to the sortable() method and tweaked the presentation of the document to accommodate multiple lists.

```
<div id='finderCategoryFileWrapper'>
    <ul id='finderCategoryFiles'>
```

The <div> element contains two <ul> elements; each, in turn, is a sortable list. Each <ul> element is also made into a column that spans the height of the <div> element. The following CSS is used to prepare the <div> element so that the <ul> elements within it can become columns.

```
div#finderCategoryFileWrapper {
    position: absolute;
    top: 0;
    right: 0;
    bottom: 23px;
    left: 0;
}
```

The <div> element is positioned absolutely, and the four offset properties are used to imply width and height, causing the <div> element to take up the entire viewport, except the bottom 23 pixels. Then styles are applied to each <ul> element. Each <ul> element is floated to the left and given fixed dimensions. This styling manages to turn both <ul> elements into columns, matching the visual look and feel that you saw in *Example 13-1*, but also managing to work around an annoying z-index bug in old versions of IE.

```css
ul#finderCategoryFiles,
ul#finderOtherCategoryFiles {
    float: left;
    height: 100%;
    width: 300px;
    border-bottom: 1px solid rgb(64, 64, 64);
    border-right: 1px solid rgb(64, 64, 64);
    background: #fff;
    list-style: none;
    margin: 0;
    padding: 0;
}
```

Going to the JavaScript, the scripting portion is straightforward. The first portion of the file deals with selection; as you saw later in the explanation for *Example 13-1*, a variable called *selectedFile* is used to keep track of which file is selected. The remainder of the script sets up two sortable lists, one in each column.

```javascript
$('ul#finderCategoryFiles').sortable({
    connectWith : 'ul#finderOtherCategoryFiles',
    placeholder : 'finderCategoryFilePlaceholder',
    opacity : 0.8,
    cursor : 'move'
});

$('ul#finderOtherCategoryFiles').sortable({
    connectWith : 'ul#finderCategoryFiles',
    placeholder : 'finderCategoryFilePlaceholder',
    opacity : 0.8,
    cursor : 'move'
});
```

The connectWith option accepts a selector as its value and enables you to connect one list to another so that you have the ability to sort items between multiple lists.

Then, the other options— placeholder, opacity, and cursor— are each used to tweak the presentation of each sortable list. The placeholder option, as you already learned, enables you to add a custom class name to the element that acts as a placeholder during sorting. The opacity option is used to control the opacity of the helper element, and it takes a standard CSS 3 opacity property value (that works in IE, too). The cursor option is used to change the cursor while the helper is being dragged, and it takes any value that the CSS cursor property can take.

Also in the preceding snippet of code, the <ul> list with the id name finderCategoryFiles is connected to the <ul> list with the id name finderOtherCategoryFiles. The connectWith option specified for this list sets up a one-way connection from the first <ul> element to the second, which lets you drag items from the first list to the second, but not vice versa. To have two-way sorting, you also need to set the connectWith option on the second <ul> list, which you also see in the preceding snippet of code. Other than the connectWith option, the second <ul> element has the same options as the first <ul> element.

As mentioned previously, this section discussed only a few of the options for Sortable. All options for Sortable are documented in Appendix K.

SAVING THE STATE OF SORTED LISTS

The Sortable API in jQuery UI wouldn't be complete without one last detail: saving the state of a sorted list. This too is covered by the Sortable plugin. In Chapter 7, "AJAX," you learned about jQuery's serialize() method, which automatically takes a selection of input elements for a form and serializes the data in those input elements into a string of data that you can then submit to a server-side script with an AJAX request. The Sortable plugin provides a similar mechanism for retrieving data from a sortable list. But instead of retrieving input form values, the Sortable plugin retrieves a specific attribute from each sortable element. By default, the Sortable plugin retrieves the value of the id attribute. In the context of the examples you've completed in this chapter, you'd give each <li> element an id attribute and then use the Sortable plugin's mechanism for serializing the data present in each id attribute into a string that you can pass on to an AJAX request to a server-side script, so you can save the sort. The following code snippet shows the code you'd use on the JavaScript side:

```
var data = $('ul').sortable(
    'serialize', {
        key: 'listItem[]'
    }
);
```

In the preceding code, to serialize the data present in the id attribute of each <li> element, you call the sortable() method, with the first argument set to 'serialize'. For the second argument, you specify an object literal of options, which decide how the serialization will be done. The key option specifies the name you want to use for each query string argument. The name listItem[] is used, which in PHP and some other server-side scripts will cause the query string of sorted items to be translated into an array or hash.

In the following example you apply the concepts you've just learned to the sortable files example that you've been working on throughout this chapter. Using *Example 13-2.html* as the basis, copy the contents of that file into a new document, and save that document as *Example 13-3.html*; then add a data-path attribute to each <li> element, as you see in the following markup. Don't forget to update each file reference to *Example 13-3*.

```
<!DOCTYPE HTML>
<html xmlns='http://www.w3.org/1999/xhtml'>
    <head>
        <meta http-equiv='content-type'
            content='application/xhtml+xml; charset=utf-8' />
        <meta http-equiv='content-language' content='en-us' />
        <title>Sortables</title>
        <script src='../jQuery.js'></script>
        <script src='../jQueryUI.js'></script>
        <script src='Example 13-3.js'></script>
        <link href='Example 13-3.css' rel='stylesheet' />
    </head>
    <body>
        <div id='finderCategoryFileWrapper'>
            <ul id='finderCategoryFiles'>
                <li class='finderCategoryFile'
                    data-path='/Blog/apple/CoreImage.html'>
                    <div class='finderCategoryFileIcon'></div>
                    <h5 class='finderCategoryFileTitle'>
```

```
            Using CoreImage to Resize and Change Formats on the Fly
        </h5>
        <div class='finderCategoryFilePath'>
            <a href='/Blog/apple/CoreImage.html'>
                /Blog/apple/CoreImage.html
            </a>
        </div>
    </li>
    <li class='finderCategoryFile'
        data-path='/Blog/php/Polymorphism.html'>
        <div class='finderCategoryFileIcon'></div>
        <h5 class='finderCategoryFileTitle'>
            Exploring Polymorphism in PHP
        </h5>
        <div class='finderCategoryFilePath'>
            <a href='/Blog/php/Polymorphism.html'>
                /Blog/php/Polymorphism.html
            </a>
        </div>
    </li>
    <li class='finderCategoryFile'
        data-path='/Blog/php/Backup Script.html'>
        <div class='finderCategoryFileIcon'></div>
        <h5 class='finderCategoryFileTitle'>
            A PHP Shell Script for Backups
        </h5>
        <div class='finderCategoryFilePath'>
            <a href='/Blog/php/Backup%20Script.html'>
                /Blog/php/Backup Script.html
            </a>
        </div>
    </li>
    <li class='finderCategoryFile'
        data-path='/Blog/web/html5_doctype.html'>
        <div class='finderCategoryFileIcon'></div>
        <h5 class='finderCategoryFileTitle'>
            HTML 5 DOCTYPE
        </h5>
        <div class='finderCategoryFilePath'>
            <a href='/Blog/web/html5_doctype.html'>
                /Blog/web/html5_doctype.html
            </a>
        </div>
    </li>
    <li class='finderCategoryFile'
        data-path='/Blog/web/ie8_beta2.html'>
        <div class='finderCategoryFileIcon'></div>
        <h5 class='finderCategoryFileTitle'>
            First Impressions of IE 8 Beta 2
        </h5>
        <div class='finderCategoryFilePath'>
            <a href='/Blog/web/ie8_beta2.html'>
                /Blog/web/ie8_beta2.html
            </a>
        </div>
```

```
                </li>
            </ul>
            <ul id='finderOtherCategoryFiles'>
            </ul>
        </div>
    </body>
</html>
```

The preceding HTML file is combined with the same CSS you used in *Example 13-2.css*, and then the following script is applied:

```
$(document).ready(
    function()
    {
        var selectedFile;

        $('li.finderCategoryFile').mousedown(
            function()
            {
                if (selectedFile && selectedFile.length)
                {
                    selectedFile.removeClass('finderCategoryFileSelected');
                }

                selectedFile = $(this);
                selectedFile.addClass('finderCategoryFileSelected');
            }
        );

        $('ul#finderCategoryFiles').sortable({
            connectWith : 'ul#finderOtherCategoryFiles',
            placeholder : 'finderCategoryFilePlaceholder',
            opacity : 0.8,
            cursor : 'move',
            update : function(event, ui)
            {
                var data = $(this).sortable(
                    'serialize', {
                        attribute : 'data-path',
                        expression : /^(.*)$/,
                        key : 'categoryFiles[]'
                    }
                );

                data += '&categoryId=1';

                alert(data);

                // Here you could go on to make an AJAX request
                // to save the sorted data on the server, which
                // might look like this:
                //
                // $.get('/path/to/server/file.php', data);
            }
        });
```

```
$('ul#finderOtherCategoryFiles').sortable({
    connectWith : 'ul#finderCategoryFiles',
    placeholder : 'finderCategoryFilePlaceholder',
    opacity : 0.8,
    cursor : 'move',
    update : function(event, ui)
    {
        var data = $(this).sortable(
            'serialize', {
                attribute : 'data-path',
                expression : /^(.*)$/,
                key : 'categoryFiles[]'
            }
        );

        data += '&categoryId=2';

        alert(data);

        // Here you could go on to make an AJAX request
        // to save the sorted data on the server, which
        // might look like this:
        //
        // $.get('/path/to/server/file.php', data);
    }
});
    }
);
```

The preceding document gives you something similar to Figure 13-3.

FIGURE 13-3

In *Example 13-3*, you add some code that retrieves data from each <li> element. However, instead of getting data from the id attribute, which is what jQuery UI uses by default, you can get data from the custom data-path attribute.

```
$('ul#finderCategoryFiles').sortable({
    connectWith : 'ul#finderOtherCategoryFiles',
    placeholder : 'finderCategoryFilePlaceholder',
    opacity : 0.8,
    cursor : 'move',
    update : function(event, ui)
    {
        var data = $(this).sortable(
            'serialize', {
                attribute : 'data-path',
                expression : /^(.*)$/,
                key : 'categoryFiles[]'
            }
        );

        data += '&categoryId=1';

        alert(data);

        // Here you could go on to make an AJAX request
        // to save the sorted data on the server, which
        // might look like this:
        //
        // $.get('/path/to/server/file.php', data);
    }
});
```

You start this project by defining a new anonymous function that is assigned to the custom *update* event of the sortable plugin. The custom sortable update event fires every time you complete a sort, and it is therefore the most useful method to save the state of sorting as sorting occurs. Within the anonymous function, you retrieve data from each <li> element by calling the sortable() method again but this time with the serialize option specified in the first argument. Then, in the options you pass in the second argument to the sortable() method, you change the attribute that jQuery UI serializes data from by using the attribute option and setting the value of that option to data-path. The rest is the same: You use the expression option to retrieve the data-path attribute's entire value from beginning to end, rather than just a substring within that value. (You can use any regular expression here.) And the key option is set to categoryFiles[], which is used to name the data in the serialized string. This results in sending something like the following query string to the server side:

```
categoryFiles[]=/Blog/apple/CoreImage.html
&categoryFiles[]=/Blog/php/Polymorphism.html
&categoryFiles[]=/Blog/web/ie8_beta2.html
&category=1
```

On the server side, you have two GET arguments. The first is an array called *categoryFiles*; the second is an integer named *category*. The syntax for creating an array is that used for PHP, and, of course, you want to adjust this syntax depending on the server-side language you're actually using.

SUMMARY

In this chapter, you learned how to make sortable lists with the jQuery UI Sortable plugin. Using the Sortable plugin, you can offer a drag-and-drop sorting API effortlessly. jQuery UI provides a plethora of options that you can use for fine-grained control.

You learned how to use options such as placeholder, cursor, and opacity to control the look and feel of a sortable list. The placeholder option takes a class name, which enables you to use CSS to customize the look of the space that's reserved for a sortable element as sorting is taking place. And you saw how the opacity and cursor options both take the same values of the CSS opacity and cursor properties.

You saw how multiple lists can be connected to each other using the connectWith option, which you provide with a selector that indicates which list you want that sortable list to exchange items with. The connectWith option creates a one-way link to another list, which means that you can drag items only to the other list, but not back to the original. To create a two-way link, you can also add the connectWith option to the other list, with a selector that references the first list.

You've also learned how to save the state of sorted lists, which is also done with the sortable() method. In the first argument, you provide the string 'serialize'. Then in the second argument, you can provide options that determine how serialization works. For example, you provide the attribute option if you want to get the value of any attribute other than the id attribute. Another option you can use is the expression option, which takes a JavaScript regular expression as its value. Then, the key option is used to name the data that's serialized.

You also learned how the update option can be provided to sortable lists, which takes a callback function that executes after a sort is completed.

EXERCISES

1. What method do you use to make a list sortable?

2. What kind of value do you provide to the placeholder option?

3. What is the purpose of the placeholder option?

4. If you want to change the cursor displayed as a sort is taking place, which option would you use?

5. What is the purpose of the helper option?

6. Which option do you use to connect multiple sortable lists to one another?

7. What kind of value do you provide to the connectWith option?

8. How do you save the state of a sortable list after every sort takes place?

14

Selectable

This chapter presents the jQuery UI Selectable plugin. The Selectable plugin fills a niche in UI functionality, and that niche is the occasion in which you need to make a selection by drawing a box. And this is a niche because you probably won't use this functionality very much in your applications. Making a selection by drawing a box is something you've probably done a few times in your operating system's file manager or a graphical editor like Photoshop.

Nonetheless, the Selectable plugin can be useful when the need arises, and in this chapter you see at least one practical application of this plugin: a continuation of the Mac OS X Finder clone that you started in Chapter 10, "Scrollbars."

INTRODUCING THE SELECTABLE PLUGIN

The Selectable plugin works similarly to the Sortable plugin presented in Chapter 13, "Sortable," and all jQuery UI plugins, as you'll have recognized by now, share a clean and consistent API that is implemented similarly from plugin to plugin.

To make elements into Selectable elements, you call the `selectable()` method on any element. The following document, which appears as *Example 14-1* in the source materials at www.wrox.com/go/webdevwithjquery, demonstrates the plugin:

```
<!DOCTYPE HTML>
<html xmlns='http://www.w3.org/1999/xhtml'>
    <head>
        <meta http-equiv='content-type'
            content='application/xhtml+xml; charset=utf-8' />
        <meta http-equiv='content-language' content='en-us' />
        <title>Finder</title>
        <script type='text/javascript' src='../jQuery.js'></script>
        <script type='text/javascript' src='../jQueryUI.js'></script>
        <script type='text/javascript' src='Example 14-1.js'></script>
        <link type='text/css' href='Example 14-1.css' rel='stylesheet' />
    </head>
    <body>
```

```html
<div id='finderFiles'>
    <div class='finderDirectory' data-path='/Applications'>
        <div class='finderIcon'><div></div></div>
        <div class='finderDirectoryName'>
            <span>Applications</span>
        </div>
    </div>
    <div class='finderDirectory' data-path='/Library'>
        <div class='finderIcon'><div></div></div>
        <div class='finderDirectoryName'>
            <span>Library</span>
        </div>
    </div>
    <div class='finderDirectory' data-path='/Network'>
        <div class='finderIcon'><div></div></div>
        <div class='finderDirectoryName'>
            <span>Network</span>
        </div>
    </div>
    <div class='finderDirectory' data-path='/Sites'>
        <div class='finderIcon'><div></div></div>
        <div class='finderDirectoryName'>
            <span>Sites</span>
        </div>
    </div>
    <div class='finderDirectory' data-path='/System'>
        <div class='finderIcon'><div></div></div>
        <div class='finderDirectoryName'>
            <span>System</span>
        </div>
    </div>
    <div class='finderDirectory' data-path='/Users'>
        <div class='finderIcon'><div></div></div>
        <div class='finderDirectoryName'>
            <span>Users</span>
        </div>
    </div>
</div>
</body>
</html>
```

The following CSS provides some styling for the finder example and jQuery UI Selectable example.

```css
html,
body {
    width: 100%;
    height: 100%;
    overflow: hidden;
}
body {
    font: 12px "Lucida Grande", Arial, sans-serif;
    background: rgb(189, 189, 189) url('images/Bottom.png') repeat-x bottom;
    color: rgb(50, 50, 50);
    margin: 0;
    padding: 0;
```

```css
}
div#finderFiles {
    border-bottom: 1px solid rgb(64, 64, 64);
    background: #fff;
    position: absolute;
    top: 0;
    right: 0;
    bottom: 23px;
    left: 0;
    overflow: auto;
}
div.finderDirectory {
    float: left;
    width: 150px;
    height: 100px;
    overflow: hidden;
}
div.finderIcon {
    height: 56px;
    width: 54px;
    margin: 10px auto 3px auto;
}
div.finderIcon div {
    background: url('images/Folder 48x48.png') no-repeat center;
    width: 48px;
    height: 48px;
    margin: auto;
}
div.finderSelected div.finderIcon,
div.finderDirectoryDrop div.finderIcon {
    background-color: rgb(196, 196, 196);
    border-radius: 5px;
}
div.finderDirectoryDrop div.finderIcon div {
    background-image: url('images/Open Folder 48x48.png');
}
div.finderDirectoryName {
    text-align: center;
}
div.finderSelected div.finderDirectoryName span,
div.finderDirectoryDrop div.finderDirectoryName span {
    background: rgb(56, 117, 215);
    border-radius: 8px;
    color: white;
    padding: 1px 7px;
}
div.ui-selectable-helper {
    position: absolute;
    background: rgb(128, 128, 128);
    border: 1px solid black;
    opacity: 0.25;
    -ms-filter:"progid:DXImageTransform.Microsoft.Alpha(Opacity=25)";
    filter: alpha(opacity=25);
}
```

The following JavaScript makes it possible to select multiple files at once by drawing a box.

```javascript
$.fn.extend({

    selectFile : function()
    {
        this.addClass('finderSelected');

        this.each(
            function()
            {
                if ($.inArray($(this), finder.selectedFiles) == -1)
                {
                    finder.selectedFiles.push($(this));
                }
            }
        );

        return this;
    },

    unselectFile : function()
    {
        this.removeClass('finderSelected');
        var files = this;

        if (finder.selectedFiles instanceof Array && finder.selectedFiles.length)
        {
            finder.selectedFiles = $.grep(
                finder.selectedFiles,
                function(file, index)
                {
                    return $.inArray(file, files) == -1;
                }
            );
        }

        return this;
    }
});

var finder = {

    selectingFiles : false,

    selectedFiles : [],

    unselectSelected : function()
    {
        if (this.selectedFiles instanceof Array && this.selectedFiles.length)
        {
            $(this.selectedFiles).each(
                function()
                {
                    $(this).unselectFile();
```

```
            }
        );
    }

    this.selectedFiles = [];
},

ready : function()
{
    $('div.finderDirectory, div.finderFile')
        .mousedown(
            function()
            {
                if (!finder.selectingFiles)
                {
                    finder.unselectSelected();
                    $(this).selectFile();
                }
            }
        )
        .draggable({
            helper : 'clone',
            opacity : 0.5
        });

    $('div.finderDirectory').droppable({
        accept : 'div.finderDirectory, div.finderFile',
        hoverClass : 'finderDirectoryDrop',
        drop : function(event, ui)
        {
            var path = ui.draggable.data('path');
            ui.draggable.remove();
        }
    });

    $('div#finderFiles').selectable({
        appendTo : 'div#finderFiles',
        filter : 'div.finderDirectory, div.finderFile',
        start : function(event, ui)
        {
            finder.selectingFiles = true;
            finder.unselectSelected();
        },
        stop : function(event, ui)
        {
            finder.selectingFiles = false;
        },
        selecting : function(event, ui)
        {
            $(ui.selecting).selectFile();
        },
        unselecting : function(event, ui)
        {
            $(ui.unselecting).unselectFile();
```

```
                }
            });
        }
    };

    $(document).ready(
        function()
        {
            finder.ready();
        }
    );
```

The preceding source code comes together to give you the document that you see in Figure 14-1.

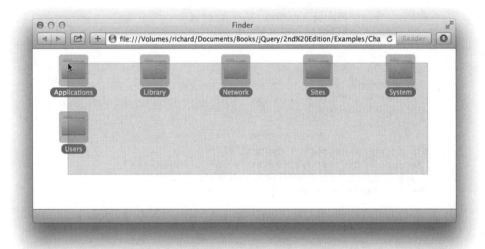

FIGURE 14-1

While this example teaches you how to draw a selection box, you'll note that you cannot drag the selection after it is made, even though you have implemented drag-and-drop on the individual folders. Although this is possible, it is beyond the scope of this example.

In this example, you applied the Selectable plugin to the Mac OS X Finder Clone example that you worked on in Chapter 12, "Draggable and Droppable." This example incorporates some jQuery functionality that you learned about in previous chapters to demonstrate how you apply jQuery in a realistic example.

You made a few changes to the style sheet that you created in Chapter 12. You added one additional rule that gives you the ability to customize the box that's drawn when a selection is made. jQuery UI's default selection box as depicted in the documentation looks like the one used in older operating systems, like Windows 98, which just provided a dotted box to indicate where the box is being drawn. In an application like Photoshop, where the selection is oftentimes also animated, this type of selection is referred to as *marching ants* because the selection box is made to resemble ants marching in a line. In this example, you changed the style of that box to look more like the selection box in Mac OS X.

```css
div.ui-selectable-helper {
    position: absolute;
    background: rgb(128, 128, 128);
    border: 1px solid black;
    opacity: 0.25;
    -ms-filter:"progid:DXImageTransform.Microsoft.Alpha(Opacity=25)";
    filter: alpha(opacity=25);
}
```

The selection box can be customized with the same selector that you see here. jQuery UI does not provide a mechanism for customizing the style of the selection box via an option within the JavaScript API. This is by design because it is best practice to keep style separated from behavior. To customize the styling, you must use CSS. The class name *ui-selectable-helper* is the class name that jQuery UI applies to the selection box, which is also a <div> element, internally, so the customization that you see simply exploits that fact. The styling that the Selectable plugin provides is limited to the necessary CSS properties that actually change as you move your mouse cursor. Those properties are top, left, width, and height. The rest you must provide for yourself, and in fact, the selection box will have no styling at all until you apply it, meaning it will be completely invisible until you provide some styling. You must first position the selection box using position: absolute, and then a border or background should be applied so that you can see a selection when you create one. In this example, I've chosen to simply imitate OS X, making the styling choice easy.

The style provides a gray background and a black border; then the whole box is made semi-transparent via the standard opacity property supported by Safari, Chrome, Firefox, and IE9; Microsoft's proprietary filter property is supported by IE6 and IE7; and Microsoft's proprietary -ms-filter property is supported by IE8 in IE8 standards mode. The IE8 syntax for the -ms-filter property is the same as previous versions; it just puts quotes around the property's value and adds the vendor-specific -ms- prefix. IE9 goes on to eliminate the need for the filter or -ms-filter property because IE9 has native support for the opacity property.

Aside from those modifications, the style sheet remains mostly the same as the style sheet you made in Chapter 12. The brunt of the elbow work in this example occurs in the JavaScript.

In this example, you rewrite the example that you saw in Chapter 12 with a few jQuery plugins, and you add some functionality that deals with keeping track of selected folders. You begin by creating two plugin methods, selectFile() and unselectFile(). As you learned in Chapter 9, "Plugins," you use $.fn to create jQuery plugins. There is also more than one way to leverage $.fn to create jQuery plugins. The method I use most often is jQuery's extend() method, which allows you to take an object and add to it. For this example, you add two new methods, which each become a new jQuery plugin.

```javascript
$.fn.extend({
```

Within the selectFile() method, you begin by adding the class name *finderSelected* to each element that selectFile() is called on, which can be just one file or many files. The class name provides you with a visual cue to let you see that a file is selected by triggering the following CSS:

```css
div.finderSelected div.finderIcon,
div.finderDirectoryDrop div.finderIcon {
    background-color: rgb(196, 196, 196);
    border-radius: 5px;
}
```

In addition to styling the folder icon, the following style is applied to the name of the file or folder:

```
div.finderSelected div.finderDirectoryName span,
div.finderDirectoryDrop div.finderDirectoryName span {
    background: rgb(56, 117, 215);
    border-radius: 8px;
    color: white;
    padding: 1px 7px;
}
```

Then, for each file object that selectFile() is called on, you see if that file object is already added to the *finder.selectedFiles* array. This array keeps track of every file that is selected at a given time by storing a reference to it. jQuery's inArray() method is designed to work like JavaScript's indexOf() method. The indexOf() is used to determine if a string contains another string. If the string is found, then indexOf() returns the offset position of the first occurrence of that string, where counting from zero, the first character in the string you're searching is number zero. If indexOf() returns an integer zero or greater, then the string is found within the second string and that number can be used to identify where in that string the second string exists. If indexOf() returns -1, then the string is not found. jQuery's inArray() works the same way it applies the same logic using arrays instead of strings. If a value is found within the array, the offset position of that value is returned. The array is also numbered starting from zero, so the first item within the array is number zero and each item is numbered from there. inArray() returns -1 if the value does not exist within the array, otherwise inArray()returns a number zero or greater.

```
        selectFile : function()
        {
            this.addClass('finderSelected');

            this.each(
                function()
                {
                    if ($.inArray($(this), finder.selectedFiles) == -1)
                    {
                        finder.selectedFiles.push($(this));
                    }
                }
            );

            return this;
        },
```

To unselect files, the first thing that you do is to remove the class name *finderSelected* using the removeClass() method. Then the elements passed to unselectFile(), which are made available in the this keyword, are assigned to a new variable called *files*. This is done to make the elements available within the anonymous function passed to the grep() method. You then verify that *finder.selectedFiles* is an array and contains one or more items. The grep() method is used to filter the *finder.selectedFiles* array. The anonymous function provided to grep() is executed once for every item in the array. If the anonymous function provided to grep() returns true, then the item remains in the array. If the anonymous function returns false, however, then the item is removed from the array. In the context of this example, if the file is among the files to be unselected, then file or files are removed from the *finder.selectedFiles* array via grep().

```
unselectFile : function()
{
    this.removeClass('finderSelected');
    var files = this;

    if (finder.selectedFiles instanceof Array && finder.selectedFiles.length)
    {
        finder.selectedFiles = $.grep(
            finder.selectedFiles,
            function(file, index)
            {
                return $.inArray(file, files) == -1;
            }
        );
    }

    return this;
}
});
```

The unselectFile() method then returns the files that were unselected so that you can potentially chain method calls together.

You next set up a new object called finder.

```
var finder = {
```

The property *finder.selectingFiles* is used to keep track of whether a selection of files is presently underway using the Selectable plugin. The default value is set to false to indicate that there is no selection of files underway.

The property *finder.selectedFiles* contains an empty array by default. As you saw with the jQuery plugins selectFile() and unselectFile(), when one or more files are selected, a reference to each selected node is stored in the *selectedFiles* property.

```
selectingFiles : false,

selectedFiles : [],
```

The method unselectSelected() unselects every file node that is presently selected, and then the property is reset to an empty array. This method is simply a quick and easy way to unselect every file.

```
unselectSelected : function()
{
    if (this.selectedFiles instanceof Array && this.selectedFiles.length)
    {
        $(this.selectedFiles).each(
            function()
            {
                $(this).unselectFile();
            }
        );
    }
}
```

```
        this.selectedFiles = [];
    },
```

As you have read, the `ready()` method is executed upon the `DOMContentLoaded` event.

```
    ready : function()
    {
```

Every directory and every file receives a `mousedown` event and is made draggable using jQuery UI's Draggable plugin. Every directory is also made a drop target using the Droppable plugin.

```
    $('div.finderDirectory, div.finderFile')
```

Within the `mousedown` event, if there is no selection presently underway, which is tracked in the `finder.selectingFiles` property, all files are unselected, and then whichever file element is receiving the `mousedown` event is selected.

```
        .mousedown(
            function()
            {
                if (!finder.selectingFiles)
                {
                    finder.unselectSelected();
                    $(this).selectFile();
                }
            }
        )
```

The Draggable plugin is enabled by calling the `draggable()` method; the dragged element is set to clone the file where the drag originated, creating a ghost of the element being dragged. The ghost element is also set to receive opacity of 50 percent, making it semi-transparent (or semi-opaque, depending on your view).

```
        .draggable({
            helper : 'clone',
            opacity : 0.5
        });
```

Even though this example contains only directory objects, you set up the example prepared to deal with both directory and ordinary file objects. Each directory is distinguished from regular files via the class name assigned. The *finderDirectory* class name is given to directories, and the *finderFile* class name is given to regular files.

Directory objects are made droppable using the Droppable jQuery UI plugin; a call to the `droppable()` method enables a directory as a drop target. As you learned in Chapter 12, jQuery UI is just one way of implementing drag and drop. The more complicated HTML5 drag-and-drop API is another option, and it's the option that I recommend if you need to drag and drop between multiple browser windows. In the interest of keeping the example simple, I stuck with the simpler jQuery UI draggable and droppable plugins.

```
    $('div.finderDirectory').droppable({
        accept : 'div.finderDirectory, div.finderFile',
        hoverClass : 'finderDirectoryDrop',
        drop : function(event, ui)
```

```
        {
            var path = ui.draggable.data('path');
            ui.draggable.remove();
        }
    });
```

An example of the Selectable jQuery UI plugin follows next. The contents of the <div> with id name *finderFiles* is made selectable. The option *appendTo* is provided a selector that tells the selectable() plugin where to put the <div> element that represents the selection box. The selection box is added to the <div> element with the id *finderFiles*.

The option *filter* is used to tell the selectable() plugin which elements it contains are selectable, and you do that by providing a selector to it to describe those selectable elements. The selector *div.finderDirectory, div.finderFile* makes the <div> elements with class names *finderDirectory* or *finderFile* selectable.

```
$('div#finderFiles').selectable({
    appendTo : 'div#finderFiles',
    filter : 'div.finderDirectory, div.finderFile',
```

The option *start* is provided a callback function that fires each time a new selection begins. As you learned in Chapter 12, each option that specifies a custom UI plugin event accepts two arguments, one for the event and another for passing additional UI plugin data. In this example, when selection begins, the property *finder.selectingFiles* is set to true, and this is used to prevent the mousedown event that you created earlier from also selecting files because that would conflict with the selection taking place using the selectable() plugin. In addition, any file selection that is already in place is completely cleared by calling finder.unselectSelected().

```
    start : function(event, ui)
    {
        finder.selectingFiles = true;
        finder.unselectSelected();
    },
```

When selection ends, the callback function provided to the option *stop* is fired. This callback function sets the property *finder.selectingFiles* to false so that selection of individual files or directories using the mousedown event you set up previously can again take place.

```
    stop : function(event, ui)
    {
        finder.selectingFiles = false;
    },
```

While selection is happening, the callback function provided to the option *selecting* is continuously fired. The objects that are experiencing a selection are provided to you and described in the selector passed in the *ui.selecting* property. Those items are in turn selected by calling selectFile() on the individual item or collection of items.

```
    selecting : function(event, ui)
    {
        $(ui.selecting).selectFile();
    },
```

While selection is happening, as items are included in a selection, sometimes items are also excluded from a selection. When items are excluded from a selection in progress, the custom event callback function assigned to the *unselecting* option is fired. Like the *selecting* option, the *unselecting* option also receives data in the *ui* argument. A selector is provided to the *ui.unselecting* property, which contains the file nodes that should be unselected; each file that should be unselected is unselected using a call to unselectFile().

```
unselecting : function(event, ui)
{
    $(ui.unselecting).unselectFile();
}
});
```

Although it is a niche feature that is not called for often in programming, the jQuery UI Selectable plugin provides useful functionality that has been with computing since the dawn of the graphical user interface.

> **NOTE** *Complete API documentation for the Selectable plugin is available in Appendix L.*

SUMMARY

In this chapter, you learned about the jQuery UI Selectable plugin, which provides functionality for making selections by drawing a box with your mouse cursor. You saw how the Selectable plugin can be applied to the Finder clone that you made in Chapter 12.

The Selectable plugin, like jQuery UI's other plugins, accepts an object literal of options that are specified in key, value form. The Selectable plugin lets you specify callback functions for selectable events. Callback functions provided to the options start and stop are executed when a selection begins and ends, respectively. Callback functions provided to the options selecting and unselecting are executed as items are added and removed from a selection while a selection is taking place.

EXERCISES

1. Which option do you use to execute the callback function when a selection begins?

2. What options do you use to execute callback functions when items are added to or removed from a selection (while a selection is taking place)?

3. When using the *selecting* and *unselecting* options, how do you access each element added to and removed from the selection?

4. What selector would you add to a style sheet to customize the look and feel of the selection box?

15

Accordion

So far you've learned about how jQuery makes dragging and dropping easy to implement, and you've learned how jQuery makes it a breeze to select items by drawing a box. You've also seen how ridiculously easy it is to implement drag-and-drop sorting with jQuery. This chapter presents another cool jQuery UI plugin, Accordion.

The jQuery UI Accordion plugin makes it easy to implement content that expands and folds like your favorite polka instrument, the accordion. Accordion UI widgets can be seen on popular websites. If you'd like to see a quick demo of the Accordion UI, look at www.jqueryui.com/accordion/. The downside of the jQuery UI Accordion plugin is that you can have only one item open at a time. It's easy to write some code that sidesteps this limitation.

In this chapter, you find out how to use the jQuery UI Accordion plugin to make your own Accordion widget and customize its look.

BUILDING AN ACCORDION UI

This section discusses how to make an Accordion UI, which is a collection of content panes that each has its own header, where only one content pane is visible at a time. When you click the other content panes, a smooth animation transitions the visible pane to closed by animating its height, leaving only its header visible, animating the other element's height, expanding that element until it is fully visible.

Now that we have briefly explained what an Accordion UI is, the following document, which can be retrieved from www.wrox.com/go/webdevwithjquery as *Example 15-1*, begins with a basic implementation of the jQuery UI Accordion plugin:

```
<!DOCTYPE HTML>
<html xmlns='http://www.w3.org/1999/xhtml'>
    <head>
        <meta http-equiv='content-type'
            content='application/xhtml+xml; charset=utf-8' />
        <meta http-equiv='content-language' content='en-us' />
        <title>Accordion Plugin</title>
```

```
            <script src='../jQuery.js'></script>
            <script src='../jQueryUI.js'></script>
            <script src='Example 15-1.js'></script>
            <link href='Example 15-1.css' rel='stylesheet' />
    </head>
    <body>
        <h4>The Beatles</h4>
        <ul>
            <li>
                <a href='#'>John Lennon</a>
                <p>
                    Lorem ipsum dolor sit amet, consectetuer adipiscing elit.
                    Vestibulum luctus rutrum orci. Praesent faucibus tellus
                    faucibus quam. Aliquam erat volutpat. Nam posuere.
                </p>
            </li>
            <li>
                <a href='#'>Paul McCartney</a>
                <p>
                    Lorem ipsum dolor sit amet, consectetuer adipiscing elit.
                    Vestibulum luctus rutrum orci. Praesent faucibus tellus
                    faucibus quam. Aliquam erat volutpat. Nam posuere.
                </p>
            </li>
            <li>
                <a href='#'>George Harrison</a>
                <p>
                    Lorem ipsum dolor sit amet, consectetuer adipiscing elit.
                    Vestibulum luctus rutrum orci. Praesent faucibus tellus
                    faucibus quam. Aliquam erat volutpat. Nam posuere.
                </p>
            </li>
            <li>
                <a href='#'>Ringo Starr</a>
                <p>
                    Lorem ipsum dolor sit amet, consectetuer adipiscing elit.
                    Vestibulum luctus rutrum orci. Praesent faucibus tellus
                    faucibus quam. Aliquam erat volutpat. Nam posuere.
                </p>
            </li>
        </ul>
    </body>
</html>
```

The following style sheet is applied to the preceding markup document:

```
body {
    font: 12px "Lucida Grande", Arial, sans-serif;
    background: #fff;
    color: rgb(50, 50, 50);
    margin: 0;
    padding: 0;
}
h4 {
    margin: 5px;
}
```

```
ul {
    list-style: none;
    margin: 0;
    padding: 15px 5px;
}
li {
    background: gold;
    padding: 3px;
    width: 244px;
    margin: 1px;
}
```

The following script makes the `<ul>` element in the markup document into an accordion with a simple function call:

```
$(document).ready(
    function()
    {
        $('ul').accordion();
    }
);
```

Figure 15-1 shows that although the accordion has been created, your work here is not yet done.

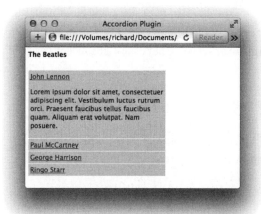

FIGURE 15-1

You see the most basic but functioning example of the Accordion plugin possible. By calling the accordion() method on the `<ul>` element, the `<ul>` element is transformed into accordion UI. When you click an `<a>` element, the corresponding text in the sibling `<p>` element is expanded by a smooth, animated transition.

Structurally speaking, jQuery's Accordion plugin wants to be applied to a collection of elements; like a `<ul>` element, after the plugin is applied, it automatically recognizes each `<a>` element as being the header portion of each content pane. Later this chapter discusses in more detail how to approach styling an accordion.

CHANGING THE DEFAULT PANE

At this point, you have a functioning Accordion UI. This section shows you how to change the content pane that's displayed by default. Out-of-the-box, the Accordion plugin displays the first content pane, but using the active option, you can force a different content pane to be displayed. The following markup document, which appears as *Example 15-2* in the source materials, demonstrates this concept:

```
<!DOCTYPE HTML>
<html xmlns='http://www.w3.org/1999/xhtml'>
    <head>
        <meta http-equiv='content-type'
            content='application/xhtml+xml; charset=utf-8' />
        <meta http-equiv='content-language' content='en-us' />
        <title>Accordion Plugin</title>
        <script src='../jQuery.js'></script>
        <script src='../jQueryUI.js'></script>
        <script src='Example 15-2.js'></script>
        <link href='Example 15-2.css' rel='stylesheet' />
    </head>
    <body>
        <h4>The Beatles</h4>
        <ul>
            <li>
                <a href='#'>John Lennon</a>
                <p>
                    Lorem ipsum dolor sit amet, consectetuer adipiscing elit.
                    Vestibulum luctus rutrum orci. Praesent faucibus tellus
                    faucibus quam. Aliquam erat volutpat. Nam posuere.
                </p>
            </li>
            <li>
                <a href='#'>Paul McCartney</a>
                <p>
                    Lorem ipsum dolor sit amet, consectetuer adipiscing elit.
                    Vestibulum luctus rutrum orci. Praesent faucibus tellus
                    faucibus quam. Aliquam erat volutpat. Nam posuere.
                </p>
            </li>
            <li>
                <a href='#'>George Harrison</a>
                <p>
                    Lorem ipsum dolor sit amet, consectetuer adipiscing elit.
                    Vestibulum luctus rutrum orci. Praesent faucibus tellus
                    faucibus quam. Aliquam erat volutpat. Nam posuere.
                </p>
            </li>
            <li>
                <a href='#'>Ringo Starr</a>
                <p>
```

```
                    Lorem ipsum dolor sit amet, consectetuer adipiscing elit.
                    Vestibulum luctus rutrum orci. Praesent faucibus tellus
                    faucibus quam. Aliquam erat volutpat. Nam posuere.
              </p>
          </li>
       </ul>
    </body>
</html>
```

The following style sheet is applied to the preceding markup document:

```
body {
    font: 12px "Lucida Grande", Arial, sans-serif;
    background: #fff;
    color: rgb(50, 50, 50);
    margin: 0;
    padding: 0;
}
h4 {
    margin: 5px;
}
ul {
    list-style: none;
    margin: 0;
    padding: 15px 5px;
}
li {
    background: gold;
    padding: 3px;
    width: 244px;
    margin: 1px;
}
```

In the following script, you see that the integer 1 is provided to the active option, which causes the second <li> element in the markup document to be used as the default content pane:

```
$(document).ready(
    function()
    {
        $('ul').accordion({
            active : 1
        });
    }
);
```

Figure 15-2 shows that the content under Paul McCartney is now the default content. The active option selects the default content when you provide it a zero offset integer (where zero is the first item, one is the second item, and so on) that represents the item in the collection that you want to select by default. In this case, *Paul McCartney* is the second item, so 1 is provided as the value to the active option to select that panel.

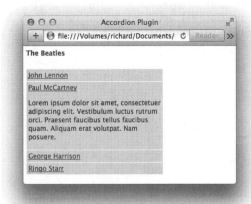

FIGURE 15-2

You can also set the option `active` to `false`, which makes no content open by default. If you set the active option to `false`, you must also set the collapsible option to `true`. This is demonstrated in the following script:

```
$(document).ready(
    function()
    {
        $('ul').accordion({
            collapsible : true,
            active : false
        });
    }
);
```

The preceding script gives you the result of having no pane open by default. This example is available in the source materials as *Example 15-3*.

When you have no default pane selected by default, when you open a panel, you may notice that the content of each pane overlaps the rest of the accordion, as shown in Figure 15-3.

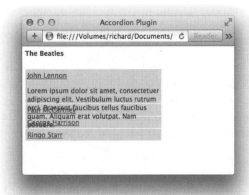

FIGURE 15-3

This problem can be corrected by specifying the `heightStyle` option. The `heightStyle` option takes three possible values: auto, fill, and content. The auto option sets the height of each panel to the height of the tallest panel. The problem with this is that because all panels are hidden when the page is rendered, this makes the height of each panel the height of the header without the additional hidden content. The fill option uses the accordion element's parent element as the basis for height. In the context of this example, that would set the height of each item based on the height of the <body> element. The content option sets the height of each panel based on the height of the content that it contains. The following example reflects changing the script to specify the `heightStyle` option with the content value:

```
$(document).ready(
    function()
    {
        $('ul').accordion({
            collapsible : true,
            active : false,
            heightStyle : "content"
        });
    }
);
```

The preceding example is available in the source materials as *Example 15-4*. With the change in the preceding script, each item opens without the content overlapping the other headings, as shown in Figure 15-4.

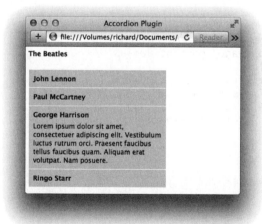

FIGURE 15-4

In the next section you learn how to change the event that triggers opening each content panel in the accordion collection.

CHANGING THE ACCORDION EVENT

Upon setup, Accordion content panes are transitioned when you click a header. You have the option of changing the event that triggers the transition using the event option. The following script shows you how to change the event to a mouseover event from a click event:

```
$(document).ready(
    function()
    {
        $('ul').accordion({
            active : 1,
            event : 'mouseover'
        });
    }
);
```

The preceding modification makes no visible change, so you see a document that looks similar to the one referred to in Figure 15-2. However, when you load it in a browser, you can transition between content panes using a mouseover event instead of a click event.

The preceding example is available in the source materials as *Example 15-5* but is not shown here.

SETTING THE HEADER ELEMENTS

By default, the Accordion uses the <a> element as a header within each <li> element. However, you don't have to use an <a> element as the header; the following example, available in the source materials as *Example 15-6*, illustrates how to use an <h4> element instead of an <a> element:

```
<!DOCTYPE HTML>
<html xmlns='http://www.w3.org/1999/xhtml'>
    <head>
        <meta http-equiv='content-type'
            content='application/xhtml+xml; charset=utf-8' />
        <meta http-equiv='content-language' content='en-us' />
        <title>Accordion Plugin</title>
        <script src='../jQuery.js'></script>
        <script src='../jQueryUI.js'></script>
        <script src='Example 15-6.js'></script>
        <link href='Example 15-6.css' rel='stylesheet' />
    </head>
    <body>
        <h4>The Beatles</h4>
        <ul>
            <li>
                <h4>John Lennon</h4>
                <p>
                    Lorem ipsum dolor sit amet, consectetuer adipiscing elit.
                    Vestibulum luctus rutrum orci. Praesent faucibus tellus
                    faucibus quam. Aliquam erat volutpat. Nam posuere.
                </p>
            </li>
            <li>
                <h4>Paul McCartney</h4>
                <p>
                    Lorem ipsum dolor sit amet, consectetuer adipiscing elit.
                    Vestibulum luctus rutrum orci. Praesent faucibus tellus
                    faucibus quam. Aliquam erat volutpat. Nam posuere.
                </p>
            </li>
```

```
        <li>
            <h4>George Harrison</h4>
            <p>
                Lorem ipsum dolor sit amet, consectetuer adipiscing elit.
                Vestibulum luctus rutrum orci. Praesent faucibus tellus
                faucibus quam. Aliquam erat volutpat. Nam posuere.
            </p>
        </li>
        <li>
            <h4>Ringo Starr</h4>
            <p>
                Lorem ipsum dolor sit amet, consectetuer adipiscing elit.
                Vestibulum luctus rutrum orci. Praesent faucibus tellus
                faucibus quam. Aliquam erat volutpat. Nam posuere.
            </p>
        </li>
    </ul>
</body>
</html>
```

The following style sheet is applied to the preceding markup document:

```
body {
    font: 12px "Lucida Grande", Arial, sans-serif;
    background: #fff;
    color: rgb(50, 50, 50);
    margin: 0;
    padding: 0;
}
ul {
    list-style: none;
    margin: 0;
    padding: 15px 5px;
}
h4,
ul h4,
ul p {
    margin: 5px;
}
li {
    background: gold;
    padding: 3px;
    width: 244px;
    margin: 1px;
}
```

In the following script, you change the element that's used as the header for each content pane by providing a selector to the header option, in this case h4, which causes the <h4> element of each <li> element to be used as a header, rather than the <a> element:

```
$(document).ready(
    function()
    {
        $('ul').accordion({
            active : 1,
```

```
            event : 'mouseover',
            header : 'h4'
        });
    }
);
```

In the preceding script, take note that you also have to change the selector provided to the header option because now you want to have a content pane that uses an <h4> header to be open by default.

Figure 15-4 demonstrates that the <h4> element is used instead of an <a> element.

SUMMARY

In this chapter, you learned how to create an Accordion UI and the various options that you can use to tweak an Accordion UI implementation. You learned that the Accordion plugin takes a list of elements, such as a <ul> element, and makes the items in that list into smoothly animated content panes, which transition one to the other by animating the height of each item in the list. By default, headers for each content pane are provided as <a> elements, but you can change the header element to something else by supplying a selector to the header option.

The active option can be used to change the default content pane that's displayed when the page first loads. You can also have no default content pane by setting the active option to false and the collapsible option to true. If no default content pane is specified, the first element in the list will be used.

The heightStyle option can each be used to tweak how the Accordion plugin defines the height for each content pane. The auto value takes the highest content and uses that height as the height for all other content panes, which may not always provide the right look and feel.

Finally, the event option is used to change the event that's used to trigger a content pane transition; click is the default event.

> **NOTE** *A quick reference of the Accordion plugin and its options appears in Appendix N, "Accordion."*

EXERCISES

1. Which option would you provide to the accordion() method to change the default content pane?

2. Which option and its values would you consider using to change how the accordion() method handles height?

3. What option would you use to make the accordion() method trigger a content transition using a mouseover event instead of a click event?

4. What option would you use to change the header element to an <h3> element?

16

Datepicker

jQuery UI offers a sophisticated and feature-rich UI component for inputting dates into a form field in its Datepicker plugin. The jQuery UI Datepicker plugin provides a graphical calendar that can be set to pop up anywhere you might need a date keyed into a form. The calendar can be customized in its look and feel. The date format it produces can be set to mirror local customs. The text it labels fields with can be swapped out with whatever text you like or translated into a foreign language, making the plugin fully capable of localization.

This chapter describes how to use and customize the Datepicker plugin.

IMPLEMENTING A DATEPICKER

A barebones implementation of the Datepicker plugin doesn't look like much; it's not styled, but it works, more or less, from the standpoint of functionality.

The following document, which can be downloaded from www.wrox.com/go/webdevwithjquery as *Example 16-1*, demonstrates a basic implementation of the jQuery UI Datepicker plugin:

```
<!DOCTYPE HTML>
<html xmlns='http://www.w3.org/1999/xhtml'>
    <head>
        <meta http-equiv='content-type'
            content='application/xhtml+xml; charset=utf-8' />
        <meta http-equiv='content-language' content='en-us' />
        <title>Datepicker Plugin</title>
        <script src='../jQuery.js'></script>
        <script src='../jQueryUI.js'></script>
        <script src='Example 16-1.js'></script>
        <link href='Example 16-1.css' rel='stylesheet' />
    </head>
    <body>
        <form action='javascript:void(0);' method='post'>
            <fieldset>
                <legend>Appointment Form</legend>
                <div class="exampleDate">
                    <label for="exampleDate">Date:</label>
```

```
                    <input type="text" name="exampleDate" id="exampleDate" />
                    <img src="images/Calendar.png" alt="Calendar Icon" />
               </div>
          </fieldset>
      </form>
  </body>
</html>
```

The following style sheet provides a little bit of styling for the preceding markup document:

```
body {
    font: 12px 'Lucida Grande', Arial, sans-serif;
    background: #fff;
    color: rgb(50, 50, 50);
}
fieldset {
    border: none;
}
input {
    background: lightblue;
}
div.exampleDate img {
    vertical-align: -5px;
}
```

In the following script, the datepicker() method is called on the <input> element in the markup document, which causes a calendar to dynamically pop up for date selection whenever the <input> element receives focus:

```
$(document).ready(
    function()
    {
        $('input#exampleDate').datepicker();
    }
);
```

As you can see in Figure 16-1, the Datepicker plugin provides an unstyled calendar provided each time the <input> field it is associated with is activated.

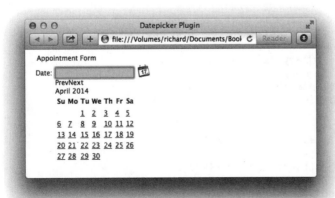

FIGURE 16-1

Custom Styling the Datepicker

By default, the Datepicker plugin doesn't provide styling. To style the Datepicker plugin, you can either use a jQuery UI theme or style it manually. This section presents how to style the Datepicker calendar manually. Before you can style the Datepicker widget, however, you need to understand how the widget is structured. A comprehensive list of customization options and a list of class names appear in Appendix O, "Datepicker."

In the following example, you examine the markup structure of the Datepicker plugin and apply some CSS to it. This example is available in this book's source code download materials available at www.wrox.com in *Example 16-2.html* and *Example 16-2.css*. This example focuses only on the markup and CSS portions of the Datepicker plugin and does not include any JavaScript. This is an example of the markup the Datepicker plugin generates with default options selected. If you provide custom options to the Datepicker plugin, you need to use something such as WebKit Inspector or Firebug to examine the markup generated by the plugin for changes.

```html
<!DOCTYPE HTML>
<html xmlns='http://www.w3.org/1999/xhtml'>
    <head>
        <meta http-equiv='content-type'
            content='application/xhtml+xml; charset=utf-8' />
        <meta http-equiv='content-language' content='en-us' />
        <title>Datepicker Plugin</title>
        <link href='Example 16-2.css' rel='stylesheet' />
    </head>
    <body>
        <div id="ui-datepicker-div"
            class="ui-datepicker
                    ui-widget
                    ui-widget-content
                    ui-helper-clearfix
                    ui-corner-all">
            <div class="ui-datepicker-header
                        ui-widget-header
                        ui-helper-clearfix
                        ui-corner-all">
                <a class="ui-datepicker-prev
                        ui-corner-all"
                    title="Prev">
                    <span class="ui-icon
                            ui-icon-circle-triangle-w">Prev</span>
                </a>
                <a class="ui-datepicker-next
                        ui-corner-all"
                    title="Next">
                    <span class="ui-icon
                            ui-icon-circle-triangle-e">Next</span>
                </a>
                <div class="ui-datepicker-title">
                    <select class="ui-datepicker-month">
                        <option value="0">Jan</option>
                        <option value="1">Feb</option>
                        <option value="2">Mar</option>
                        <option value="3" selected="selected">Apr</option>
```

```
            <option value="4">May</option>
            <option value="5">Jun</option>
            <option value="6">Jul</option>
            <option value="7">Aug</option>
            <option value="8">Sep</option>
            <option value="9">Oct</option>
            <option value="10">Nov</option>
            <option value="11">Dec</option>
        </select>
        <select class="ui-datepicker-year">
            <option value="2004">2004</option>
            <option value="2005">2005</option>
            <option value="2006">2006</option>
            <option value="2007">2007</option>
            <option value="2008">2008</option>
            <option value="2009">2009</option>
            <option value="2010">2010</option>
            <option value="2011">2011</option>
            <option value="2012">2012</option>
            <option value="2013">2013</option>
            <option value="2014" selected="selected">2014</option>
            <option value="2015">2015</option>
            <option value="2016">2016</option>
            <option value="2017">2017</option>
            <option value="2018">2018</option>
            <option value="2019">2019</option>
            <option value="2020">2020</option>
            <option value="2021">2021</option>
            <option value="2022">2022</option>
            <option value="2023">2023</option>
            <option value="2024">2024</option>
        </select>
    </div>
</div>
<table class="ui-datepicker-calendar">
    <thead>
        <tr>
            <th class="ui-datepicker-week-end">
                <span title="Sunday">S</span>
            </th>
            <th>
                <span title="Monday">M</span>
            </th>
            <th>
                <span title="Tuesday">T</span>
            </th>
            <th>
                <span title="Wednesday">W</span>
            </th>
            <th>
                <span title="Thursday">T</span>
            </th>
            <th>
                <span title="Friday">F</span>
```

```
            </th>
            <th class="ui-datepicker-week-end">
                <span title="Saturday">S</span>
            </th>
        </tr>
    </thead>
    <tbody>
        <tr>
            <td class="ui-datepicker-week-end
                        ui-datepicker-other-month
                        ui-datepicker-unselectable
                        ui-state-disabled"> </td>
            <td class="ui-datepicker-other-month
                        ui-datepicker-unselectable
                        ui-state-disabled"> </td>
            <td>
                <a class="ui-state-default" href="#">1</a>
            </td>
            <td>
                <a class="ui-state-default" href="#">2</a>
            </td>
            <td>
                <a class="ui-state-default" href="#">3</a>
            </td>
            <td>
                <a class="ui-state-default" href="#">4</a>
            </td>
            <td class="ui-datepicker-week-end">
                <a class="ui-state-default" href="#">5</a>
            </td>
        </tr>
        <tr>
            <td class="ui-datepicker-week-end">
                <a class="ui-state-default" href="#">6</a>
            </td>
            <td class="ui-datepicker-days-cell-over
                        ui-datepicker-today">
                <a class="ui-state-default
                            ui-state-highlight
                            ui-state-hover" href="#">7</a>
            </td>
            <td>
                <a class="ui-state-default" href="#">8</a>
            </td>
            <td>
                <a class="ui-state-default" href="#">9</a>
            </td>
            <td>
                <a class="ui-state-default" href="#">10</a>
            </td>
            <td>
                <a class="ui-state-default" href="#">11</a>
            </td>
            <td class="ui-datepicker-week-end">
```

```
                <a class="ui-state-default" href="#">12</a>
            </td>
        </tr>
        <tr>
            <td class="ui-datepicker-week-end">
                <a class="ui-state-default" href="#">13</a>
            </td>
            <td>
                <a class="ui-state-default" href="#">14</a>
            </td>
            <td>
                <a class="ui-state-default" href="#">15</a>
            </td>
            <td>
                <a class="ui-state-default" href="#">16</a>
            </td>
            <td>
                <a class="ui-state-default" href="#">17</a>
            </td>
            <td>
                <a class="ui-state-default" href="#">18</a>
            </td>
            <td class="ui-datepicker-week-end">
                <a class="ui-state-default" href="#">19</a>
            </td>
        </tr>
        <tr>
            <td class="ui-datepicker-week-end">
                <a class="ui-state-default" href="#">20</a>
            </td>
            <td>
                <a class="ui-state-default" href="#">21</a>
            </td>
            <td>
                <a class="ui-state-default" href="#">22</a>
            </td>
            <td>
                <a class="ui-state-default" href="#">23</a>
            </td>
            <td>
                <a class="ui-state-default" href="#">24</a>
            </td>
            <td>
                <a class="ui-state-default" href="#">25</a>
            </td>
            <td class="ui-datepicker-week-end">
                <a class="ui-state-default" href="#">26</a>
            </td>
        </tr>
        <tr>
            <td class="ui-datepicker-week-end">
                <a class="ui-state-default" href="#">27</a>
            </td>
            <td>
```

```
                    <a class="ui-state-default" href="#">28</a>
                </td>
                <td>
                    <a class="ui-state-default" href="#">29</a>
                </td>
                <td>
                    <a class="ui-state-default" href="#">30</a>
                </td>
                <td class="ui-datepicker-other-month
                            ui-datepicker-unselectable
                            ui-state-disabled"> </td>
                <td class="ui-datepicker-other-month
                            ui-datepicker-unselectable
                            ui-state-disabled"> </td>
                <td class="ui-datepicker-week-end
                            ui-datepicker-other-month
                            ui-datepicker-unselectable
                            ui-state-disabled"> </td>
            </tr>
        </tbody>
    </table>
</div>
</body>
</html>
```

The preceding markup document is styled with the following CSS:

```css
body {
    font: 12px "Lucida Grande", Arial, sans-serif;
    background: rgb(255, 255, 255);
    color: rgb(50, 50, 50);
    margin: 0;
    padding: 0;
}
div#ui-datepicker-div {
    border: 1px solid rgb(128, 128, 128);
    background: rgb(255, 255, 255);
    width: 180px;
    margin: 30px;
    position: relative;
}
div.ui-datepicker-control div a {
    color: rgb(0, 0, 0);
}
div.ui-datepicker-links {
    position: relative;
    height: 16px;
    padding: 0;
    background: rgb(255, 255, 255);
    text-align: center;
}
div.ui-datepicker-clear,
a.ui-datepicker-prev {
    position: absolute;
    top: 0;
```

```
        left: 0;
}
div.ui-datepicker-close,
a.ui-datepicker-next {
        position: absolute;
        top: 0;
        right: 0;
}
div.ui-datepicker-header {
        padding-top: 16px;
}
a.ui-datepicker-next,
a.ui-datepicker-prev {
        display: block;
        text-indent: -10000px;
        width: 58px;
        height: 16px;
        border-left: 1px solid rgb(186, 186, 186);
        border-bottom: 1px solid rgb(186, 186, 186);
        background: rgb(233, 233, 233);
}
a.ui-datepicker-next span,
a.ui-datepicker-prev span {
        display: block;
        width: 0;
        height: 0;
        border-top: 6px solid rgb(77, 77, 77);
        border-left: 7px solid transparent;
        border-right: 7px solid transparent;
        position: relative;
        top: 4px;
        left: 23px;
}
a.ui-datepicker-next:active ,
a.ui-datepicker-prev:active {
        background: rgb(200, 200, 200);
}
a.ui-datepicker-prev  {
        border-right: 1px solid rgb(186, 186, 186);
        border-left: none;
}
a.ui-datepicker-prev span {
        border-top: none;
        border-bottom: 6px solid rgb(77, 77, 77);
}
a.ui-datepicker-next:active span,
a.ui-datepicker-prev:active span {
        border-top-color: rgb(255, 255, 255);
}
a.ui-datepicker-prev:active span {
        border-top-color: transparent;
        border-bottom-color: rgb(255, 255, 255);
```

```
}
div.ui-datepicker-title {
    margin-top: 5px;
    text-align: center;
}
div.ui-datepicker-title select {
    margin: 0 3px;
}
table.ui-datepicker-calendar {
    width: 100%;
    border-collapse: collapse;
    margin: 10px 0 0 0;
}
table.ui-datepicker-calendar td {
    padding: 3px;
    text-align: center;
    color: rgb(255, 255, 255);
    background: rgb(158, 158, 158);
    border-bottom: 1px solid rgb(255, 255, 255);
    font-size: 11px;
}
table.ui-datepicker-calendar td a {
    color: rgb(255, 255, 255);
    text-decoration: none;
    display: block;
}
table.ui-datepicker-calendar thead th {
    text-align: center;
    font-weight: bold;
    font-size: 11px;
    color: rgb(0, 0, 0);
}
table.ui-datepicker-calendar td.ui-datepicker-today {
    background: rgb(230, 230, 230);
}
table.ui-datepicker-calendar td.ui-datepicker-today a {
    color: rgb(0, 0, 0);
}
table.ui-datepicker-calendar td.ui-datepicker-current-day {
    background: rgb(0, 0, 0);
}
table.ui-datepicker-calendar td.ui-datepicker-current-day a {
    color: rgb(255, 255, 255);
}
table.ui-datepicker-calendar td.ui-datepicker-other-month {
    background: rgb(230, 230, 230);
    border-bottom: 1px solid rgb(255, 255, 255);
    font-size: 11px;
}
```

When you load the document in a browser, the preceding example results in something similar to Figure 16-2.

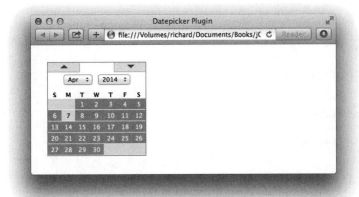

FIGURE 16-2

In the preceding example, you learned how to style the default Datepicker widget without using a premade jQuery UI theme, which would otherwise style the widget for you. Other aspects of the Datepicker concerning which dates you are allowed to pick from, how dates are formatted, and which controls are present in the widget may also be customized. You learn more about these things in the "Localizing the Datepicker" section later in this chapter.

To style the Datepicker, you can reference the markup provided, using the various id and class names to create styling for the pop-up calendar.

The styles provided are nothing extraordinary, just run-of-the-mill CSS. In the following sections, you take a look at how to further customize the Datepicker widget.

Setting the Range of Allowed Dates

By default, the jQuery UI Datepicker plugin allows you to select from a range of dates that goes 10 years into the future and 10 years into the past. You can customize the range of dates that are allowed by the widget, however, by specifying the range via options that you set upon calling the `datepicker()` method:

➤ `minDate` and `maxDate` set the minimum and maximum possible dates a user can enter into the date field. These options are set by providing a JavaScript `Date` object.

➤ `changeMonth` and `changeYear` are both boolean options that toggle regardless of whether the month and year are drop-down menus, which allow the user to jump to a particular date more quickly.

➤ `yearRange` sets the range of years made available in the year drop-down menu. This option is a string with the beginning and end year separated by a colon. For example, `"1900:2000"` would populate a drop-down menu with every year from 1900 to 2000.

The following example is a demonstration of the preceding options and is available in the source materials as *Example 16-3.html*, and it uses a style sheet based on the example provided in *Example 16-2.css*.

```
<!DOCTYPE HTML>
<html xmlns='http://www.w3.org/1999/xhtml'>
```

```
<head>
    <meta http-equiv='content-type'
        content='application/xhtml+xml; charset=utf-8' />
    <meta http-equiv='content-language' content='en-us' />
    <title>Datepicker Plugin</title>
    <script src='../jQuery.js'></script>
    <script src='../jQueryUI.js'></script>
    <script src='Example 16-3.js'></script>
    <link href='Example 16-3.css' rel='stylesheet' />
</head>
<body>
    <form action='javascript:void(0);' method='post'>
        <fieldset>
            <legend>Appointment Form</legend>
            <div class="exampleDate">
                <label for="exampleDate">Date:</label>
                <input type="text" name="exampleDate" id="exampleDate" />
                <img src="images/Calendar.png" alt="Calendar Icon" />
            </div>
        </fieldset>
    </form>
</body>
</html>
```

The date field in the preceding markup is made into a Datepicker with the following JavaScript:

```
$(document).ready(
    function()
    {
        $('input#exampleDate').datepicker({
            changeMonth : true,
            changeYear : true,
            minDate : new Date(1900, 1, 1),
            maxDate : new Date(2020, 12, 31),
            yearRange : "1900:2020"
        });

        $('div.exampleDate img').click(
            function()
            {
                $(this)
                    .prev('input')
                    .focus();
            }
        );
    }
);
```

The preceding results are shown in Figure 16-3.

The preceding script sets up five options for the Datepicker. The first two options, changeMonth and changeYear, toggle whether the month or year, respectively, are <select> inputs in the pop-up Datepicker. If these options are set to false, as in the following script, which is available in the source materials as *Example 16-4*, the month and year become static:

```
$('input#exampleDate').datepicker({
    changeMonth : false,
```

```
        changeYear : false,
        minDate : new Date(1900, 1, 1),
        maxDate : new Date(2020, 12, 31),
        yearRange : "1900:2020"
});
```

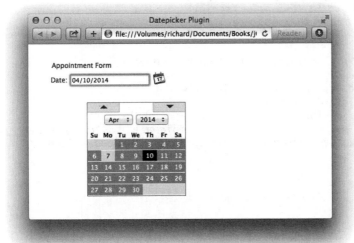

FIGURE 16-3

Figure 16-4 shows the difference in providing changeMonth with the false versus the true value.

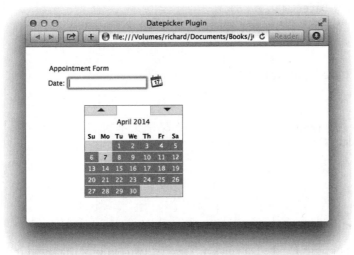

FIGURE 16-4

It is also possible to make only the month a `<select>` input or only the year. In the next section you learn how to localize the Datepicker.

LOCALIZING THE DATEPICKER

The Datepicker plugin has many localization options that allow you to completely change how the calendar looks, the text that it uses, the date format that it uses, and the weekday the calendar starts on. The following sections describe how to localize a Datepicker implementation.

Setting the Date Format

You can change the date format displayed as the value of the `<input>` element to whatever format you like. The following script, *Example-16-5*, demonstrates how to change the date format so that the day is placed before the month, as is done with dates in much of the world:

```
$(document).ready(
    function()
    {
        $('input#exampleDate').datepicker({
            changeMonth : true,
            changeYear : true,
            minDate : new Date(1900, 1, 1),
            maxDate : new Date(2020, 12, 31),
            yearRange : "1900:2020",
            dateFormat : "dd/mm/yy"
        });

        $('div.exampleDate img').click(
            function()
            {
                $(this)
                    .prev('input')
                    .focus();
            }
        );
    }
);
```

In the preceding script, the date format is set using the `dateFormat` option; in this case, it specifies the day, month, and year—the day and month with leading zeroes and the year in four-digit format. A full list of options is available in Appendix O, in the "Format Options" section. Figure 16-5 shows that the day appears first, then the month, and then the year.

Localizing Datepicker Text

You can use the following options to localize, customize, or translate an implementation of Datepicker:

➤ `appendText`—The text to display after each date field.

➤ `buttonText`—The text to display on the button element that triggers the Datepicker.

➤ closeText—The text to display for the close link. The default is "Close".

➤ currentText—The text to display for the current day link. The default is "Today".

➤ dayNames—The list of long day names, starting from Sunday, for use as requested via the dateFormat setting. Day names also appear as pop-up hints when hovering over the corresponding column headings. The default is ["Sunday", "Monday", "Tuesday", "Wednesday", "Thursday", "Friday", "Saturday"].

➤ dayNamesMin—The list of minimized day names, starting from Sunday, for use as column headers within the Datepicker. The default is ["Su", "Mo", "Tu", "We", "Th", "Fr", "Sa"].

➤ dayNamesShort—The list of abbreviated day names, starting from Sunday, for use as requested via the dateFormat setting. The default is ["Sun", "Mon", "Tue", "Wed", "Thu", "Fri", "Sat"].

➤ monthNames—The list of full month names, as used in the month header on each Datepicker and as requested via the dateFormat setting. The default is ["January", "February", "March", "April", "May", "June", "July", "August", "September", "October", "November", "December"].

➤ monthNamesShort—The list of abbreviated month names, for use as requested via the dateFormat setting. The default is ["Jan", "Feb", "Mar", "Apr", "May", "Jun", "Jul", "Aug", "Sep", "Oct", "Nov", "Dec"].

➤ nextText—The text to display for the next month link. The default is "Next".

➤ prevText—The text to display for the previous month link. The default is "Prev".

➤ weekHeader—The column header for the week of the year (see showWeeks). The default is "wk".

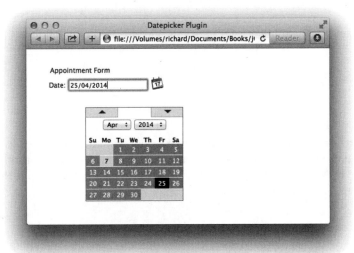

FIGURE 16-5

Changing the Starting Weekday

In some places in the world, the calendar begins with Monday and ends with Sunday. Whichever day you want to use as the starting weekday is also customizable via the firstDay option. The following script, *Example 16-6*, demonstrates how to change the starting weekday:

```
$(document).ready(
    function()
    {
        $('input#exampleDate').datepicker({
            changeMonth : true,
            changeYear : true,
            minDate : new Date(1900, 1, 1),
            maxDate : new Date(2020, 12, 31),
            yearRange : "1900:2020",
            dateFormat : "dd/mm/yy",
            firstDay : 1
        });

        $('div.exampleDate img').click(
            function()
            {
                $(this)
                    .prev('input')
                    .focus();
            }
        );
    }
);
```

In the preceding script, the firstDay option changes the starting calendar day from Sunday (which is number 0) to Monday (which is number 1). Figure 16-6 shows the result of the change.

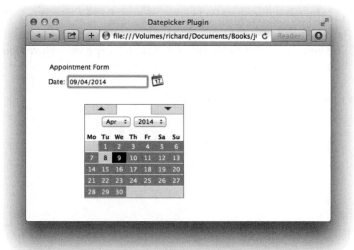

FIGURE 16-6

SUMMARY

In this chapter, you learned a little about what the jQuery UI Datepicker plugin offers. This chapter covered only some of the options allowed because of constraints on resources; however, a comprehensive reference containing all the options that you can use with the datepicker() method appears in Appendix O.

In this chapter, you learned that the Datepicker plugin does not come with much styling, and whatever styling you want must be implemented either manually or using one of the premade jQuery UI themes. You saw how the widget's markup is structured and a sample style sheet that could be applied to it.

You learned that the Datepicker can limit the range of selectable dates. To limit what dates the user can put in the date field, the minDate and maxDate options can be used. To set the range of years the Datepicker displays, the yearRange option can be used. To toggle whether the month and year options are drop-down menus, you use the changeMonth and changeYear options.

You learned a little about the options available to you for localizing the Datepicker. You can change the date format any of the text labels, and the starting weekday displayed in the calendar.

EXERCISES

1. Name the two options that you can potentially use to limit the dates the user can input into the Datepicker.

2. Which option sets the years populated in the year drop-down menu? What is an example value?

3. Which options provide the month and year options as drop-down menus?

4. Which option would you use to change the date format?

5. Does the Datepicker plugin give you the ability to translate its text into Spanish? How would you translate the weekday labels into Spanish?

6. Which option would you use to change the starting weekday?

Dialog

This chapter presents how to work with the jQuery UI Dialog plugin, which provides pseudo-pop-up windows created using markup, CSS, and JavaScript.

Unlike pop-up windows, which require that you open a new document in a separate browser window that is increasingly saddled with security limitations, such as being unable to hide the URL of the document and being unable to hide the status bar at the bottom of the window, dialogs created using markup, CSS, and JavaScript can be styled in any way that you like and can impose any limitations that you like. For example, you have the ability to make a modal dialog, which provides a dialog and prevents the user from continuing to interact with the document until the dialog is closed.

Another difference between pop-up windows and dialogs (as I will now refer to this widget for the remainder of this chapter—without reiterating the fact that they are generated by markup, CSS, and JavaScript) is that dialogs cannot leave the browser window in which they reside. So a dialog cannot be minimized to your operating system's taskbar, although you could possibly create your own minimization script so that the dialog can be minimized within the browser window.

As with many of the things that you learned in this book, jQuery UI again leaves little to be desired in its implementation of dialogs.

IMPLEMENTING A DIALOG

As with every other jQuery UI plugin, this discussion of the Dialog plugin begins with a demonstration of what the plugin does in its default state. *Example 17-1* demonstrates the out-of-the-box implementation:

```
<!DOCTYPE HTML>
<html xmlns='http://www.w3.org/1999/xhtml'>
    <head>
```

```
        <meta http-equiv='content-type'
            content='application/xhtml+xml; charset=utf-8' />
        <meta http-equiv='content-language' content='en-us' />
        <title>Dialog Plugin</title>
        <script src='../jQuery.js'></script>
        <script src='../jQueryUI.js'></script>
        <script src='Example 17-1.js'></script>
        <link href='Example 17-1.css' rel='stylesheet' />
    </head>
    <body>
        <div id='exampleDialog' title='Lorem Ipsum'>
            <p>
                Lorem ipsum dolor sit amet, consectetuer adipiscing elit. In
                sagittis commodo ipsum. Donec est. Mauris eget arcu. Suspendisse
                tincidunt aliquam velit. Maecenas libero. Aliquam dapibus
                tincidunt eros. Donec suscipit tincidunt odio. Maecenas congue
                tortor non ligula. Phasellus vel elit. Suspendisse potenti. Nunc
                odio quam, hendrerit ac, imperdiet sit amet, venenatis sed, enim.
            </p>
        </div>
    </body>
</html>
```

The following style sheet is applied to the preceding markup document:

```
body {
    font: 12px "Lucida Grande", Arial, sans-serif;
    background: #fff;
    color: rgb(50, 50, 50);
}
```

In the following script, you see how the `<div>` element with an id name `exampleDialog` is made into a dialog by selecting that `<div>` element and then calling the `dialog()` method:

```
$(document).ready(
    function()
    {
        $('div#exampleDialog').dialog();
    }
);
```

In Figure 17-1, you can see that the dialog doesn't look like much out-of-the-box. The title of the dialog is set by placing the title in the `title` attribute of the element that you want to transform into a dialog. The title of the dialog may also be set by passing a `title` option to the `dialog()` method; either method of setting the title can be used. If both methods are used, the `title` option to the `dialog()` method will be used.

FIGURE 17-1

> **NOTE** *Lipsum text can be copied and pasted from* www.lipsum.com.

STYLING A DIALOG

Before you can learn how to style a dialog, you need to see how it is constructed and assembled in markup. The following markup is the basic structure used for a typical jQuery UI dialog after the dialog() method has finished modifying the document:

```
<!DOCTYPE HTML>
<html xmlns='http://www.w3.org/1999/xhtml'>
    <head>
        <meta http-equiv='content-type'
            content='application/xhtml+xml; charset=utf-8' />
        <meta http-equiv='content-language' content='en-us' />
        <title>Dialog Plugin</title>
        <script src='../jQuery.js'></script>
        <script src='../jQueryUI.js'></script>
        <link href='Example 17-2.css' rel='stylesheet' />
    </head>
    <body>
        <div class="ui-dialog
```

```
                ui-widget
                ui-widget-content
                ui-corner-all
                ui-front
                ui-draggable
                ui-resizable"
 tabindex="-1"
 role="dialog"
 aria-describedby="exampleDialog"
 aria-labelledby="ui-id-1">
<div class="ui-dialog-titlebar
            ui-widget-header
            ui-corner-all
            ui-helper-clearfix">
    <span id="ui-id-1" class="ui-dialog-title">
        Lorem Ipsum
    </span>
    <button type="button"
            class="ui-button
                    ui-widget
                    ui-state-default
                    ui-corner-all
                    ui-button-icon-only
                    ui-dialog-titlebar-close"
            role="button"
            aria-disabled="false"
            title="close">
        <span class="ui-button-icon-primary
                     ui-icon
                     ui-icon-closethick"></span>
        <span class="ui-button-text">close</span>
    </button>
</div>
<div id="exampleDialog" class="ui-dialog-content ui-widget-content">
    <p>
        Lorem ipsum dolor sit amet, consectetuer adipiscing elit. In
        sagittis commodo ipsum. Donec est. Mauris eget arcu.
        Suspendisse tincidunt aliquam velit. Maecenas libero.
        Aliquam dapibus tincidunt eros. Donec suscipit tincidunt
        odio. Maecenas congue tortor non ligula. Phasellus vel elit.
        Suspendisse potenti. Nunc odio quam, hendrerit ac, imperdiet
        sit amet, venenatis sed, enim.
    </p>
</div>
<div class="ui-resizable-handle
            ui-resizable-n">
</div>
<div class="ui-resizable-handle
            ui-resizable-e">
</div>
<div class="ui-resizable-handle
            ui-resizable-s">
</div>
<div class="ui-resizable-handle
            ui-resizable-w">
</div>
```

```
            <div class="ui-resizable-handle
                        ui-resizable-se
                        ui-icon
                        ui-icon-gripsmall-diagonal-se">
            </div>
            <div class="ui-resizable-handle
                        ui-resizable-sw">
            </div>
            <div class="ui-resizable-handle
                        ui-resizable-ne">
             <div class="ui-resizable-handle
                        ui-resizable-nw">
            </div>
        </div>
    </body>
</html>
```

The preceding markup can be accessed in this book's source code download materials in the *Example 17-2.html* file.

As you can see in the preceding markup, the `dialog()` method adds a title bar, resize handles, and a `<button>` element for closing the dialog. The dialog can also be moved by dragging the dialog from the title bar, as well as resized from its edges (after the resize handles have been positioned in place).

Like the Datepicker in Chapter 16, "Datepicker," you can style a jQuery UI Dialog either by applying a jQuery UI theme style sheet provided from the jQuery UI website or by manually styling the dialog markup. In *Example 17-3*, you do just that:

```
<!DOCTYPE HTML>
<html xmlns='http://www.w3.org/1999/xhtml'>
    <head>
        <meta http-equiv='content-type'
            content='application/xhtml+xml; charset=utf-8' />
        <meta http-equiv='content-language' content='en-us' />
        <title>Dialog Plugin</title>
        <script src='../jQuery.js'></script>
        <script src='../jQueryUI.js'></script>
        <script src='Example 17-3.js'></script>
        <link href='Example 17-3.css' rel='stylesheet' />
    </head>
    <body>
        <div id='exampleDialog' title='Lorem Ipsum'>
            <p>
                Lorem ipsum dolor sit amet, consectetuer adipiscing elit. In
                sagittis commodo ipsum. Donec est. Mauris eget arcu. Suspendisse
                tincidunt aliquam velit. Maecenas libero. Aliquam dapibus
                tincidunt eros. Donec suscipit tincidunt odio. Maecenas congue
                tortor non ligula. Phasellus vel elit. Suspendisse potenti. Nunc
                odio quam, hendrerit ac, imperdiet sit amet, venenatis sed, enim.
            </p>
        </div>
    </body>
</html>
```

The preceding markup document is saved as *Example 17-3.html* and is styled with the following style sheet, *Example 17-3.css*:

```css
body {
    font: 12px "Lucida Grande", Arial, sans-serif;
    background: #fff;
    color: rgb(50, 50, 50);
}
div.ui-dialog {
    box-shadow: 0 7px 100px rgba(0, 0, 0, 0.6);
    border-radius: 4px;
    outline: none;
    position: fixed;
    z-index: 1000;
    background: #fff;
}
div.ui-dialog-titlebar {
    height: 23px;
    background: url('images/Titlebar Right.png')
                no-repeat
                top right,
                url('images/Titlebar Left.png')
                no-repeat
                top left;

    position: relative;
    z-index: 10;
}
span.ui-dialog-title {
    display: block;
    font-size: 13px;
    text-align: center;
    margin: 0 9px;
    padding: 4px 0 0 0;
    height: 19px;
    background: url('images/Titlebar.png')
                repeat-x
                top;
    position: relative;
    z-index: 10;
}
div.ui-dialog-container {
    background: #fff
                url('images/Titlebar Left.png')
                no-repeat
                top left;
}
button.ui-dialog-titlebar-close {
    position: absolute;
    width: 14px;
    height: 15px;
    top: 5px;
```

```
            left: 10px;
            border: none;
            background: url('images/Close Off.png')
                        no-repeat
                        top left;
            z-index: 10;
}
button.ui-dialog-titlebar-close:hover {
            background: url('images/Close On.png')
                        no-repeat
                        top left;
}
button.ui-dialog-titlebar-close span {
            display: none;
}
button.ui-dialog-titlebar-close:focus {
            border: none;
            outline: none;
}
div.ui-dialog-content  {
            padding: 10px;
}
div.ui-resizable-handle {
            border: none;
            position: absolute;
            z-index: 1;
}
div.ui-resizable-nw {
            width: 10px;
            height: 10px;
            top: -10px;
            left: -10px;
            cursor: nw-resize;
}
div.ui-resizable-n {
            height: 10px;
            top: -10px;
            left: 0;
            right: 0;
            cursor: n-resize;
}
div.ui-resizable-ne {
            width: 10px;
            height: 10px;
            top: -10px;
            right: -10px;
            cursor: ne-resize;
}
div.ui-resizable-w {
            width: 10px;
            left: -10px;
            top: 0;
```

```
        bottom: 0;
        cursor: w-resize;
    }
div.ui-resizable-e {
        width: 10px;
        right: -10px;
        top: 0;
        bottom: 0;
        cursor: e-resize;
    }
div.ui-resizable-sw {
        width: 10px;
        height: 10px;
        bottom: -10px;
        left: -10px;
        cursor: sw-resize;
    }
div.ui-resizable-s {
        height: 10px;
        bottom: -10px;
        left: 0;
        right: 0;
        cursor: s-resize;
    }
div.ui-resizable-se {
        width: 10px;
        height: 10px;
        bottom: -10px;
        right: -10px;
        cursor: se-resize;
    }
```

The preceding style sheet and XHTML are joined with the following JavaScript, *Example 17-3.js*:

```
$(document).ready(
    function()
    {
        $('div#exampleDialog').dialog({
            title : "Example Dialog"
        });
    }
);
```

The preceding styles the jQuery UI Dialog similar to a Mac OS X application window, as shown in Figure 17-2.

In the preceding example, you learned how to apply styling to the jQuery UI Dialog plugin, which is inspired by the look of application windows found on Mac OS X.

The example referred to in Figure 17-2 works great in every modern browser, but there is no drop shadow in older versions of IE, which cannot render the box-shadow property.

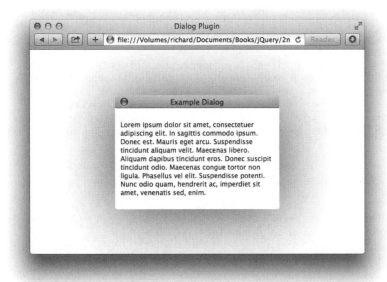

FIGURE 17-2

MAKING A MODAL DIALOG

A *modal dialog* is a dialog that upon activation prevents interaction with the document until the dialog is closed. *Example 17-4* demonstrates how to make a jQuery UI Dialog with modal behavior:

```
<!DOCTYPE HTML>
<html xmlns='http://www.w3.org/1999/xhtml'>
    <head>
        <meta http-equiv='content-type'
            content='application/xhtml+xml; charset=utf-8' />
        <meta http-equiv='content-language' content='en-us' />
        <title>Dialog Plugin</title>
        <script src='../jQuery.js'></script>
        <script src='../jQueryUI.js'></script>
        <script src='Example 17-4.js'></script>
        <link href='Example 17-4.css' rel='stylesheet' />
    </head>
    <body>
        <p>
            Lorem ipsum dolor sit amet, consectetuer adipiscing elit. In
            sagittis commodo ipsum. Donec est. Mauris eget arcu. Suspendisse
            tincidunt aliquam velit. Maecenas libero. Aliquam dapibus
            tincidunt eros. Donec suscipit tincidunt odio. Maecenas congue
            tortor non ligula. Phasellus vel elit. Suspendisse potenti. Nunc
```

```
            odio quam, hendrerit ac, imperdiet sit amet, venenatis sed, enim.
        </p>
        <div id='exampleDialog' title='Lorem Ipsum'>
            <p>
                Lorem ipsum dolor sit amet, consectetuer adipiscing elit. In
                sagittis commodo ipsum. Donec est. Mauris eget arcu. Suspendisse
                tincidunt aliquam velit. Maecenas libero. Aliquam dapibus
                tincidunt eros. Donec suscipit tincidunt odio. Maecenas congue
                tortor non ligula. Phasellus vel elit. Suspendisse potenti. Nunc
                odio quam, hendrerit ac, imperdiet sit amet, venenatis sed, enim.
            </p>
        </div>
    </body>
</html>
```

The CSS rule for `div.ui-widget-overlay` is added to the style sheet that you created in *Example 17-3*; this file is available in the source materials as *Example 17-4.css*:

```css
body {
    font: 12px "Lucida Grande", Arial, sans-serif;
    background: #fff;
    color: rgb(50, 50, 50);
}
div.ui-widget-overlay {
    background: rgba(255, 255, 255, 0.7);
    position: fixed;
    top: 0;
    right: 0;
    bottom: 0;
    left: 0;
}
div.ui-dialog {
    box-shadow: 0 7px 100px rgba(0, 0, 0, 0.6);
    border-radius: 4px;
    outline: none;
    position: fixed;
    z-index: 1000;
    background: #fff;
}
div.ui-dialog-titlebar {
    height: 23px;
    background: url('images/Titlebar Right.png')
                no-repeat
```

Then the JavaScript file applies the `modal` option to create a modal dialog:

```javascript
$(document).ready(
    function()
    {
        $('div#exampleDialog').dialog({
            title : 'Example Dialog',
            modal : true
        });
    }
);
```

In the preceding script, you turn on the `modal` option by setting it to `true`. When you set the `modal` option to `true` along with the application of the `div.ui-widget-overlay` CSS rule, you disable inter-action with background content while the dialog is open. Interaction with background content is disabled because the `<div>` element with the `ui-widget-overlay` class name is added dynamically to the document when the `modal` option is enabled. This element then blocks access to background content because it is positioned to take up the entire window and is positioned in front of background content, but behind the open dialog.

Figure 17-3 shows that the background is draped in a semitransparent white background to indicate that it is disabled.

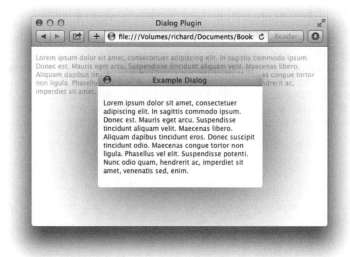

FIGURE 17-3

AUTO-OPENING THE DIALOG

By default, upon calling the `dialog()` method, the dialog is automatically opened. This behavior can be controlled by setting the `autoOpen` option to `false`. When the `autoOpen` option is set to `false`, you can programmatically open a dialog by calling the `dialog()` method with the string `'open'` in its first argument or `dialog('open')`. Likewise, `dialog('close')` can be used to close the dialog.

Example 17-5 demonstrates the `autoOpen` option:

```
<!DOCTYPE HTML>
<html xmlns='http://www.w3.org/1999/xhtml'>
    <head>
        <meta http-equiv='content-type'
            content='application/xhtml+xml; charset=utf-8' />
        <meta http-equiv='content-language' content='en-us' />
        <title>Dialog Plugin</title>
        <script src='../jQuery.js'></script>
```

```
        <script src='../jQueryUI.js'></script>
        <script src='Example 17-5.js'></script>
        <link href='Example 17-5.css' rel='stylesheet' />
    </head>
    <body>
        <p>
            Lorem ipsum dolor sit amet, consectetuer adipiscing elit. In
            sagittis commodo ipsum. Donec est. Mauris eget arcu. Suspendisse
            tincidunt aliquam velit. Maecenas libero. Aliquam dapibus
            tincidunt eros. Donec suscipit tincidunt odio. Maecenas congue
            tortor non ligula. Phasellus vel elit. Suspendisse potenti. Nunc
            odio quam, hendrerit ac, imperdiet sit amet, venenatis sed, enim.
        </p>
        <input type='submit' id='exampleDialogOpen' value='Open Dialog' />
        <div id='exampleDialog' title='Lorem Ipsum'>
            <p>
                Lorem ipsum dolor sit amet, consectetuer adipiscing elit. In
                sagittis commodo ipsum. Donec est. Mauris eget arcu. Suspendisse
                tincidunt aliquam velit. Maecenas libero. Aliquam dapibus
                tincidunt eros. Donec suscipit tincidunt odio. Maecenas congue
                tortor non ligula. Phasellus vel elit. Suspendisse potenti. Nunc
                odio quam, hendrerit ac, imperdiet sit amet, venenatis sed, enim.
            </p>
        </div>
    </body>
</html>
```

The CSS document from *Example 17-4* is applied to the preceding markup document, along with
the following script:

```
$(document).ready(
    function()
    {
        $('div#exampleDialog').dialog({
            title : 'Example Dialog',
            modal : true,
            autoOpen : false
        });

        $('input#exampleDialogOpen').click(
            function(event)
            {
                event.preventDefault();

                $('div#exampleDialog')
                    .dialog('open');
            }
        );
    }
);
```

In the preceding script, you prevent the dialog from being opened automatically by setting the autoOpen option to false. To open the dialog, you attach a click event to the <input> element, and when that event takes place, you make a call to $('div#exampleDialogOpen').dialog('open') to open the dialog programmatically. Figure 17-4 displays the preceding example.

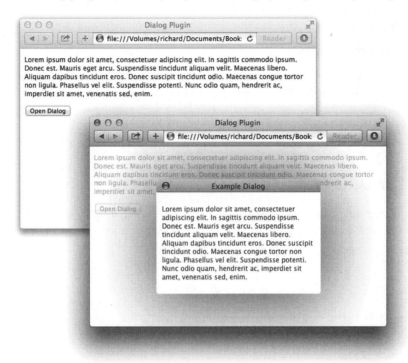

FIGURE 17-4

CONTROLLING DYNAMIC INTERACTION

By default, the jQuery UI Dialog plugin enables you to resize and drag the dialog window. Both types of dynamic interaction with a dialog can be disabled by passing options to the dialog() method. For example, the draggable option can be set to false to disable dragging the dialog, and the resizable option can also be set to false to disable resizing a dialog. Disabling these options is demonstrated in the following script, *Example 17-6*:

```
$(document).ready(
    function()
    {
        $('div#exampleDialog').dialog({
            title : 'Example Dialog',
            modal : true,
```

```
            autoOpen : false,
            resizable : false,
            draggable : false
    });

    $('input#exampleDialogOpen').click(
        function(event)
        {
            event.preventDefault();

            $('div#exampleDialog')
                .dialog('open');
        }
    );
    }
);
```

ANIMATING THE DIALOG

Opening or closing a dialog can also be animated using one of the effects listed in Appendix M, "Effects." Animation can be introduced by providing an effect to the show option.

The following script, *Example 17-7*, demonstrates how to do this:

```
$(document).ready(
    function()
    {
        $('div#exampleDialog').dialog({
            title : 'Example Dialog',
            modal : true,
            autoOpen : false,
            resizable : true,
            draggable : true,
            show : 'explode'
        });

        $('input#exampleDialogOpen').click(
            function(event)
            {
                event.preventDefault();

                $('div#exampleDialog')
                    .dialog('open');
            }
        );
    }
);
```

The preceding script applies an animation upon opening the dialog using the jQuery explode effect. Figure 17-5 captures the explode effect mid-animation.

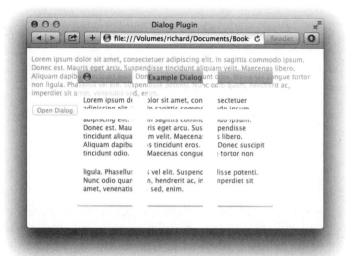

FIGURE 17-5

Appendix P, "Dialog," provides a complete list of options that can be provided to the show option.

WORKING WITH DIALOG EVENTS

The Dialog plugin supports a variety of events. You can set up events that are executed when the dialog is opened, when the dialog is focused, when the dialog is resized, when the dialog is dragged, or when the dialog is closed. The following document, *Example 17-8*, demonstrates attaching close and open events to the dialog, but a full list of events is available in Appendix P:

```
$(document).ready(
    function()
    {
        $('div#exampleDialog').dialog({
            title : 'Example Dialog',
            modal : true,
            autoOpen : false,
            resizable : true,
            draggable : true,
            show : 'explode',
            close : function(event, ui)
            {
                alert('Dialog Closed');
            },
            open : function(event, ui)
            {
                alert('Dialog Opened');
```

```
            }
        });

        $('input#exampleDialogOpen').click(
            function(event)
            {
                event.preventDefault();

                $('div#exampleDialog')
                    .dialog('open');
            }
        );
    }
);
```

The preceding script demonstrates the attachment of the close and open options to the dialog, which causes a callback function to be executed when the dialog is opened or closed. The callback function is executed within the context of the dialog element it is attached to, making that element available in the this keyword, as shown in Figure 17-6.

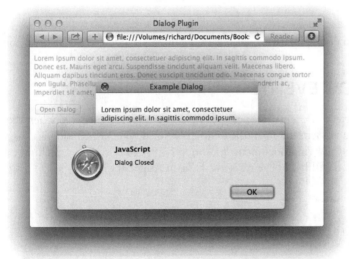

FIGURE 17-6

SUMMARY

In this chapter, you learned how to implement a dialog using the jQuery UI Dialog plugin. The Dialog plugin doesn't come with much styling, so you learned how the markup is structured and implemented your own styling for a dialog. An alternative and easier way of styling a dialog is to also download and apply a jQuery UI theme from the www.jqueryui.com website.

You learned how to make a modal dialog using the modal option: You can use the modal option to prevent interaction with the document in the background when the requisite CSS is added to the style sheet.

You learned how to disable automatically opening a dialog using the autoOpen option. After automatically opening a dialog has been disabled, you can programmatically open a dialog by calling dialog('open') or close a dialog by calling dialog('close').

You can disable resizing a dialog or dragging a dialog using the resizable and draggable options.

You can animate opening and closing a dialog by providing an effect (documented in Appendix P) to the show option.

Finally, there are a variety of events associated with a dialog that you can attach callback functions to. You saw an example of the close event, but a full list of options is in Appendix P.

EXERCISES

1. What option would you use to disable interaction with the document while a dialog is open?

2. How do you disable automatically opening a dialog?

3. How do you open a dialog when automatically opening the dialog is disabled?

4. How do you close a dialog?

5. How do you disable resizing and dragging a dialog?

6. What option would you use to animate opening or closing a dialog?

Tabs

This installment of my introduction to jQuery and jQuery UI presents how to work with the jQuery UI Tabs plugin, a plugin that makes it easier to implement tabbed functionality, in which you click a series of tabs that toggles the display of content that either already exists in the document or is loaded dynamically via an AJAX request.

jQuery UI provides all the functional aspects that you need to implement a tabbed user interface. For styling the interface, like Dialog and the Datepicker, you can either use a jQuery UI theme or create your own style sheet.

Implementing a tabbed user interface, like much of the plugin functionality that jQuery UI offers, is easy and straightforward. You need learn about only a few fundamentals, such as how to structure markup destined to become tabs and, of course, the various options that the Tabs plugin offers to allow tweaking the implementation to cover the variations in use as well as callback events.

This chapter covers how to implement and style a tabbed user interface and covers a few of the options offered by the Tabs plugin that you're most likely to be interested in using. Like the other jQuery UI plugins, a comprehensive reference of options, callback events, and arguments are covered in Appendix Q, "Tabs."

IMPLEMENTING TABS

To start with your tabbed user interface implementation, here's a remedial demonstration of the jQuery UI Tabs plugin without any options or styling. The objective is to present where you stand using the plugin out-of-the-box, which is the purpose of the following example (*Example 18-1* in the source code download materials at www.wrox.com/go/webdevwithjquery):

```
<!DOCTYPE HTML>
<html xmlns='http://www.w3.org/1999/xhtml'>
    <head>
        <meta http-equiv='content-type'
            content='application/xhtml+xml; charset=utf-8' />
        <meta http-equiv='content-language' content='en-us' />
        <title>Tabs Plugin</title>
```

```
        <script src='../jQuery.js'></script>
        <script src='../jQueryUI.js'></script>
        <script src='Example 18-1.js'></script>
        <link href='Example 18-1.css' rel='stylesheet' />
    </head>
    <body>
        <div id='exampleTabs'>
            <ul>
                <li>
                    <a href='#exampleTabFirst'>
                        <span>First Tab</span>
                    </a>
                </li>
                <li>
                    <a href='#exampleTabSecond'>
                        <span>Second Tab</span>
                    </a>
                </li>
                <li>
                    <a href='#exampleTabThird'>
                        <span>Third Tab</span>
                    </a>
                </li>
            </ul>
            <div id='exampleTabFirst'>
                <p>
                    Lorem ipsum dolor sit amet, consectetuer adipiscing elit.
                    Suspendisse id sapien. Suspendisse rutrum libero sit amet dui.
                    Praesent pede elit, tincidunt pellentesque, condimentum nec,
                    mollis et, lacus. Donec nulla ligula, tempor vel, eleifend ut.
                </p>
            </div>
            <div id='exampleTabSecond'>
                <p>
                    Cras eu metus orci. Nam pretium neque ante. In eu mattis sem,
                    Ut euismod nulla. Curabitur a diam eget risus vestibulum
                    mattis et at turpis. Etiam semper, orci sit amet semper
                    molestie, nibh sem hendrerit est, auctor varius arcu purus ut
                    enim. Curabitur nisi nunc, ullamcorper a placerat a, faucibus
                    imperdiet urna. Maecenas cursus ullamcorper dolor, ac viverra
                    nibh consectetur eget.
                </p>
            </div>
            <div id='exampleTabThird'>
                <p>
                    Mauris sollicitudin, sem non tempor molestie, quam nunc
                    blandit lectus, quis molestie dui arcu in lectus. In id
                    fringilla elit. Ut auctor lectus eget orci malesuada, et
                    lacinia ligula interdum. Pellentesque bibendum, orci eget
                    euismod scelerisque, nibh nulla posuere mi, quis commodo
                    purus sem et arcu.
                </p>
            </div>
        </div>
```

```
        </body>
   </html>
```

The preceding document is styled with the following style sheet:

```css
body {
    font: 12px 'Lucida Grande', Arial, sans-serif;
    background: #fff;
    color: rgb(50, 50, 50);
}
div#exampleTabFirst {
    background: lightblue;
    padding: 5px;
}
div#exampleTabSecond {
    background: lightgreen;
    padding: 5px;
}
div#exampleTabThird {
    background: yellow;
    padding: 5px;
}
```

The following script demonstrates a call to the jQuery UI's `tabs()` method:

```javascript
$(document).ready(
    function()
    {
        $('div#exampleTabs').tabs();
    }
);
```

Figure 18-1 shows that the preceding actually doesn't look like much so far, but some groundwork had been laid in preparation of creating a proper tabbed user interface.

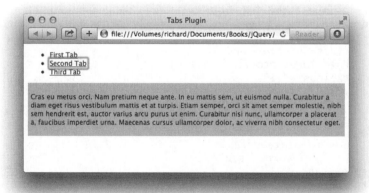

FIGURE 18-1

STYLING THE TABBED USER INTERFACE

Because the Tabs plugin requires either a theme or a custom style sheet to be applied, you need to examine the markup document after the tabs() method has been executed to see how the Tabs plugin modifies the markup. The modified markup document is presented in the following example, which is *Example 8-2* in the source code download materials:

```
<!DOCTYPE HTML>
<html xmlns='http://www.w3.org/1999/xhtml'>
    <head>
        <meta http-equiv='content-type'
            content='application/xhtml+xml; charset=utf-8' />
        <meta http-equiv='content-language' content='en-us' />
        <title>Tabs Plugin</title>
        <script src='../jQuery.js'></script>
        <script src='../jQueryUI.js'></script>
        <script src='Example 18-2.js'></script>
        <link href='Example 18-2.css' rel='stylesheet' />
    </head>
    <body>
        <div id="exampleTabs"
            class="ui-tabs
                    ui-widget
                    ui-widget-content
                    ui-corner-all">
            <ul class="ui-tabs-nav
                    ui-helper-reset
                    ui-helper-clearfix
                    ui-widget-header
                    ui-corner-all"
                role="tablist">
                <li class="ui-state-default
                            ui-corner-top"
                    role="tab"
                    tabindex="0"
                    aria-controls="exampleTabFirst"
                    aria-labelledby="ui-id-1"
                    aria-selected="true">
                    <a href="#exampleTabFirst"
                        class="ui-tabs-anchor"
                        role="presentation"
                        tabindex="-1"
                        id="ui-id-1">
                        <span>First Tab</span>
                    </a>
                </li>
                <li class="ui-state-default
                            ui-corner-top"
                    role="tab"
                    tabindex="-1"
                    aria-controls="exampleTabSecond"
                    aria-labelledby="ui-id-2"
                    aria-selected="false">
                    <a href="#exampleTabSecond"
                        class="ui-tabs-anchor"
```

```
        role="presentation"
        tabindex="-1"
        id="ui-id-2">
          <span>Second Tab</span>
      </a>
  </li>
  <li class="ui-state-default
            ui-corner-top"
      role="tab"
      tabindex="-1"
      aria-controls="exampleTabThird"
      aria-labelledby="ui-id-3"
      aria-selected="false">
      <a href="#exampleTabThird"
        class="ui-tabs-anchor"
        role="presentation"
        tabindex="-1"
        id="ui-id-3">
          <span>Third Tab</span>
      </a>
  </li>
</ul>
<div class="ui-tabs-panel
            ui-widget-content
            ui-corner-bottom"
    id="exampleTabFirst"
    aria-labelledby="ui-id-1"
    role="tabpanel"
    aria-expanded="true"
    aria-hidden="false">
  <p>
      Lorem ipsum dolor sit amet, consectetuer adipiscing elit.
      Suspendisse id sapien. Suspendisse rutrum libero sit amet dui.
      Praesent pede elit, tincidunt pellentesque, condimentum nec,
      mollis et, lacus. Donec nulla ligula, tempor vel, eleifend ut.
  </p>
</div>
<div class="ui-tabs-panel
            ui-widget-content
            ui-corner-bottom"
    id="exampleTabSecond"
    aria-labelledby="ui-id-2"
    role="tabpanel"
    aria-expanded="false"
    aria-hidden="true">
  <p>
      Cras eu metus orci. Nam pretium neque ante. In eu mattis sem,
      Ut euismod nulla. Curabitur a diam eget risus vestibulum
      mattis et at turpis. Etiam semper, orci sit amet semper
      molestie, nibh sem hendrerit est, auctor varius arcu purus ut
      enim. Curabitur nisi nunc, ullamcorper a placerat a, faucibus
      imperdiet urna. Maecenas cursus ullamcorper dolor, ac viverra
      nibh consectetur eget.
  </p>
</div>
<div class="ui-tabs-panel
```

```
                        ui-widget-content
                        ui-corner-bottom"
                id="exampleTabThird"
                aria-labelledby="ui-id-3"
                role="tabpanel"
                aria-expanded="false"
                aria-hidden="true">
            <p>
                Mauris sollicitudin, sem non tempor molestie, quam nunc
                blandit lectus, quis molestie dui arcu in lectus. In id
                fringilla elit. Ut auctor lectus eget orci malesuada, et
                lacinia ligula interdum. Pellentesque bibendum, orci eget
                euismod scelerisque, nibh nulla posuere mi, quis commodo
                purus sem et arcu.
            </p>
        </div>
    </div>
</body>
</html>
```

The preceding markup document contains all the class name and attribute changes that the Tabs plugin makes to the document. The additional class names and attributes are not necessary to style the document because these are all automatically added by the Tabs plugin upon calling the `tabs()` method. I have included the additional class names and attributes to illustrate what happens to the markup document after the `tabs()` method has completed execution. The following style sheet is applied to the preceding example.

```css
body {
    font: 12px 'Lucida Grande', Arial, sans-serif;
    background: #fff;
    color: rgb(50, 50, 50);
}
div#exampleTabFirst {
    background: lightblue;
    padding: 5px;
}
div#exampleTabSecond {
    background: lightgreen;
    padding: 5px;
}
div#exampleTabThird {
    background: yellow;
    padding: 5px;
}
.ui-tabs-hide {
    display: none;
}
ul.ui-tabs-nav {
    list-style: none;
    padding: 0;
    margin: 0;
    height: 22px;
    border-bottom: 1px solid darkgreen;
}
```

```
ul.ui-tabs-nav li {
    float: left;
    height: 17px;
    padding: 4px 10px 0 10px;
    margin-right: 5px;
    border: 1px solid rgb(200, 200, 200);
    border-bottom: none;
    position: relative;
    background: yellowgreen;
}
ul.ui-tabs-nav li a {
    text-decoration: none;
    color: black;
}
ul.ui-tabs-nav li.ui-tabs-active {
    background: darkgreen;
    border-bottom: 1px solid darkgreen;
}
ul.ui-tabs-nav li.ui-tabs-active a {
    color: white;
    outline: none;
}
div     {
    display: none;
}
```

The style sheet and XHTML are joined with the following JavaScript:

```
$(document).ready(
    function()
    {
        $('div#exampleTabs').tabs({
            active : 1
        });
    }
);
```

Figure 18-2 shows the results.

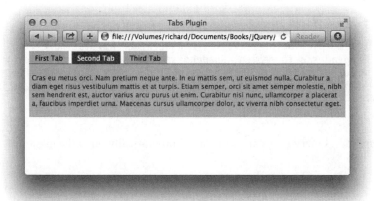

FIGURE 18-2

In Figure 18-2, you can see that the tabs are laid out in a manner that's more consistent with what you might expect from a tabbed UI. With the addition of the active option with the value of 1, the second content panel is visible by default when the page loads. The active option toggles the selected tab, counting from zero.

The class name ui-state-active references the selected tab. The class name ui-state-hover references the tab the mouse cursor is hovering over. Both class names are applied to the <li> elements that eventually become tabs.

When you click the labels in the <ul> element, you toggle between the different content panels. Making tabs requires some structural rules. First, you have a list of items, and in that list you have hyperlinks to anchors.

```
<ul>
    <li>
        <a href='#exampleTabFirst'>
            <span>First Tab</span>
        </a>
    </li>
    <li>
        <a href='#exampleTabSecond'>
            <span>Second Tab</span>
        </a>
    </li>
    <li>
        <a href='#exampleTabThird'>
            <span>Third Tab</span>
        </a>
    </li>
</ul>
```

In the preceding snippet of markup, each hyperlink links to an anchor that appears elsewhere in the document, by including a pound sign, followed by that element's id name. Structuring the document in this way makes your scripting unobtrusive. If scripting is disabled, the user can still navigate the tabs by clicking a link to an anchor, instead of toggling the display of a content pane.

Following the list, you have three <div> elements, each having an id name that corresponds to the anchor link, which makes those elements anchors.

```
<div id='exampleTabFirst'>
    <p>
        Lorem ipsum dolor sit amet, consectetuer adipiscing elit.
        Suspendisse id sapien. Suspendisse rutrum libero sit amet dui.
        Praesent pede elit, tincidunt pellentesque, condimentum nec,
        mollis et, lacus. Donec nulla ligula, tempor vel, eleifend ut.
    </p>
</div>
```

When you call the tabs() method, jQuery looks at the list and automatically pulls the id names from the hyperlinks.

LOADING REMOTE CONTENT VIA AJAX

Loading remote content instead of local content is easy to do. The following document shows an example, which is *Example 8-3* in the source code download materials, of how to set up a tab that loads remote content using AJAX, instead of having that content already loaded in your document.

```html
<!DOCTYPE HTML>
<html xmlns='http://www.w3.org/1999/xhtml'>
    <head>
        <meta http-equiv='content-type'
            content='application/xhtml+xml; charset=utf-8' />
        <meta http-equiv='content-language' content='en-us' />
        <title>Tabs Plugin</title>
        <script src='../jQuery.js'></script>
        <script src='../jQueryUI.js'></script>
        <script src='Example 18-3.js'></script>
        <link href='Example 18-3.css' rel='stylesheet' />
    </head>
    <body>
        <div id='exampleTabs'>
            <ul>
                <li>
                    <a href='#exampleTabFirst'>
                        <span>First Tab</span>
                    </a>
                </li>
                <li>
                    <a href='#exampleTabSecond'>
                        <span>Second Tab</span>
                    </a>
                </li>
                <li>
                    <a href='#exampleTabThird'>
                        <span>Third Tab</span>
                    </a>
                </li>
                <li>
                    <a href='Fourth Tab.html'>
                        <span>Fourth Tab</span>
                    </a>
                </li>
            </ul>
            <div id='exampleTabFirst'>
                <p>
                    Lorem ipsum dolor sit amet, consectetuer adipiscing elit.
                    Suspendisse id sapien. Suspendisse rutrum libero sit amet dui.
                    Praesent pede elit, tincidunt pellentesque, condimentum nec,
                    mollis et, lacus. Donec nulla ligula, tempor vel, eleifend ut.
                </p>
            </div>
            <div id='exampleTabSecond'>
                <p>
```

```
                    Cras eu metus orci. Nam pretium neque ante. In eu mattis sem,
                    Ut euismod nulla. Curabitur a diam eget risus vestibulum
                    mattis et at turpis. Etiam semper, orci sit amet semper
                    molestie, nibh sem hendrerit est, auctor varius arcu purus ut
                    enim. Curabitur nisi nunc, ullamcorper a placerat a, faucibus
                    imperdiet urna. Maecenas cursus ullamcorper dolor, ac viverra
                    nibh consectetur eget.
                </p>
            </div>
            <div id='exampleTabThird'>
                <p>
                    Mauris sollicitudin, sem non tempor molestie, quam nunc
                    blandit lectus, quis molestie dui arcu in lectus. In id
                    fringilla elit. Ut auctor lectus eget orci malesuada, et
                    lacinia ligula interdum. Pellentesque bibendum, orci eget
                    euismod scelerisque, nibh nulla posuere mi, quis commodo
                    purus sem et arcu.
                </p>
            </div>
        </div>
    </body>
</html>
```

A new markup document is created to contain the content of the fourth tab, and it is called *Fourth Tab.html*, which is also referenced in the href attribute of the <a> element for the new tab in the preceding markup document.

```
<p>
    Quisque tempus euismod justo vitae ultrices. Nam in
    ligula sit amet mi molestie luctus. Aenean et
    egestas arcu. Mauris dictum tortor sit amet purus
    aliquam condimentum. Integer fermentum at odio vitae
    sollicitudin.
</p>
```

The following style sheet is applied to the AJAX-enabled example. This style sheet adds a new rule for a <div> element with the id name ui-tabs-1.

```
body {
    font: 12px 'Lucida Grande', Arial, sans-serif;
    background: #fff;
    color: rgb(50, 50, 50);
}
div#exampleTabFirst {
    background: lightblue;
    padding: 5px;
}
div#exampleTabSecond {
    background: lightgreen;
    padding: 5px;
}
div#exampleTabThird {
    background: yellow;
    padding: 5px;
```

```css
}
div#ui-tabs-1 {
    background: pink;
    padding: 5px;
}
.ui-tabs-hide {
    display: none;
}
ul.ui-tabs-nav {
    list-style: none;
    padding: 0;
    margin: 0;
    height: 22px;
    border-bottom: 1px solid darkgreen;
}
ul.ui-tabs-nav li {
    float: left;
    height: 17px;
    padding: 4px 10px 0 10px;
    margin-right: 5px;
    border: 1px solid rgb(200, 200, 200);
    border-bottom: none;
    position: relative;
    background: yellowgreen;
}
ul.ui-tabs-nav li a {
    text-decoration: none;
    color: black;
}
ul.ui-tabs-nav li.ui-tabs-active {
    background: darkgreen;
    border-bottom: 1px solid darkgreen;
}
ul.ui-tabs-nav li.ui-tabs-active a {
    color: white;
    outline: none;
}
div.ui-tabs-panel {
    display: none;
}
```

The JavaScript has no changes from *Example 18-2* because the bits that enable AJAX loading occur entirely in the markup and in the Tabs plugin.

```javascript
$(document).ready(
    function()
    {
        $('div#exampleTabs').tabs({
            active : 1
        });
    }
);
```

Figure 18-3 shows the results.

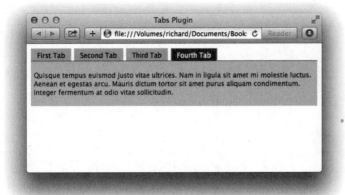

FIGURE 18-3

In the preceding markup document, there are a few minor modifications made to add a new tab that has content loaded via AJAX. You set up the tab with the href attribute referencing the document that you want to load by AJAX. The id attribute is not necessary and is automatically generated by the Tabs plugin. (It does this for all the tabs if you want to structure your document using automatically generated id names.)

Using a server-side script, you can add logic on the server side that presents content within your normal template depending on whether scripting is enabled on the client side. To do that, by default, make the link content.html?noscript=true. Then, in your JavaScript, automatically remove the query string portion ?noscript=true at page load, which would then signal your server-side script to serve only the content, rather than the content within a template. Without this, if scripting is disabled, your visitors can still see the content; it will simply be plain, unstyled, and unbranded.

Finally, the class name ui-tabs-loading is applied to the <li> element during the time that the content is loading from the server up until the time the Tabs plugin loads and displays it.

ANIMATING TAB TRANSITIONS

Most things in jQuery UI can be customized with any of the animation effects provided by jQuery, and the Tabs plugin is no exception. Like the Dialog plugin, the Tabs plugin also accepts show and hide options, which can specify an effect when a tab is opened and when a tab is closed, respectively.

The following script demonstrates how to animate a tab transition:

```
$(document).ready(
    function()
    {
        $('div#exampleTabs').tabs({
            active : 1,
            show : 'explode',
```

```
        hide : 'fade'
    });
  }
);
```

The preceding script adds an explode effect when tabs are opened and fades out when tabs are closed. This example is available in this book's source code materials in *Example 18-4.html*. Comprehensive documentation of animation options is provided in Appendix Q.

SUMMARY

Several additional options can also be used with a Tabs implementation. I've covered some of the more useful options in this chapter, and you can find a full reference of all options available for the Tabs plugin in Appendix Q.

In this chapter, you learned how to implement a tabbed user interface using the jQuery UI Tabs plugin. By default, the Tabs plugin offers no presentational styling. You learned how to approach styling a tabbed user interface so that you can apply your own custom styling. Another option is to use a jQueryUI theme, which you can download from the jQuery UI website at www.jqueryui.com.

You learned that the Tabs plugin supports loading content remotely using AJAX; you need to add only a little markup to accomplish this.

And finally, you also learned that the Tabs plugin supports animated transitions between tabs via the show and hide options.

EXERCISES

1. Which option would you use to change the default tab that is displayed after the tabs() method has been applied?

2. What class names are used to style the active tab and the hover tab?

3. What do you have to do to load content via an AJAX call?

4. What options can you use to animate tab transitions?

PART III
Popular Third-Party jQuery Plugins

19

Tablesorter

The Tablesorter plugin is a popular third-party jQuery plugin available from `http://www.tablesorter.com`. The plugin does what the name implies; the plugin is attached to any `<table>` element that you like, and then it can sort that table's columns, one or more at a time. For example, you can sort by name only, by name and then by age, or by name, age, and then by date. How many columns are sorted is entirely up to you.

The `$.tablesorter()` plugin allows for some configuration and customization; whatever isn't covered in this chapter explicitly is documented both on the Tablesorter website at `http://www.tablesorter.com` as well as in Appendix T, "Tablesorter."

SORTING A TABLE

The `$.tablesorter()` plugin is straightforward. It functions well out-of-the-box and dropped in a document; with only a call to the plugin's method and some styling, you can be off sorting tables in no time.

The following example (*Example 19-1* in the code downloads at www.wrox.com/go/webdevwith-jquery) sets up the basic, out-of-the-box `$.tablesorter()` plugin:

```
<!DOCTYPE HTML>
<html lang='en'>
    <head>
        <meta charset='utf-8' />
        <title>Tablesorter</title>
        <script src='../jQuery.js'></script>
        <script src='../jQueryUI.js'></script>
        <script src='../Tablesorter/Tablesorter.js'></script>
        <script src='Example 19-1.js'></script>
        <link href='Example 19-1.css' rel='stylesheet' />
    </head>
    <body>
        <table>
            <colgroup>
                <col style="width: 100px;" />
                <col />
```

```
            <col style="width: 150px;" />
    </colgroup>
    <thead>
        <tr>
            <th>
                Track #
                <span class='tableSorterDescending'>&darr;</span>
                <span class='tableSorterAscending'>&uarr;</span>
            </th>
            <th>
                Name
                <span class='tableSorterDescending'>&darr;</span>
                <span class='tableSorterAscending'>&uarr;</span>
            </th>
            <th>
                Album
                <span class='tableSorterDescending'>&darr;</span>
                <span class='tableSorterAscending'>&uarr;</span>
            </th>
        </tr>
    </thead>
    <tbody>
        <tr>
            <td>1</td>
            <td>Come Together</td>
            <td>Abbey Road</td>
        </tr>
        <tr>
            <td>2</td>
            <td>Something</td>
            <td>Abbey Road</td>
        </tr>
        <tr>
            <td>3</td>
            <td>Maxwell's Silver Hammer</td>
            <td>Abbey Road</td>
        </tr>
        <tr>
            <td>4</td>
            <td>Oh! Darling</td>
            <td>Abbey Road</td>
        </tr>
        <tr>
            <td>5</td>
            <td>Octopus's Garden</td>
            <td>Abbey Road</td>
        </tr>
        <tr>
            <td>6</td>
            <td>I Want You (She's So Heavy)</td>
            <td>Abbey Road</td>
        </tr>
        <tr>
            <td>7</td>
            <td>Here Comes The Sun</td>
            <td>Abbey Road</td>
```

```
        </tr>
        <tr>
            <td>8</td>
            <td>Because</td>
            <td>Abbey Road</td>
        </tr>
        <tr>
            <td>9</td>
            <td>You Never Give Me Your Money</td>
            <td>Abbey Road</td>
        </tr>
        <tr>
            <td>10</td>
            <td>Sun King</td>
            <td>Abbey Road</td>
        </tr>
        <tr>
            <td>11</td>
            <td>Mean Mr. Mustard</td>
            <td>Abbey Road</td>
        </tr>
        <tr>
            <td>12</td>
            <td>Polythene Pam</td>
            <td>Abbey Road</td>
        </tr>
        <tr>
            <td>13</td>
            <td>She Came In Through The Bathroom Window</td>
            <td>Abbey Road</td>
        </tr>
        <tr>
            <td>14</td>
            <td>Golden Slumbers</td>
            <td>Abbey Road</td>
        </tr>
        <tr>
            <td>15</td>
            <td>Carry That Weight</td>
            <td>Abbey Road</td>
        </tr>
        <tr>
            <td>16</td>
            <td>The End</td>
            <td>Abbey Road</td>
        </tr>
        <tr>
            <td>17</td>
            <td>Her Majesty</td>
            <td>Abbey Road</td>
        </tr>
        <tr>
            <td>1</td>
            <td>Drive My Car</td>
            <td>Rubber Soul</td>
        </tr>
```

```
    <tr>
        <td>2</td>
        <td>Norwegian Wood (This Bird Has Flown)</td>
        <td>Rubber Soul</td>
    </tr>
    <tr>
        <td>3</td>
        <td>You Won't See Me</td>
        <td>Rubber Soul</td>
    </tr>
    <tr>
        <td>4</td>
        <td>Nowhere Man</td>
        <td>Rubber Soul</td>
    </tr>
    <tr>
        <td>5</td>
        <td>Think For Yourself</td>
        <td>Rubber Soul</td>
    </tr>
    <tr>
        <td>6</td>
        <td>The Word</td>
        <td>Rubber Soul</td>
    </tr>
    <tr>
        <td>7</td>
        <td>Michelle</td>
        <td>Rubber Soul</td>
    </tr>
    <tr>
        <td>8</td>
        <td>What Goes On</td>
        <td>Rubber Soul</td>
    </tr>
    <tr>
        <td>9</td>
        <td>Girl</td>
        <td>Rubber Soul</td>
    </tr>
    <tr>
        <td>10</td>
        <td>I'm Looking Through You</td>
        <td>Rubber Soul</td>
    </tr>
    <tr>
        <td>11</td>
        <td>In My Life</td>
        <td>Rubber Soul</td>
    </tr>
    <tr>
        <td>12</td>
        <td>Wait</td>
        <td>Rubber Soul</td>
    </tr>
    <tr>
```

```
                <td>13</td>
                <td>If I Needed Someone</td>
                <td>Rubber Soul</td>
            </tr>
            <tr>
                <td>14</td>
                <td>Run For Your Life</td>
                <td>Rubber Soul</td>
            </tr>
        </tbody>
    </table>
</body>
</html>
```

The preceding HTML is styled with the following CSS:

```css
body {
    font: 12px 'Lucida Grande', Arial, sans-serif;
    background: #fff;
    color: rgb(50, 50, 50);
    padding: 20px;
    margin: 0;
}
table {
    table-layout: fixed;
    border: 1px solid rgb(200, 200, 200);
    border-collapse: collapse;
    padding: 0;
    margin: 0;
    width: 600px;
}
table th {
    text-align: left;
    background: rgb(244, 244, 244);
}
table th,
table td {
    border: 1px solid rgb(200, 200, 200);
    padding: 5px;
}
span.tableSorterDescending,
span.tableSorterAscending {
    display: none;
    float: right;
}
table th.headerSortDown {
    background: rgb(150, 150, 150);
}
table th.headerSortUp {
    background: rgb(200, 200, 200);
}
th.headerSortDown span.tableSorterDescending {
    display: inline;
}
th.headerSortUp span.tableSorterAscending {
    display: inline;
}
```

Finally, this example is enabled for table sorting using the following JavaScript.

```
$(document).ready(
    function()
    {
        $('table').tablesorter();
    }
);
```

The preceding example creates the screen shot that you see in Figure 19-1.

Track #	Name	Album
1	Come Together	Abbey Road
2	Something	Abbey Road
3	Maxwell's Silver Hammer	Abbey Road
4	Oh! Darling	Abbey Road
5	Octopus's Garden	Abbey Road
6	I Want You (She's So Heavy)	Abbey Road
7	Here Comes The Sun	Abbey Road
8	Because	Abbey Road
9	You Never Give Me Your Money	Abbey Road
10	Sun King	Abbey Road
11	Mean Mr. Mustard	Abbey Road
12	Polythene Pam	Abbey Road
13	She Came In Through The Bathroom Window	Abbey Road
14	Golden Slumbers	Abbey Road
15	Carry That Weight	Abbey Road
16	The End	Abbey Road
17	Her Majesty	Abbey Road
1	Drive My Car	Rubber Soul
2	Norwegian Wood (This Bird Has Flown)	Rubber Soul
3	You Won't See Me	Rubber Soul
4	Nowhere Man	Rubber Soul
5	Think For Yourself	Rubber Soul
6	The Word	Rubber Soul
7	Michelle	Rubber Soul
8	What Goes On	Rubber Soul
9	Girl	Rubber Soul
10	I'm Looking Through You	Rubber Soul
11	In My Life	Rubber Soul
12	Wait	Rubber Soul
13	If I Needed Someone	Rubber Soul
14	Run For Your Life	Rubber Soul

FIGURE 19-1

Figure 19-2 shows how to sort by multiple columns. To do this, sort the first column by clicking the column header; then hold down the Shift key to click a second column header.

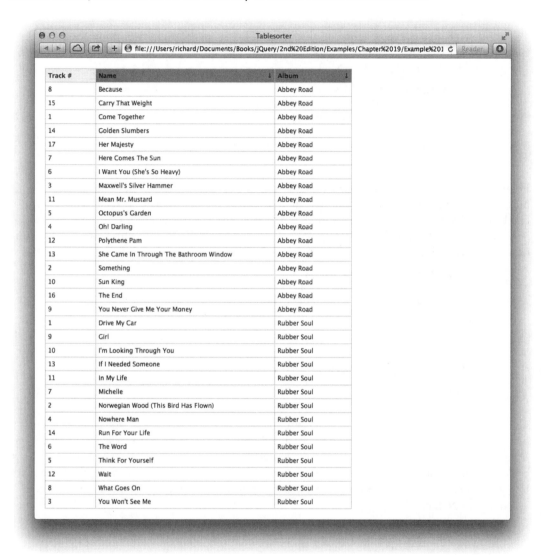

FIGURE 19-2

This example is primarily about setting up the proper HTML and then styling it with CSS. The `$.tablesorter()` plugin's default functionality provides the rest as soon as it is applied.

You can customize several aspects of `$.tablesorter()` using the options documented in Appendix T. For example, you can change which keyboard key you have to press to select a second column for sorting using the option `sortMultiSortKey`. The default value is `'shiftKey'`; to make it the Option (Mac) or Alt (Windows) key, you would change the value to `'altKey'`.

```
$('table').tablesorter({
    sortMultiSortKey : 'altKey'
});
```

You can also change the class names applied to the <th> elements using the options cssHeader, cssAsc, and cssDesc. The default value of cssHeader is header. The default value of cssAsc is header-SortUp, and the default value of cssDesc is headerSortDown.

```
$('table').tablesorter({
    sortMultiSortKey : 'altKey',
    cssHeader : 'tableSorterHeader',
    cssAsc : 'tableSorterAscending',
    cssDesc : 'tableSorterDescending'
});
```

Finally, if your table contains additional markup in the table cells, you need to account for the markup using the textExtraction option. The textExtraction option can be the string 'simple' or it can be a callback function. Whatever method you use, it should be as fast and as optimized as possible. The method provided would be slow because it uses jQuery and the numerous chains of function calls that entails.

```
$('table').tablesorter({
    sortMultiSortKey : 'altKey',
    cssHeader : 'tableSorterHeader',
    cssAsc : 'tableSorterAscending',
    cssDesc : 'tableSorterDescending',
    textExtraction : function(node)
    {
        return $(node).text();
    }
});
```

The initial sorting of a table is controlled with the sortList option. This options allows you to provide an array that describes how a table should be sorted after the $.tablesorter() plugin has been applied. The default behavior is to not change the sorting of the table until the user explicitly clicks a header to sort a column. The following example sorts the table by default, the same way it is sorted in Figure 19-2, which is to say, it is first sorted ascending by Album and then sorted ascending by Name.

```
$('table').tablesorter({
    sortList : [
        [2, 0],
        [1, 0]
    ]
});
```

Each column is referenced by number, offset from zero. The first column sorted is the third column. Then you specify ascending or descending by specifying 0 for ascending and 1 for descending. So, [2, 0] sorts the third column ascending, and [1, 0] sorts the second column ascending after that.

Additional options for customizing a $.tablesorter() plugin implementation are available in Appendix T.

SUMMARY

Using the $.tablesorter() plugin is an easy and straightforward experience of adding the plugin's code to your document and then enabling $.tablesorter() on whatever <table> elements you would like to make sortable.

You learned in this chapter that the out-of-the-box experience for sorting tables includes the ability to sort one or more columns. To do this you need little more than the right HTML structure and some CSS.

You learned that the hot key for selecting multiple columns can be customized easily using the sort-MultiSortKey option.

You also learned that the various class names that $.tablesorter() uses for <th> elements can be customized using the cssHeader, cssAsc, and cssDesc options.

If you have a more complicated table and use markup in your table cells, you can control how text is extracted from each cell for sorting using the textExtraction option. You can use the 'simple' method, which just takes the content of the cell wholesale, regardless if it includes markup. You can also use a callback function that specifies explicitly how you'd like the text to be extracted. For example, you could walk the DOM yourself and get the text node using JavaScript APIs directly, instead of jQuery.

Finally, the sortList option defines how a table should be sorted by default when the $.table-sorter() plugin is applied.

EXERCISES

1. How is a table sorted by default?

2. How would you use the Control key on a Mac or Windows keyboard as the key you press when selecting a second column to sort?

3. How would you customize the class names used on the <th> elements by the $.tablesorter() plugin?

20

Creating an Interactive Slideshow

Slideshows are a common sight on homepages today. Typically, you have three or more panels set to transition automatically between the slides, one after another. When the slideshow finishes, it starts over again. These slideshows are typically used for marketing, displaying multiple banners.

In this chapter you learn how to use a slideshow plugin that I wrote for my open source PHP framework, Hot Toddy. It has no options but is a demonstration of how to create a reusable jQuery plugin that can accommodate multiple instances of the plugin on a single page.

CREATING A SLIDESHOW

In this section, you learn both how to create a slideshow using a plugin and how to code the plugin itself. The plugin that I've created provides only a fade transition between slides. Your goal in this chapter is to understand how the plugin works well enough to modify it to suit your needs, which should include how to use a different animation.

The principle of the slideshow is simple: Provide two or more frames that can transition between one another. The number of slides is variable; you can include as few or as many as you like, and the plugin automatically numbers them and transitions between them.

This plugin is designed to accommodate the possibility of multiple slideshows on the same page; each slideshow is called a *collection*. The code is designed to instantiate a new instance of the slideshow object for each collection so that they can operate independently of one another.

Use the following example (*Example 20-1* in the source code download materials at www.wrox. com/go/webdevwithjquery) to start creating a slideshow:

```
<!DOCTYPE HTML>
<html lang='en'>
    <head>
        <meta charset='utf-8' />
        <title>Slideshow</title>
        <script src='../jQuery.js'></script>
        <script src='../jQueryUI.js'></script>
        <script src='Example 20-1.js'></script>
        <link href='Example 20-1.css' rel='stylesheet' />
    </head>
    <body>
        <div id='slides' class='slideshow'>
            <div class='slide'>
                <a href='#'>
                    <img src='images/Faces of Autumn.jpg'
                        alt="Faces of Autumn" />
                </a>
            </div>
            <div class='slide'>
                <a href='#'>
                    <img src='images/Key.png' alt="Key" />
                </a>
            </div>
            <div class='slide'>
                <a href='#'>
                    <img src='images/Pencil Drawing.jpg'
                        alt="Pencil Drawing" />
                </a>
            </div>
        </div>
    </body>
</html>
```

The preceding HTML is joined with the following CSS:

```
body {
    font: 12px 'Lucida Grande', Arial, sans-serif;
    background: #fff;
    color: rgb(50, 50, 50);
}
div#slides {
    position: relative;
    border: 1px solid black;
    height: 200px;
    width: 500px;
}
div.slide {
    position: absolute;
    top: 0;
    left: 0;
    width: 500px;
    height: 200px;
    background: black;
    overflow: hidden;
    z-index: 1;
```

```
}
ul.slideshowControls {
    list-style: none;
    padding: 0;
    margin: 0;
    position: absolute;
    z-index: 2;
}
ul.slideshowControls li {
    float: left;
    width: 10px;
    height: 10px;
    margin: 5px 0 0 5px;
    border-radius: 5px;
    background: black;
    text-indent: -2000000px;
    cursor: pointer;
    border: 1px solid white;
    overflow: hidden;
}
ul.slideshowControls li.slideshowControlActive {
    background: white;
    border: 1px solid black;
}
div#slide-1-1 img {
    position: relative;
    top: -200px;
}
div#slide-1-2 img {
    position: relative;
    top: -200px;
}
div#slide-1-3 img {
    position: relative;
    top: -600px;
}
```

The preceding style sheet and HTML are accompanied by the following JavaScript, which completes this example:

```
var slideshows = [];

$.fn.extend({
    slideshow : function()
    {
        return this.each(
            function()
            {
                var node = $(this);

                if (typeof node.data('slideshow') === 'undefined')
                {
                    var slideCollection = slideshows.length + 1;
```

```
                         slideshows[slideCollection] =
                             new slideshow(node, slideCollection);

                         node.data('slideshow', slideCollection);
                     }
                 }
             );
         }
    });

    // From John Resig's awesome class instantiation code.
    // http://ejohn.org/blog/simple-class-instantiation/
    var hot = {

        factory : function()
        {
            return function(args)
            {
                if (this instanceof arguments.callee)
                {
                    if (typeof(this.init) == 'function')
                    {
                        this.init.apply(this, args && args.callee? args : arguments);
                    }
                }
                else
                {
                    return new arguments.callee(arguments);
                }
            }
        }
    };

    var slideshow = hot.factory();

    slideshow.prototype.init = function(node, slideCollection)
    {
        this.counter = 1;
        this.isInterrupted = false;
        this.transitioning = false;
        this.resumeTimer = null;

        if (!node.find('ul.slideshowControls').length)
        {
            node.prepend(
                $('<ul/>').addClass('slideshowControls')
            );
        }

        node.find('ul.slideshowControls').html('');

        var slideInCollection = 1;

        node.find('.slide').each(
```

```javascript
function()
{
    this.id = 'slide-' + slideCollection + '-' + slideInCollection;

    node.find('ul.slideshowControls')
        .append(
            $('<li/>')
                .attr(
                    'id',
                    'slideshowControl-' + slideCollection + '-' +
                        slideInCollection
                )
                .html(
                    $('<span/>').text(slideInCollection)
                )
        );

    slideInCollection++;
}
);

node.find('ul.slideshowControls li:first')
    .addClass('slideshowControlActive');

node.find('ul.slideshowControls li')
    .hover(
        function()
        {
            $(this).addClass('slideshowControlOn');
        },
        function()
        {
            $(this).removeClass('slideshowControlOn');
        }
    )
    .click(
        function()
        {
            if (!slideshows[slideCollection].transitioning)
            {
                if (slideshows[slideCollection].resumeTimer)
                {
                    clearTimeout(slideshows[slideCollection].resumeTimer);
                }

                slideshows[slideCollection].transitioning = true;
                slideshows[slideCollection].isInterrupted = true;

                var li = $(this);

                node.find('ul.slideshowControls li')
                    .removeClass('slideshowControlActive');

                node.find('.slide:visible')
```

```
                            .fadeOut('slow');

                var slideInCollection = parseInt($(this).text());

                var counter = slideInCollection + 1;

                var resetCounter = (
                    (slideInCollection + 1) >
                    node.find('ul.slideshowControls li').length
                );

                if (resetCounter)
                {
                    counter = 1;
                }

                slideshows[slideCollection].counter = counter;

                $('#slide-' + slideCollection + '-' + slideInCollection)
                    .fadeIn(
                    'slow',
                    function()
                    {
                        li.addClass('slideshowControlActive');

                        slideshows[slideCollection].transitioning = false;

                        slideshows[slideCollection].resumeTimer = setTimeout(
                            'slideshows[' + slideCollection + '].resume();',
                            5000
                        );
                    }
                );
            }
        }
    );

    this.resume = function()
    {
        this.isInterrupted = false;
        this.transition();
    };

    this.transition = function()
    {
        if (this.isInterrupted)
        {
            return;
        }

        node.find('.slide:visible')
            .fadeOut('slow');
```

```
            node.find('ul.slideshowControls li')
                .removeClass('slideshowControlActive');

        $('#slide-' + slideCollection + '-' + this.counter).fadeIn(
            'slow',
            function()
            {
                node.find('ul.slideshowControls li').each(
                    function()
                    {
                        if (parseInt($(this).text()) ==
                            slideshows[slideCollection].counter)
                        {
                            $(this).addClass('slideshowControlActive');
                        }
                    }
                );

                slideshows[slideCollection].counter++;

                var resetCounter = (
                    slideshows[slideCollection].counter >
                    node.find('ul.slideshowControls li').length
                );

                if (resetCounter)
                {
                    slideshows[slideCollection].counter = 1;
                }

                setTimeout(
                    'slideshows[' + slideCollection + '].transition();',
                    5000
                );
            }
        );
    };

    this.transition();
};

$(document).ready(
    function()
    {
        if ($('.slideshow').length)
        {
            $('.slideshow').slideshow();
        }
    }
);
```

The preceding example results are shown in Figure 20-1.

FIGURE 20-1

The HTML in this example is designed to allow the author to specify as little as possible about the slideshow. The number of slides is automatically calculated from the plugin, and they are transitioned in the order that they appear in the document. Because each slide is a <div> element, you can have any HTML you like within each slide, including text for a marketing message. The slideshow controls are also automatically generated by the plugin.

The remainder of this chapter examines the JavaScript in this example in detail, explaining how each bit comes together to create the larger plugin.

You begin with a simple global variable declaration.

```
var slideshows = [];
```

This variable, slideshows, contains each instance of a slideshow object that has been created, making it possible to have as many slideshows as you like within the same DOM.

The next section of code creates a jQuery plugin called $.slideshow(). Unlike most of the jQuery plugins you've seen so far, this plugin has no option parameters. You could add options for pausing a slideshow, destroying a slideshow, and so on—whatever configurable parameters you want to add. Doing so would be a simple matter of adding optional arguments for the jQuery $.slideshow() method, and then deciding how those arguments should act upon the correct corresponding slideshow() object that gets instantiated for each instance of a slideshow on the page.

```
$.fn.extend({
    slideshow : function()
    {
        return this.each(
            function()
            {
                var node = $(this);

                if (typeof node.data('slideshow') === 'undefined')
                {
```

```
                        var slideCollection = slideshows.length + 1;

                        slideshows[slideCollection] =
                            new slideshow(node, slideCollection);

                        node.data('slideshow', slideCollection);
                    }
                }
            );
        }
    });
```

Presently, the $.slideshow() method is called on each HTML element with a class name of slideshow, and that happens automatically when the DOM is ready. When $.slideshow() is called, a variable called slideCollection is created based on the number of slideshows already created. This variable keeps track of each collection and makes it possible to go back and reference an existing collection. Each slideshow in the document is numbered offset from one, and this data is stored with each instance of the slideshow using the jQuery data API. If an instance does not have the associated *slideshow* data attached to it, then it hasn't been processed by the plugin. This makes it possible to call the $.slideshow() plugin method as many times as you need to call it to create a slideshow over the life of a document or application. New slideshows are created and added to the existing collection of slideshows as needed.

The next bit of code is lifted from the website of John Resig (the creator of jQuery). It provides an easy-to-reference factory method for creating prototype objects, which is to say a single object that you can instantiate again and again, creating multiple copies, each with their own properties, timers, and settings, individually intact.

```
// From John Resig's awesome class instantiation code.
// http://ejohn.org/blog/simple-class-instantiation/
var hot = {

    factory : function()
    {
        return function(args)
        {
            if (this instanceof arguments.callee)
            {
                if (typeof this.init == 'function')
                {
                    this.init.apply(this, args && args.callee? args : arguments);
                }
            }
            else
            {
                return new arguments.callee(arguments);
            }
        }
    }
};

var slideshow = hot.factory();
```

The next section of code begins the `slideshow.prototype.init` function. When the slideshow is instantiated with `new slideshow(node, slideCollection)`, the `slideshow.prototype.init` function is executed to create a new copy of the `slideshow` object.

The names of the arguments are the same so that you can easily associate `new slideshow(node, slideCollection)` with `slideshow.prototype.init = function(node, slideCollection)`. When a new `slideshow` object is created, some variables are created to keep track of different states.

The `this.counter` property keeps track of which slide is presently being displayed. The `this.isInterrupted` property keeps track of whether the slideshow has been interrupted by the user clicking a slide control. When a slideshow is interrupted, the slideshow pauses for 5 seconds on the slide the user clicked to see, and then the slideshow automatically resumes.

The `this.transitioning` property keeps track of whether an animated transition is occurring. This property prevents multiple animations from stacking up by ignoring any additional animation requests until the current one has completed.

The `this.resumeTimer` property keeps a reference to timers created when the user interrupts a slideshow. This timer occasionally needs to be cleared or created based on what the user does.

```
slideshow.prototype.init = function(node, slideCollection)
{
    this.counter = 1;
    this.isInterrupted = false;
    this.transitioning = false;
    this.resumeTimer = null;
```

The next line creates the slideshow controls. At this point, the element created is a `<ul>` element with the class name `slideshowControls`; it does not yet have any child elements.

```
    if (!node.find('ul.slideshowControls').length)
    {
        node.prepend(
            $('<ul/>').addClass('slideshowControls')
        );
    }
```

If the `<ul>` with the class name `slideshowControls` does already exist, its children are removed.

Next, you iterate over each element existing within the slideshow container element with the class name `slide`. This block of code begins with the declaration of a variable, `slideInCollection`, which is a counter to keep track of which slide in this slideshow is presently under consideration. The counter creates id names as well as creates the slideshow controls.

```
    var slideInCollection = 1;

    node.find('.slide').each(
        function()
        {
            this.id = 'slide-' + slideCollection + '-' + slideInCollection;

            node.find('ul.slideshowControls')
                .append(
```

```
$('<li/>')
    .attr(
        'id',
        'slideshowControl-' + slideCollection + '-' +
            slideInCollection
    )
    .html(
        $('<span/>').text(slideInCollection)
    )
);

slideInCollection++;
        }
    );
);
```

First, each element with the slide class name is given an id name that identifies the collection's offset and the slide's offset. The <ul> with the class name slideshowControls is given a new <li> element for each slide. Each <li> element is populated with a <span> element, which in turn contains the numbered offset of the slide.

You can find the first <li> element within the <ul> slideshowControls with the following code, and it is given a class name slideshowControlActive.

```
node.find('ul.slideshowControls li:first')
    .addClass('slideshowControlActive');
```

Next, each <li> element within <ul> slideshowControls is provided with hover and click events. The hover event simply toggles the presence of the slideshowControlOn class name.

```
node.find('ul.slideshowControls li')
    .hover(
        function()
        {
            $(this).addClass('slideshowControlOn');
        },
        function()
        {
            $(this).removeClass('slideshowControlOn');
        }
    )
```

The click event controls what happens when the user clicks a slideshow control, indicating that the user wants to see that particular slide again.

Within the callback function to the click event, you can use the existing slideshows global variable to refer to the correct instance of the slideshow object. You can do this in many ways—this is the method that best illustrates what is happening.

The first statement within this block of code checks whether an animation is in progress using the transitioning property. If an animation is occurring, then nothing happens and the click event is ignored.

```
.click(
    function()
    {
        if (!slideshows[slideCollection].transitioning)
        {
```

Next, you check to see if there is a resumeTimer active; the resumeTimer controls the interval between slide transitions. If a timer is active, it is cleared by calling the native clearTimeout() method.

```
if (slideshows[slideCollection].resumeTimer)
{
    clearTimeout(slideshows[slideCollection].resumeTimer);
}
```

The transitioning property is set to true to indicate that a slide animation is taking place. Then the isInterrupted property is set to true to indicate that the user clicked a slide control and interrupted the slideshow.

```
slideshows[slideCollection].transitioning = true;
slideshows[slideCollection].isInterrupted = true;
```

A reference to the <li> element's jQuery object is stored in the variable named li.

```
var li = $(this);
```

All <li> elements within the current slideshow slideshowControlActive class have that class removed.

```
node.find('ul.slideshowControls li')
    .removeClass('slideshowControlActive');
```

The currently visible slide identified with the class name slide and the :visible pseudo-class (proprietary to jQuery) is faded out with an animation.

```
node.find('.slide:visible')
    .fadeOut('slow');
```

A reference to the current slide's offset number is retrieved from the text inside the current <li> element.

```
var slideInCollection = parseInt($(this).text());
```

A counter variable is created so that when the slideshow resumes, the counter property contains the correct reference to the correct slide.

```
var counter = slideInCollection + 1;
```

If the number contained in slideInCollection + 1 exceeds the length of slides in the collection, then the counter is reset to 1. This moves the slideshow forward from the last slide to the first slide in a loop.

```
var resetCounter = (
    (slideInCollection + 1) >
    node.find('ul.slideshowControls li').length
```

```
        );

        if (resetCounter)
        {
            counter = 1;
        }
```

The value of the counter variable is moved to the counter property so that the slideshow can continue to function properly when it resumes automatically.

```
slideshows[slideCollection].counter = counter;
```

Then the slide the user clicked is faded in with an animation. The slide is referenced by its collection number and its slide number.

```
$('#slide-' + slideCollection + '-' + slideInCollection)
    .fadeIn(
    'slow',
    function()
    {
```

The slideshowControlActive class name is added to the li variable holding a reference to the current <li> element's jQuery object.

```
li.addClass('slideshowControlActive');
```

Now that the animation has completed, the transitioning property is set to false to indicate that there is no animation taking place right now.

```
slideshows[slideCollection].transitioning = false;
```

Because the animation has completed, the next step is to resume the timer. A call to setTimeout() triggers a slideshow transition to occur automatically after 5 seconds, as though the slideshow had never been interrupted. The next slide transition occurs after an additional 5 seconds.

```
                slideshows[slideCollection].resumeTimer = setTimeout(
                    'slideshows[' + slideCollection + '].resume();',
                    5000
                );
            }
        );
    }
}
);
```

The next block of code is an API method. It resumes the slideshow if the slideshow has been interrupted.

```
this.resume = function()
{
    this.isInterrupted = false;
    this.transition();
};
```

This method is used only when the user clicks a control to manually flip to a slide. It resets the isInterrupted property to false and then triggers the next transition by calling the transition() method.

The transition() method is used for the normal transition of one slide to the next, repeating display of all slides on a loop, endlessly.

```
this.transition = function()
{
```

If the isInterrupted property is true, the method returns and nothing happens. This means that the process of interrupting the slideshow has not completed and should not be interfered with.

```
if (this.isInterrupted)
{
    return;
}
```

Like in the block that handled clicking a slide control, the first thing you do is hide the currently visible slide with a call to fadeOut(). You can find the slide within the current slideshow by the class name slide and the :visible pseudo-class.

```
node.find('.slide:visible')
    .fadeOut('slow');
```

Then, all the <li> slideshowControls within the current slideshow lose the class name slideshowControlActive.

```
node.find('ul.slideshowControls li')
    .removeClass('slideshowControlActive');
```

Finally, the new slide is animated with a call to fadeIn(); it is referenced by its collection number (slideCollection) and its slide number (this.counter).

```
$('#slide-' + slideCollection + '-' + this.counter).fadeIn(
    'slow',
    function()
    {
```

When the new slide completes the fadeIn() animation, the current slide's corresponding <li> control within <ul> slideshowControls receives the class name slideshowControlActive. You can find the current control by comparing the text of each <li> element with the current value of the counter property.

```
node.find('ul.slideshowControls li').each(
    function()
    {
        if (parseInt($(this).text()) ==
            slideshows[slideCollection].counter)
        {
            $(this).addClass('slideshowControlActive');
        }
    }
);
```

The counter property is incremented by 1 to prepare for the next slide.

```
slideshows[slideCollection].counter++;
```

If the counter property's new value is greater than the total number of slides, it is reset to 1 so that the counter property goes from referencing the last slide to the first slide, when the last slide is displayed.

```
var resetCounter = (
    slideshows[slideCollection].counter >
    node.find('ul.slideshowControls li').length
);

if (resetCounter)
{
    slideshows[slideCollection].counter = 1;
}
```

A new timer is created that runs from this transition to the next one.

```
            setTimeout(
                'slideshows[' + slideCollection + '].transition();',
                5000
            );
        }
    );
};
```

A call to `this.transition();` starts the slideshow running:

```
this.transition();
```

Finally, at the end of the script, a ready event fires when the DOM is ready. It checks to see whether there are any items with the class name slideshow; if there are, the `$.slideshow()` jQuery plugin method is called on each of those elements.

```
$(document).ready(
    function()
    {
        if ($('.slideshow').length)
        {
            $('.slideshow').slideshow();
        }
    }
);
```

SUMMARY

In this chapter you learned how to create and use a plugin for creating interactive slideshows, like those used to display advertising on many websites' homepages. The plugin that you created can handle one or more distinct slideshows within a document, each with two or more slides. Using a prototype style of programming, you can create distinct objects for each slideshow, each with their own properties and states of being.

EXERCISES

1. What is the purpose of keeping track of whether a slideshow has been interrupted by the user using the `isInterrupted` property?

2. What is the purpose of keeping track of whether a transition is in progress with the `transitioning` property?

3. Describe how the plugin automatically creates controls to click a specific slide. What information is contained in the id name of each control? What information is available in the text of each control?

Extra Credit: Create your own version of the slideshow plugin with options to

➤   Start, pause, or resume a slideshow.

➤   Destroy a slideshow.

➤   Set a custom amount of time between slide transitions.

➤   Set a custom animation.

Working with HTML5 Audio and Video

From its early days, the true rise of the World Wide Web began when textual information could be displayed with formatting on the same page as media elements such as graphics. Continuing in this tradition, HTML5 has introduced simple and standard <video> and <audio> elements for using media of the named types. Unfortunately, support within browsers is an ongoing struggle.

In this chapter you learn how to use the MediaElement plugin, which harnesses the media functionality available in today's browsers and includes several custom plugins to provide support for older browsers.

DOWNLOADING THE MEDIAELEMENT PLUGIN

The MediaElement plugin is conveniently located at http://www.mediaelementjs.com/. All the needed materials are available in one download. From the build directory of the download, obtain the mediaelement-and-player.min.js and mediaelement.min.css files for use in your project. These files are the minimum required for functionality; additional files that might be required for your use cases are described later in this chapter in the section "Implementing h.264 Video Content."

CONFIGURING THE MEDIAELEMENT PLUGIN

The MediaElement plugin provides nearly two dozen configuration options. Here you focus on a few of the options; the entire list is available in Appendix U, "MediaElement." To begin, create the following markup, from *Example 21-1.html* in the source materials at www.wrox.com/go/webdevwithjquery:

```
<!DOCTYPE HTML>
<html xmlns='http://www.w3.org/1999/xhtml'>
    <head>
        <meta http-equiv='content-type'
            content='application/xhtml+xml; charset=utf-8' />
```

```
        <meta http-equiv='content-language' content='en-us' />
        <title>MediaElement Plugin</title>
        <script src='../jQuery.js'></script>
        <script src='../MediaElement/mediaelement-and-player.min.js'></script>
        <script src='Example 21-1.js'></script>
        <link href='../MediaElement/mediaelementplayer.min.css' rel='stylesheet' />
        <link href='Example 21-1.css' rel='stylesheet' />
    </head>
    <body>
        <div id='container'>
            <video src='testvideo1.mp4' width='320' height='240'></video>
        </div>
    </body>
</html>
```

CSS is referenced, but the rules do not influence the presentation of this example. The following JavaScript (in *Example 21-1.js*) is included for configuring and activating the MediaElement plugin:

```
$(document).ready(
    function()
    {
        $('video,audio').mediaplayerelement(
            {
                clickToPlayPause: true,
                features: ['playpause', 'current', 'progress', 'volume'],
                poster: 'images/FilmMarker.jpg'
            }
        );
    }
);
```

The code results are shown in Figure 21-1.

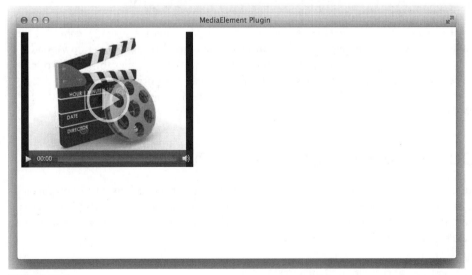

FIGURE 21-1

Start by using the HTML5 `<video>` element to specify the media file and dimensions.

```
<video src='testvideo1.mp4' width='320' height='240'></video>
```

Then use jQuery to select all `<video>` and `<audio>` elements on the page, activating the MediaElement plugin on them with the `clickToPlayPause`, `features`, and `poster` configuration options.

```
$('video,audio').mediaplayerelement(
    {
        clickToPlayPause: true,
        features: ['playpause', 'current', 'progress', 'volume'],
        poster: 'images/FilmMarker.jpg'
    }
    );
```

The `features` option is discussed in the section "Customizing Player Controls." The `clickToPlayPause` option is nearly self-explanatory; like the well-known YouTube feature, you can click anywhere on the video to play or pause the video. The `poster` option enables you to display an image before the video starts playing. Without this option, the MediaElement plugin would display the first frame of the video by default. Common uses include showing a frame from the middle of the video (previously saved to an image file) or showing a flashy Check Out Our Video marketing graphic.

CREATING AN HTML STRUCTURE THAT ENABLES FALLBACK VIDEO/AUDIO PLUGINS FOR OLDER BROWSERS

You might have noticed that an h.264 (MP4) video file was used in the last example. The next section discusses this format, which is one of three formats (h.264, Ogg, and WebM) supported in the HTML5 video specification. In this discussion, you see one of the best reasons to use the MediaElement plugin: its capability to display media files in browsers that do not have native support for those formats, all without losing the capability for newer browsers to natively play the content. The plugin enables a fallback to supported formats by supplying multiple sources until a supported one is found. Review the following markup (from *Example 21-2.html*):

```
<!DOCTYPE HTML>
<html xmlns='http://www.w3.org/1999/xhtml'>
    <head>
        <meta http-equiv='content-type'
            content='application/xhtml+xml; charset=utf-8' />
        <meta http-equiv='content-language' content='en-us' />
        <title>MediaElement Plugin</title>
        <script src='../jQuery.js'></script>
        <script src='../MediaElement/mediaelement-and-player.min.js'></script>
        <script src='Example 21-2.js'></script>
        <link href='../MediaElement/mediaelementplayer.min.css' rel='stylesheet' />
        <link href='Example 21-2.css' rel='stylesheet' />
    </head>
    <body>
        <div id='container'>
            <video width='320' height='240'>
```

```
                    <source type='video/mp4' src='testvideo1.mp4'></source>
                    <source type='video/wmv' src='testvideo1.wmv'></source>
                    <object width='320' height='240'
                            type='application/x-shockwave-flash'
                        data='flashmediaelement.swf'>
                        <param name='movie' value='flashmediaelement.swf' />
                        <param name='flashvars'
                                value='controls=true&file=testvideo1.mp4' />
                    </object>
                </video>
            </div>
        </body>
    </html>
```

Note that the source is no longer specified in the <video> element; instead, you now have multiple <source> elements. The MediaElement plugin first attempts to load natively supported formats and then formats supported by the Silverlight plugin. In addition, this example markup includes a fallback to the Flash plugin if none of the <source> elements were supported.

IMPLEMENTING H.264 VIDEO CONTENT

The h.264 video format has become the new de facto standard for digital video. It is used by YouTube, Apple, and over-the-air HDTV providers. It is also one of the encoding standards for Blu-ray discs. In this section, you learn how to convert and distribute your video content in this format.

Encoding Using Handbrake or QuickTime

The format of your video content depends on whether you obtain or generate the video content (and from which device the content is generated). If you want to use the h.264 format and need to convert from another video format, you need to obtain a video conversion utility. Recommended utilities are Handbrake (`https://handbrake.fr/`) and QuickTime (`https://www.apple.com/quick-time/`). Handbrake is explicitly recommended if you are not using a Mac. In addition, QuickTime Player (v. 10+) on a Mac enables you to Export from the File menu, but Apple recently (since version 10.3) reduced the available functionality. Each tool contains device presets to produce the expected video size and quality when targeting users on desktop computers and mobile devices of various capabilities.

Using the HTML5 <video> Element

The HTML5 <video> element specification allows for multiple <source> elements, as shown in the previous section. In this manner, you can add an element for each of the three supported formats (h.264, Ogg, and WebM) and be certain of content playback on all modern browsers.

Using the Flash Player Plugin

To avoid encoding your video content in multiple formats, you can instead add fallback markup to specify that the MediaElement plugin should use Flash to play your h.264 video file:

```
                    <object width='320' height='240'
                            type='application/x-shockwave-flash'
                        data='flashmediaelement.swf'>
```

```
            <param name='movie' value='flashmediaelement.swf' />
            <param name='flashvars'
                value='controls=true&file=testvideo1.mp4' />
        </object>
```

This plugin utilizes the `flashmediaelement.swf` Flash video to play your content, where your filename is passed in the `flashvars` param.

Using Microsoft's Silverlight Plugin

Although you can include `<object>` element markup for the Silverlight plugin in a manner similar to that for the Flash plugin, Silverlight requires many additional parameters that are generally best created by the MediaElement plugin. Silverlight provides support for formats such as Windows Media Video in browsers where such formats are not supported.

CUSTOMIZING PLAYER CONTROLS

As previously discussed, the MediaElement plugin provides many configuration options. The `features` option customizes which controls display to the user.

```
features: ['playpause', 'current', 'progress', 'duration', 'volume',
'fullscreen']
```

Most of the available controls or features are self-explanatory, with the preceding code indicating a play/pause button and displaying the current position, progress bar, video length, volume control, and full-screen button, respectively.

Following are common options that can be provided in the `features` array:

➤ `playpause`—A control button to play or pause the media, switching its icon to appropriate action for the media's state.

➤ `current`—A display of the media's current position, in typical HH:MM:SS format.

➤ `progressbar`—A filled bar control to display the current position of the media against its duration.

➤ `duration`—A display of the media's length, in typical HH:MM:SS format.

➤ `volume`—A control button with an integrated slider for setting the volume.

➤ `tracks`—A control button to toggle display of captions or subtitles specified by `<track>` elements inside the `<video>` element. It is important to note that browsers have differing security policies for local text track files.

➤ `speed`—A speed control button with options menu for setting the playback speed.

CONTROLLING WHEN THE DOWNLOAD OF MEDIA BEGINS

A few concerns should factor into the decision for when your media content should download (or buffer) within the user's browser; among them are the size of the video and the expected probability that the user will play the media. The actual control is indicated by the value of the optional `preload` attribute of the `<video>` or `<audio>` element.

```
<video src='testvideo1.mp4' width='320' height='240'
        preload='metadata'></video>
```

Following are the possible values:

➤ (no `preload` attribute specified)—Enables the browser to determine whether the media data should be preloaded.

➤ `none`—No media data should be preloaded. A `poster` image attribute or option for video content would be recommended unless you prefer that the user sees a solid, black frame until content playback activates.

➤ `metadata`—Metadata for the content should be downloaded, but the media data should not be preloaded. This value enables the element to display the content's first frame, duration, and track information and is a recommended minimum value.

➤ `auto` (also a blank value or attribute with no value) —The full media data should be downloaded.

You might have noticed the word "should" in each value definition. The HTML specification states that browsers should consider these values as hints instead of requirements. For instance, mobile device browsers often avoid preloading data regardless of the value.

SUMMARY

In this chapter, you learned about the MediaElement plugin and how to use it to enable consistent audio and video content in browsers. You learned about the HTML5 `<video>` and `<audio>` elements.

You learned about the three video formats supported by the HTML5 `<video>` element in various browsers. You learned more about one of these formats, h.264, and wrote code to display this video format.

You learned about additional MediaElement plugins to support Flash and Silverlight content and saw how multiple `<source>` elements enable browser fallback to a supported format.

Finally, you learned about common configuration options for the MediaElement plugin and the ability to request control of content download timing with the `preload` attribute.

EXERCISES

1. The MediaElement plugin standardizes browser support for which two HTML5 elements?

2. Which HTML5 element can be repeated inside a media element to allow the browser to render a supported format?

3. Which three video formats are supported in the HTML5 specification?

4. Name the MediaElement configuration option that enables captions or subtitles.

5. Which HTML5 attribute specifies when media content should download to the browser?

22

Creating a Simple WYSIWYG Editor

Many web-based WYSIWYG (what-you-see-is-what-you-get) editors have risen in popularity only to be later supplanted by editors with better interfaces or more features. Some of these editors used `<textarea>` elements or modified the `innerHTML` of DOM elements when formatting features were used.

In this chapter you learn an attribute that changed the face of web-based editors and how you can use it with jQuery to create a simple WYSIWYG editor in a few steps.

MAKING AN ELEMENT EDITABLE WITH THE CONTENTEDITABLE ATTRIBUTE

Although those comfortable with HTML editors can find it easy to be underwhelmed by the HTML5 `contenteditable` attribute, its impact should not be underestimated. It is another intuitive feature; when added to a DOM element, the content of that element becomes editable by the user directly in the browser. If you've ever used a settings page to perform an action such as changing the text of a button you commonly use, imagine instead toggling your web application to editable and then typing the text directly on the button. This is the type of feature that becomes not only possible but also easy with the `contenteditable` attribute.

Start with an HTML example of the attribute (*Example 22-1.html*):

```
<!DOCTYPE HTML>
<html xmlns='http://www.w3.org/1999/xhtml'>
    <head>
        <meta http-equiv='content-type'
            content='application/xhtml+xml; charset=utf-8' />
        <meta http-equiv='content-language' content='en-us' />
        <meta charset='utf-8' />
        <title>WYSIWYG Editor 1</title>
        <link href='Example 22-1.css' rel='stylesheet' />
    </head>
    <body>
        <div id='container' contenteditable='true'>
        </div>
    </body>
</html>
```

Add the following CSS for presentation (*Example 22-1.css*):

```
body {
    font: 12px Arial, sans-serif;
    background: #fff;
    color: rgb(50, 50, 50);
}

div#container {
    position: absolute;
    top: 10%;
    left: 10%;
    height: 80%;
    width: 80%;
    padding: 5px;
    border: 1px solid black;
    border-radius: 3px;
}
```

That completes the code for the example. Although you can use JavaScript to dynamically toggle whether an element is editable, you don't need any JavaScript for the simplest example of the contenteditable attribute. You simply add the attribute to a <div> element.

```
<div id='container' contenteditable='true'>
```

The CSS sets some default styles for the <body> and then positions the editable element in the center of the page with a thin, rounded (in most browsers) border and a little padding to keep the text off the border.

The preceding code results in the document shown in Figure 22-1.

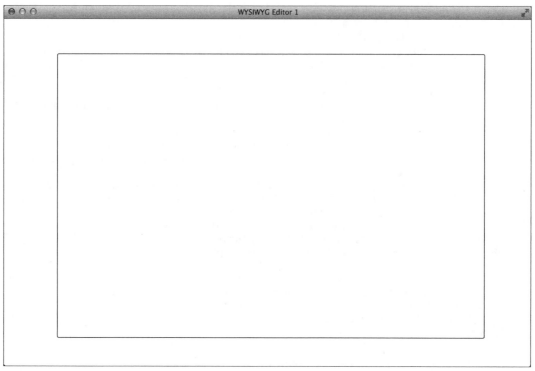

FIGURE 22-1

CREATING BUTTONS TO APPLY BOLD, ITALIC, UNDERLINE, FONT, AND FONT SIZE

So far, you have a text editor; in this section, you learn how to add rich-text features for formatting the text. You build a toolbar to house these features. Begin with the following HTML (*Example 22-2.html*):

```
<!DOCTYPE HTML>
<html xmlns='http://www.w3.org/1999/xhtml'>
    <head>
        <meta http-equiv='content-type'
            content='application/xhtml+xml; charset=utf-8' />
        <meta http-equiv='content-language' content='en-us' />
        <meta charset='utf-8' />
        <title>WYSIWYG Editor 2</title>
        <link href='Example 22-2.css' rel='stylesheet' />
        <script type='text/javascript' src='../jQuery.js'></script>
        <script type='text/javascript' src='Example 22-2.js'></script>
```

```
    </head>
    <body>
        <div id='toolbar'>
            <button class='toolbar-btn bold' data-format='bold'>B</button>
            <button class='toolbar-btn italic' data-format='italic'>I</button>
            <button class='toolbar-btn underline'
                    data-format='underline'>U</button>
            <select class='toolbar-ddl fontname' data-format='fontname'>
                <option value=''></option>
                <option value='Arial'>Arial</option>
                <option value='Courier New'>Courier New</option>
                <option value='Times New Roman'>Times New Roman</option>
            </select>
            <select class='toolbar-ddl fontsize' data-format='fontsize'>
                <option value=''></option>
                <option value='2'>Small</option>
                <option value='3'>Normal</option>
                <option value='4'>Big</option>
                <option value='5'>Bigger</option>
            </select>
        </div>
        <div id='container' contenteditable='true'>
        </div>
    </body>
</html>
```

Combine the preceding HTML with the following CSS (*Example 22-2.css*):

```
body {
    font: 16px Arial, sans-serif;
    background: #fff;
    color: rgb(50, 50, 50);
}

div#container {
    position: absolute;
    top: 17%;
    left: 10%;
    height: 75%;
    width: 80%;
    padding: 5px;
    border: 1px solid black;
    border-radius: 3px;
}

div#toolbar {
    position: absolute;
    top: 10%;
    left: 10%;
    height: 5%;
    width: 80%;
    padding: 5px;
```

```
        border: 1px solid black;
        border-radius: 3px;
    }

    button.bold {
        font-weight: bold;
    }

    button.italic {
        font-style: italic;
    }

    button.underline {
        text-decoration: underline;
    }
```

Finally, include the following JavaScript (*Example 22-2.js*) for handling the events for the toolbar buttons:

```
$(document).ready(
    function()
    {
        $('button.toolbar-btn').click(
            function()
            {
                var data = this && $(this).data && $(this).data();
                if (data && data.format && document.execCommand)
                {
                    document.execCommand(data.format, false, null);
                    $('div#container').focus();
                }
            }
        );
        $('select.toolbar-ddl').change(
            function()
            {
                var data = this && $(this).data && $(this).data();
                if (data && data.format && document.execCommand)
                {
                    document.execCommand(data.format, false,
                        this[this.selectedIndex].value);
                    this.selectedIndex = 0;
                    $('div#container').focus();
                }
            }
        );
    }
);
```

This code results in the document shown in Figure 22-2.

FIGURE 22-2

You added a `<div>` element for the toolbar and updated the CSS to account for positioning this toolbar. On the toolbar, you included three `<button>` elements for the bold, italic, and underline features, respectively, along with two `<select>` elements for the font name and size features. Note the `data-format` attribute added to these elements.

```
<button class='toolbar-btn bold' data-format='bold'>B</button>
```

This construction uses the `$.data()` feature of jQuery, which provides access to the `dataset` property mapping of the HTML5 data, attributes for use without requesting attribute values individually. The toolbar button click event handler starts with some sanity checks:

```
var data = this && $(this).data && $(this).data();
```

This line of code uses the JavaScript shortcut of combining logical checks and assignment. The variable `data` is assigned when `this` (the clicked button) exists and its wrapped jQuery object `$(this)` contains a `data` member. Unlike other programming languages, the value assigned is not the boolean (true or false) result of the conditional expression on the right side of the `=` assignment operator, but rather the result of the rightmost argument: `$(this).data()`.

```
if (data && data.format && document.execCommand)
```

Again, you check that the $(this).data() function returned valid information, that it contains a format member, and finally that the HTML document object supports the execCommand function, which is a shortcut for JavaScript to tell the browser to handle specific functions using its native features.

```
document.execCommand(data.format, false, null);
$('div#container').focus();
```

After these checks pass, you send the format value to the document.execCommand function with the additional parameters false (no user interface prompt for the user) and null (no value needed for bold, italic, or underline). Finally, because the button click removed focus from the editable element, you send the focus back to the editable element.

The <select> element drop-down list event handler differs slightly:

```
document.execCommand(data.format, false,
    this[this.selectedIndex].value);
this.selectedIndex = 0;
```

For the font name and size, you need to pass those values to the function. The this keyword now refers to the changed <select> element, so the indicated pattern is used as a shortcut to the selected item's value, which is then passed as the data value.

```
this.selectedIndex = 0;
```

For the purposes of this simple editor, the blank item at the top of each list is then selected. Although it does add the inconvenience of not seeing the last selected item, it also prevents some possible confusion. Without this line, a user might expect that you would detect the font name and size when you select text in the editable element.

CREATING A SELECTION

While working with the previous examples, you might have noticed the ability to change existing content by selecting it in the editable element. JavaScript offers the ability to work with selections, including options for creating a selection programmatically, storing information about a current selection, and restoring a selection that has been deselected. The next set of example code is fairly large to account for these cases, but each is discussed in turn.

Begin with the example markup (*Example 21-3.html*):

```
<!DOCTYPE HTML>
<html xmlns='http://www.w3.org/1999/xhtml'>
    <head>
        <meta http-equiv='content-type'
            content='application/xhtml+xml; charset=utf-8' />
        <meta http-equiv='content-language' content='en-us' />
        <meta charset='utf-8' />
        <title>WYSIWYG Editor 3</title>
        <link href='Example 22-3.css' rel='stylesheet' />
```

```html
<script type='text/javascript' src='../jQuery.js'></script>
<script type='text/javascript' src='Example 22-3.js'></script>
</head>
<body>
    <div id='toolbar'>
        <button class='toolbar-btn bold' data-format='bold'>B</button>
        <button class='toolbar-btn italic' data-format='italic'>I</button>
        <button class='toolbar-btn underline'
               data-format='underline'>U</button>
        <select class='toolbar-ddl fontname' data-format='fontname'>
            <option value=''></option>
            <option value='Arial'>Arial</option>
            <option value='Courier New'>Courier New</option>
            <option value='Times New Roman'>Times New Roman</option>
        </select>
        <select class='toolbar-ddl fontsize' data-format='fontsize'>
            <option value=''></option>
            <option value='2'>Small</option>
            <option value='3'>Normal</option>
            <option value='4'>Big</option>
            <option value='5'>Bigger</option>
        </select>
        <button id='btnCreateSelection'>Create Selection</button>
        <button id='btnStoreSelection'>Store Selection</button>
        <button id='btnRestoreSelection'>Restore Selection</button>
    </div>
    <div id='container' contenteditable='true'>
    </div>
</body>
</html>
```

The CSS remains unchanged from the previous example, so refer to it if needed. The updated markup is, however, enhanced with the updated JavaScript (*Example 22-3.js*):

```javascript
$(document).ready(
    function()
    {
        $('div#container').focus();
        $('button.toolbar-btn').click(
            function()
            {
                var data = this && $(this).data && $(this).data();
                if (data && data.format && document.execCommand)
                {
                    document.execCommand(data.format, false, null);
                    $('div#container').focus();
                }
            }
        );
        $('select.toolbar-ddl').change(
            function()
            {
                var data = this && $(this).data && $(this).data();
                if (data && data.format && document.execCommand)
                {
```

```javascript
                    document.execCommand(data.format, false,
                        this[this.selectedIndex].value);
                    this.selectedIndex = 0;
                    $('div#container').focus();
                }
            }
        );
        $('button#btnCreateSelection').click(
            function()
            {
                var container = document.getElementById('container');
                container.innerHTML = 'Here is some sample text for selection';
                var range = document.createRange();
                range.setStart(container.firstChild, 5);
                range.setEnd(container.firstChild, 17);
                setSelectionRange(range);
            }
        );
        $('button#btnStoreSelection').click(
            function()
            {
                window.selectedRange = getSelectionRange();
            }
        );
        $('button#btnRestoreSelection').click(
            function()
            {
                if (window.selectedRange)
                {
                    setSelectionRange(window.selectedRange);
                }
            }
        );
    }
);

function getSelectionRange()
{
    if (window.getSelection)
    {
        var sel = window.getSelection();
        if (sel.getRangeAt && sel.rangeCount)
        {
            return sel.getRangeAt(0);
        }
        else // Safari
        {
            var range = document.createRange();
            range.setStart(sel.anchorNode, sel.anchorOffset);
            range.setEnd(sel.focusNode, sel.focusOffset);
            return range;
        }
    }
    return null;
```

```
    }

    function setSelectionRange(range)
    {
        if (range && window.getSelection)
        {
            var sel = window.getSelection();
            sel.removeAllRanges();
            sel.addRange(range);
        }
    }
```

This code results in the document shown in Figure 22-3.

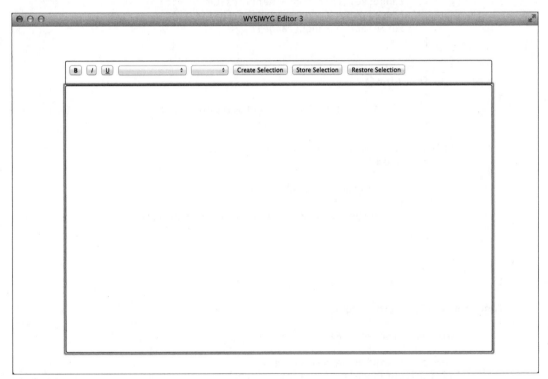

FIGURE 22-3

The markup now includes a button for creating a selection within the editable element:

```
<button id='btnCreateSelection'>Create Selection</button>
```

You added a click event handler for this button to the JavaScript code:

```
$('button#btnCreateSelection').click(
    function()
    {
        var container = document.getElementById('container');
```

```
                           container.innerHTML = 'Here is some sample text for selection';
                           var range = document.createRange();
                           range.setStart(container.firstChild, 5);
                           range.setEnd(container.firstChild, 17);
                           setSelectionRange(range);
                   }
           );
```

First, you obtain the editable element and place in a variable for ease of use:

```
           var container = document.getElementById('container');
```

To maintain the simplicity of this example, the handler sets the contents of the editable element before creating the selection. Although it is fairly easy to select edited and formatted content, it can become tedious quickly.

```
           container.innerHTML = 'Here is some sample text for selection';
```

Next, you create a Range object, which corresponds to a selection range.

```
           var range = document.createRange();
```

You set the bounds of the Range object. In this example, you set the contents of the element; therefore, you know the values that would typically be determined or calculated. The start of the Range is set to the sixth character of the text, and the end is set to the eighteenth character as the offsets are zero-based.

```
           range.setStart(container.firstChild, 5);
           range.setEnd(container.firstChild, 17);
```

Now that you have a Range object with its bounds set, you can call your first helper function for selection ranges:

```
           setSelectionRange(range);
```

The `setSelectionRange` function was added as a utility method to assist with this section of the chapter and the "Restoring a Selection" section:

```
       function setSelectionRange(range)
       {
           if (range && window.getSelection)
           {
               var sel = window.getSelection();
               sel.removeAllRanges();
               sel.addRange(range);
           }
       }
```

As is good practice, you start with some sanity checks. Ensure that a range was provided and that the browser supports the modern `window.getSelection` method:

```
       if (range && window.getSelection)
```

You then obtain the current Selection object.

```
var sel = window.getSelection();
```

The Selection object may contain zero to many selection ranges. In general, it contains zero until the page is clicked and one thereafter. You start by removing any existing selection ranges:

```
sel.removeAllRanges();
```

Finally, you add the programmatically created range to the Selection object, which finally selects the text "is some samp" within the editable element.

STORING A SELECTION

Within the previous example code, the markup was updated to add a button to the toolbar for storing the current position of a selection range:

```
<button id='btnStoreSelection'>Store Selection</button>
```

You updated the JavaScript to add a click event handler for this button. The handler performs the incredibly simple task of setting a window-level variable to store information about the currently selected content:

```
$('button#btnStoreSelection').click(
    function()
    {
        window.selectedRange = getSelectionRange();
    }
);
```

Notice that you used your second helper function:

```
function getSelectionRange()
{
    if (window.getSelection)
    {
        var sel = window.getSelection();
        if (sel.getRangeAt && sel.rangeCount)
        {
            return sel.getRangeAt(0);
        }
        else // Safari
        {
            var range = document.createRange();
            range.setStart(sel.anchorNode, sel.anchorOffset);
            range.setEnd(sel.focusNode, sel.focusOffset);
            return range;
        }
    }
    return null;
}
```

After dispensing with the `window.getSelection` sanity check (feature detection), you obtain the current Selection object as with the other helper function. This time, you access additional information about the object. In most cases, the Selection object supports the `getRangeAt` method; you check for support as well as the existence of selection ranges. If the tests pass, return the first Range object within the Selection object:

```
if (sel.getRangeAt && sel.rangeCount)
{
    return sel.getRangeAt(0);
}
```

If the logic tests fail (as is the case with Safari, which does not support `getRangeAt`), use familiar code to create a Range object, this time using bound information from the Selection object to specify the start and end containers and offsets:

```
else // Safari
{
    var range = document.createRange();
    range.setStart(sel.anchorNode, sel.anchorOffset);
    range.setEnd(sel.focusNode, sel.focusOffset);
    return range;
}
```

Finally, if basic feature detection indicated a lack of support for the modern Selection object, simply return `null` and move on. This is one of those instances in which it might be a good idea to alert the user that a better experience can be obtained with a newer browser.

```
return null;
```

Unless you hit the last case in which the Selection object was not available, you should have stored enough information about the selected content for later use.

RESTORING A SELECTION

The last button added in the previous code example's markup enabled the restoration of a previous selection within the editable element.

```
<button id='btnRestoreSelection'>Restore Selection</button>
```

You included one final JavaScript event handler for the click of this button. First, you test for the existence of the previously stored selection. If it does exist, pass it to the previously discussed helper function, which deselects any current selections and restores the saved selection.

```
$('button#btnRestoreSelection').click(
    function()
    {
        if (window.selectedRange)
        {
            setSelectionRange(window.selectedRange);
        }
    }
);
```

One caveat of storing and restoring selection information is that the process can be a bit fragile; in particular, the bound node information is stored. If the element content is changed, that information could become invalid, even if the content is reset to the exact same state.

SUMMARY

In this chapter, you created a simple WYSIWYG editor in the browser. Along the way, you learned about the powerful HTML5 contenteditable attribute, which can make nearly any DOM element editable. You learned to use the document.execCommand function for processing the formatting options within your editor.

You learned some of the structure of the current browser selection model and created Range objects programmatically. Although you might not have created the next giant of word processing software, you created a stable code base for additional exploration.

EXERCISES

1. Which HTML5 attribute is the basis for most modern web-based WYSIWYG editors?

2. Which JavaScript command asks the browser to perform actions using native functionality?

3. Name two options that require additional information when passed to the command described in Exercise 2.

4. Describe the structure in which most browsers store information about currently selected content.

5. Which jQuery method provides access to HTML5 data attributes?

PART IV
Appendices

- ▶ **APPENDIX A:** Exercise Answers

- ▶ **APPENDIX B:** jQuery Selectors

- ▶ **APPENDIX C:** Selecting, Traversing, and Filtering

- ▶ **APPENDIX D:** Events

- ▶ **APPENDIX E:** Manipulating Content, Attributes, and Custom Data

- ▶ **APPENDIX F:** More Content Manipulation

- ▶ **APPENDIX G:** AJAX Methods

- ▶ **APPENDIX H:** CSS

- ▶ **APPENDIX I:** Utilities

- ▶ **APPENDIX J:** Draggable and Droppable

- ▶ **APPENDIX K:** Sortable

- ▶ **APPENDIX L:** Selectable

Exercise Answers

CHAPTER 2

1. CSS and XPath are both acceptable answers.

2. `parents()`

3. `prev()`

4. `children()` for immediate descendants and `find()` for any elements in the descendant hierarchy

5. `not()`

6. `eq()`

7. `siblings()`, `prev()`, `next()`, `prevAll()`, `nextAll()`

8. `add()`

CHAPTER 3

1. You can use the `mouseover()` or `on('mouseover')` method. If you use deprecated methods, in addition, you can use `bind('mouseover')` or `live('mouseover')`.

   Extra Credit: Use the `hover()` method.

2. The `on()` method.

3. The `event.target` property is used to check to see which descendant element has received the event. The event then bubbles up from that element to the element that the event handler is attached to.

4. Provide a selector argument to the `on()` method describing the element you want the event to apply to on the parent or container element that contains the elements you want the event to apply to. This can also be the `document` object.

5. Naming an instance of an event handler can be done by applying the event name, a dot, and then the namespace you want to use. You can apply multiple event names by repeating the same process.

6. The off() method.

7. Yes.

8. You can use either click() with no arguments or trigger('click').

9. A custom event handler begins with any event name not already in use in JavaScript; you can attach a custom event handler using that name using the on() method. The trigger() method can be used to fire the custom event handler, as well as to send custom data to the event handler.

CHAPTER 4

1. One possibility:

```
$('input').attr(
    'value' : 'Some Value'.
    'class' : 'someClass'
);
```

Another possibility:

```
$('input').addClass('someClass').val('Some Value');
```

2. It might look like this:

```
$('a').attr('href', 'http://www.example.com');
```

3. removeAttr()

4. hasClass()

5. No, HTML tags will not be present in the return value, only the element's text content.

6. Yes, HTML tags will be escaped and treated like text content.

7. One bug that jQuery's append() and prepend() methods work around in IE is how IE makes innerHTML Read Only on <table> elements.

8. One bug that jQuery's append() and prepend() methods work around in Firefox is how Firefox occasionally loses form input values when appending or prepending HTML content using innerHTML.

9. insertBefore()

10. wrapAll()

11. outerHTML

12. `remove()`
13. `clone(true)`

CHAPTER 5

1. It might look like this:
   ```
   $(nodes).each(
       function() {
       }
   );

   $.each(
       nodes,
       function() {
       }
   );
   ```

2. `return false;`

3. The items referenced by the selector are kept in the selection; items not referenced by the selector are discarded.

4. Keeps the current item in the selection; returning `false` removes the current item from the selection.

5. A value that evaluates to `true`. Returning `false` will remove an item from the array.

6. It replaces the value of the item passed to the callback function during that iteration.

7. −1 means that the value does not exist within the array; a return value of zero or greater means that the value exists within the array.

CHAPTER 6

1. `$('div').css('color');`

2. Specifying any color in the second argument, the code would look something like this:
   ```
   $('body').css('backgroundColor', 'yellow');
   ```

3.
   ```
   $('div').css({
       padding: '5px',
       margin: '5px',
       border: '1px solid grey'
   });
   ```

4. `outerWidth()`

5. `outerHeight(true)`

CHAPTER 7

1. In the context of an AJAX request, the only difference between GET and POST requests is that a GET request has a concrete limitation on the amount of data you can pass; the actual limit varies from browser to browser. A GET request can also be slightly more efficient.

2. A REST service implements more meaning in HTTP requests by providing additional methods that describe data manipulation, such as ADD or DELETE. In addition, a REST service may also be implemented to standardize server responses so that they utilize the proper HTTP error codes.

3. An optional second argument to the `$.get()` method allows you to pass data along with the request, either as a query string or as a JavaScript object literal.

4. You access the JSON object in the variable that you assign to the first argument of the callback function that you specify for the `$.getJSON()` method. This variable can have any name you like.

5. Accessing the contents of the `<response>` element looks something like this:

```
$.get(
    '/url/to/request.xml',
    function(xml)
    {
        alert($(xml).text());
    }
);
```

6. The `load()` method.

7. In the JavaScript, jQuery sets AJAX events globally via a call to the `$.ajaxSetup()` method, which takes a list of options that are formatted as a JavaScript object literal. The `before-Send` property specifies a callback function that is executed before every AJAX request. The `success` property specifies a callback function that is executed upon every successful AJAX request. The `error` property specifies a callback function that is invoked upon encountering an HTTP error. Finally, the `complete` callback function is executed when the request has completed, after the `success` or `error` callbacks have been executed, depending on whether the request was successful.

8. One method is by using jQuery's AJAX event methods like `ajaxStart()` and `ajaxSuccess()`; another is via jQuery's `$.ajax()` method.

9. Select the form elements you want to get the values of; then call the `serialize()` method.

10. You use the `type` property to set the request method to DELETE. You use the `contentType` property to set the MIME type of the request to signal to the server that the body of the request is a JSON object. Then you pass the JSON data to send in the body of the request within the `data` property. An example of creating this call using the `$.ajax()` method follows:

```
$.ajax({
    url : '/Server/Example',
    contentType : "application/json; charset=utf-8",
    type : 'DELETE',
```

```
            dataType : 'json',
            data : JSON.stringify({
                dataForTheServerHere : true
            }),
            success : function(json, status, request)
            {

            },
            error : function(request, status)
            {

            }
        });
```

CHAPTER 8

1. An integer value in milliseconds or the strings `'slow'`, `'normal'`, or `'fast'`.

2. It animates an element's `height` property when displaying an element.

3. The `fadeIn()`, `fadeOut()`, and `fadeToggle()` methods all animate an element's opacity to display or hide an element.

4. The `animate()` method.

5. The *linear* and *swing* easings are included in jQuery core.

CHAPTER 9

1. `$.fn.extend()` or `$.fn.prototype`.

2. `console.log($.fn);` Then examine the object in Firefox or Chrome.

3. Define my functions or objects inside the closure used to define my plugin.

4. They are defined in the keyword `this`.

5. It should attempt to return `this` (the selection in context), or jQuery, if possible.

6. It allows me to remove my own events explicitly, without touching other people's or other projects' events.

7. Answers may vary but include any valid code that meets the specified criteria.

CHAPTER 10

1. `scrollTop()` and `scrollLeft()`.

2. The top (or offset top) of the wanted element, the top (or offset top) of its container, and the current vertical scrollbar position (or `scrollTop`).

3. Any syntactically correct code implementing something similar to the following:

```
$('#myScroller').scrollTop(0);
```

4. Answers will vary but should describe calculating the element's scrollHeight and using an arbitrary value expected to be larger than the scrollHeight.

5. 0.

CHAPTER 11

1. Depending on the browser, you use the –webkit-user-drag CSS property with a value of element for older versions of Webkit-based browsers such as Safari and Chrome. You use the draggable HTML attribute, which is the official method sanctioned by the HTML5 specification and supported by all modern browsers. Or you can use the dragDrop() method on the element's DOM object, which enables drag and drop in IE5 through IE8.

2. The drag events in the order that they fire are dragstart, drag, and dragend.

3. The drop events in the order that they fire are dragenter, dragover, drop, and dragleave.

4. You look for event.originalEvent.dataTransfer.files within the drop event. Without using jQuery to attach the event listener, you look for event.dataTransfer.files within the drop event.

5. A base64-encoded data URI is assigned to the value of the src attribute of an <img /> element. The data URI can also be used with the CSS background and background-image properties.

6. The progress and load events can be attached to the upload property of an XMLHttpRequest object to monitor the upload progress of files.

7. The event.lengthComputable, event.loaded, and event.total properties.

8. First, you instantiate the FormData object; the instantiated object is stored in a variable. Then use the append() method on the instantiated object to create custom POST variables.

9. You attach a load event to the XMLHttpRequest object. This event is fired when the upload is successful.

CHAPTER 12

1. draggable()

2. Any syntactically correct program, which implements the following (or similar enough to the following):

```
draggable({
    helper : 'clone',
    opacity : 0.5
});
```

3. `droppable()`

4. Any syntactically correct program implementing something similar to this:

   ```
   droppable({
       hoverClass : 'theHoverClassYouUsed'
   });
   ```

5. You would use the accept option, and the value that you provide to the accept option would be a valid selector.

CHAPTER 13

1. The `sortable()` method.

2. A CSS class name that will be applied to the *placeholder*.

3. It creates blank space within a sortable list that represents a reservation for the item currently being dragged during a sort.

4. The `cursor` option.

5. It allows you to create a custom drag image for the element being dragged during a sort; this drag image is also known as the `helper`.

6. The `connectWith` option.

7. A selector, a selection, an element, or a callback function that returns an element or selection.

8. By providing a callback function to the `update` event, which contains logic that sends an AJAX request to a server-side script.

CHAPTER 14

1. The `start` option.

2. The `selecting` and `unselecting` options.

3. The added elements are accessed from the `ui.selecting` selector, and the removed elements are accessed from the `ui.unselecting` selector.

4. `div.ui-selectable-helper`

CHAPTER 15

1. The `active` option.

2. The `heightStyle` option with the values `auto`, `fill`, or `content`.

3. The `event` option with the value `mouseover`.

4. The `header` option with the value `h3`.

CHAPTER 16

1.   The `minDate` and `maxDate` options.

2.   The `yearRange` option. Example value: "1900:2020"

3.   The `changeMonth` and `changeYear` options.

4.   The `dateFormat` option.

5.   Yes. By providing an array of the Spanish translated weekdays to the `dayNames`, `dayNamesMin`, or `dayNamesShort` options.

6.   Use the `firstDay` option to provide the starting day of the week. Sunday is number 0 and Saturday is number 6. For example, to change the starting day to Tuesday, you would set `firstDay : 2`.

CHAPTER 17

1.   The modal option with positioning the `<div>` with class name `ui-widget-overlay`. It must be positioned to take up the entire window in front of the document's content but behind the opened dialog.

2.   Set the `autoOpen` option to `false`.

3.   By calling `dialog('open')`.

4.   By calling `dialog('close')`.

5.   By setting the `draggable` and `resizing` options to `false`.

6.   The `show` option with an animation preset such as `'explode'`.

CHAPTER 18

1.   The `active` tab with a value indicating the tab to display, offset from zero.

2.   The class names are `ui-tabs-active` and `ui-tabs-hover`.

3.   Add a new tab that references the content you want to load in the `href` attribute of the `<a>` element. The jQuery Tabs plugin takes care of the rest.

4.   The `show` and `hide` options.

CHAPTER 19

1.   No sorting occurs until you explicitly sort by a header unless you specify the `sortList` option, which specifies how default sorting should be handled.

2.   You would use the `sortMultiSortKey` option with the value `'ctrlKey'`.

3.   You use the `cssHeader`, `cssAsc`, and `cssDesc` options to specify custom class names.

CHAPTER 20

1. You must keep track of whether the slideshow has been interrupted to prevent the normal transition from occurring.

2. The `transitioning` property prevents multiple animations from occurring simultaneously. It ensures that only one animation happens at a time.

3. The number of items with the slideshow element with the class name `slide` is iterated, and controls are created for each of these items. The controls are given an id name that contains a reference to the collection and a reference to the slide. Finally, the slide's offset number is made the text of the control.

CHAPTER 21

1. `<audio>` and `<video>`

2. `<source>`

3. h.264, Ogg, and WebM

4. The `tracks` option. (Extra credit for specifying that it displays the text from HTML5 `<track>` elements.)

5. The `preload` attribute.

CHAPTER 22

1. `contenteditable`

2. `document.execCommand`

3. Any options that require a user interface prompt or data value when used with `document.execCommand`, such as `fontname` or `fontsize`.

4. Answers will vary but should describe a Selection object that contains a collection of Range objects, which, in turn, stores information about bounding nodes and positions within them.

5. `$(this).data()`

jQuery Selectors

The following table contains the selector syntax that you can use with jQuery's Selector API, which is implemented using the open source Sizzle engine.

SELECTOR	DESCRIPTION
SIMPLE SELECTORS	
The following selectors are the most basic, commonly used selectors.	
`#idName` `div#idName`	Selects a single element via the id name specified in the element's `id` attribute.
`div`	Selects one or more elements by the element name—for example, `form`, `div`, `input`, and so on.
`div.className` `.className`	Selects one or more elements via a class name present in the element's `class` attribute. Individual elements may also have multiple class names.
`*`	The universal or wildcard selector; selects all elements.
`div.body, div.sideColumn,` `h1.title`	Selects one or more elements by chaining multiple selectors together with commas.
HIERARCHY	
The following selectors are used based on hierarchical context.	
`div.outerContainer` `table.form`	Selects one or more elements based on an ancestral relationship.
`div#wrapper > h1.title`	Selects one or more elements based on a parent, child relationship.
`h3 + p`	Selects the sibling immediately following an element.
`h3 ~ p`	Selects any siblings immediately following an element.

CONTEXT FILTERS

The following selectors are applied based on the context elements that appear in the document.

`:root`	Selects the root element of the document; in an HTML document this will be the `<html>` element. In an XML document, it will be whatever name is given the root element.
`:first`	Selects the first element that occurs in the selection.
`:last`	Selects the last element that occurs in the selection.
`:not(selector)`	Reduces a selection by specifying what you want to exclude from a selection.
`:even`	Selects only elements falling within even numbering. jQuery calculates position, offset from zero. Item one would be considered number zero, item two would be considered number one, and so on; so `:even` matches numbers 0, 2, 4, and so on.
`:odd`	Selects only elements falling within odd numbering. jQuery calculates position offset from zero. Item one would be number 0, item two would be number 1; so `:odd` matches numbers 1, 3, 5, and so on.
`:eq(index)`	Selects a single element based on its offset in the selection counting from 9; for example, `:eq(0)` matches the first item in the selection, `:eq(1)` matches the second item in the selection, and so on.
`:gt(index)`	Selects all elements where each element's offset is greater than the number specified. Specifying `:gt(4)` selects elements with offset 5 or greater, where the count is offset from 0.
`:lt(index)`	Selects all elements where each element's offset is less than the number specified. For example, specifying `:lt(4)` would select element's with offset 0, 1, 2, and 3.
`:header`	Selects all elements that are headers, for example, `h1`, `h2`, `h3`, `h4`, `h5`, or `h6`.
`:animated`	Selects all elements that are currently animated.
`:lang("en")` `:lang("en-us")`	Selects all elements of the specified language, such as `<div id="en">` or `<div id="en-us">`.

`:target`	Selects the element based on the URI fragment, if a fragment exists. For example, if you have the URL: `http://www.example.com#idName` `:target` would select the element in the document with the id name idName.
`:contains(text)`	Selects elements based on whether the text specified is present in the element's content. For example, `:contents("Lorem Ipsum")` matches: `<p>Lorem Ipsum</p>` and any other element containing *Lorem Ipsum* anywhere in its text content.
`:empty`	Selects elements that have no children (including text nodes). For example, `:empty` matches `<div></div>`, `<a></a>`, or `<span></span>`.
`:has(selector)`	Selects elements that match the specified selector. For example, `input:has(':checked')` matches any element that has a check box or radio `<input>` with the attribute `checked="checked"`.
`:parent`	Selects an element's parent. Therefore, `div:parent` matches all parents that have `<div>` children.
VISIBILITY FILTERS	
The following selectors make selections based on whether an element is visible or invisible.	
`:hidden`	Selects all elements that are hidden or `<input>` elements that are of `type="hidden"`, depending on the context of the selection. The concept of *hidden* applies to either elements with CSS `visibility: hidden;` or `display: none;`.
`:visible`	Selects all elements that are visible—for example, they are not hidden with `visibility: hidden;` or `display: none;`.
ATTRIBUTE FILTERS	
The following selectors make selections based on attribute presence or strings contained within attribute values.	
`[attribute]`	Selects all elements where the specified attribute is present. For example, the selector `[href]` selects all elements in a document that have an `href` attribute.
`[attribute=value]`	Selects all elements where the attribute has an exact match for the specified value. For example, `[href="#"]` matches all `href="#"` attributes in the document (regardless of what element the attribute is attached to).

continues

(continued)

`[attribute!=value]`	Selects all elements where the attribute does not have the specified value. For example, given the selector `[src!="about:blank"]` all elements with a `src` attribute that does not contain the value `about:blank` will be matched.
`[attribute^=value]`	Selects all elements where the attribute's value begins with the specified string. One example might be the selector `[href^="https://"]`, which would match all `href` attributes that reference a secure HTTP connection.
`[attribute$=value]`	Selects all elements where the attribute's value ends with the specified string. For example, the selector: `[href$=".pdf"]` matches all `href` attributes that link to pdf documents (assuming there are no query string parameters or URL fragments).
`[attribute*=value]`	Selects all elements where the attribute's value contains the specified string anywhere within the value. If you were searching for `href` attributes that might have query string permanents or URL fragments, you could use the selector `[href*=".pdf"]` to find PDF documents where the string `".pdf"` might occur somewhere within the attribute's value.
`[attribute~=value]`	Selects all elements where the attribute's value contains the specified word. This is useful for situations like class names where there are multiple values separated by spaces. This selector is intended to match one space-separated value. Take, for example, this selector: `[class~="selected"]`; this selector would match the following attribute: `class="disabled selected bodyContainer"`.
`[href] [title] [class] [target]`	Selects all elements where the element has each attribute. In this example, any element that contains all four attributes, `href`, `title`, `class`, and `target`, would be matched. Chaining attribute selectors works with any type of attribute selector mentioned here, so you can test if an attribute is present, if another attribute contains a particular value, and if another attribute begins with a value, and so on.

CHILD FILTERS

The following selectors make selections based on the position of children elements relative to their siblings and their parents.

`:nth-child(offset)`
`:nth-child(even)`
`:nth-child(odd)`
`:nth-child(equation)`
	Selects all elements where the element is a certain off-set counting from zero, or elements that are in even or odd positions (also determined by counting offset from zero). You can also provide a mathematical expression that will be evaluated to determine which elements are matches.

`:nth-last-child(offset)`
`:nth-last-child(even)`
`:nth-last-child(odd)`
`:nth-last-child(equation)`
	Similar to nth-child, but elements are selected based on their offset position counting backward from the last child of the parent.

`:first-child`	Selects all elements where the element is the first child of its parent.
`:last-child`	Selects all elements where the element is a last child of its parent.
`:only-child`	Selects all elements where the element is the only child of its parent.
`:first-of-type`	Matches the first element of the specified type, wherever it may occur within the context of the selection. If the selection is within the context of the entire document and the selection `div:first-of-type` is used, the first occurrence of `<div>` in relation to its parent element, wherever it may be, is matched.
`:last-of-type`	Matches the last element of the specified type within the context of that element's parent and siblings.

`:nth-of-type(offset)`
`:nth-of-type(even)`
`:nth-of-type(odd)`
`:nth-of-type(equation)`
	Selects elements in relation to their parent and siblings counting offset from zero, the first element of the same type.

`:nth-last-of-type(offset)`
`:nth-last-of-type(even)`
`:nth-last-of-type(odd)`
`:nth-last-of-type(equation)`
	Selects elements in relation to their parent and siblings of the same type, counting from the last element of that type.

continues

(continued)

`:only-of-type`	Selects elements of the specified type that have no siblings of the same type.

FORMS ELEMENTS

The following selectors can be used to select various form input elements.

`:input`	Selects all `<input>`, `<select>`, `<textarea>`, and `<button>` elements.
`:text`	Selects all `<input>` elements where `type="text"`.
`:password`	Selects all `<input>` elements where `type="password"`.
`:radio`	Selects all `<input>` elements where `type="radio"`.
`:checkbox`	Selects all `<input>` elements where `type="checkbox"`.
`:submit`	Selects all `<input>` elements where `type="submit"`.
`:image`	Selects all `<input>` elements where `type="image"`
`:reset`	Selects all `<input>` elements where `type="reset"`.
`:button`	Selects all `<button>` elements and `<input>` elements where `type="button"`.
`:file`	Selects all `<input>` elements where `type="file"`.
`:hidden`	Selects all elements that are hidden using `visibility: hidden;` or `display: none;` or `<input>` elements where `type="hidden"`.

FORM STATE SELECTORS

The following selectors are used to select form elements based on their state.

`:enabled`	Selects all elements that are enabled.
`:disabled`	Selects all elements that are disabled with the attribute `disabled="disabled"`.
`:checked`	Selects all elements that are checked, for example, check box and radio inputs, where the attribute `checked="checked"` is present.
`:selected`	Selects all elements that are selected, for example, options in a select drop-down where the attribute `selected="selected"` is present.
`:focus`	Selects whatever element currently has focus.

Note that selectors marked with an asterisk (*) are jQuery extensions to the standard Selector API, which utilizes the built-in browser Selector API `document.querySelector()` and `document.querySelectorAll()` and may not perform as well as natively supported selectors. Wherever possible, jQuery's selector engine, Sizzle, transforms these extended features into natively supported selectors at run time, so in many cases the performance impact is negligible, but there is still the additional overhead of parsing the selector and transforming the selector into one that the native selector API understands.

Having said that, to get the best possible performance out of jQuery, it is best to first perform a selection using a highly efficient selector (the most efficient selector is an id selector), and then filter the selection from within the context of that selection using filtering methods such as `find()`, `filter()`, and so on. This is good practice not just for jQuery extensions to the selector API but for any selection. Id selectors are the most efficient selectors because ids are meant to be unique (you should never assign the same id name to multiple elements) and, when done correctly, id selections result in only one possible match within a document.

C

Selecting, Traversing, and Filtering

METHOD/PROPERTY	DESCRIPTION	RETURN VALUE
SELECTING		
`$(selector)`	Makes a selection from the document.	jQuery
`jQuery(selector)`	An alternative name for the preceding dollar sign method.	jQuery
`length`	The number of selected elements.	Number
`get()`	Returns all selected elements as an array, rather than as a jQuery object.	Array
`get(index)`	Returns a single element from the selection; the `index` argument is the element's position in the selection, offset from zero.	Element
`index(subject)`	Searches the selection for the specified element and returns that element's position in the selection offset from zero.	Number
TRAVERSING AND FILTERING		
`add(selector)`	Adds one or more elements to the selection by virtue of an additional selector.	jQuery
`add(elements)`	Adds one or more elements to the selection by virtue of one or more element object references.	jQuery

continues

(continued)

add(*html*)	Adds one or more elements to the selection by virtue of an HTML fragment string that is parsed and converted into DOM element object references.	jQuery
add(*selection*)	Adds one or more elements to the selection by virtue of an existing selection reference.	jQuery
add(*selector, context*)	Adds one or more elements to the selection by virtue of a selector. A context provides the relative point in the document where the selector should be carried out.	jQuery
addBack(*[selector]*)	Adds a set or selection of elements to the current selection; this can optionally be filtered by a selection.	jQuery
andSelf()	Adds the previous selection to the current selection. *Deprecated in jQuery 1.8.*	jQuery
children(*[selector]*)	Makes a selection within the context of the matched elements' children. The `selector` argument is optional; to select all children of all the selected elements, simply omit the `selector` argument.	jQuery
closest(*selector[, context]*)	Similar to the `parents()` method, except this method begins with the element itself, rather than its parent, and either matches the element itself or travels up the DOM to find the right ancestor. If the optional *context* argument is provided, it provides a DOM element within which a matching element can be found.	jQuery
closest(*selection*)	The `closest()` method may also use an existing selection reference.	jQuery
closest(*element*)	The `closest()` method may also use a DOM element object reference directly.	jQuery
contents()	Gets children elements of each matched element, including text and comment nodes, which are normally excluded from jQuery method operations.	jQuery

`each(function(key, value))`	Executes a callback function for every element in a selection. As with most jQuery callback functions, `this` refers to the current element within the callback function, and the callback function is provided the argument list: `offset, element`. Returning `true` from the callback function provides a result similar to a `continue` statement. Returning `false` provides a result similar to a `break` statement.	jQuery

`$(Array).each(`
    `function(key, value)`
`)`
`$.each(Array, function)`
`$.each(Object, function)`
	Executes a callback function for every element in an array.
	
	As with most jQuery callback functions, `this` refers to the current item within the callback function, and the callback function is provided the argument list: `key, value`.
	
	Returning `true` from the callback function provides a result similar to a `continue` statement. Returning `false` provides a result similar to a `break` statement.
		Object

`end()`	Ceases any filtering that took place and returns the current selection to its previous state.	jQuery
`eq(index)`	Reduces a selection to a single element, where `index` is the number representing the element's position in the selection offset from zero.	jQuery
`eq(-index)`	Reduces a selection to a single element, where index is a negative number representing the element's position from the last element in the selection.	jQuery
`filter(selector)`	Removes all elements that do not match the specified selector.	jQuery

continues

(continued)

`filter(function(index))`	The `filter()` method may alternatively accept a function as its first argument, which works identically to the jQuery `$.each()` method. The function is executed for each item selected. The function must return a boolean value, where `true` indicates that the element should remain in the result set, and `false` indicates that the element should be removed from the result set. As with most jQuery callback functions, `this` refers to the current element within the callback function, and the callback function is provided the argument list: `offset, element`.	jQuery
`filter(element)`	Filters the selection based on the JavaScript node passed in the `element` argument, elements that match the node remain in the selection; elements that do not match the node are dropped from the selection. One or more DOM element object references can be passed in.	jQuery
`filter(selection)`	Filters the selection based on the jQuery object passed in the `selection` object (the result of a jQuery selection) argument. If elements in the selection match the jQuery object, they remain in the selection; if not, those elements are removed from the selection.	jQuery
`find(selector)`	Makes a selection within the context of matched elements' descendants.	jQuery
`find(selection)`	Finds element descendants using an existing selection object to match element descendants against.	jQuery
`find(element)`	Finds element descendants using an existing DOM element object to match descendants against.	jQuery
`first()`	Removes all elements from the selection, except the first.	jQuery

`has(selector)`	Reduces a previous selection based on whether the selection matches the selector provided in the selector argument.	jQuery
`has(element)`	Reduces a selection based on whether the selection matches the DOM element provided in the element argument.	jQuery
`is(selector)`	Returns `true` if one or more elements match the condition specified in the selector. For example: `$('input').is(':checked')`	Boolean
`is(function(index))`	Returns `true` if the callback function returns `true` for one or more elements. Returns `false` if the callback function returns `false` for every item passed to the callback function. As with most jQuery callback functions, `this` refers to the current element within the callback function, and the callback function is provided the argument list: `offset, element`.	Boolean
`is(selection)`	Returns `true` if the selection matches one or more items present using an existing jQuery selection.	Boolean
`is(elements)`	Returns `true` if the selection matches any of the DOM element object reference(s) provided.	Boolean
`last()`	Removes all elements from the selection, except the last.	jQuery

continues

(continued)

`map(function(index, element))`	Like `each()`, each matched element is passed into a callback function. The return value of each callback function is used to build a new jQuery object, creating a mapping to a new array of element references. Returning the item or array of items includes it in the new array. Returning `null` or `undefined` results in no item added to the new array. As with most jQuery callback functions, `this` refers to the current element within the callback function, and the callback function is provided the argument list: `offset, element`. Returning `true` from the callback function provides a result similar to a `continue` statement. Returning `false` provides a result similar to a `break` statement.	jQuery

`$(Array).map(`
    `function(key, value)`
`)`
	Like `each()`, each array item is passed into a callback function. The return value of each callback function is used to build a new array, creating a mapping to a new array. Returning the item or array of items includes it in the new array. Returning `null` or `undefined` results in no item added to the new array.
	
	As with most jQuery callback functions, `this` refers to the current item within the callback function, and the callback function is provided the argument list: `key, value`.
	
	Returning `true` from the callback function provides a result similar to a `continue` statement. Returning `false` provides a result similar to a `break` statement.
		Array

`next([selector])`	Selects the next sibling element; the `selector` argument is optional.	jQuery
`nextAll([selector])`	Selects all subsequent sibling elements; the `selector` argument is optional.	jQuery

nextUntil([selector] [, filter])	Selects all subsequent sibling elements up to but not including the element matched by the selector.	jQuery
	If the optional filter argument is specified, the matched elements are further filtered against the selector you provide to the filter argument.	
nextUntil([element] [, filter])	Selects all subsequent sibling elements up to but not including the element object reference provided.	jQuery
	If the optional filter argument is specified, the matched elements are further filtered against the selector you provide to the filter argument.	
not(selector)	Removes elements from the selection that match the specified selector.	jQuery
not(elements)	Removes elements from the selection that match the specified DOM element object reference(s).	jQuery
not(function(index))	Removes elements from the selection based on the whether the callback function returns true or false. If the callback function returns true, the element current is excluded from the selection; if the callback function returns false, it is included in the selection.	jQuery
	As with most jQuery callback functions, this refers to the current element within the callback function, and the callback function is provided the argument list: offset, element.	
not(selection)	Removes elements from the selection based on whether the elements in the selection match elements in the provided selection object.	jQuery
offsetParent()	Gets the closest ancestor element that is positioned with position absolute, relative or fixed.	jQuery
parent([selector])	Selects all immediate parent elements; the selector argument is optional.	jQuery

continues

(continued)

`parents([selector])`	Selects all ancestor elements; the `selector` argument is optional.	jQuery
`parentsUntil([selector] [, filter])`	Matches parent or ancestor elements up to but not including the element that matches the selector. If the optional `filter` argument is specified, the matched elements are further filtered via the selector that you provide in the `filter` argument.	jQuery
`parentsUntil([element] [, filter])`	Matches parent or ancestor elements up to but not including the element that matches the provided DOM element object reference. If the optional `filter` argument is specified, the matched elements are further filtered via the selector that you provide in the `filter` argument.	jQuery
`prev([selector])`	Selects the previous sibling element; the `selector` argument is optional.	jQuery
`prevAll([selector])`	Selects all preceding sibling elements; the `selector` argument is optional.	jQuery
`prevUntil([selector] [, filter])`	Selects all preceding sibling elements up to but not including the element matched by the selector. If the optional `filter` argument is specified, the matched elements are further filtered against the selector you provide to the `filter` argument.	jQuery
`prevUntil([element] [, filter])`	Selects all preceding sibling elements up to but not including the element object reference provided. If the optional `filter` argument is specified, the matched elements are further filtered against the selector you provide to the `filter` argument.	jQuery
`siblings([selector])`	Selects all sibling elements; the `selector` argument is optional.	jQuery
`slice(start [, end])`	Selects a subset of the selection, where each `index` is a number representing the element's position in the selection offset from zero.	jQuery

Events

The following table contains all the event methods supported by jQuery as listed in jQuery's official documentation at www.jquery.com.

All the event methods return the jQuery object.

METHOD	DESCRIPTION
PAGE LOAD	
ready(*function*) function(event)	Attaches a function that is executed when the DOM is completely loaded; that is, all markup, CSS, and JavaScript are loaded, but not necessarily images.
EVENT HANDLING	
bind(***events, function***) string events function(event)	Attaches a function that is executed when the event occurs. Multiple events can be specified in the event argument; if you specify multiple events, each event must be separated with a single space. The on() method is preferred over bind() in jQuery 1.7 or later.
bind(***events [, data]*** ***[, function]***) string events object data function(event)	The bind() method accepts an optional data argument. The data argument is an object that allows you to pass custom data to the event, which is available in the event handler, in the event argument as event.data. The on() method is preferred over bind() in jQuery 1.7 or later.

continues

(continued)

`bind(events[, data]` `[, preventBubble])`
 	
`string events`
 	
`object data`
 	
`boolean preventBubble`
	When calling the `bind()` method with the *preventBubble* argument, an event handler is automatically created, which prevents bubbling, as well as the default action.
	
	`bind(eventName, false);`
	or
	`bind(eventName);`
	is equivalent to creating the following:
	
	`bind(`
	`    eventName,`
	`    function(event)`
	`    {`
	`        event.preventDefault();`
	`        event.stopPropagation();`
	`    }`
	`);`
	
	The `on()` method is preferred over `bind()` in jQuery 1.7 or later.

`bind(events)`
 	
`object events`
	Allows multiple events to be bound by passing an object where the property is the name of the event and the value is the callback function. For example:
	
	`bind({`
	`    click : function(event)`
	`    {`
	
	`    },`
	`    mouseover : function(event)`
	`    {`
	
	`    },`
	`    mouseout : function(event)`
	`    {`
	
	`    }`
	`})`
	The `on()` method is preferred over `bind()` in jQuery 1.7 or later.

`delegate(selector,` `events, function)`
 	
`string selector`
 	
`string events`
 	
`function(event)`
	Provides the same functionality as the `on()` method in jQuery 1.4.2 and later. The `on()` method is preferred over `delegate()` in jQuery 1.7 or later.

delegate(*selector, events, data, function*) string selector string events object data function(event)	Provides the same functionality as the on() method in jQuery 1.4.2 and later. The on() method is preferred over delegate() in jQuery 1.7 or later.
delegate(*selector, events*) string selector string events	Provides the same functionality as the on() method in jQuery 1.4.2 and later. The on() method is preferred over delegate() in jQuery 1.7 or later.
off(*events[, selector] [, function]*) string events string selector function(event)	Removes an event handler.
off(*events[, selector]*) string events string selector	Removes an event handler.
off()	Removes all event handlers.
on(*events[, selector] [, data], function*) string events string selector object data function(event)	Attaches an event handler for the selected elements; the elements referenced in the selection must exist at the time on() is called. If a selector is provided in the second argument, descendant element(s) referenced by the selector will be the element(s) receiving the event(s), rather than the original selection. Elements referenced by the selector may or may not exist when on() is called. If new descendant elements matching the selector are created after the attachment of the event(s), those element(s) automatically receive the event(s) when they exist. Custom data can be passed in the data argument;, if custom data is provided, it will be available in the event handler, in the event argument, as event.data.

continues

(continued)

on(*events* **[,** *selector]* **[,** *data]***)**
 	
`string events`
 	
`string selector`
 	
`object data`
	Attaches an event handler for the selected elements; the elements referenced in the selection must exist at the time `on()` is called.
	
	If a selector is provided in the second argument, descendant element(s) referenced by the selector will be the element(s) receiving the event(s), rather than the original selection. Elements referenced by the selector may or may not exist when `on()` is called. If new descendant elements matching the selector are created after the attachment of the event(s), those element(s) automatically receive the event(s) when they exist.
	
	Custom data can be passed in the data argument; if custom data is provided it will be available in the event handler, in the `event` argument, as `event.data`.

one(*events,* *function***)**
 	
`string events`
 	
`function(event)`
	Attaches a function to be fired for the specified event. The function is executed only once. Subsequent events will not execute the specified function.

one(*events* **[,** *data]***,** *function***)**
 	
`string events`
 	
`object data`
 	
`function(event)`
	The `one()` method accepts an optional data argument. The data argument is an object that is passed to the `event` object of the attached function as `event.data`.

one(*events* **[,** *selector]* **[,** *data]***,** *function***)**
 	
`string events`
 	
`string selector`
 	
`object data`
 	
`function(event)`
	Attaches an event handler that is always executed just once per element and event.
	
	If a selector is provided in the second argument, descendant element(s) referenced by the selector will be the element(s) receiving the event(s), rather than the original selection. Elements referenced by the selector may or may not exist when `one()` is called. If new descendant elements matching the selector are created after the attachment of the event(s), those element(s) automatically receive the event(s) when they exist.
	
	Custom data can be passed in the data argument; if custom data is provided, it will be available in the event handler, in the `event` argument, as `event.data`.

trigger(*events***)** `string events`	Triggers the specified event on matched elements.

trigger(*events,*** ***parameters***) string events array *parameters*	The trigger() method accepts an optional data argument. The data argument is an object that is passed to event object functions being triggered as event.data.
triggerHandler(*events***)** string events	Triggers the specified event on matched elements while canceling the browser's default action for any given event.
triggerHandler(*events,*** ***parameters***)** string events array parameters	The triggerHandler() method accepts an optional data argument. The data argument is an object that is passed to event object functions being triggered as event.data.
unbind()	Removes all events from the selected element(s).
unbind(*events***)** string events	Removes the specified event from the selected element(s).
unbind(*events, function***)** string events function(event)	Removes by event and event handler.
unbind(*events, false***)** string events	Removes the specified events.
undelegate()	Provides the same functionality as the off() method in jQuery 1.4.2 and later. The off() method is preferred over undelegate() in jQuery 1.7 or later.
undelegate(*selector,*** ***events***)** string selector string events	Provides the same functionality as the off() method in jQuery 1.4.2 and later. The off() method is preferred over undelegate() in jQuery 1.7 or later.
undelegate(*selector,*** ***events, function***)** string selector string events function(event)	Provides the same functionality as the off() method in jQuery 1.4.2 and later. The off() method is preferred over undelegate() in jQuery 1.7 or later.

continues

(continued)

undelegate(*namespace*)	Provides the same functionality as the off() method in jQuery 1.4.2 and later. The off() method is preferred over undelegate() in jQuery 1.7 or later.

EVENT HELPERS

hover(*mouseoverFunction, mouseoutFunction*) mouseoverFunction(event) mouseoutFunction(event)	Attaches a function for mouseover and a function for mouseout to the same element.
toggle(*function1, function2[, function3] . . .*) function1(event) function2(event) function3(event) . . .	Upon first click, the first function is executed; upon second click, the second function is executed; upon third click, the third function is executed, and so on. A minimum of two functions must be specified; an unlimited number of total functions may be specified. The toggle() method was deprecated in jQuery 1.8 and removed altogether in version 1.9.

EVENT METHODS

blur()	Triggers the blur event of each selected element.
blur(*[data,]function*)	Attaches a function to the blur event of each selected element. Optionally, custom data can be passed if the data argument is specified, which is available in turn as event.data.
change()	Triggers the change event of each selected element.
change(*[data,]function*)	Attaches a function to the change event of each selected element. Optionally, custom data can be passed if the data argument is specified, which is available in turn as event.data.
click()	Triggers the click event of each selected element.
click(*[data,]function*)	Attaches a function to the click event of each selected element. Optionally, custom data can be passed if the data argument is specified, which is available in turn as event.data.
dblclick()	Triggers the dblclick (double-click) event of each selected element.
dblclick(*[data,] function*)	Attaches a function to the dblclick event of each selected element. Optionally, custom data can be passed if the data argument is specified, which is available in turn as event.data.

`error()`	Triggers the `error` event of each selected element.
`error([data, ]function)`	Attaches a function to the `error` event of each selected element. Optionally, custom data can be passed if the data argument is specified, which is available in turn as `event.data`.
`focus()`	Triggers the `focus` event of each selected element.
`focus([data, ]function)`	Attaches a function to the `focus` event of each selected element. Optionally, custom data can be passed if the data argument is specified, which is available in turn as `event.data`.
`focusin()`	Triggers the `focusin` event of each selected element.
`focusin([data, ]function)`	Attaches an event handler to the `focusin` event of each selected element. Optionally, custom data can be passed if the data argument is specified, which is available in turn as `event.data`.
`focusout()`	Triggers the `focusout` event of each selected element.
`focusout([data, ]function)`	Attaches an event handler to the `focusout` event of each selected element. Optionally, custom data can be passed if the data argument is specified, which is available in turn as `event.data`.
`keydown()`	With no arguments, the `keydown` event of each selected element is triggered.
`keydown([data, ]function)`	With only a callback function, the callback function is executed upon the `keydown` event of each selected element. Optionally, custom data can be passed if the data argument is specified, which is available in turn as `event.data`.
`keypress()`	Triggers the `keypress` event of each selected element.
`keypress([data, ]function)`	Attaches a keypress event handler to each selected element. Optionally, custom data can be passed if the data argument is specified, which is available in turn as `event.data`.
`keyup()`	Triggers the `keyup` event of each selected element.
`keyup([data, ]function)`	Attaches a function to the `keyup` event of each selected element. Optionally, custom data can be passed if the data argument is specified, which is available in turn as `event.data`.

continues

(continued)

`load(function)`
 	
`load([data, ]function)`
	Attaches a function to the `load` event of each selected element. Optionally, custom data can be passed if the data argument is specified, which is available in turn as `event.data`.

`mousedown()`
 	
`mousedown([data, ]`
`function)`
	Triggers the `mousedown` event of each selected element.
	
	Attaches a function to the `mousedown` event of each selected element. Optionally, custom data can be passed if the data argument is specified, which is available in turn as `event.data`.

`mouseenter()`
 	
`mouseenter([data, ]`
`function)`
	Triggers the `mouseenter` event of each selected element.
	
	Attaches a function to the `mouseenter` event of each selected element. Optionally, custom data can be passed if the data argument is specified, which is available in turn as `event.data`.

`mouseleave()`
 	
`mouseleave([data, ]`
`function)`
	Triggers the `mouseleave` event of each selected element.
	
	Attaches a function to the `mouseleave` event of each selected element. Optionally, custom data can be passed if the data argument is specified, which is available in turn as `event.data`.

`mousemove()`
 	
`mousemove([data, ]`
`function)`
	Triggers the `mousemove` event of each selected element.
	
	Attaches a function to the `mousemove` event of each selected element. Optionally, custom data can be passed if the data argument is specified, which is available in turn as `event.data`.

`mouseout()`
 	
`mouseout([data, ]`
`function)`
	Triggers the `mouseout` event of each selected element.
	
	Attaches a function to the `mouseout` event of each selected element. Optionally, custom data can be passed if the data argument is specified, which is available in turn as `event.data`.

`mouseover()`
 	
`mouseover([data, ]`
`function)`
	Triggers the `mouseover` event of each selected element.
	
	Attaches a function to the `mouseover` event of each selected element. Optionally, custom data can be passed if the data argument is specified, which is available in turn as `event.data`.

`mouseup()`
 	
`mouseup([data, ]`
`function)`
	Triggers the `mouseup` event of each selected element.
	
	Attaches a function to the `mouseup` event of each selected element. Optionally, custom data can be passed if the data argument is specified, which is available in turn as `event.data`.

`resize()`	Triggers the `resize` event of each selected element.
`resize([data, ]function)`	Attaches a function to the `resize` event of each selected element. Optionally, custom data can be passed if the data argument is specified, which is available in turn as `event.data`.
`scroll()`	Triggers the `scroll` event of each selected element.
`scroll([data, ]function)`	Attaches a function to the `scroll` event of each selected element. Optionally, custom data can be passed if the data argument is specified, which is available in turn as `event.data`.
`select()`	Triggers the `select` event of each selected element.
`select([data, ]function)`	Attaches a function to the `select` event of each selected element. Optionally, custom data can be passed if the data argument is specified, which is available in turn as `event.data`.
`submit()`	Triggers the `submit` event of each selected element.
`submit([data, ]function)`	Attaches a function to the `submit` event of each selected element. Optionally, custom data can be passed if the data argument is specified, which is available in turn as `event.data`.
`unload()`	Triggers the `unload` event of each selected element.
`unload([data, ]function)`	Attaches a function to the `unload` event of each selected element. Optionally, custom data can be passed if the data argument is specified, which is available in turn as `event.data`.

EVENT OBJECT

The following table documents event methods and properties supported both by jQuery's event object provided to jQuery events and by regular JavaScript events without jQuery. You can access the regular JavaScript event object from any jQuery event object by using the `event.originalEvent` object. If you find a method or property listed below missing from the jQuery event object, it is likely to be found within the `event.originalEvent` object.

METHOD/PROPERTY	DESCRIPTION
`event.altKey` `boolean`	Indicates whether the Option key (Mac) or Alt key (Windows) is being pressed.
`event.bubbles` `boolean`	Indicates whether the event bubbles up through the DOM.

continues

(continued)

`event.cancelable` `boolean`	Indicates whether the event can be canceled.
`event.clientX, event.clientY` `integer`	Provides x, y coordinates, indicating where the mouse cursor is located relative to the window.
`event.createEvent()`	Creates a new event, which must be initialized by calling its `init()` method.
`event.ctrlKey` `boolean`	Indicates whether the Control key is being pressed (Mac and Windows).
`event.currentTarget` `object`	The DOM element that is presently the target of the event. Usually this refers to the same element as the `this` keyword.
`event.data`	An object passed to the function acting as an event handler. See the data argument specified for various methods under "Event Handling" in the previous table.
`event.defaultPrevented` `boolean`	Indicates whether the `event.preventDefault()` method has been called.
`event.detail` `integer`	A numeric property that indicates how many times a mouse has been clicked in the same location. Applies to the *click*, *dblclick*, *mousedown*, and *mouseup* events.
`event.delegateTarget`	A reference to the element the event handler is ultimately attached to.

`event.eventPhase`
`integer`
	A numeric property that indicates the phase of the event execution process.
	`event.NONE = 0`
	`event.CAPTURING_PHASE = 1`
	`event.AT_TARGET = 2`
	`event.BUBBLING_PHASE = 3`

`event.initKeyEvent()`
`type`
`bubbles`
`cancelable`
`view`
`ctrlKey`
`altKey`
`shiftKey`
`metaKey`
`keyCode`
`charCode`
	The `initKeyEvent()` method is used to initialize the value of an event created using `document.createEvent`.

`event.initMouseEvent()`
`type`
`canBubble`
`cancelable`
`view`
`detail`
`screenX`
`screenY`
`clientX`
`clientY`
`ctrlKey`
`altKey`
`shiftKey`
`metaKey`
`button`
`relatedTarget`
	The `initMouseEvent()` method initializes the value of a mouse event when it's been created using `document.createEvent`.

`event.initUIEvent()`
`type`
`canBubble`
`cancelable`
`view`
`detail`
	The `initUIEvent()` method initializes a UI event when it has been created, for example, through `document.createEvent`.

`event.isChar` `boolean`	Indicates whether the event produced a `keyCode`.

continues

(continued)

`event.isDefaultPrevented()` `returns boolean`	Determines whether `preventDefault()` was ever called on the `event` object.

`event.isImmediatePropaga-`
`tionStopped()`
`returns boolean`
	Determines whether `stopImmediatePropagation()` was ever called on the `event` object.

`event.isPropagationStopped()` `returns boolean`	Determines whether `stopPropagation()` was ever called on the `event` object.
`event.keyCode` `integer`	The numeric offset representing which key on the keyboard is currently being pressed.
`event.layerX, event.layerY` `integer`	Coordinates of the event relative to the current layer.
`event.metaKey` `boolean`	Whether the Command key (Mac) or Windows key (Windows) is pressed.
`event.namespace`	The namespace specified when the event was triggered.
`event.originalEvent`	A copy of the browser's original event object, before jQuery's modifications were made to it.
`event.originalTarget`	The original target of the event before any retargeting.
`event.pageX, event.pageY` `integer`	The mouse coordinates relative to the document.
`event.preventDefault()`	Prevents the browser's default action for a given event, for example, submitting a form or navigating to the `href` attribute of an `<a>` element.
`event.relatedTarget`	Finds another element involved in the event, if applicable.
`event.result`	The last value returned by an event handler that was triggered by this event, unless the value was `undefined`.
`event.screenX, event.screenY` `integer`	Returns the horizontal coordinates of the event within the context of the entire screen.
`event.shiftKey` `boolean`	Whether the Shift key (Mac and Windows) is pressed.
`event` `.stopImmediatePropagation()`	Prevents other attached listeners for the same event from being called.

`event.stopPropagation()`	Stops the propagation of an event from a child or descendent element to its parent or ancestor elements, which prevents the same event from running on the later ancestor elements.
`event.target`	The DOM element that triggered the event.
`event.timeStamp`	The difference in milliseconds between the time the browser created the event and the UNIX epoch (January 1st, 1970, 12:00:00 AM).
`event.type`	Provides the type of event, for example, `click`, `mouseover`, `keyup`, and so on.
`event.view`	Returns the Window object the event happened in. In non-browsers, this may be referred to as the AbstractView.
`event.which`	Returns the numeric `keyCode` of the key pressed, or the character code, or `charCode`, for an alphanumeric key that was pressed.

Manipulating Content, Attributes, and Custom Data

METHOD/PROPERTY	DESCRIPTION	RETURN VALUE
ATTRIBUTES		
`attr(name)`	Returns the attribute value for the specified attribute from the first element present in a selection. If no element is present, the method returns `undefined`.	String, Undefined

`attr(object)`	Allows you to set attributes via the specification of key, value pairs. For example:
	
	`attr({`
	`    id : 'idName',`
	`    href : '/example.html',`
	`    title : 'Tooltip text.'`
	`});`
		jQuery

`attr(key, value)`	Allows you to specify an attribute by providing the name of the attribute in the `key` argument and its value in the `value` argument.	jQuery
`attr(key, function)`	Sets an attribute's value depending on the return value of the callback function that you specify. The callback function is executed within the context of each selected element, where each selected element can be accessed within the function via `this`.	jQuery

continues

(continued)

`removeAttr(name)`	Removes the specified attribute from the element(s).	jQuery
CLASS NAMES		
`addClass(className)`	Adds the specified class name to each selected element. Elements can have one or more class names.	jQuery
`addClass(function())`	Adds one or more space separated class names returned from a callback function.	jQuery
`hasClass(className)`	Returns `true` if the specified class name is present on at least one of the selected elements.	Boolean
`removeClass([className])`	Removes the specified class name from each selected element. If multiple class names are provided, each is separated by a single space.	jQuery
`removeClass(function())`	Removes the specified class name from each selected element by executing a callback function to determine whether the class should be removed. The function should return one or more class names to be removed. If multiple class names are removed, they should be separated by a single space.	jQuery
`toggleClass(className[, switch])`	Adds the specified class name if it is not present, and removes the specified class name if it is present. If the switch argument is provided, it explicitly tells `toggleClass()` whether the class name should be added or removed. `true` adds the class, and `false` removes it.	jQuery
`toggleClass([switch])`	*switch* explicitly tells `toggleClass()` whether the class name should be added or removed. `true` adds the class, and `false` removes it.	jQuery
`toggleClass(function()[, switch])`	If a function is provided, it returns one or more space separated class names to be toggled. If the `switch` argument is provided, it explicitly tells `toggleClass()` whether the class name should be added or removed. `true` adds the class, and `false` removes it.	jQuery

HTML		
`html()`	Returns the HTML contents, or `innerHTML`, of the first element of the selection. This method does not work on XML documents but does work on XHTML documents.	String
`html(htmlString)`	Sets the HTML contents of every selected element.	jQuery
`html(function())`	If a function is provided, it returns the HTML content to set for each selected element. As with most jQuery callback functions, `this` refers to the current element within the callback function, and the callback function is provided the argument list: `offset, oldHTML`.	jQuery
TEXT		
`text()`	Returns the text content of each selected element.	String
`text(value)`	Sets the text content of each selected element. HTML source code will not be rendered.	jQuery
`text(function())`	If a function is provided, it returns the text content to set for each selected element. As with most jQuery callback functions, `this` refers to the current element within the callback function, and the callback function is provided the argument list: `offset, oldText`.	jQuery
VALUE		
`val()`	Returns the contents of the `value` attribute for the first element of the selection. For `<select>` elements with attribute `multiple="multiple"`, an array of selected values is returned.	String, Number, Array
`val(value)`	When providing a single value, this method sets the contents of the `value` attribute for each selected element.	jQuery

continues

(continued)

`val(valuesArray)`	When providing multiple values, this method checks or selects radio buttons, check boxes, or select options that match the set of values.	jQuery
`val(function())`	If a function is provided, it returns the content to set as the value for each selected element. As with most jQuery callback functions, `this` refers to the current element within the callback function, and the callback function is provided the argument list: `offset, oldValue`.	jQuery

CUSTOM DATA ATTRIBUTES

`data()`	Returns all custom data attributes set on the selected element(s) as a simple object.	Object
`data(object)`	Sets custom data on all selected elements, where the key portion is used to name the data, and the corresponding value sets the value of that attribute.	jQuery
`data(key)`	Returns data stored for an element by the specified name for the selected elements.	Mixed
`data(key, value)`	Stores data with the specified name and value for each selected element(s).	jQuery
`$.data(element, key, value)`	Associates data by the specified name with the specified value with the specified DOM element object reference.	Object
`removeData([name])`	Removes the data by the specified name from the selected elements. If no name is specified then all data is removed.	jQuery
`removeData([list])`	Removes data by specifying an array of data names to remove, or a space-separated list of data names to remove. If no list is provided, all data is removed.	jQuery
`$.removeData(element [, name])`	Removes data from the specified DOM element object reference going by the specified name.	jQuery

More Content Manipulation

METHOD/PROPERTY	DESCRIPTION	RETURN VALUE
HTML		
after(*content* [, *content*])	Inserts the specified content after each selected element. One or more content items can be specified for inclusion and will be inserted sequentially. Content items can be an HTML snippet, a DOM element object reference, or a jQuery object.	jQuery
after(*function ()*)	Executes a function that returns content to be inserted after the selected element(s). The content returned by the function can be an HTML string, a DOM element object reference, an Array of DOM element object references, or a jQuery object.	jQuery
	As with most jQuery callback functions, this refers to the current element within the callback function, and the callback function is provided with the argument list: *offset*, *html*.	
append(*content* [, *content*])	Appends the specified content after any existing content for each selected element. One or more content items can be specified for inclusion and will be inserted sequentially. Content items can be an HTML snippet, a DOM element object reference, or a jQuery object.	jQuery

continues

(continued)

`append(function())`	Executes a function that returns content to be appended. The content returned by the function can be an HTML string, a DOM element object reference, an Array of DOM element object references, or a jQuery object. As with most jQuery callback functions, `this` refers to the current element within the callback function, and the callback function is provided with the argument list: `offset, html`.	jQuery
`appendTo(selector)`	Appends all the selected elements to the elements specified by the `selector` argument.	jQuery
`before(content [, content])`	Inserts the specified content before each selected element. One or more content items can be specified for inclusion and will be inserted sequentially. Content items can be an HTML snippet, a DOM element object reference, or a jQuery object.	jQuery
`before(function())`	Executes a function that returns content to be inserted before the selected element(s). The content returned by the function can be an HTML string, a DOM element object reference, an Array of DOM element object references, or a jQuery object. As with most jQuery callback functions, `this` refers to the current element within the callback function, and the callback function is provided with the argument list: `offset, html`.	jQuery
`clone([withDataAndEvents])`	Clones the selected elements; returns the jQuery object including the clones you created. If the optional `withDataAndEvents` argument is `true`, then events and data are cloned as well.	jQuery

`clone(`
 	
   `[withDataAndEvents],`
 	
`[deepWithDataAndEvents]`
 	
`)`
	Clones the selected elements; returns the jQuery object including the clones you created. If the optional `withDataAndEvents` argument is `true`, then events and data are cloned as well.
	
	If the optional second argument is provided, the `deepWithDataAndEvents` argument controls whether children elements also have their events and data cloned. By default, this argument matches whatever is provided for the first value. The first value's default value is `false`.
		jQuery

`detach([selector])`	Removes the selected elements from the DOM. This method keeps jQuery data for the associated elements around, which can be useful when it is desired to reinsert the elements in the DOM at a later time.	jQuery
`empty()`	Removes all child nodes from the selected elements.	jQuery
`insertAfter(selector)`	Inserts the selected elements after the elements specified by the `selector` argument.	jQuery
`insertBefore(selector)`	Inserts the selected elements before the selectors specified by the `selector` argument.	jQuery
`prepend(content [,` `content])`	Prepends the specified content before any existing content for each selected element. One or more content items can be specified for inclusion and will be inserted sequentially. Content items can be an HTML snippet, a DOM element object reference, or a jQuery object.	jQuery
`prepend(function())`	Executes a function that returns content to be prepended. The content returned by the function can be an HTML string, a DOM element object reference, an Array of DOM element object references, or a jQuery object. As with most jQuery callback functions, `this` refers to the current element within the callback function, and the callback function is provided with the argument list: `offset`, `html`.	jQuery

continues

(continued)

`prependTo(selector)`	Prepends all the selected elements to the elements specified by the `selector` argument.	jQuery
`remove([selector])`	Removes the selected elements from the DOM. An optional selector can be provided to further filter the selection.	jQuery
`replaceAll(selector)`	Replaces the elements specified in the `selector` argument with the selected elements.	jQuery
`replaceWith(content)`	Replaces each selected element(s) with the specified HTML or DOM element(s). This method returns the jQuery object, which includes the element that was replaced.	jQuery
`replaceWith(function())`	A callback function that returns content that will replace the selected elements. The content returned by the callback function can be an HTML snippet, a DOM element reference, an Array of DOM element references, or a jQuery object. As with most jQuery callback functions, `this` refers to the current element within the callback function, and the callback function is provided with the argument list: `offset`, `html`.	jQuery
`unwrap()`	Removes the selected element(s) parent element.	jQuery
`wrap(wrappingElement)`	Wraps each selected element with the specified element. The element can be a selector referencing another element, an HTML snippet, a DOM element object reference, or a jQuery object. Note the distinction that the element must be capable of wrapping another element—for example, you couldn't use an `<img/>` element to wrap another element.	jQuery

`wrap(function())`	A callback function that returns content that wraps the selected elements. The content returned by the callback function can be an HTML snippet, a DOM element reference, or a jQuery object.	jQuery
	As with most jQuery callback functions, `this` refers to the current element within the callback function, and the callback function is provided with the argument list: `offset`.	
	Note the distinction that the element must be capable of wrapping another element—for example, you couldn't use an `<img/>` element to wrap another element.	
`wrapAll(wrappingElement)`	Wraps all the selected elements. The element used to wrap each element can be a selector referencing an element, an HTML snippet, a DOM element object reference, or a jQuery object.	jQuery
	Note the distinction that the element must be capable of wrapping another element—for example, you couldn't use an `<img/>` element to wrap another element.	
`wrapInner(wrappingElement)`	Wraps the inner contents of each selected element. The element used to wrap each element can be a selector referencing an element, an HTML snippet, a DOM element object reference, or a jQuery object.	jQuery
	Note the distinction that the element must be capable of wrapping another element—for example, you couldn't use an `<img/>` element to wrap another element.	
`wrapInner(function())`	A callback function that returns content that wraps the selected elements. The content returned by the callback function can be an HTML snippet, a DOM element reference, or a jQuery object.	jQuery
	As with most jQuery callback functions, `this` refers to the current element within the callback function, and the callback function is provided with the argument list: `offset`.	
	Note the distinction that the element must be capable of wrapping another element—for example, you couldn't use an `<img/>` element to wrap another element.	

G

AJAX Methods

METHOD	DESCRIPTION	RETURN VALUE
AJAX REQUESTS		
`$.ajax([options])` `$.ajax(url[, options])`	Allows you to pass an object literal specifying various options in key, value pairs. For the complete list of options, see the "AJAX Options" table. This method is used by jQuery's other AJAX methods to make AJAX requests. You should use this method only if you require finer-grained control over an AJAX request than is possible with jQuery's other methods.	jQuery XMLHttpRequest
`ajaxComplete(function())`	Attaches a function to be executed when an AJAX request is completed.	jQuery
`ajaxError(function())`	Attaches a function that is executed when an error occurs.	jQuery

`$.ajaxPrefilter(`
`    [dataTypes],`
`    function()`
`)`
	The dataTypes argument is optional and should contain one or more space-separated `dataTypes`.
	
	The callback function argument sets default values for future AJAX requests. Its argument list is `options, originalOptions, jqXHR`.
		Undefined

continues

(continued)

`ajaxSend(function())`	Attaches a function to be executed before an AJAX request is sent.	jQuery
`$.ajaxSetup(options)`	Configures the default options for AJAX requests. The `option` argument is passed as an object literal, in key, value pairs. See the "AJAX Options" table.	jQuery
`ajaxStart(function())`	Attaches a function to be executed when the first AJAX request begins (if not already active).	jQuery
`ajaxStop(function())`	Attaches a function to be executed when all AJAX requests have completed.	jQuery
`ajaxSuccess(function())`	Attaches a function to be executed when an AJAX request has completed successfully.	jQuery
`$.ajaxTransport()`	Creates the AJAX transport object used internally to issue AJAX requests. You should use this method only if you require finer-grained control over an AJAX request than is possible with jQuery's other methods.	undefined

`$.get(`
    `url`
    `[, data]`
    `[, onSuccessFunction]`
    `[, dataType]`
`)`
	Initiates and sends to the server an HTTP GET request.	jQuery
		XMLHttpRequest

`$.getJSON(`
    `url`
    `[, data]`
    `[, function]`
`)`
	Initiates and sends an HTTP GET request, in which the response will be JSON-formatted data.	jQuery
		XMLHttpRequest

`$.getScript(url,` `[function])`	Loads and executes a new JavaScript file via the GET method asynchronously.	jQuery XMLHttpRequest

`load(`
 	
    `url`
 	
    `[, data]`
 	
    `[,`
`onCompleteFunction]`
 	
`)`
	Loads HTML from a remote file and inserts the HTML inside of the selected elements. The `data` argument (optional) is specified as an object literal, defining the data you want to pass to the server in key, value pairs. The `function` argument (also optional) is the callback method that handles the data when it is returned from the server.	jQuery

`$.param(object[,` `traditional])`	Creates a serialized representation of an object or an array, which can then be used in a URL or AJAX request. The optional `traditional` argument indicates whether serialization should be a traditional shallow serialization.	String

`$.post(`
 	
    `url`
 	
    `[, data]`
 	
    `[, onSuccessFunction]`
 	
    `[, dataType]`
 	
`)`
	Initiates and sends to the server an HTTP POST request.	jQuery
		XMLHttpRequest

`serialize()`	Serializes a set of input elements into a string of data.	String
`serializeArray()`	Serializes all forms and form elements into a JSON structure.	Array

AJAX OPTIONS		
Option	Description	Type
`accepts`	The content type sent in the request header to the server that tells the server what kind of response the browser can accept in its response. The default value depends on `dataType`.	Object

continues

(continued)

`async`	By default, jQuery sends all AJAX requests asynchronously. To send a synchronous request, set this property to `false`. Default value: `true`	Boolean
`beforeSend`	A callback function that is executed before the AJAX request is sent, which can be used to modify the jQuery XMLHttpRequest object, as well as to set custom headers. The arguments passed to this function are *jqXHR* and *settings*. Returning `false` from this function cancels the request.	Function
`cache`	If the value of the cache setting is set to `false`, the browser is forced to not cache the request. The default value is `true`, `false` for *dataType* `'script'` and `'jsonp'`.	Boolean
`complete`	A function that is executed when the AJAX request has completed after the `success` or `error` callbacks have been executed. This callback is passed two arguments: *jqXHR* and *status*. The *status* argument will be any of the following strings: `'success'`, `'notmodified'`, `'error'`, `'timeout'`, `'abort'`, and `'parsererror'`.	Function
`contents`	An object of string, regular expression pairs that determine how jQuery parses the server's response, given the specified `dataType`.	Object

`contentType`	The MIME type of data being sent to the server.
	
	If a `contentType` is explicitly set, then it is always sent to the server.
	
	The character set is defined as UTF-8 by the W3C specification. Using a different character set will not force the browser to change the encoding sent back to the server.
	
	Default value:
	
	`application/x-www-form-`
	`urlencoded; charset=UTF-8`
		String

`context`	The object provided to this option is used to set the context of all AJAX-related callbacks. Default value: an object used to call `$.ajaxSettings()` merged with the settings passed to `$.ajax()`.	Object

`converters`	An object that specified `dataType` to `dataType` conversions. Each data type references a handler capable of processing that response.
	
	Default value:
	
	`{`
	    `"* text" :`
	      `window.String,`
	    `"text html" : true,`
	    `"text json" :`
	      `$.parseJSON`
	    `"text xml" : $.parseXML`
	`}`
		Object

`crossDomain`	Used to force or prevent a cross-domain request. The default value is `false` for same-domain requests and `true` for cross-domain requests.	Boolean

continues

(continued)

data	The data to be sent to the server with a GET or POST request. Can be specified as either a string of ampersand-delimited arguments or as an object literal in key, value pairs. If the value is an Array, jQuery serializes based on the value of the `traditional` option. Automatic processing of data can be modified with the `processData` option.	Object, String, Array

dataFilter	A callback function executed to handle the raw response data of `XMLHttpRequest`. This is a prefiltering function used to sanitize the response. You should return the sanitized data from this callback function. The function has two arguments: *responseText* and *dataType*.
	
	`function (responseText,`
	`    dataType)`
	`{`
	`    // do something`
	`    // return the sanitized`
	`    // data`
	`    return data;`
	`}`
		Function

dataType	The type of data that you expect to receive in your response from the server. jQuery attempts to automatically infer the `dataType` based on the MIME type of the data returned by the server. See the "Data Types" table at the end of this appendix for a list of allowed data types. Default value: *Educated Guess*	String

error	A callback function that is executed if the AJAX request fails. The callback function has the following three arguments: *jqXHR*, *errorType*, and *errorThrown*. The *errorType* argument can contain any of the following values: null, 'timeout', 'error', 'abort', and 'parsererror'. The *errorThrown* argument contains the HTTP status if an HTTP error were thrown, such as "Not Found" or "Internal Server Error".	Function
global	Whether to trigger the global AJAX event handlers for the request, for example, the handlers set by the various AJAX Event methods. Default value: true	Boolean
headers	An object of additional headers to include in the AJAX request. Headers should be specified in key, value pairs where the key is the name of the header, and the value is the header's value. Default value: { }	Object
ifModified	Allows the request to be successful only if the request has been modified since the last request. This is determined by checking the time specified in the Last-Modified HTTP header. Default value: false (ignore the Last-Modified header).	Boolean

continues

(continued)

`isLocal`	Allows the current environment to be recognized as a local environment. The following protocols are currently recognized by jQuery as being local: `file`, `*-extension`, and `widget`. If this option requires modification, jQuery recommends doing so once in the `$.ajaxSetup()` method.	Boolean
`jsonp`	Overrides the callback function name in a jsonp request. This value will be used instead of `'callback'` in the `'callback=?'` part of the query string in the URL for a GET or POST request. So `{jsonp:'onJsonPLoad'}` would result in `onJsonPLoad=?` sent on to the server as part of the URL.	String
`jsonpCallback`	Used to specify a callback function for a JSONP request. The name specified here will be used instead of the randomly generated name created by jQuery for this purpose by default.	String, Function
`mimeType`	A MIME type you want to use to override the default XHR MIME type.	String
`password`	A password to use in response to an HTTP access authentication request.	String
`processData`	By default, data passed in to the `data` option will be processed and transformed into a query string, fitting to the default content-type `application/x-www-form-urlencoded; charset=URF-8`. If you want to send DOMDocuments or other nonprocessed data, set this option to `false`. Default value: `true`	Boolean

`scriptCharset`	For GET requests where the `dataType` is set to `script` or `jsonp`. Forces the request to be interpreted with the specified charset. This is needed only if the charset of local content is different from the remote content being loaded.	String

`statusCode`	An object of numeric HTTP codes and corresponding callback functions that should be called when that status code is encountered.
	
	`$.ajax({`
	  `statusCode : {`
	    `404 : function()`
	    `{`
	       `alert('URL not found.');`
	    `}`
	  `}`
	`});`
		Object

`success`	A function that is executed upon success of the AJAX request.	Function
`timeout`	Sets the amount of time in milliseconds (ms) to allow before a timeout occurs.	Number
`traditional`	Determines how parameters for GET or POST requests will be serialized. If set to `true`, a shallow traditional serialization is used.	Boolean
`type`	The type of HTTP request, one of GET or POST. You can also specify PUT or DELETE. However, those methods are not supported by all browsers.	String
`url`	The URL to request.	String

continues

(continued)

`username`	A username to specify in response to an HTTP authentication required request.	String
`xhr`	Callback for creating the `XMLHttpRequest` object. Defaults to the ActiveXObject when available (IE), the `XMLHttpRequest` otherwise. Override to provide your own implementation for `XMLHttpRequest` or enhancements to the factory.	Function
`xhrFields`	An object of key, value pairs that should be set on the native XMLHttpRequest object.	Object

DATA TYPES

Type	Description
`xml`	Returns an XML document that can be processed with jQuery.
`html`	Returns HTML as plain text. `<script>` elements are evaluated upon insertion into the DOM.
`script`	Evaluates the response as JavaScript and returns the script as plain text to the callback function. Disables caching unless the `cache` option is used. Note: This type of request will make POST requests into GET requests.
`json`	Evaluates the response as JSON and returns a JavaScript object.
`jsonp`	Loads in a JSON block using JSONP. Adds an extra `?callback=?` to the end of your URL to specify the callback.
`text`	Returns the server response as a plain text string.
multiple, space-separated values	Converts what jQuery received in the Content-Type header to what you require. For example, to text a text response and treat it like XML, the value `"text xml"` should be used. In addition, it is possible to send a JSONP request, receive the response as text, and then interpret the response as XML, which would be done using the value `"jsonp text xml"`.

H

CSS

METHOD	DESCRIPTION	RETURN VALUE
CSS		
css(*property*)	Returns the specified CSS property value from the first selected element—for example: `$('div').css('background-color')`	String

css(*properties*)	Sets the specified CSS properties. The `properties` argument is defined as an object literal of key, value pairs—for example:
	
	`$('div').css({`
	`  backgroundColor : 'red',`
	`  marginLeft : '10px'`
	`});`
		jQuery

css(*property, value*)	Sets the specified CSS property value—for example: `$('div').css('background', 'red');`	jQuery
CLASS NAMES		
addClass()	Adds the specified class name(s) to the selected element(s). Multiple class names are separated by spaces.	jQuery
hasClass(*className*)	Determines whether the selected element(s) have the specified class name. This method does not support multiple class names at the time of this writing.	Boolean

continues

(continued)

`removeClass(className)`	Removes the class name(s) from the selected element(s). Multiple class names are separated by spaces.	jQuery
`toggleClass(className)`	Adds or removes one or more class names from the selected elements. Multiple class names are separated by spaces.	jQuery
POSITIONING		

`offset()`	Returns the offset position of the first selected element relative to the viewport—for example:
	
	`var offset = $('div').offset();`
	
	`alert('Left: ' + offset.left);`
	
	`alert('Top: ' + offset.top);`
		Object

`position()`	Gets the coordinates of the element relative to the offset parent—for example:
	
	`var position = $('div').position();`
	
	`alert('Left: ' + position.left);`
	
	`alert('Top: ' + position.top);`
		Object

HEIGHT AND WIDTH		
`height()`	Returns the pixel height (CSS height, excluding borders and padding) of the first selected element.	Integer
`height(value)`	Sets the height (CSS height) of the first selected element. If no unit of measurement is provided, px (pixels) is used.	jQuery
`innerHeight()`	Gets the inner height of the element, including padding, but not the border.	Integer
`innerWidth()`	Gets the inner width of the element, including padding, but not the border.	Integer
`width()`	Returns the pixel width (CSS width, excluding borders and padding) of the first selected element.	Integer
`width(value)`	Sets the width (CSS width) of the first selected element. If no unit of measurement is provided, px (pixels) is used.	jQuery

`outerHeight(`*`options`*`)`	Returns the `offsetHeight` (includes the pixel height, borders, and padding) of the first selected element. The `options` argument is a JavaScript object literal of options. See the "Options" section for more information.	Integer
`outerWidth(`*`options`*`)`	Returns the `offsetWidth` (includes the pixel width, borders, and padding) of the first selected element. The `options` argument is a JavaScript object literal of options. See the "Options" section for more information.	Integer

SCROLLING

`scrollLeft()`	Gets the horizontal position of the scrollbar for the first selected element.	Integer
`scrollLeft(`*`position`*`)`	Sets the horizontal position of the scrollbar for each selected element.	jQuery
`scrollTop()`	Gets the vertical position of the scrollbar for the first selected element.	Integer
`scrollTop(`*`position`*`)`	Sets the vertical position of the scrollbar for each selected element.	jQuery

JQUERY

`$.cssHooks`	Used to provide an API for jQuery to describe how a particular CSS property should be handled internally, by jQuery.

```
$.cssHooks['WebkitBorderRadius'] = {
    get : function(element, computed, extra)
    {
        // Code for getting the CSS property
    },
    set : function(element, value)
    {
        // Code for setting the CSS property
    }
};
```

Utilities

METHOD/PROPERTY	DESCRIPTION	RETURN VALUE
`$.clearQueue([queue])`	Removes from the queue all items that have not yet been executed.	jQuery

`$.contains(`
   `container,`
   `contained`
`)`
	Determines whether a DOM element is a descendant of another DOM element.	Boolean

`$.dequeue(element`
   `[, queue]`
`)`
	Executes the next function in the queue for the matched element.	Undefined

`$.extend(`
   `target`
   `[, object1]`
   `[, . . .]`
`)`
	Extends the target object with one or more specified objects.	Object

`$.extend(`
   `[deep,]`
   `target`
   `[, object1]`
   `[, . . .]`
`)`
	Extends the target object with one or more specified objects. If the optional *deep* argument is true, then the objects are merged recursively (aka deep copy).	Object

`$.fn.extend(object)`	Merges an object into jQuery itself. This is used, for example, to create jQuery plugins.	Object

continues

(continued)

`$.globalEval(code)`	Executes the specified JavaScript code in the global scope.	Undefined

`$.grep(`
　`array,`
　`function()`
　`[, invert]`
`)`
	Filters items out of an array using a callback function. If the optional `invert` argument is `false` or not provided, `grep` returns an array of items where the callback function has returned `true` for each of those items. If the `invert` argument is `true`, it returns an array where the callback function for each item has returned `false`.	Array

`$.inArray(value, array`
　`[, fromIndex]`
`)`
	Determines whether the specified value appears in the specified array, optionally starting at the offset provided to the `fromIndex` argument (counting from zero).	Array

`$.isArray(array)`	Determines if the item provided is an array.	Boolean
`$.isEmptyObject(object)`	Determines whether the item provided is an empty object.	Boolean
`$.isFunction(object)`	Determines whether the item provided is a function.	Boolean
`$.isNumeric(value)`	Determines whether the item provided is numeric.	Boolean
`$.isPlainObject(object)`	Determines whether the item provided is a plain object.	Boolean
`$.isWindow(object)`	Determines whether the item provided is a Window.	Boolean
`$.isXMLDoc(node)`	Determines whether the item provided is an XML document.	Boolean
`$.makeArray(object)`	Turns anything into an array (instead of an Object or a StaticNodeList).	Array
`$.merge(array1,` `array2)`	Merges two arrays into one.	Array
`$.noop()`	An empty function, use this function reference if you want a function that does nothing.	Undefined

`$.now()`	Returns a number representing the current time. The number returned is a shorthand for: `(new Date).getTime()`	Number
`$.parseHTML(html)`	Parses an HTML string into an array of DOM nodes.	Array
`$.parseJSON(json)`	Parses a JSON string and returns the resulting JavaScript object.	Object
`$.parseXML(xml)`	Parses an XML string into an XML document.	XMLDocument

`$.proxy(`
   `function(),`
   `context`
   `[, arguments]`
`)`
	Takes a function and returns a new one with the provided context. `this` becomes what you provide to `context`.
	
	If the `arguments` argument is specified, those arguments will be sent on to the function.
		Function

`$.proxy(`
   `context,`
   `functionName`
   `[, arguments]`
`)`
	Takes a function and returns a new one with the provided context. `this` becomes what you provide to `context`.
	
	`functionName` is a string referencing the function you want to change the context of.
	
	If the `arguments` argument is specified, those arguments will be sent on to the function.
		Function

`$.queue(element` `[, queue])`	Shows the queue of functions to be executed on the element.	Array
`$.support()`	Returns an object containing properties that describe the browser's features or bugs for jQuery's internal use.	Object
`$.trim(string)`	Removes white space (newline characters, spaces, tabs, and carriage returns) from the beginning and end of a string.	String
`$.type(object)`	Determines the internal JavaScript class of an object.	String
`$.unique(array)`	Removes duplicate values from the specified array.	Array

Draggable and Droppable

DRAGGABLE AND DROPPABLE METHODS		
METHOD	**DESCRIPTION**	**RETURNS**
draggable(*options*)	Makes the selected element(s) draggable. Options can be specified by passing an object literal as the first argument using key, value pairs. For a complete list of options, see the "Draggable Options" table later in this appendix.	jQuery
draggable('destroy')	Completely removes draggable functionality from the selected element(s).	jQuery
draggable('disable')	Disables draggable functionality on the selected element(s).	jQuery
draggable('enable')	Enables draggable functionality on the selected element(s).	jQuery
draggable('option')	Returns an object literal containing key, value pairs representing the value of each currently set option.	Object
draggable('option', *option*)	Returns the currently set value of the provided option name.	Mixed
draggable('option', *option*, *value*)	Sets the value of provided *option* to *value*.	jQuery
draggable('widget')	Returns a jQuery object containing the draggable element.	jQuery

continues

(continued)

`droppable(options)`	Makes the selected element(s) droppable. Options can be specified by passing an object literal as the first argument using key, value pairs. For a complete list of options, see the "Droppable Options" section later in this appendix.	Dropset
`droppable('destroy')`	Completely removes droppable functionality from the selected element(s).	jQuery
`droppable('disable')`	Disables droppable functionality on the selected element(s).	jQuery
`droppable('enable')`	Enables droppable functionality on the selected element(s).	jQuery
`droppable('option')`	Returns an object literal containing key, value pairs representing the value of each currently set option.	Object
`droppable('option', option)`	Returns the currently set value of the provided option name.	Mixed
`droppable('option', option, value)`	Sets the value of the provided *option* to *value*.	jQuery
`droppable('widget')`	Returns a jQuery object containing the droppable element.	jQuery

DRAGGABLE OPTIONS

OPTION	DESCRIPTION	TYPE
`addClasses`	If set to `false`, this option prevents the class *ui-draggable* from being added to the draggable element. Default value: `true`	Boolean
`appendTo`	For a draggable with a `helper` option specified, the matched element passed to the `appendTo` option is used as the helper's container. If not specified, the helper is appended to the same container as the draggable. Default value: `"parent"`	jQuery, Element, Selector, String
`axis`	Contains dragging to either the *x* or *y* axis. Default value: `false`	String, Boolean

`cancel`	Prevents dragging, if you start dragging within elements matching the selector. Default value: `"input, textarea, button, select, option"` Default value: `false`	Selector
`connectToSortable`	Allows the draggable element to be dropped on the sortable elements specified in the provided selector. Default value: `false`	Selector, Boolean
`containment`	Contains dragging within the bounds of the specified element or selection. If a string is provided, the possible values are `"window"`, `"document"`, or `"parent"`. If an array is provided, the values represent the four coordinates of the containing box in the form of `[x1, y1, x2, y2]`. Default value: `false`	Element, Selector, String, Array, Boolean
`cursor`	The CSS `cursor` to be used during the operation. Any value suitable for use with the CSS `cursor` property may be provided. Default value: `"auto"`	String
`cursorAt`	Moves the dragging element/helper, so the cursor always appears to drag from the same position. Coordinates can be given as an object literal using the keys: `top`, `left`, `right`, `bottom`. Default value: `false`	Object, Boolean
`delay`	Time in milliseconds (ms) to delay the start of a drag. This helps prevent unwanted dragging from occurring when clicking an element. Default value: `0`	Integer
`disabled`	Disables the draggable if set to `true`. Default value: `false`	Boolean
`distance`	Tolerance in pixels for when dragging should start. Prevents dragging from taking place until the mouse cursor has reached the pixel distance from the point the drag began. Default value: `1`	Integer

continues

(continued)

`grid`	Snaps the dragging element or helper to a grid. The value is provided in the form of an array `[x, y]`. Default value: `false`	Array, Boolean
`handle`	Restricts the drag start to the specified element. This lets you make a large element draggable, but only when a smaller element within it is used as the "handle." Default value: `false`	Element, Selector
`helper`	Allows for a `helper` element to be used for dragging display. The `clone` option produces a ghosting effect. Possible values are `original` and `clone`. The default value is `original`. If you supply a function, it must return a valid DOM node. Default value: `"original"`	String, Function
`iframeFix`	Prevents an `<iframe>` from capturing mouse events. When set to `true`, all `<iframe>` elements are covered with a transparent overlay while dragging is taking place. If a selector is provided, only the `<iframe>` elements referenced by the selector are covered with a transparent overlay. Default value: `false`	Boolean, Selector
`opacity`	The CSS `opacity` for the element being dragged, specified as a float between 0 and 1. Default value: `false`	Float, Boolean
`refreshPositions`	By default, the positions of all droppable elements are cached and saved for reference for the best possible performance. Setting this option to `true` disables this caching, and the positions of droppable elements are recalculated in real time as the mouse moves. Default value: `false`	Boolean

revert	If set to `true`, the element returns to its start position when dragging stops.	Boolean, String, Function
	Also accepts the strings `valid` and `invalid`. If set to `invalid`, revert occurs only if the draggable has not been dropped on a droppable. If set to `valid`, it's the other way around.	
	If a function is provided, the function determines whether the element should be returned to its starting position. If you use a function, the function should return a boolean value.	
	Default value: `false`	
revertDuration	The duration of the `revert` animation provided in milliseconds. This option is ignored if the `revert` option is `false`.	Integer
	Default value: `500`	
scope	This option is used to group sets of draggable and droppable items. Used with the `accept` option on a droppable element, the scope option.	String
	Default value: `"default"`	
scroll	If set to `true`, the draggable's container auto-scrolls while dragging.	Boolean
	Default value: `true`	
scrollSensitivity	Distance in pixels from the edge of the viewport after which the viewport should scroll. Distance is relative to the pointer, not the draggable.	Integer
	Default value: `20`	
scrollSpeed	The speed at which the window should scroll when the mouse pointer gets within the `scrollSensitivity` distance.	Integer
	Default value: `20`	
snap	If set to a selector or to `true` (same as selector `.ui-draggable`), the new draggable snaps to the edges of the selected elements when coming to an edge of the element.	Boolean, Selector
	Default value: `false`	

continues

(continued)

snapMode	If set, the dragged element snaps only to the outer edges or to the inner edges of the element. Possible values are inner, outer, and both. Default value: "both"	String
snapTolerance	The distance in pixels from the snapping elements before the snapping should occur. Default value: 20	Integer
stack	Used for window managers or window manger-like applications. This feature controls the z-index of draggable elements that match the provided selector. This feature ensures that the draggable element the user clicks on is always on top. Default value: false	Selector, Boolean
zIndex	The z-index value for the helper element, while it is being dragged. Default value: false	Integer
DRAGGABLE EVENTS		
create		function(event, ui)
drag	A function that is executed while the element is being dragged.	function(event, ui)
start	A function that is executed when the element begins a drag.	function(event, ui)
stop	A function that is executed when the element's drag ends.	function(event, ui)

DRAGGABLE UI OBJECT OPTIONS

The callback functions specified for various draggable options specify a ui object in the second argument. Following are the properties exposed in the ui object.

OPTION	DESCRIPTION	TYPE
ui.options	Options used to initialize the draggable element.	Object
ui.helper	The jQuery object representing the helper being dragged.	Object

`ui.position`	The current position of the `helper` as an object literal relative to the offset element.	Object {top, left}
`ui.absolutePosition`	The current absolute position of the `helper` relative to the page.	Object {top, left}

DROPPABLE OPTIONS		
OPTION	**DESCRIPTION**	**TYPE**
accept	If a function is provided, the function is executed each time a draggable is dropped on a droppable. This lets you filter which elements can be dropped. The function should return `true` if the dragged element should be accepted and `false` if it should not. If a selector is provided, draggables that match the specified selector will be accepted by the droppable. Default value: `"*"`	function(draggable) Selector
activeClass	A class name that is added to the droppable element while a draggable element is being dragged. Default value: `false`	String Boolean
addClasses	If the value provided is set to `false`, this feature prevents the `ui-droppable` class name from being added to droppable elements. Default value: `true`	Boolean
Disabled	Disables the droppable element if the value is set to `true`. Default value: `false`	Boolean
greedy	If `true`, this property prevents event propagation on nested droppables. Default value: `false`	Boolean
hoverClass	A class name that is added to the droppable element while a draggable element is being dragged over the droppable element. Default value: `false`	String, Boolean

continues

(continued)

`scope`	Used to group draggable and droppable elements into sets, with the accept option. Draggables and droppables can interact only with other draggables and droppables of the same scope. Default value: `"default"`	String
`tolerance`	Specifies which method to use for determining whether a draggable element is over a droppable element. Possible values are `fit`, `intersect`, `pointer`, or `touch`. Default value: `"intersect"`	String
DROPPABLE EVENTS		
`activate`	A function that is executed any time an acceptable draggable element begins a drag.	function(event, ui)
`create`	A function that is executed when a droppable is created.	function(event, ui)
`deactivate`	A function that is executed any time an acceptable draggable element's drag ends.	function(event, ui)
`Drop`	A function that is executed when an accepted draggable element is dropped on a droppable element. ("On" is defined by the `tolerance` option.) Within the function, `this` refers to the droppable element, and `ui.draggable` refers to the draggable element.	function(event, ui)
`Out`	A function that is executed when an acceptable draggable element leaves a droppable element. (":eave" is defined by the `tolerance` option.)	function(event, ui)
`Over`	A function that is executed when an acceptable draggable element is dragged over a droppable element. ("Over" is defined by the `tolerance` option.)	function(event, ui)

DROPPABLE UI OBJECT OPTIONS

The callback functions specified for various droppable options specify a `ui` object in the second argument. Following are the properties exposed by the `ui` object.

OPTION	DESCRIPTION	TYPE
`ui.options`	The options used to initialize the droppable element.	Object
`ui.position`	The current position of the draggable `helper`.	Object {top, left}
`ui.absolutePosition`	The current absolute position of the draggable `helper`.	Object {top, left}
`ui.draggable`	The current draggable element.	Object
`ui.helper`	The current draggable `helper`.	Object

Sortable

SORTABLE METHODS		
METHOD	**DESCRIPTION**	**RETURN VALUE**
sortable(*options*)	Makes the selected element(s) sortable. Options can be specified by passing an object literal as the first argument using key, value pairs. For a complete list of options, see the "Sortable Options" section later in this appendix.	jQuery
sortable('cancel')	Cancels a change in the state of a sortable and reverts it back to what it was prior to sorting.	jQuery
sortable('destroy')	Completely removes sortable functionality from the selected element(s).	jQuery
sortable('disable')	Disables sortable functionality on the selected element(s).	jQuery
sortable('enable')	Enables sortable functionality on the selected element(s).	jQuery
sortable('option', *optionName*)	Returns the value of the specified option.	Mixed
sortable('option')	Returns an object containing all values of all options.	Object
sortable('option', *optionName*, *optionValue*)	Sets the specified option to the specified value.	jQuery

continues

(continued)

`sortable('option', object)`	Sets the specified options to the specified values by providing an object representing all of the options you'd like to set.	jQuery
`sortable('refresh')`	Refreshes the sortable items.	jQuery
`sortable ('refreshPositions')`	Refreshes the cached positions of sortable items.	jQuery
`sortable ('serialize', options)`	Returns a string of serialized IDs for each sortable item, which can then be used in an AJAX request or input form. For a complete list of options, see the "Serialize Options" section later in this appendix.	String

`sortable('toArray', options)`	Serializes all the sortable items' element `id` properties into an array. An object of options can be provided in the second argument; the only option that can be customized is changing which attribute is used.
	
	 `{`
	    `attribute : 'data-custom'`
	`}`
		Array

`sortable('widget')`	Returns a jQuery object that contains the sortable element.	jQuery

SORTABLE OPTIONS

OPTION	DESCRIPTION	TYPE
`appendTo`	Defaults to the parent; defines where the helper that moves with the mouse is being appended to during the drag (for example, to resolve overlap/zIndex issues). Default value: `'parent'`	jQuery Element Selector String
`axis`	If specified, the items can be dragged only along either the X- or Y-axis. Only allows the values `'x'` or `'y'`. Default value: `false`	String Boolean
`cancel`	Prevents sorting from the beginning on elements that match the selector. Default selector: `"input, textarea, button, select, option"`	Selector

connectWith	A selector that references other sortable elements you'd like to connect a sortable with.	Selector
		Boolean
	Default value: `false`	
containment	Constrains the dragging of sortable elements within the bounds of the specified or selected element. If using a string, the possible values are `'parent'`, `'document'`, and `'window'`.	Element
		Selector
		String
		Boolean
	Default value: `false`	
cursor	Specifies the cursor that should be shown while sortable elements are being dragged. The string provided should be a value suitable for the CSS `cursor` property.	String
	Default value: `'auto'`	
cursorAt	Specifies coordinates for the cursor that should be shown while sortable elements are being dragged.	Object
	Default value: `false`	
delay	Defines a delay time in milliseconds (ms), which helps to prevent unwanted drags.	Integer
	Default value: `0`	
disabled	Whether or not the sortable is disabled.	Boolean
	Default value: `false`	
distance	A tolerance in pixels, for where the threshold sorting should take place. If this option is specified, sorting won't take place until the mouse cursor is dragged beyond the specified distance.	Integer
	Default value: `1`	
dropOnEmpty	If set to `true`, this option allows a sortable item to be dropped from a linked selectable.	Boolean
	Default value: `true`	
forceHelperSize	If the value provided is `true`, this option forces the helper element to have a size.	Boolean
	Default value: `false`	

continues

(continued)

forcePlaceholderSize	If `true`, this option forces the placeholder for the sortable to have a size. Default value: `false`	Boolean
grid	Snaps the dragging element/helper to a grid, every x and y pixels, where x and y are specified as an Array [x, y]. Default value: `false`	Array
handle	Restricts sorting from starting unless it begins on the specified element. Default value: `false`	Selector Element
helper	This option allows a helper element to be displayed while dragging is taking place. If a callback function is specified, it should return a valid DOM node that can be used for display. Default value: `'original'`	Element function (event, element)
items	Which items sorting should be applied to. Default value: `'> *'`	Selector
opacity	Defines the opacity of the helper while sorting using a CSS `opacity` value, where 0 is fully transparent, 1 is fully opaque, and floating points between are semitransparent. For example, 0.5 would be half-transparent (or half-opaque). Default value: 1	Float
placeholder	Applies a class name to the placeholder element (which would otherwise be empty white space). Default value: `false`	String, Boolean
revert	This option triggers the dragged item to be reverted back to its original position using a smooth animation. If the value provided is `true`, a default animation is used. If a number is provided, it represents the duration in milliseconds. Default value: `true`	Boolean, Number

scroll	This option causes the page to scroll when a dragged element comes to an edge. Default value: `true`	Boolean
scrollSensitivity	This option defines how close to an edge a dragged element must be before scrolling occurs. Measured in pixels. Default value: `20`	Number
scrollSpeed	This option defines the speed that the container is scrolled. Default value: `20`	Number
tolerance	This option defines what mode to use to determine whether a dragged element is above another item. The possible values are `'intersect'` and `'pointer'`. Default value: `'intersect'`	String
zIndex	The z-index for the `drag` element. Default value: `1000`	Integer
EVENTS		
activate bind('sortactivate') on('sortactivate')	A function that executes when a drag on a sortable item begins. This function propagates to all connected lists.	function (event, ui)
beforeStop bind('sortbeforestop') on('sortbeforestop')	A function that executes when sorting ends, but while the `placeholder` or `helper` is still available.	function (event, ui)
change bind('sortchange') on('sortchange')	A function that executes when a change in sorting takes place.	function (event, ui)
create bind('sortcreate') on('sortcreate')	A function that executes when a sortable is created.	function (event, ui)
deactivate bind('sortdeactivate') on('sortdeactivate')	A function that executes when sorting ends. This function propagates to all connected lists.	function (event, ui)

continues

(continued)

out bind('sortout') on('sortout')	A function that executes when a sortable item is moved out of the boundaries of a sortable list.	function (event, ui)
over bind('sortover') on('sortover')	A function that executes when an item is moved over a connected list.	function (event, ui)
receive bind('sortreceive') on('sortreceive')	A function that executes when an item from this sortable list is dragged to a connected (separated) sortable list.	function (event, ui)
remove bind('sortremove') on('sortremove')	A function that executes when an item from this sortable list is dragged to a connected (separated) sortable list.	function (event, ui)
sort bind('sort') on('sort')	A function that executes while sorting is taking place.	function (event, ui)
start bind('sortstart') on('sortstart')	A function that executes when sorting begins.	function (event, ui)
stop bind('sortstop') on('sortstop')	A function that executes when sorting ends.	function (event, ui)
update bind('sortupdate') on('sortupdate')	A function that executes when sorting ends and the DOM position of the dragged element has changed.	function (event, ui)

SERIALIZE OPTIONS		
OPTION	**DESCRIPTION**	**TYPE**
attribute	The attribute value that is retrieved from each sortable element. Default: id	String
expression	A regular expression used to extract a string from within the attribute value. Default: /(.+)[-=_](.+)/	Regular Expression
key	The key in the URL hash. If not specified, it takes the first result of the expression.	String

UI OBJECT		
PROPERTY	DESCRIPTION	TYPE
ui.helper	A jQuery object representing the helper for the element being sorted.	jQuery
ui.item	A jQuery object representing the element being dragged.	jQuery
ui.offset	The absolute position of the helper element represented as an object with properties top and left.	Object
ui.position	The position of the helper element represented as an object with the properties top and left.	Object
ui.originalPosition	The original position of the element represented as an object with the properties top and left.	Object
ui.sender	A jQuery object containing the original sortable element, if the item is being moved to a different sortable element.	jQuery
ui.placeholder	A jQuery object representing the placeholder element, if one is in use.	jQuery

L

Selectable

METHOD	DESCRIPTION	RETURN VALUE
SORTABLE METHODS		
selectable(*options*)	Turns the children of selected element(s) into selectable elements. Options can be specified by passing an object literal as the first argument using key, value pairs. For a complete list of options, see the "Selectable Options" section later in this appendix.	jQuery
selectable('option')	Returns an object containing key value pairs representing the current selection of options.	Object
selectable(*optionName*)	Returns the current value of the specified option.	Mixed
selectable(*optionName*, *value*)	Sets the value of the specified option.	jQuery
selectable('disable')	Disables selectable functionality on the selected element(s).	jQuery
selectable('destroy')	Completely removes the selectable functionality.	jQuery
selectable('enable')	Enables selectable functionality on the selected element(s).	jQuery
selectable('refresh')	Refreshes the position and size of each selected element.	jQuery
selectable('widget')	Returns a jQuery object containing the selectable element.	jQuery

SELECTABLE OPTIONS		
OPTION	**DESCRIPTION**	**TYPE**
appendTo	This option determines what element the selection box will be appended to. Default selector: *"body"*	Selector
autoRefresh	This option determines whether to refresh (the cached) the position and size of each selectable element at the beginning of a select operation. If you have experienced performance degradation (as you would if you have a lot of selectable elements), you might want to set this option to `false` and refresh positions manually, as needed. Default value: `true`	Boolean
cancel	The cancel option provides a selector of elements that are omitted from the action of beginning a selection. If the user clicks and drags on one of the specified elements, no selection occurs. Default selector: `"input, textarea, button, select, option"`	Selector
delay	Allows you the option of specifying the number of milliseconds that should pass before a selection is allowed to take place. The default is zero (no delay).	Integer
disabled	Determines whether the selectable is disabled. Default value: `false`	Boolean
distance	Specifies the number of pixels the mouse cursor should move before a selection begins. Default value: `0`	Number
filter	The matching child elements will be made into selectable elements. Default value: `*` (all child elements)	Selector

`tolerance`	Defines how a selection should occur. The two options at the time of this writing are `"fit"` and `"touch"`. The value `"fit"` means that the selection box should completely contain the item being selected before a selection takes place. The option `"touch"` means that merely coming into contact with the item makes the item selected. Default value: `"touch"`	String

`create`
`bind('selectablecreate')`
`on('selectablecreate')`
	This function is executed when the selectable is created.	function (event, ui)

`selected`
`bind('selectableselected')`
`on('selectableselected')`
	This function is executed at the end of a select operation (when the mouse button has been released), on each element added to the selection. Selected elements are available in the `ui` argument as `ui.selected`. The `this` keyword refers to the parent selectable element.	function (event, ui)

`selecting`
`bind('selectableselecting')`
`on('selectableselecting')`
	This function is executed as elements are selected during a select operation (while the selection box is being drawn). Selected elements are available in the `ui` argument as `ui.selecting`. The `this` keyword refers to the parent selectable element.	function (event, ui)

`start`
`bind('selectablestart')`
`on('selectablestart')`
	This function is executed at the beginning of a select operation (when the mouse button is first pressed down). The `this` keyword refers to the parent selectable element.	function (event, ui)

`stop`
`bind('selectablestop')`
`on('selectablestop')`
	This function is executed at the end of a select operation (when the mouse button is released). The `this` keyword refers to the parent selectable element.	function (event, ui)

continues

(continued)

`unselected`
 	
`bind('selectableunselected')`
 	
`on('selectableunselected')`
	This function is executed at the end of a select operation (when the mouse button has been released), for each element removed from the selection. The element removed from the selection is available in the `ui` argument as `ui.unselected`. The `this` keyword refers to the parent selectable element.	function
		(event, ui)

`unselecting`
 	
`bind('selectableunselecting')`
 	
`on('selectableunselecting')`
	This function is executed during a select operation (while the selection box is being drawn). Selected elements are available in the `ui` argument as `ui.unselecting`. The `this` keyword refers to the parent selectable element.	function
		(event, ui)

NOTES

In the `ui` argument of each of the callback functions documented here, the parent selectable element is also available as `ui.selectable`.

The Selectable plugin currently does not provide a way to customize the box being drawn—for example, by adding a class name to it via a Selectable option. Despite this limitation, you do have the ability to customize the selection box, and you can do that by adding a rule to your style sheet that references the selector, `div.ui-selectable-helper`.

Animation and Easing Effects

METHOD	DESCRIPTION	RETURN VALUE

animate(
    css
    [, duration]
    [, easing]
    [, function()]
)
	Animates an element's styles, from the styles an element begins with, to the styles specified in an object literal provided to the first argument. At the time of this writing, only CSS properties with numeric values are supported. Animating color transitions is supported with additional plugin support.
	
	The easing argument accepts two possible values using the default easing library, "linear" and "swing". However, you may download and enable a plethora of additional easing options, which are documented later in this appendix.
	
	The optional callback function is executed once the animation has completed. this refers to the element animated.
		jQuery

animate(
    css,
    options
)
	Animates an element's styles, from the styles an element begins with to the styles specified in an object literal provided to the first argument. See the "Animation Options" section later in this appendix.	jQuery

clearQueue ([queue])	Removes from the queue all items that have not been executed yet. If a queue is specified, only that queue is cleared.	jQuery
delay(duration [, queue])	Sets a timer to delay the execution of subsequent items in the queue. If a queue is specified, the delay is initiated on that queue item.	jQuery

continues

(continued)

`dequeue ( [queue] )`	Executes the next function in the queue for the matched elements. If the optional *queue* argument is specified, that queue item is executed.	jQuery

`fadeIn (`
 	
    `[duration]`
 	
    `[, function()]`
 	
`)`
	Fades in (shows) each selected element by adjusting the element's opacity. The duration is either a time in milliseconds or a time preset: `"slow"`, `"normal"`, or `"fast"`.
	
	The optional callback function is executed when the animation has completed. `this` refers to the element animated.
		jQuery

`fadeIn (options)`	Fades in (shows) each selected element by adjusting the element's opacity. See the "Animation Options" section later in this appendix.	jQuery

`fadeIn (`
 	
    `[duration]`
 	
    `[, easing]`
 	
    `[, function()`
 	
`)`
	Fades in (shows) each selected element by adjusting the element's opacity. The duration is either a time in milliseconds or a time preset: `"slow"`, `"normal"`, or `"fast"`.
	
	The *easing* can be either default easings `"linear"` or `"swing"`, or any easing documented below, assuming you have installed the requisite additional easings as part of jQuery UI.
	
	The optional callback function is executed when the animation has completed. `this` refers to the element.
		jQuery

`fadeOut (`
 	
    `[duration]`
 	
    `[, function()]`
 	
`)`
	Fades out (hides) each selected element by adjusting the element's opacity. The duration is either a time in milliseconds or a time preset: `"slow"`, `"normal"`, or `"fast"`.
	
	The optional callback function is executed when the animation has completed. `this` refers to the element animated.
		jQuery

`fadeOut (options)`	Fades out (hides) each selected element by adjusting the element's opacity. See the "Animation Options" section later in this appendix.	jQuery

`fadeOut (`
`    [duration]`
`    [, easing]`
`    [, function()`
`)`
	Fades out (hides) each selected element by adjusting the element's opacity. The duration is either a time in milliseconds or a time preset: `"slow"`, `"normal"`, or `"fast"`.
	
	The *easing* can be either default easings `"linear"` or `"swing"`, or any easing documented below, assuming you have installed the requisite additional easings as part of jQuery UI.
	
	The optional callback function is executed when the animation has completed. `this` refers to the element.
		jQuery

`fadeTo (`
`    [duration]`
`    [, easing]`
`    [, function()`
`)`
	Fades in each selected element by adjusting the element's opacity. The duration is either a time in milliseconds or a time preset: `"slow"`, `"normal"`, or `"fast"`.
	
	The *easing* can be either default easings `"linear"` or `"swing"`, or any easing documented below, assuming you have installed the requisite additional easings as part of jQuery UI.
	
	The optional callback function is executed after the animation has completed. `this` refers to the element.
		jQuery

`fadeToggle (`
`    [duration]`
`    [, easing]`
`    [, function()`
`)`
	Toggles the display of each selected element by fading in or out by adjusting the element's opacity. The duration is either a time in milliseconds or a time preset: `"slow"`, `"normal"`, or `"fast"`.
	
	The *easing* can be either default easings `"linear"` or `"swing"`, or any easing documented below, assuming you have installed the requisite additional easings as part of jQuery UI.
	
	The optional callback function is executed after the animation has completed. `this` refers to the element.
		jQuery

`fadeToggle` `(options)`	Toggles the display of each selected element by fading in or out by adjusting the element's opacity using the specified Animation Options. See the "Animation Options" section later in this appendix for more information.	jQuery

continues

(continued)

`finish([queue])`	Stop the currently running animation, remove all queued animations, and complete all animations for the matched elements. If the optional *queue* argument is specified, animations are stopped, removed, and completed only for the referenced queue.	jQuery
`hide()`	Hides each selected element if the element is not already hidden.	jQuery

`hide(`
    `[duration]`
    `[, function()]`
`)`
	Hides each selected element using an animation. The duration is either a time in milliseconds or a time preset: `"slow"`, `"normal"`, or `"fast"`.
	
	An optional callback function can be executed when hiding has completed. `this` refers to the element being hidden within the callback function.
		jQuery

`hide(options)`	The hide animation is carried out with the specified object of options. See the "Animation Options" section later in this appendix.	jQuery

`hide(`
    `[duration]`
    `[, easing]`
    `[, function()]`
`)`
	Hides each selected element using a preset animation. The duration is either a time in milliseconds or a time preset: `"slow"`, `"normal"`, or `"fast"`.
	
	The *easing* can be either default easings `"linear"` or `"swing"`, or any easing documented below, assuming you have installed the requisite additional easings as part of jQuery UI.
	
	The optional callback function is executed when the animation has completed. `this` refers to the element.
		jQuery

`$.fx.interval`	The rate in milliseconds that specifies how often animations fire. Default value: `13 milliseconds`	Number
`$.fx.off`	Globally disable all animations.	Boolean
`queue([queue])`	Shows the queue of functions to be executed on the matched elements.	Array
`queue([queue],` `newQueue)`	Manipulates the queue of functions to be executed, once for each matched element. The *newQueue* argument should contain an array of functions to replace the current queue contents.	jQuery

`queue([queue],` `function())`	Manipulates the queue of functions to be executed, once for each matched element. The `function` argument refers to the new function to add to the queue, with a function to call that will dequeue the next item.	jQuery
`show()`	Displays each selected element if the element is hidden.	jQuery

`show(`
    `[duration]`
    `[, function()]`
`)`
	Shows each selected element using an animation. The duration is either a time in milliseconds or a time preset: `"slow"`, `"normal"`, or `"fast"`.
	
	An optional callback function can be executed when showing has completed. `this` refers to the element being shown within the callback function.
		jQuery

`show(options)`	The `show` animation is carried out with the specified object of options. See the "Animation Options" section later in this appendix.	jQuery

`show(`
    `[duration]`
    `[, easing]`
    `[, function()]`
`)`
	Shows each selected element using a preset animation. The duration is either a time in milliseconds or a time preset: `"slow"`, `"normal"`, or `"fast"`.
	
	The `easing` can be either default easings `"linear"` or `"swing"`, or any easing documented below, assuming you have installed the requisite additional easings as part of jQuery UI.
	
	The optional callback function is executed when the animation has completed. `this` refers to the element.
		jQuery

`slideDown(`
    `[duration]`
    `[, function()]`
`)`
	Slides down (shows) each selected element using an animation. The duration is either a time in milliseconds or a time preset: `"slow"`, `"normal"`, or `"fast"`.
	
	An optional callback function can be executed when sliding has completed. `this` refers to the element being slid within the callback function.
		jQuery

`slideDown(options)`	The `slideDown` animation is carried out with the specified object of options. See the "Animation Options" section later in this appendix.	jQuery

continues

(continued)

`slideDown(`
 	
    `[duration]`
 	
    `[, easing]`
 	
    `[, function()]`
 	
`)`
	Slides down (shows) each selected element using a preset animation. The duration is either a time in milliseconds or a time preset: `"slow"`, `"normal"`, or `"fast"`.
	
	The *easing* can be either default easings `"linear"` or `"swing"`, or any easing documented below, assuming you have installed the requisite additional easings as part of jQuery UI.
	
	The optional callback function is executed when the animation has completed. `this` refers to the element.
		jQuery

`slideToggle(`
 	
    `[duration]`
 	
    `[, function()]`
 	
`)`
	Toggles each selected element between displayed and hidden by animating the element's height. The duration is either a time in milliseconds or a time preset: `"slow"`, `"normal"`, or `"fast"`. An optional callback function can be executed when sliding has completed. This refers to the element being slid within the callback function.	jQuery

`slideToggle(`*`options`*`)`	Toggles each selected element between displayed and hidden by animating each element's height. Animation is carried out with the specified object of options. See the "Animation Options" section later in this appendix.	jQuery

`slideToggle(`
 	
    `[duration]`
 	
    `[, easing]`
 	
    `[, function()]`
 	
`)`
	Toggles the sliding animation for each selected element using a preset animation. The duration is either a time in milliseconds or a time preset: `"slow"`, `"normal"`, or `"fast"`.
	
	The *easing* can be either default easings `"linear"` or `"swing"`, or any easing documented below, assuming you have installed the requisite additional easings as part of jQuery UI.
	
	The optional callback function is executed when the animation has completed. `this` refers to the element.
		jQuery

`slideUp(`
 	
    `[duration]`
 	
    `[, function()]`
 	
`)`
	Slides up (hides) each selected element using an animation. The duration is either a time in milliseconds or a time preset: `"slow"`, `"normal"`, or `"fast"`.
	
	An optional callback function can be executed when sliding has completed. `this` refers to the element being slid within the callback function.
		jQuery

`slideUp(`*`options`*`)`	The `slideUp` animation is carried out with the specified object of options. See the "Animation Options" section later in this appendix.	jQuery

`slideUp(`
    `[duration]`
    `[, easing]`
    `[, function()]`
`)`
	Slides up (hides) each selected element using a preset animation. The duration is either a time in milliseconds or a time preset: `"slow"`, `"normal"`, or `"fast"`.
	
	The *easing* can be either default easings `"linear"` or `"swing"`, or any easing documented below, assuming you have installed the requisite additional easings as part of jQuery UI.
	
	The optional callback function is executed when the animation has completed. `this` refers to the element.
		jQuery

`stop(`
    `[clearQueue]`
    `[,`
`jumpToTheEnd]`
`)`
	Stops all the currently running animations on all the specified elements.
	
	If the *clearQueue* argument is specified, it indicates whether to remove queued animation as well. This argument defaults to `false`.
	
	The *jumpToTheEnd* argument is a boolean that indicates whether the current animation should be completed immediately. This argument defaults to `false`.
		jQuery

`stop(`
    `[queue]`
    `[, clearQueue]`
    `[,`
`jumpToTheEnd]`
`)`
	Stops all the currently running animations on all the specified elements.
	
	The *queue* argument specifies which queue to stop animations within.
	
	If the *clearQueue* argument is specified, it indicates whether to remove queued animation as well. This argument defaults to `false`.
	
	The *jumpToTheEnd* argument is a boolean that indicates whether the current animation should be completed immediately. This argument defaults to `false`.
		jQuery

`toggle()`	Toggles each selected element between displayed and hidden.	jQuery

`toggle(`
    `[duration]`
    `[, function()]`
`)`
	Toggles selected element using an animation. The duration is either a time in milliseconds or a time preset: `"slow"`, `"normal"`, or `"fast"`.
	
	An optional callback function can be executed when sliding has completed. `this` refers to the element being slid within the callback function.
		jQuery

`toggle(`*options*`)`	A `toggle` animation is carried out with the specified object of options. See the "Animation Options" section later in this appendix.	jQuery

continues

(continued)

`toggle(`
`    [duration]`
`    [, easing]`
`    [, function()]`
`)`
	Toggles each selected element using a preset animation. The duration is either a time in milliseconds or a time preset: `"slow"`, `"normal"`, or `"fast"`.
	
	The *easing* can be either default easings `"linear"` or `"swing"`, or any easing documented below, assuming you have installed the requisite additional easings as part of jQuery UI.
	
	The optional callback function is executed when the animation has completed. `this` refers to the element.
		jQuery

`toggle(showOrHide)`	Toggles each element using the boolean *showOrHide* argument to explicitly determine if an element should be shown or hidden.	jQuery

ANIMATION OPTIONS

OPTION	DESCRIPTION	TYPE
`duration`	Any one of `"slow"`, `"normal"`, `"fast"`, or the time specified in milliseconds (ms).	String, Number
`easing`	The name of the easing effect that you want to use (plugin required). There are two built-in values, `"linear"` and `"swing"`.	String
`queue`	Setting this to `false` makes the animation skip the queue and begin running immediately.	Boolean
`specialEasing`	A map of one or more CSS properties that are already defined in the `css` (or properties) argument, which are each mapped to the easing that should be used to animate that particular property.	Object
`step`	A function that is called for each animated property of each animated element. This function provides an opportunity to modify the Tween object.	Function
`progress`	A function to be called after each step of the animation, only once per animated element, regardless of how many properties are animated. The function provides the following arguments: *animation*, *progress*, and *remainingMilliseconds*.	Function
`complete`	A function that is executed when the animation completes.	Function

`start`	A function that is executed when animation starts. The function provides the following argument: *animation*.	Function
`done`	A function that is executed when animation completes and its `Promise` object is resolved. The function provides the following arguments: *animation* and *jumpedToTheEnd*.	Function
`fail`	A function that is executed when animation fails to complete and its `Promise` object is rejected. The function provides the following arguments: *animation* and *jumpedToTheEnd*.	Function
`always`	A function that is executed when the animation completes or stops without completing, its `Promise` object is either resolved or rejected. The function provides the following arguments: *animation* and *jumpedToTheEnd*.	Function

EASINGS

`linear`	
`swing`	
`easeInQuad`	
`easeOutQuad`	
`easeInOutQuad`	
`easeInCubic`	

continues

(continued)

easeOutCubic	
easeInOutCubic	
easeInQuart	
easeOutQuart	
easeInOutQuart	
easeInQuint	
easeOutQuint	
easeInOutQuint	
easeInExpo	
easeOutExpo	
easeInOutExpo	
easeInSine	

easeOutSine	
easeInOutSine	
easeInCirc	
easeOutCirc	
easeInOutCirc	
easeInElastic	
easeOutElastic	
easeInOutElastic	
easeInBack	
easeOutBack	

continues

(continued)

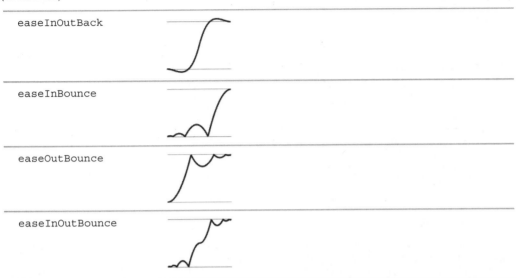

easeInOutBack	
easeInBounce	
easeOutBounce	
easeInOutBounce	

EFFECTS

OPTION	DESCRIPTION
Effects that can be used with Show/Hide/Toggle:	
blind	Blinds the element away or shows it by blinding it in.
clip	Clips the element on or off, vertically or horizontally.
drop	Drops the element away or shows it by dropping it in.
explode	Explodes the element into multiple pieces.
fold	Folds the element like a piece of paper.
puff	Scale and fade out animations create the puff effect.
slide	Slides the element out of the viewport.
scale	Shrinks or grows an element by a percentage factor.
size	Resizes an element to a specified width and height.
pulsate	Pulsates the opacity of the element multiple times.
Effects that can be used only as standalones:	
bounce	Bounces the element vertically or horizontally n-times.
highlight	Highlights the background with a defined color.
shake	Shakes the element vertically or horizontally n-times.
transfer	Transfers the outline of an element to another.

Accordion

METHOD	DESCRIPTION	RETURN VALUE
SHOWING AND HIDING METHODS		
accordion(*options*)	Makes the selected elements into accordions (see "Accordion Options").	jQuery
accordion('destroy')	Destroys the selected accordion.	jQuery
accordion('disable')	Disables the selected accordion.	jQuery
accordion('enable')	Enables the selected accordion.	jQuery
accordion('option')	Returns an object containing all the options and their values.	Object
accordion('refresh')	Recalculates accordion panels, headers, and heights after modifying an accordion.	jQuery
accordion('widget')	Returns a jQuery object that contains the accordion.	jQuery

ACCORDION OPTIONS		
OPTION	DESCRIPTION	TYPE
active	Determines which panel is open, if any. If the value is set to `false`, all panels are collapsed. (This requires the `collapsible` option to be set `true`. If the value is set to an integer, it opens the corresponding panel, offset from zero.) Default value: `0`	Boolean, Integer
animate	Options for animating the panels. Setting the value to `false` disables animation. Setting the value to a number sets the length of the animation in milliseconds with the easing effect. If the value is a string, the string is the type of easing animation (see Appendix M, "Effects"). An object can also be provided with `easing` and `duration` properties. Default value: `{ }`	Boolean, Number, String, Object
collapsible	Whether all the accordion sections can be closed at once. Default value: `false`	Boolean
disabled	Whether the accordion is disabled. Default value: `false`	Boolean
event	The event used to trigger the accordion. Default value: `click`	String
header	Selector referencing the element to use for the header element for each content panel. Default value: `"> li > :first-child,> :not(li):even"`	Selector, Element, jQuery
heightStyle	Determines how the height of each panel is calculated. `"auto"`—The height of each panel will be the height of the tallest panel. `"fill"`—The height of each panel is determined by the accordion's parent element. `"content"`—The height of each panel is determined by the content within each panel. Default value: `"auto"`	String

icons	Icons to use for headers.
	Default value:
	{
	  "header" :
	    "ui-icon-triangle-1-e",
	  "activeHeader" :
	    "ui-icon-triangle-1-s"
	}
		Object

ACCORDION EVENTS		
activate	Triggered once a panel is activated (after the animation has finished).	function (event, ui)
beforeActivate	Triggered once a panel is opened, before animation begins. Can be canceled to prevent a panel from activating.	function (event, ui)
create	Triggered when an accordion is created.	function (event, ui)

ACCORDION UI OBJECT OPTIONS

The callback functions specified for various accordion events specify a ui object in the second argument. Following are the properties exposed in the ui object.

OPTION	DESCRIPTION	TYPE
ui.header	The active header.	jQuery
ui.newHeader	The header of the panel about to be activated.	jQuery
ui.newPanel	The panel about to be activated.	jQuery
ui.oldHeader	The header of the panel about to be deactivated.	jQuery
ui.oldPanel	The panel about to be deactivated.	jQuery
ui.panel	The active panel.	jQuery

Datepicker

DATEPICKER METHODS

METHOD	DESCRIPTION	RETURN VALUE
`datepicker(options)`	Makes the selected elements into Datepickers (see "Datepicker Options").	jQuery
`datepicker('destroy')`	Destroys the Datepicker.	jQuery
`datepicker('dialog', date [, onSelect][, settings] [, pos])`	Opens a Datepicker in a dialog box.	jQuery
`datepicker('getDate')`	Retrieves the current date(s) for a Datepicker.	Date
`datepicker('hide', speed)`	Closes a previously open Datepicker.	jQuery
`datepicker('isDisabled')`	Determines whether a Datepicker field has been disabled.	Boolean
`datepicker('option')`	Returns an object of all options as key, value pairs.	Object
`datepicker('option', optionName)`	Returns the specified option.	Mixed
`datepicker('option', optionName, value)`	Sets the specified option to the specified value.	jQuery
`datepicker('option', optionObject)`	Sets options using an option object.	jQuery

continues

(continued)

`datepicker('setDate', date, endDate)`	Sets the current date(s) for a Datepicker.	jQuery
`datepicker('show')`	Opens a Datepicker.	jQuery
`datepicker('widget')`	Returns a jQuery object containing the Datepicker.	jQuery

DATEPICKER OPTIONS		
OPTION	**DESCRIPTION**	**TYPE**
`altField`	The jQuery selector for another field that is to be updated with the selected date from the Datepicker. Use the `altFormat` setting below to change the format of the date within this field. Leave as blank for no alternative field. Default value: `' '`	String
`altFormat`	The `dateFormat` to be used for the `altField` above. This allows one date format to be shown to the user for selection purposes, whereas a different format is actually sent behind the scenes. Default value: `' '`	String
`appendText`	The text to display after each date field, for example, to show the required format. Default value: `' '`	String
`autoSize`	Set to true to automatically resize the input field to accommodate dates in the current dateFormat. Default value: `false`	Boolean
`beforeShow`	Can be a function that takes an input field and current Datepicker instance and returns a settings (anonymous) object to update the Datepicker with. It is called just before the Datepicker is displayed. Default value: `null`	`function (input, obj)`
`beforeShowDay`	The function takes a date as a parameter and must return an array, with `[0]` equal to `true/false` indicating whether this date is selectable, `[1]` equal to a CSS class name(s) or `' '` for the default presentation. It is called for each day in the Datepicker before it is displayed. Default value: `null`	`function (date)`

`buttonImage`	The URL for the pop-up button image. If set, button text becomes the alt value and is not directly displayed. Default value: `' '`	String
`buttonImageOnly`	Set to `true` to place an image after the field to use as the trigger without it appearing on a button. Default value: `false`	Boolean
`buttonText`	The text to display on the trigger button. Use with `showOn` equal to `'button'` or `'both'`. Default value: `'...'`	String
`calculateWeek`	Performs the week of the year calculation. This function accepts a `Date` as a parameter and returns the number of the corresponding week of the year. The default implementation uses the ISO 8601 definition of a week: Weeks start on a Monday, and the first week of the year contains January 4. This means that up to 3 days from the previous year may be included in the first week of the current year, and that up to 3 days from the current year may be included in the last week of the previous year. Default value: `$.datepicker.iso8601Week`	`function()`
`changeMonth`	Whether the month should be rendered as a drop-down instead of as text. Default value: `false`	Boolean
`changeYear`	Whether the year should be rendered as a drop-down instead of as text. Default is value: `false`	Boolean
`closeText`	The text to display for the `close` link. Use the `showButtonPanel` option to display this button. Default value: `'Done'`	String
`constrainInput`	`true` if the input field is constrained to the current date format. Default value: `true`	Boolean
`currentText`	The text to display for the current day link. Default value: `'Today'`	String

continues

(continued)

`dateFormat`	The format for parsed and displayed dates. For a full list of the possible formats, see "Format Options." Default value: `'mm/dd/yy'`	String
`dayNames`	The list of long day names, starting from Sunday, for use as requested via the `dateFormat` setting. Day names also appear as pop-up hints when hovering over the corresponding column headings. Default value: `['Sunday', 'Monday', 'Tuesday', 'Wednesday', 'Thursday', 'Friday', 'Saturday']`	Array
`dayNamesMin`	The list of minimized day names, starting from Sunday, for use as column headers within the Datepicker. Default value: `['Su', 'Mo', 'Tu', 'We', 'Th', 'Fr', 'Sa']`	Array
`dayNamesShort`	The list of abbreviated day names, starting from Sunday, for use as requested via the `dateFormat` setting. Default value: `['Sun', 'Mon', 'Tue', 'Wed', 'Thu', 'Fri', 'Sat']`	Array
`defaultDate`	Sets the date to display on first opening if the field is blank. Specifies either an actual date via a Date object, or relative to today with a number (for example, `+7`) or a string of values and periods (`'y'` for years, `'m'` for months, `'w'` for weeks, `'d'` for days; for example, `'+1m +7d'`) or `null` for today. Default value: `null`	Date, Number, String
`duration`	Controls the speed at which the Datepicker appears. It may be a time in milliseconds (ms), a string representing one of the three predefined speeds (`'slow'`, `'normal'`, and `'fast'`) or `''` for immediately. Default value: `'normal'`	String, Number
`firstDay`	Sets the first day of the week: Sunday is 0, Monday is 1. Default value: `0`	Integer

gotoCurrent	If `true`, the current day link moves to the currently selected date instead of today. Default value: `false`	Boolean
hideIfNoPrevNext	By default, the previous and next links are disabled with not applicable; setting this attribute to `true` hides them altogether. Default value: `false`	Boolean
isRTL	`true` if the current language is drawn from right to left. Default value: `false`	Boolean
maxDate	Sets a maximum selectable date via a Date object, or relative to today with a number (for example, `+7`) or a string of values and periods (`'y'` for years, `'m'` for months, `'w'` for weeks, and `'d'` for days; for example, `'+1m +1w'`), or `null` for no limit. Default value: `null`	Number, String, Date
minDate	Sets a minimum selectable date via a Date object, or relative to today with a number (for example, `+7`) or a string of values and periods (`'y'` for years, `'m'` for months, `'w'` for weeks, `'d'` for days; for example, `'-1y -1m'`), or `null` for no limit. Default value: `null`	Number, String, Date
monthNames	The list of full month names, as used in the month header on each Datepicker and as requested via the `dateFormat` setting. Default value: `['January', 'February', 'March', 'April', 'May', 'June', 'July', 'August', 'September', 'October', 'November', 'December']`	Array
monthNamesShort	The list of abbreviated month names, for use as requested via the `dateFormat` setting. Default value: `['Jan', 'Feb', 'Mar', 'Apr', 'May', 'Jun', 'Jul', 'Aug', 'Sep', 'Oct', 'Nov', 'Dec']`	Array
navigationAs-DateFormat	When set to `true`, the `formatDate` function is applied to the `prevText`, `nextText`, and `currentText` values before display, allowing them to display the target month names, for example. Default value: `false`	Boolean

continues

(continued)

`nextText`	The text to display for the next month link. Default value: `'Next'`	String
`numberOfMonths`	Sets how many months to show at once. The value can be a number, or it can be an array to define the number of rows and columns to display. Default value: `1`	Number, Array

`onChangeMonth-`
`Year`
	Allows you to define your own event when the Datepicker moves to a new month and/or year. The function receives the date of the first day of the first displayed month and the Datepicker instance as parameters. `this` refers to the associated input field.
	Default value: `null`
		`function`
		`(year,`
		`month,`
		`inst)`

`onClose`	Allows you to define your own event when the Datepicker is closed, regardless if a date is selected. The function receives the selected date(s) as a date or array of dates and the Datepicker instance as parameters. `this` refers to the associated input field.
	Default value: `null`
		`function`
		`(dateText,`
		`inst)`

`onSelect`	Allows you to define your own event when the Datepicker is selected. The function receives the selected date(s) as text and the Datepicker instance as parameters. `this` refers to the associated input field.
	Default value: `null`
		`function`
		`(dateText,`
		`inst)`

`prevText`	The text to display for the previous month link. Default value: `'Prev'`	String
`select-` `OtherMonths`	Displayed dates in other months shown before or after the current month are selectable. Default value: `false`	Boolean

`shortYearCutoff`	Sets the cutoff year for determining the century for a date (used with `dateFormat 'y'`). If a numeric value (0–99) is provided, then this value is used directly. If a string value is provided, then it is converted to a number and added to the current year. When the cutoff year is calculated, any dates entered with a year value less than or equal to it are considered to be in the current century, whereas those greater than it are deemed to be in the previous century. Default value: `'+10'`	String, Number
`showAnim`	Sets the name of the animation used to show/hide the Datepicker. Uses `'show'` (the default), `'slideDown'`, and `'fadeIn'`, or any of the show/hide jQuery UI effects. Default value: `'show'`	String
`showButtonPanel`	Whether to display a button pane underneath the calendar. Default value: `false`	Boolean
`showCurrent-AtPos`	When displaying multiple months via the `numberOfMonths` option, the `showCurrentAtPos` option defines which position to display the current month in. Default value: `0`	Number
`showMonth-AfterYear`	Whether to show the month after the year in the header. Default value: `false`	Boolean
`showOn`	Has the Datepicker appear automatically when the field receives focus, `'focus'`; appear only when a button is clicked, `'button'`; or appear when either event takes place, `'both'`. Default value: `'focus'`	String
`showOptions`	If using one of the jQuery UI effects for `showAnim`, you can provide additional settings for that animation via this option. Default value: `{ }`	Options

continues

(continued)

showOtherMonths	Whether to display dates in other months (nonselectable) at the start or end of the current month. To make these dates selectable use the selectOtherMonths option. Default value: false	Boolean
showWeek	Displays the week of the year alongside each month. The column header is specified by the weekHeader setting. The week number is calculated based on the first date shown in each row in the Datepicker and thus may not apply to all days in that row. The calculateWeek setting allows you to change the week of the year calculation from the default ISO 8601 implementation. Default value: false	Boolean
stepMonths	Sets how many months to move when clicking the Previous/Next links. Default value: 1	Number
weekHeader	The column header for the week of the year (see showWeeks). Default value: 'wk'	String
yearRange	Controls the range of years displayed in the year drop-down. Sets a range of years relative to the current year '-nn:+nn', where n is the number of years forward or backward; or an arbitrary range of years 'nnnn:nnnn', where n is the beginning and ending year. Default value: 'c-10:c+10'	String
yearSuffix	Additional text to display after the year in the month headers. Default value: ''	String

DATEPICKER UTILITIES		
METHOD	DESCRIPTION	RETURN VALUE

`$.datepicker`
`.formatDate(`
    `format,`
    `date,`
    `options`
`)`
	Formats a date into a string value with a specified format. For the `format` argument, see "Format Options." The optional `options` argument can be provided with an object literal of settings that include the `dayNamesShort`, `dayNames`, `monthNamesShort`, or `monthNames` options.	String

`$.datepicker` `.iso8601Week(date)`	Determines the week of the year for a given date: 1 to 53.	Number
`$.datepicker` `.noWeekends`	Used to set the `beforeShowDay` function with a predefined function that excludes weekends.	Function

`$.datepicker`
`.parseDate(`
    `format,`
    `value,`
    `options`
`)`
	Extracts a date from a string value with a specified format. For the `format` option, see "Format Options." The optional `options` argument can be provided with an object literal that includes the `shortYearCutoff`, `dayNamesShort`, `dayNames`, `monthNamesShort`, or `monthNames` options.	Date

`$.datepicker` `.setDefaults(options)`	Changes the default settings for all Datepickers. For the options argument, see "Datepicker Options."	Datepicker

FORMAT OPTIONS FOR `$.datepicker.formatDate()`	
OPTION	DESCRIPTION
d	Day of the month with no leading zero
dd	Day of the month with leading zero
o	Day of the year (no leading zeros)
oo	Day of the year (three digit)
D	Day name short
DD	Day name long

continues

(continued)

m	Month of the year with no leading zero
mm	Month of the year with leading zero
M	Month name short
MM	Month name long
y	Two-digit year
yy	Four-digit year
@	UNIX timestamp (seconds elapsed since 01/01/1970)
...	Literal text
' '	Single quote
Anything else	Literal text
ATOM	yy-mm-dd (same as RFC 3339/ISO 8601)
COOKIE	D, dd M yy
ISO_8601	yy-mm-dd
RFC_822	D, d M y
RFC_850	DD, dd-M-y
RFC_1036	D, d M y
RFC_1123	D, d M yy
RFC_2822	D, d M yy
RSS	D, d M y
TICKS	!
TIMESTAMP	@ (UNIX timestamp; seconds elapsed since 01/01/1970)
W3C	yy-mm-dd (same as ISO 8601)

P

Dialog

DIALOG METHODS		
METHOD	DESCRIPTION	RETURN VALUE
dialog(*options*)	Makes the selected elements into dialog boxes.	jQuery
dialog('close')	Closes the dialog.	jQuery
dialog('destroy')	Completely removes the dialog.	jQuery
dialog('isOpen')	Determines if the dialog is open.	Boolean
dialog('moveToTop')	Moves the specified dialog on top of the dialogs stack.	jQuery
dialog('open')	Opens the dialog.	jQuery
dialog('option', *optionName*)	Returns the value of the specified option.	Mixed
dialog('option', optionName, value)	Sets the specified option to the specified value.	jQuery
dialog('option')	Returns an object of options in key, value pairs.	Object
dialog('option', *optionObject*)	Sets the specified options as an object of key, value pairs.	jQuery
dialog('widget')	Returns a jQuery object containing the dialog.	jQuery

DIALOG OPTIONS		
OPTION	**DESCRIPTION**	**TYPE**
`appendTo`	What element the dialog should be appended to. Default value: `'body'`	Selector
`autoOpen`	When set to `true`, the dialog opens automatically when the dialog is called. If set to `false`, it stays hidden until `dialog('open')` is called on it. Default value: `true`	Boolean
`buttons`	Specifies which buttons should display on the dialog. The property key is the text of the button. The value is the callback function for when the button is clicked. The context of the callback is the dialog element; if you need access to the button, it is available as the target of the `event` object. Default value: `{ }`	Object, Array
`closeOnEscape`	Specifies whether the dialog should close when the user presses the [Escape] key. Default value: `true`	Boolean
`closeText`	Specifies the text for the close button. Default value: `'close'`	String
`dialogClass`	The specified class name(s) will be added to the dialog, for additional styling. Default value: `' '`	String
`draggable`	When set to `true`, the resulting dialog will be draggable. If `false`, the dialog will not be draggable. Default value: `true`	Boolean
`height`	The height of the dialog, in pixels. Default value: `200`	Number, String

hide	Whether and how to animate the closing of a dialog.	Boolean, Number, String, Object
	If a boolean value is provided, `false` indicates no animation, and the dialog closes immediately. If `true` is provided, the dialog fades out with the default duration and default easing.	
	If a number is provided, it indicates how long the fade animation should take place with the default easing.	
	If a string is provided, it indicates what animation or UI effect to use. For example, `'slideUp'` or `'fold'`. This animation will be applied with default duration and default easing.	
	If an object is provided, you may specify the following properties: `effect`, `delay`, `duration`, and `easing`.	
	Default value: `null`	
maxHeight	The maximum height to which the dialog can be resized, in pixels.	Number
	Default value: `false`	
maxWidth	The maximum width to which the dialog can be resized, in pixels.	Number
	Default value: `false`	
minHeight	The minimum height to which the dialog can be resized, in pixels.	Number
	Default value: `150`	
minWidth	The minimum width to which the dialog can be resized, in pixels.	Number
	Default value: `150`	
modal	When `modal` is set to `true`, the dialog will have modal behavior; other items on the page will be disabled (that is, cannot be interacted with). Modal dialogs create an overlay below the dialog but above other page elements. Custom style values for the overlay (for example, changing its color or opacity) can be set by overriding the styles for the `ui-widget-overlay` class.	Boolean
	Default value: `false`	

continues

(continued)

`position`	Specifies where the dialog should be displayed. If an object is specified, it uses the jQuery UI Position Utility (`http://api.jqueryui.com/position/`). If a string is specified, the possible values are: `'center'`, `'left'`, `'right'`, `'top'`, and `'bottom'`. If an array is specified, it should contain a coordinate pair (in pixel offset from the top, left of viewport) or the possible string values (for example, `['right', 'top']` for top-right corner). Default value: `{my: 'center', at: 'center', of: 'window'}`	Object, String, Array
`resizable`	Specifies whether the dialog will be resizable. Default value: `true`	Boolean
`show`	Whether and how to animate the opening of a dialog. If a boolean value is provided, `false` indicates no animation, and the dialog closes immediately. If `true` is provided, the dialog fades out with the default duration and default easing. If a number is provided, it indicates how long the fade animation should take place with the default easing. If a string is provided, it indicates what animation or UI effect to use,. for example, `'slideUp'` or `'fold'`. This animation will be applied with default duration and default easing. If an object is provided, you may specify the following properties: `effect`, `delay`, `duration`, and `easing`. Default value: `null`	Boolean, Number, String, Object

`title`	Specifies the title of the dialog. The title can also be specified by the `title` attribute on the dialog source element. Default value: `null`	String
`width`	The width of the dialog, in pixels. Default value: `300`	Number

DIALOG EVENTS		
OPTION	**DESCRIPTION**	**VALUE**

`beforeClose`
`bind('dialogbeforeclose')`
`on('dialogbeforeclose')`
	A function that's executed before a dialog is closed.	`function (event, ui)`

`close`
`bind('dialogclose')`
`on('dialogclose')`
	A function that's executed when a dialog is closed.	`function (event, ui)`

`create`
`bind('dialogcreate')`
`on('dialogcreate')`
	A function that's executed when a dialog is created.	`function (event, ui)`

`drag`
`bind('dialogdrag')`
`on('dialogdrag')`
	A function that's executed while a dialog is dragged.	`function (event, ui)`

`dragStart`
`bind('dialogdragstart')`
`on('dialogdragstart')`
	A function that's executed when a dialog is at the beginning of a dialog drag.	`function (event, ui)`

`dragStop`
`bind('dialogdragstop')`
`on('dialogdragstop')`
	A function that's executed when a dialog drag ends.	`function (event, ui)`

`focus`
`bind('dialogfocus')`
`on('dialogfocus')`
	A function that's executed at the dialog `focus` event. The function gets passed two arguments in accordance with the `triggerHandler` interface. The data passed is the focused dialog options object.	`function (event, ui)`

continues

(continued)

`open`
`bind('dialogopen')`
`on('dialogopen')`
	A function that's executed when a dialog is opened.	`function (event, ui)`

`resize`
`bind('dialogresize')`
`on('dialogresize')`
	A function that's executed during a dialog resize.	`function (event, ui)`

`resizeStart`
`bind('dialogresizestart')`
`on('dialogresizestart')`
	A function that's executed when a dialog resize begins.	`function (event, ui)`

`resizeStop`
`bind('dialogresizestop')`
`on('dialogresizestop')`
	A function that's executed when a dialog resize ends.	`function (event, ui)`

UI OBJECT		
OPTION	**DESCRIPTION**	**TYPE**
`ui.position`	The current CSS position of the dialog.	Object
`ui.offset`	The current offset position of the dialog.	Object
`ui.originalPosition`	The CSS position of the dialog prior to being resized.	Object
`ui.originalSize`	The size of the dialog prior to being resized.	Object
`ui.size`	The current size of the dialog.	Object

Tabs

TAB METHODS		
METHOD	**DESCRIPTION**	**RETURN VALUE**
`tabs(options)`	Makes the selected elements into tabs (see "Tab Options").	jQuery
`tabs('destroy')`	Removes the tabs' functionality completely from the document.	jQuery
`tabs('disable')`	Disables all tabs.	jQuery
`tabs('disable', index)`	Disables a tab by offset index. To disable multiple tabs, use the option method to set the disabled option with an Array of tab indices.	jQuery
`tabs('enable')`	Enables all tabs.	jQuery
`tabs('enable', index)`	Enables a tab by offset index. To enable multiple tabs, use the option method to set the disabled option with an Array of tab indices you wish to remain disabled.	jQuery
`tabs('load', index)`	Loads the content of a tab provided via AJAX programmatically.	jQuery
`tabs('option')`	Returns an object of key, value pairs for every set option.	Object
`tabs('option', optionName, value)`	Sets the specified option to the specified value.	jQuery

continues

(continued)

`tabs('refresh')`	Refreshes the positions of tabs that were added or removed from the DOM.	jQuery
`tabs('widget')`	Returns a jQuery object of the tabs container.	jQuery

TAB OPTIONS

OPTION	DESCRIPTION	TYPE
`active`	Determines which tab panel should be open. If a boolean value is provided, setting to `false` collapses all panels. If an integer is provided, setting to a zero-based offset representing the tab will open that panel. A negative value selects the active panel counting from the last tab instead of the beginning. Default value: `0`	Boolean, Integer
`collapsible`	When the value is `true`, the active panel can be closed (meaning it is possible to have no active panel at all). Default value: `false`	Boolean
`disabled`	If a boolean is provided, it indicates whether all tabs are enabled or disabled. If an Array is provided, it contains the position of each tab (zero-based) that should be disabled upon initialization. Default value: `false`	Boolean, Array
`event`	The type of event to be used for selecting a tab. For example, to activate a tab when the user's mouse enters the tab, use the value `'mouseover'`. Default value: `'click'`	String

heightStyle	Controls how the height of each tab and each panel are applied. The options are:	String
	'auto': All tab panels will be set the height of the tallest panel.	
	'fill': Expands the tab widget's height to fill the height of the parent element.	
	'content': Each tab panel will be only as tall as the content it contains.	
	Default value: 'content'	
hide	Whether and how to animate the closing of a tab panel.	Boolean, Number, String, Object
	If a boolean value is provided, false indicates no animation and the panel closes immediately. If true is provided, the panel fades out with the default duration and default easing.	
	If a number is provided, it indicates how long the fade animation should take place with the default easing.	
	If a string is provided, it indicates what animation or UI effect to use, for example, 'slideUp' or 'fold'. This animation will be applied with default duration and default easing.	
	If an object is provided, you may specify the following properties: effect, delay, duration, and easing.	
	Default value: null	

continues

(continued)

show	Whether and how to animate the opening of a tab panel.	Boolean, Number, String, Object
	If a boolean value is provided, `false` indicates no animation , and the panel closes immediately. If `true` is provided, the panel fades out with the default duration and default easing.	
	If a number is provided, it indicates how long the fade animation should take place with the default easing.	
	If a string is provided, it indicates what animation or UI effect to use, for example, `'slideUp'` or `'fold'`. This animation will be applied with default duration and default easing.	
	If an object is provided, you may specify the following properties: `effect`, `delay`, `duration`, and `easing`.	
	Default value: `null`	

TAB EVENTS		
OPTION	**DESCRIPTION**	**VALUE**
activate bind('tabsactivate') on('tabsactivate')	A function executed when a tab has been activated.	function (event, ui)
beforeActivate bind('tabsbeforeactivate') on('tabsbeforeactivate')	A function executed before a tab has been activated.	function (event, ui)
beforeLoad bind('tabsbeforeload') on('tabsbeforeload')	A function executed before a tab is loaded.	function (event, ui)
create bind('tabscreate') on('tabscreate')	A function executed when tabs are created.	function (event, ui)
load bind('tabsload') on('tabsload')	A function executed when a tab has been loaded.	function (event, ui)

UI OBJECT		
OPTION	DESCRIPTION	TYPE
ui.ajaxSettings	The settings used by jQuery.ajax to request content.	Object
ui.jqXHR	The jQuery AJAX request object that is requesting content.	jQuery AJAX
ui.newPanel	The panel that was just activated or about to be activated.	jQuery
ui.newTab	The tab that was just activated or about to be activated.	jQuery
ui.oldPanel	The panel that was just deactivated or about to be deactivated.	jQuery
ui.oldTab	The tab that was just deactivated or about to be deactivated.	jQuery
ui.panel	The panel being loaded or the active panel.	jQuery
ui.tab	The tab being loaded or the active tab.	jQuery

TAB STYLING	
CLASS	DESCRIPTION
ui-tabs-nav	This is the whole menu. Use this as a base class.
ui-tabs-selected	This is the current tab. It's very important to create a strong visual indication of which tab is the current one.
ui-tabs-unselect	This is the class for all the tabs that are not selected but selectable.
ui-tabs-deselectable	This is the class for all tabs that can be deselected.
ui-tabs-disabled	For when a tab is disabled. Highly recommended to appear somewhat transparent or disabled. This is often done by graying the color.
ui-tabs-panel	These are the boxes that will have their visibility toggled.
ui-tabs-hide	This class hides the boxes (perhaps the most important class).

ELEMENT	DESCRIPTION
<span>	<span> elements are there to facilitate tricks like rounded corners and resizable backgrounds.

Resizable

RESIZABLE METHODS		
METHOD	**DESCRIPTION**	**RETURN VALUE**
resizable(*options*)	Makes the selected elements into resizable elements (see "Resizable Options").	jQuery
resizable('destroy')	Completely removes resizable functionality.	jQuery
resizable('disable')	Temporarily disables resizable functionality.	jQuery
resizable('enable')	Enables resizable functionality.	jQuery
resizable('option')	Returns an object of all currently set options as an object of key, value pairs.	Object
resizable('option', *optionName*)	Returns the specified option's value.	Mixed
resizable('option', *optionName*, *value*)	Sets the specified option to the specified value.	jQuery

RESIZABLE OPTIONS		
OPTION	**DESCRIPTION**	**TYPE**
alsoResize	One or more elements that should be resizing simultaneously with the resizable element. Default value: false	Selector, jQuery, Element
animate	Animates to the final size after resizing. Default value: false	Boolean

continues

(continued)

animateDuration	Duration time for animating. Accepts the time in milliseconds (ms), or one of `'slow'`, `'normal'`, or `'fast'`. Default value: `'slow'`	Number, String
animateEasing	Easing effect for animation. Default value: `'swing'`	String
aspectRatio	When set to `true`, resizing is constrained by the original aspect ratio. If an alternative ratio is wanted, you can submit a number and then the aspect ratio will be constrained by height\ width. Default value: `false`	Boolean, Number
autoHide	When set to `true`, automatically hides the handles except when the mouse hovers over the element. Default value: `false`	Boolean
cancel	Prevents resizing if you start on elements matching the selector. Default value: `'input, textarea, button, select, option'`	Selector
containment	Constrains resizing to within the bounds of the specified element. This can be a DOM element, `'parent'`, `'document'`, or a selector. Default value: `false`	Boolean, Element, Selector, String
delay	Time in milliseconds (ms) to define when dragging should start. It helps prevent unwanted drags when clicking an element. Default value: `0`	Number
disabled	Disables the resizable if the value is set to `true`. Default value: `false`	Boolean
distance	Tolerance in pixels, for when resizing should start. If specified, resizing will not start until after the mouse is moved beyond the specified distance. Default value: `1`	Number

ghost	When set to `true`, a substitute element is displayed while resizing. Default value: `false`	Boolean
grid	Snaps the resizing element to a grid size, every x and y pixel. Default value: `false`	Array[x, y]
handles	Customizes handles used for resizing. If an object is specified the potential keys are `n, e, s, w, ne, se, sw, nw,` and `all`. Values for these keys should reference an element, selection, or jQuery object that should be used to represent that particular handle. If a string is provided, the string is a comma separated list of the following `'n, e, s, w, ne, se, sw, nw,` and `all'`. Default value: `'e, s, se'`	String, Object
helper	This is the CSS class that will be added to a proxy element to outline the resize during the drag of the resize handle. When the resize is complete, the original element is sized. Default value: `false`	Boolean, String
maxHeight	This is the maximum height the resizable should be allowed to resize to. Default value: `null`	Number
maxWidth	This is the maximum width the resizable should be allowed to resize to. Default value: `null`	Number
minHeight	This is the minimum height the resizable should be allowed to resize to. Default value: `10`	Number
minWidth	This is the minimum width the resizable should be allowed to resize to. Default value: `10`	Number

RESIZABLE EVENTS		
OPTION	**DESCRIPTION**	**VALUE**
create bind('resizecreate') on('resizecreate')	A function executed when a resizable element is created.	function (event, ui)
resize bind('resize') on('resize')	This function is called during the resize, on the drag of any resize handle.	function (event, ui)
start bind('resizestart') on('resizestart')	This function is executed when a resize starts.	function (event, ui)
stop bind('resizestop') on('resizestop')	This function is called at the end of a resize operation.	function (event, ui)

UI OBJECT		
OPTION	**DESCRIPTION**	**TYPE**
ui.element	A jQuery object representing the resizable element.	jQuery
ui.helper	A jQuery object representing the helper that's being resized.	jQuery
ui.originalElement	A jQuery object representing the original element before it was wrapped with the resizable plugin.	jQuery
ui.originalPosition	An object representing the original position with the keys left and top.	Object
ui.originalSize	An object containing the original width and height, before an element was resized.	Object
ui.position	An object containing the current position with the keys left and top.	Object
ui.size	An object containing the current size of the resizable element with the keys width and height.	Object

Slider

Slider Methods		
Method	Description	Return Value
slider(*options*)	Makes the selected elements into slider elements (see "Slider Options").	jQuery
slider('destroy')	Completely removes the sliding functionality.	jQuery
slider('disable')	Disables the slider.	jQuery
slider('enable')	Enables the slider.	jQuery
slider('option')	Returns an object of key, value pairs representing all options presently set for that instance of the slider plugin.	Object
slider('option', *optionName*)	Returns the value of the specified option.	Mixed
slider('option', *optionName, value*)	Sets the value of the specified option to the specified value.	jQuery
slider('option', *optionObject*)	Sets multiple options using an object of key, value pairs.	jQuery
slider('value')	Returns the value of the slider.	Number
slider('value', *value*)	Sets the value of the slider.	jQuery
slider('values')	Returns all values for all handles.	Array
slider('values', *index*)	Returns the value for the specified handle.	Number

continues

(continued)

`slider('values', index, value)`	Sets the value of the specified handle.	jQuery
`slider('values', valuesArray)`	Sets the values of the specified handles using an array.	jQuery
`slider('widget')`	Returns a jQuery object containing the slider.	jQuery

Slider Options		
Option	Description	Type
`animate`	Whether slide handles smoothly when the user clicks outside the handle on the bar. Default value: `false`	Boolean
`disabled`	Disables the slider if set to `true`. Default value: `false`	Boolean
`max`	The maximum value of the slider. Useful for tracking values via callback and to set steps. Default value: `100`	Number
`min`	The minimum value of the slider. Default value: `0`	Number
`orientation`	Determines whether the slider is moved horizontally or vertically. The possible values are `horizontal` and `vertical`. Default value: `horizontal`	String
`range`	If a boolean is provided and set to `true`, the slider will detect if you have two handles and creates a stylable range element between these two. You now also have access to `ui.range` in your callbacks to get the amount of the range. If a string is provided the potential values are `min` and `max`. Default value: `false`	Boolean, String
`step`	Determines the interval between each step the slider takes between min and mx. The full range should be easily divided by the step. Default value: `1`	Number

value	The value of the slider. If multiple handles are present, this value will be used for the first handle. Default value: `0`	Number
values	If multiple handles are desired, an array containing the value for each handle can be provided within this option. Default value: `null`	Array

SLIDER EVENTS		
OPTION	**DESCRIPTION**	**VALUE**
change	A function that is executed when the slider's value or values change.	`function (event, ui)`
create	A function executed when a slider is created.	`function (event, ui)`
slide	A function executed upon every mouse move while a slider is being dragged.	`function (event, ui)`
start	A function that gets called when the user starts sliding.	`function (event, ui)`
stop	A function that gets called when the user stops sliding.	`function (event, ui)`

UI OBJECT		
OPTION	**DESCRIPTION**	**TYPE**
ui.handle	A jQuery object representing the handle being moved.	jQuery
ui.value	The value that the handle will move to if the event is not canceled.	Number
ui.values	An array of the current values of a multihandled slider.	Array

Tablesorter

TABLESORTER OPTIONS		
OPTION	**DESCRIPTION**	**TYPE**
cancelSelection	Determines whether text in table header <th> elements should be selectable. Default value: true	Boolean
cssAsc	The class name to apply to a table header <th> that represents a column sorted ascending. Default value: 'headerSortUp'	String
cssDesc	The class name to apply to a table header <th> that represents a column sorted descending. Default value: 'headerSortDown'	String
cssHeader	The class name applied to a table header <th> representing a column in an unsorted state. Default value: 'header'	String
debug	Determines whether additional debugging information should be displayed, which is useful for development. Default value: false	Boolean

continues

(continued)

| headers | An object representing options that can be provided for each column. The object is defined counting each column offset from zero. The only option allowed at the time of this writing is indicating whether a column is sortable.<br><br>An example object that disables sorting on the first column:<br><br>```
headers : {
    0 : {
        sorter : false
    }
}
```<br>Default value: `null` | Object |
| sortForce | This option is used to assist with multicolumn sorting. For example, it can assist with sorting by name after sorting by other criteria such as by date or account balance or other criteria. The value used to specify this option follows the same pattern as the `sortList` option.

Default value: `null` | Array |
| sortList | This option defines an initial sorting for columns. Each column is defined in an array in order from the column sorted first to the column sorted last. For example:<br><br>```
sortList : [
    [0, 0],
    [2, 1]
]
```<br>This setting sorts first by the first column, ascending. The first column is offset zero with another zero for ascending `[0, 0]`. Then the third column is sorted descending. The third column is offset two followed by one for descending `[2, 1]`.<br><br>Default value: `null` | Array |

`sortMultiSortKey`	This option indicates which keyboard modifier to use to select more than one column for sorting. Default value: `'shiftKey'`	String

`textExtraction`	Defines which method to use to grab text from a table cell for sorting. String options include `'simple'` and `'complex'`. `'simple'` does not take into account any markup that might be present preceding table cell text. `'complex'` takes markup into account but can be slow when dealing with large data sets.
	
	An additional option is to write your own function for text extraction. This function has a signature like so:
	
	`function(node)`
	
	`{`
	
	    `return $(node).text();`
	
	`}`
	
	Keep in mind that using jQuery over JavaScript directly will impact performance on a large table.
	
	Default value: `'simple'`
		String, Function

`widthFixed`	Determines whether fixed widths should be used for columns. Note this can also be accomplished with the CSS `table-layout: fixed;` declaration applied to the `<table>` element. Default value: `false`	Boolean

MediaElement

MEDIAELEMENT OPTIONS		
OPTION	**DESCRIPTION**	**TYPE**
`alwaysShowControls`	Determines whether controls are hidden when the mouse cursor leaves a video. Default value: `false`	Boolean
`alwaysShowHours`	Determines whether the hour marker is present in video time, for example, HH:MM:SS. This option shows the HH: portion. Default value: `false`	Boolean
`AndroidUseNativeControls`	Determines whether native controls are used on Android devices. Default value: `false`	Boolean
`audioWidth`	If a value is provided, it overrides the `width` of the `<audio>` element. Default value: `-1`	Integer
`audioHeight`	If a value is provided, it overrides the `height` of the `<audio>` element. Default value: `-1`	Integer
`autosizeProgress`	Determines whether the size of the progress bar should be automatically calculated based on the size of other elements. Default value: `true`	Boolean

continues

(continued)

autoRewind	Returns to the beginning when media ends. Default value: true	Boolean
clickToPlayPause	Determines whether clicking a `<video>` element toggles play/pause. Default value: true	Boolean
defaultAudioHeight	The default height in pixels of an `<audio>` player. This value is used if no `height` is specified on the element. Default value: 30	Integer
defaultAudioWidth	The default width in pixels of an `<audio>` player. This value is used if no `width` is specified on the element. Default value: 400	Integer

defaultSeekBackwardInterval	The default amount of time to move backward when a key is pressed.
	
	The default value is:
	
	`function(media)`
	`{`
	`    return (media.duration *`
	`    0.5);`
	`}`
		Function

defaultSeekForwardInterval	The default amount of time to move forward when a key is pressed.
	
	The default value is:
	
	`function(media)`
	`{`
	`    return (media.duration *`
	`    0.5);`
	`}`
		Function

defaultVideoHeight	The default height in pixels of a `<video>` player. This value is used if no `height` is specified on the element. Default value: 270	Integer

`defaultVideoWidth`	The default width in pixels of a `<video>` player. This value is used if no `width` is specified on the element. Default value: `480`	Integer
`enableAutosize`	Enables Flash and Silverlight players to resize to content size. Default value: `true`	Boolean
`enableKeyboard`	Enables and disables keyboard support. Default value: `true`	Boolean
`features`	The order of controls or plugins on the control bar. Default value: `['playpause', 'current', 'progress', 'duration', 'tracks', 'volume', 'fullscreen']`	Array
`framesPerSecond`	This option is used when the `showTimecodeFrameCount` option is set to true. It indicates the number of frames per second. Default value: `25`	Integer
`hideVideoControlsOnLoad`	Determines whether video controls should hide when a video loads. Default value: `false`	Boolean
`iPadUseNativeControls`	Determines whether to use native controls on an iPad. Default value: `false`	Boolean
`iPhoneUseNativeControls`	Determines whether to use native controls on an iPhone. Default value: `false`	Boolean
`keyActions`	An array of keyboard commands. The default value is an array that initializes the following key actions: space key to play or pause the media; up and down arrow keys to increase or decrease the volume; left and right arrows to seek backward or forward; F to enter or exit full-screen model and M to mute or unmute the volume.	Array

continues

(continued)

loop	Determines whether to loop an audio track. Default value: `false`	Boolean
pauseOtherPlayers	Determines whether to pause other players on the page when the player starts. Default value: `true`	Boolean
poster	URL to a poster image. Default value: `' '`	String
showPosterWhenEnded	Determines whether to show the poster when the video has ended. Default value: `false`	Boolean
showTimecodeFrameCount	Show the frame rate in the time code. FF:HH:MM:SS. This option adds the FF: portion. The `framesPerSecond` option determines the value. Default value: `false`	Boolean
startVolume	The volume level when the player starts. Default value: `0.8`	Float
videoWidth	If a value is provided, it overrides the `width` of the `<video>` element. Default value: `-1`	Integer
videoHeight	If a value is provided, it overrides the `height` of the `<video>` element. Default value: `-1`	Integer

INDEX

Q-R